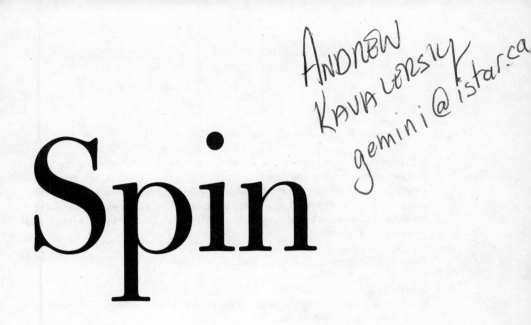

Spin

How to Turn the Power of the Press to Your Advantage

Michael S. Sitrick

with Allan Mayer

REGNERY PUBLISHING, INC.
Washington, D.C.

Library of Congress Cataloging-in-Publication Data

Sitrick, Michael S. (Michael Steven), 1947–
     Spin : how to turn the power of the press to your advantage / Michael
S. Sitrick, with Allan Mayer.
        p.   cm.
     Includes index.
     ISBN 0-89526-411-0 (alk. paper)
     1. Public relations. I. Mayer, Allan J. II. Title. III. Title:
Turning the power of the press to your advantage.
     HD59.S458   1998
     659.2--DC21   98-12114
                                                                  CIP

Published in the United States by
Regnery Publishing, Inc.
An Eagle Publishing Company
One Massachusetts Avenue, NW
Washington, DC 20001

Distributed to the trade by
National Book Network
4720-A Boston Way
Lanham, MD 20706

Printed on acid-free paper.
Manufactured in the United States of America

Book design by Dori Miller

10 9 8 7 6 5 4 3 2 1

Books are available in quantity for promotional or premium use. Write to Director of Special Sales, Regnery Publishing, Inc., One Massachusetts Avenue, NW, Washington, DC 20001, for information on discounts and terms or call (202) 216-0600.

This book is dedicated to my wife, my best friend, and my soul mate, Nancy, without whose love and support during all these years, none of what I have accomplished would have been possible.

▌ Contents

Preface   vii

PART I: The Art of Spin

1. Why Good People Get Bad Press   3
2. The Education of a Spin Doctor   19
3. Inside a Reporter's Head   39
4. The Truth About Spin   53

PART II: The Rules of Spin

5. News Media Abhor a Vacuum   61
6. Always Respond   81
7. Preempt the Situation   103
8. The Facts Don't Speak for Themselves   123
9. Think Strategically   147
10. Find a Lead Steer...   161
11. Fight Back   175
12. Face Forward   185
13. The Most Important Rule   197

Acknowledgments   205
Index   211

Preface

WHEN THE IDEA OF WRITING this book was first broached to me, my greatest concern was not, as some people suggested, that I might wind up revealing to my competitors all my trade secrets. As we make clear in the pages that follow, practicing public relations at the level we do is not all that different from practicing law. And the fact is, you can read all the law books, study all the cases, and even watch the great masters perform in court, but that won't make you a great lawyer. It takes years of studying, more years of under-studying, and then still more time to refine your own style and skills. You not only have to be able to execute the tactics, you also have to know how to develop and implement the strategies. And in order to do that, you have to know how to identify and understand the problem. Public relations, as I tell people both inside and outside of my firm, is a business of subtleties—and it is one's ability to appreciate those subtleties that often makes the difference between winning and losing in the court of public opinion.

No, my greatest concern in writing this book was to what extent and in how much detail I would be able to discuss the cases I've been involved with over the years that have helped me develop and test my ideas about the art of spin. People in my business cannot kiss and tell—at least not without permission. Maintaining client confidentiality is a basic responsibility that simply cannot be breached. What that means is that some of the most interesting cases in our files must stay under wraps, while others can be recounted only in part. Fortunately, having been involved as of this writing in upwards of five hundred or so cases (I really haven't kept count), I was able to come up with more than enough usable examples simply by combining what was already available in the public record with previously off-the-record insights and information that my clients gave me permission to share. To all of those clients, thank you once again.

PART I

The Art of Spin

CHAPTER 1

Why Good People Get Bad Press

"What we've got here is a failure to communicate."
—Strother Martin, in *Cool Hand Luke*

BACK IN THE AUTUMN OF 1995, radar operators aboard a U.S. Navy aircraft carrier steaming off the coast of Newfoundland signaled the bridge that their ship seemed to be getting dangerously close to an approaching Canadian vessel. The captain promptly got on the radio, and the following exchange ensued.

> U.S. CAPTAIN: Please divert your course five degrees to the south to avoid a collision.
>
> CANADIAN RADIO OPERATOR: Recommend you divert *your* course fifteen degrees to the south to avoid a collision.
>
> U.S. CAPTAIN: This is the captain of a U.S. Navy ship. I say again, divert your course.

CANADIAN RADIO OPERATOR: No. I say again, you divert *your* course!

U.S. CAPTAIN: *This is the aircraft carrier USS* Coral Sea. *We are a large warship of the U.S. Navy. Divert your course now!!!*

CANADIAN RADIO OPERATOR: This is a lighthouse. Your call.

In this era of mass global telecommunications, when just about anyone with access to a telephone line and a computer can transmit just about any message he wants to just about the whole world, getting the word out no longer presents much of a challenge. Being understood, on the other hand, having your message elicit the response you want, can be a bit more problematic. As the captain of the *Coral Sea* discovered, it's not enough merely to be heard. In order to get the results you're looking for, you've got to know something about exactly whom it is you happen to be addressing.

This, of course, is the dilemma faced by everyone who operates in the public eye or depends in some way on public acceptance. How do you win the regard and understanding of what amounts to an audience of strangers? Until quite recently, this question has been of real concern only to a relatively small group of people—for the most part, those deliberately conspicuous types who have chosen to live in the glare of mass exposure and media attention: entertainers, politicians, marketers, and other such professional extroverts whose livelihoods depend on their ability to communicate effectively with a broad range of people. But in a media-fixated culture such as ours, the problems of celebrity are no longer limited just to celebrities. These days, the challenge of relating to an audience that extends far beyond one's personal circle of relatives, friends, and immediate colleagues is something more and more of us need to worry about.

As any reader of *People* or viewer of *60 Minutes* can tell you, we live in a world in which, virtually overnight, almost any individual can become a public figure; any organization, a target of public inquiry. This is, after all, the Information Age (or so we are constantly reminded). For the most part, we like to think about what this means in terms of the good things it brings us—

> **Almost any individual can become a public figure; any organization, a target of public inquiry.**

namely, unprecedented access to all kinds of data and entertainment that allows us to do business more efficiently and relax more imaginatively. But there is (inevitably) a downside, a price we must pay for it all as individuals. Specifically, in a culture that has come to prize information as the most valuable of commodities, one can no longer assume that any part of one's life or business is inherently private— that is, safely off limits to public interest, or even mere curiosity. Sooner or later, the news media are bound to point their probing lenses and inquisitive microphones in our direction—at us personally or at some company or group with which we're connected. And if we don't know how to respond, we are going to regret it.

Anyone who has ever been the target of unflattering rumors or undeserved innuendo will never forget what a potent—and painful— combination of emotions such an experience provokes: shame, anger, frustration, and despair are the least of it. Imagine, then, what it must feel like to be, say, the chief executive of a struggling company that's just begun to hit its stride when, without warning, disaster strikes. It could be anything from a poisoned product (as happened to Tylenol some years back) to a faulty microchip (Intel) to an outright catastrophe (TWA or ValuJet). Suddenly, you are catapulted onto every front page and television screen on the planet. Suddenly, you personify the company—not only to the public at large, but to your family and friends, your butcher and your minister. Rightly or wrongly, fairly or unfairly, you are being held accountable for whatever may have happened by the self-appointed credibility police, those relentless reporters who keep sticking microphones in your face and refusing to take "No comment" for an answer.

Do you find it maddening? Frustrating? Insulting? Intolerable?

It may be all of the above, and then some. But, hey, you're the boss. You wanted the job, and accountability goes with the territory. Command has its pains as well as its privileges. The point is, if ever you've needed to demonstrate your ability to take charge—to make sure your story is presented in such a way that the world can't help but understand it correctly—it's now.

One thing is certain: You're in the hot seat, and there's no easy way out. Once the press decides that an individual or an organization is newsworthy, there is no point in disagreeing. Dismissing the media as irrelevant is like insisting the world is flat. Nor will you get very far trying to bully reporters or treating them as impolitely as they treat you. (It may feel good at the time, but over the long haul, it's about as useful as throwing gasoline on a campfire.)

So what do you do? If experience is any guide, probably the wrong thing.

More often than you might think, otherwise smart, shrewd, sophisticated executives react to the sudden glare of the media spotlight by shooting themselves squarely in the foot. Rather than making a virtue of necessity and regarding the press's interest as an opportunity, they see it as a threat. Why else would the normally astute chief executive officer (CEO) of one of the world's largest banks have allowed himself to become the target of such hostile coverage that it ultimately cost him his job? How else did the previously respected chairman of one of the country's premier investment banks wind up the subject of a ruinous cover story in *New York* magazine? What else led the chairman of a major airline to appear evasive and uncaring after one of the worst flight disasters in recent history? And why else did the CEO of one of America's top computer com-

> **Many "victims" of the press could have averted disaster had they known how to manage the process.**

panies let story after unanswered story erode his company's once brilliant reputation to the point at which its very survival is now in question?

The sad fact is that many so-called victims of the press could have averted the disasters that engulfed them, if only they had known how to manage the process. But too many of them refused to recognize that they were involved in a process. They didn't see that the maelstrom swirling around them was, in fact, nothing more or less than a particular, predictable kind of situation, one that passes through a series of readily recognized stages, is shaped by an array of clearly identifiable forces, and follows a number of easily understood rules.

Being for the most part hard-headed types, corporate bosses like to think the facts alone will save them. Unfortunately, while "Just the facts, ma'am" may have been good enough for *Dragnet's* Sergeant Friday, it doesn't get you very far today. When it comes to mass communications, the most salient fact of all is that the same set of facts can be interpreted in many different ways—some of them positive, some of them extremely negative. What matters— what ultimately determines how a story is told and, more to the point, how it will eventually be understood—is the way in which those facts are presented. Or, to use the currently fashionable phrase, how they are spun.

■ ■ ■

To understand how the art of spin works, it's probably worth taking a brief look at where it came from.

Public relations (PR) is a touchy subject. Some people consider it a science; others insist it's a scam. In fact, it's neither. Like journalism, with which it is inextricably (if uneasily) linked, PR lies somewhere on the spectrum between a profession and a craft. As a coherent discipline, it dates back to the beginning of the twentieth century, and its development parallels that of modern business. Indeed, it's probably not too much to say that without PR, modern business as we know it would not be possible.

Perhaps it strikes you as obvious that relating to the public is an essential ingredient in any successful commercial or civic enterprise. If so, you're one up on your great-grandfather, for the notion that public relations is something that needs to be continuously monitored and cultivated hasn't been around all that long. It first arose partly in reaction to, partly as a consequence of, the huge social and economic shifts that began to transform the United States toward the end of the nineteenth century. Before then, most of the country's business and political leaders didn't really care very much what the "average American" thought about or wanted out of life. Certainly not the robber barons who then dominated the business landscape. The fact was, old-fashioned tycoons like Rockefeller, Morgan, and Gould didn't need to. They made their money not from selling products to a broad mass of consumers, but in primary activities such as oil, finance, and mining that involved little if any contact with the general public. As a result, they didn't have to be concerned about what most people thought about them or their enterprises. Indeed, one might even say they regarded public opinion and their own public images with an indifference that bordered on contempt—except that, in their day, concepts like public opinion and public image didn't yet exist.

All that started to change around the turn of the century, when increasing prosperity, spreading literacy, and evolving democratic values began to create the first glimmerings of an American mass culture. Stock ownership was expanding beyond the confines of small Wall Street cabals, with the result that Main Street increasingly found itself with a voice in the nation's economic destiny. At the same time, a new breed of consumer-oriented companies with names like AT&T and General Electric were coming to the fore; to sell their services and appliances, they needed to understand and influence the wants, needs, attitudes, and opinions of a fast-growing mass of middle-class householders. Politics, too, began to reinvent itself, as newspaper chains proliferated and the new communications technologies of, first, telegraphy and, later, radio began to make it possible for astute leaders to mobilize huge masses of previously scattered voters. The net result of all this was a profound shift in the social balance of power. For the first time, the once imperious lords of business and politics found themselves forced to contend with a new entity known as the "public."

The first generation of PR professionals consisted essentially of damage-control experts, brought in to help put down what amounted to popular uprisings against their clients. (The most famous of these early PR pros was probably Ivy Lee, who made his name defending the Rockefeller interests after the infamous Ludlow

Massacre of 1914, in which fourteen striking miners and their families were killed by company goons.) But after World War I—and particularly after the Wall Street Crash of 1929—the idea began spreading that PR was something both business and government needed to work on all the time.

There was nothing new, of course, about publicity-mongering. Press agentry was an ancient, if not exactly honorable, occupation. But public relations, as the former theatrical press agent Edward Bernays dubbed the new discipline in the early 1920s, was

> **Many people trip up in the media glare for two main reasons: ignorance and arrogance.**

something different. If the publicist's job was simply to call attention to something, the PR man's aim was to create nothing less than an emotional and intellectual climate. The publicist, operating in the tradition of the old-fashioned carnival barker, relied on his street-smart sense of human nature, his understanding of humankind's perennial fascination with the bright, the shiny, the loud, and the unusual; the PR man, steeped in the new sciences of psychology and sociology, drew on the theories of Freud and William James. The name really said it all. Boiled down to its essence, all the publicist wanted was a one-night stand; the PR man, by contrast, was looking for a *relationship*.

Viewed in this sense, modern PR developed along three fronts. The first was corporate, pushed along by the new consumer-oriented behemoths that were remaking the American economy in the initial decades of the twentieth century. The real trailblazer in this regard—the first company to devote major resources and executive attention to public relations—was AT&T, which back then, of course, owned the entire Bell System, and was struggling to secure a nationwide telephone monopoly. As early as 1903 AT&T was hiring outside publicity experts, and by 1907 it had established its own in-house PR department. The department's mission was simple—though, for a corporate concern, revolutionary. As a privately held public utility with a potentially enormous customer base, AT&T needed to win the support not just of a relatively small constituency of investors, bankers, and clients, but also of a broad swath of the general population. The firm's strategy had to be appropriately visionary, and so it was. "Educate the public" was the mandate handed down by company president Theodore Newton Vail. (Of course, what Vail meant by that was, "Make the public appreciate the situation from our point of view.") In any case, what followed over the ensuing decades was a mind-boggling—and hugely effective—avalanche of articles, ads, films, lectures, television specials, school curricula, and other pedagogical and promotional ephemera that flogged the AT&T line.

If AT&T set the standard for the private sector—and its early efforts were quickly emulated by other large, consumer-oriented firms such as General Electric and Ford—Franklin D. Roosevelt established PR's second front in the public sector. Woodrow Wilson was actually the first major American political leader to take advantage of modern PR techniques; in April 1917, just a week after the United States entered World War I, he established a huge propaganda ministry known as the Committee on Public Information (CPI). Headed by a former journalist and staffed by a cadre of enthusiastic (if somewhat cynical) PR and advertising specialists, the CPI's mission was to persuade the public to follow into battle a president who had been reelected just the previous year on the slogan "He kept us out of war." Not only did the CPI succeed, but in the process it developed an arsenal of brilliantly effective PR techniques and attitudes, many of which remain in use to this day. For all that, however, the CPI and its accomplishments paled in comparison to the exploits of the massive publicity juggernaut President Roosevelt built fifteen years later to sell himself and his New Deal to a frightened and skeptical nation.

Uniquely for his time and class, FDR understood that successful mass communication required far more than simply proclaiming a message and presenting an argument. You also had to cultivate the press and charm the public. And that FDR did, as no president had done before him (and few since). To be sure, he had some advantages—a natural buoyancy, an apparently effortless gift for radio (his broadcast "fireside chats" made millions of Americans feel as if he were speaking to them individually, rather than addressing a multitude), and an instinctive appreciation of the importance of symbolic gestures. Even his infirmity helped; had polio not robbed him of the use of his legs, his aristocratic bearing might have been too much for mass consumption.

At the same time that Roosevelt was "writing the book" on political PR, the discipline's third front was taking shape in, of all places, Hollywood. Through the 1930s, as the national economy plunged deeper into depression, the motion-picture industry's star-making machinery grew more and more proficient at creating, imposing, and maintaining public images for its contract players—images that had little if anything to do with the reality on which they were overlaid. Whether taking an awkward pharmacist's son from Glendale named Marion Morrison and turning him into John Wayne, or reinventing a chubby high-school girl with mousy brown hair as a blonde Venus called Lana Turner, Hollywood raised the art of image-making to such heights that even the subjects of its magic themselves often couldn't tell where nature left off and artifice began.

Though the old-fashioned, studio-dominated star system began to fade out in the 1960s, Hollywood's ability to manufacture and market celebrities has continued apace. And increasingly—in particular over the past two decades—its flair for drama (and occasionally melodrama), not to mention its technical expertise, began to seep into the worlds of politics and business,

> **The successful spin doctor gets the press to *want* to go where he'd like it to go.**

and vice versa. Before long, politicians were being groomed like movie stars, businessmen were wooing public constituencies like political candidates, and entertainment figures were merchandising themselves like consumer goods.

No individual or institution better illustrates the merging of these three aspects of modern PR than Ronald Reagan. Reagan, of course, first came to prominence as a movie actor. From the late 1930s through the mid-1950s, he learned from the inside just how a star's image was constructed and an appealing personality projected. In the late 1950s and early 1960s, he became a corporate spokesman (for General Electric and the National Association of Manufacturers), mastering firsthand what it took to sell an audience not simply a character but an ideology as well. And finally, in the mid-1960s, he entered politics, getting himself elected, first, governor of California and, later, president of the United States by deftly combining the skills he had acquired in his previous lines of work.

Like FDR, whom he greatly admired (if not ideologically, then certainly as a charismatic leader), Reagan knew that in a media-dominated world, one prevailed as much by seeming as by doing. In the words of his resident spinmeister Michael Deaver, he recognized that "image is sometimes as useful as substance. Not as

important, but as useful...." As a former film actor, he was also genuinely gifted at communicating what he represented not through
words but via visual images; thus, just as Roosevelt had excelled on
radio, Reagan was an acknowledged master of the dominant
medium of his time, television. In this, he was aided by his visceral
understanding of how much the public hated complexity, how
uncomfortable it was with subtlety or indirection (indeed, he
recoiled from that sort of thing himself). It didn't matter how
intrinsically correct your position might be, Reagan would tell his
aides, if you couldn't explain it—and yourself—simply and clearly,
you'd lose the debate. (To be fair, neither Reagan nor his spin doctors ever went so far as to proclaim that substance was irrelevant;
they simply held—as, indeed, experience had taught them—that by
itself, it wasn't nearly enough.)

This emphasis on presentation and style reflected Reagan's
shrewd take on the central question that has faced everyone who has
ever had to function in the public eye: Which is the most effective way
to win over a crowd of strangers—through a rational presentation of
facts or by an emotional appeal to human passions and prejudices?

The earliest practitioners of modern PR held that facts and
logic were what mattered. As AT&T's Theodore Vail had implied,
all that was needed in order for right to triumph was for the public
to be educated. Even as cynical an operator as Ivy Lee insisted (to
a government commission investigating the carnage at Ludlow)
that his basic mission was nothing more or less than to "get [the]
facts before the greatest number of people...."

Like so much else, this notion was turned on its head by World
War I. What President Wilson's CPI discovered was that messages
that tugged at people's heartstrings were far more effective than
those meant to engage their intellects. In the years after the war, this

attitude became more and more entrenched, as pundits as varied as Walter Lippmann (the Progressive intellectual turned Washington mandarin) and Edward Bernays (the erstwhile Broadway press agent) insisted that the average man did not reflect upon events but merely reacted to them, that passion and drama were what moved people, not reason and logic.

Over the next decade or two, the argument raged inconclusively. By the 1930s, the factual approach was once again in vogue. Indeed, the Roosevelt administration based its PR efforts on behalf of the New Deal largely on the belief that the public would respond to straight talk and fact-filled presentations. It was in this spirit, for example, that new federal agencies such as the Resettlement Administration and the Farm Security Administration commissioned a corps of photographers to document the horrendous conditions afflicting the nation's dust bowl. The idea, of course, was that the debate over the government's unprecedented activism could be won merely by "showing" the public the truth. (The flaw in this logic was pointed out by photographer Lewis Hine, who wryly reminded his employers that "while photographs may not lie, liars may photograph.")

In any case, even before the United States entered World War II, the PR pendulum was swinging back toward the efficacy of emotional appeals. And after the war, Edward Bernays set what would become the dominant tone in a classic essay called "The Engineering of Consent." As his title implied, Bernays believed that public opinion was an artificial construct that could be (indeed, *should* be) manufactured by trained experts. Moreover, he held that the key to doing this effectively was not by arguing the facts, but by understanding the conscious and subconscious emotional desires that move most people. Though in retrospect his faith in the unambiguous ability of science and technology to fathom the ways of the human heart seems almost touchingly naive, Bernays's basic view of the public as myopic, illogical, and easily led (or misled) prevails among many PR practitioners to this day.

■ ■ ■

So why is it, then, if we know so much about what moves people, that so many supposedly sophisticated professionals flounder so badly when they find themselves thrust into the public spotlight?

Or to put it more simply, why do good people get bad press?

The answer is actually buried in that second formulation. What trips people up is the press—or more precisely, the tricky business of *dealing* with the press. Even at the best of times, media attention can be difficult to handle; when it arrives unsought and unwanted on the heels of some personal or professional crisis, it can be positively traumatic. Unfortunately, it is at just these sorts of moments that the penalties for imprudent behavior are most severe. Like it or not, the press is the pipeline through which most of us learn most of what we know about the world—and more to the point, it's the conduit through which the world learns everything it knows about us.

Some of the worst offenders in this regard are business people—in particular, senior corporate types who are used to being in charge. As longtime *Wall Street Journal* bureau chief Steve Sansweet puts it, "Corporate executives tend to be control freaks, and they don't react well to an inherently uncontrollable press." Instead of figuring out how to get the press to work with them, they tend to treat it as an adversary—only to wonder later why they and their companies invariably wind up being portrayed in such a hostile light.

There are two main reasons why so many business people do this to themselves: ignorance and arrogance. Some executives regard the press as an inscrutable and unpredictable force of nature. When lightning strikes, their instinct is to hunker down and wait for the storm to pass. That seems to have been what the head of one major entertainment conglomerate did not too long ago when he was forced out of his job. As veteran entertainment-industry reporter Nikki Finke recalls, "When he got fired, there was no one spinning for him, so all we got was the company's perspective." The result was what amounted to a journalistic crucifixion. Other executives seem to regard the press as a noisy but ultimately spineless beast that can be bullied or cowed into submission. The *Wall Street Journal*'s Sansweet tells a typical story of receiving three increasingly enraged phone calls in a row from a prominent CEO, who had "worked himself into a frenzy" over a *Journal* article that he felt might be unfair to his company. "By the third one," Sansweet recalls, "he was cursing up a storm and threatening that if the article ran no one at his company would ever speak to the *Journal* again." Needless to say, the article did run, and his company did not retaliate.

In fact, the press is neither a force of nature nor an easily manipulated animal. Unlike earthquakes or tornadoes, news people are usually quite predictable. But though their habits, haunts, and appetites are generally well known and easily satisfied, that doesn't mean they can be led around by the ear. Quite the contrary, as a group, the press can be relentless in its pursuit of a story—and when provoked, unforgiving. What the successful spin doctor does is figure out a way to get it to *want* to go where he'd like it to go— or at least get it to lose interest in going where he'd rather it not poke its nose.

We're not talking necromancy here. It's really just a matter of what *Newsweek*'s Wall Street editor Allan Sloan calls "common sense and calmness." The challenge, as Kipling noted, is to keep your head while everyone else around you is losing theirs. Granted, that's not easy when the roof is falling in. But as the saying goes, no guts, no glory.

The thing to remember is that the press doesn't have to be an adversary. In fact, if approached properly, it can be your best ally in a hostile world. Exactly how to do that is something we'll explore in the coming chapters.

CHAPTER 2

The Education of
a Spin Doctor

*"If an idea is worth having once, it's worth
having twice."*
—Tom Stoppard

EVEN AS A KID, I had the makings of a spin doctor. At least that's what
my two younger brothers insist. David and Ronald are both successful lawyers now, so I suppose they must know something about
spinning. And I admit I was a pretty good talker, an asset that was
not without its uses in our often turbulent southside Chicago neighborhood. Still, despite what they say, I never planned on a career in
public relations. Growing up in the 1950s and early 1960s, my main
interest (aside from baseball) was blues and jazz guitar.

David and I played together in a band. We performed mainly
at neighborhood parties—well enough to be offered a recording
contract shortly after I turned eighteen. I was tempted (what
eighteen-year-old wouldn't be?), but my parents were adamant.
College came first.

I began college at the University of Alabama. My parents had just moved to Birmingham, Alabama, from Chicago in 1964. For most of my childhood, my dad had been one of the top sales–management executives at WGN, the big Chicago radio station. But then, during my senior year in high school, he was offered the chance to run a chain of radio stations headquartered in Birmingham, and the next thing I knew a moving truck was pulling up in front of our house.

Talk about culture shock. With the civil-rights movement just hitting its stride, Birmingham wasn't exactly the most congenial place for a Jewish kid from the north. I remember a classroom discussion, shortly after I started school there, in which another student asked me whether I had gone to school with any "niggers" back in Chicago.

"Yes," I replied carefully, "we had Negroes in our classes."

Our teacher glared at me, clearly irritated by my obvious alien sympathies. "No, boy," he snapped. "You're in Birmingham now. It's *niggers*, not Negroes."

Anyway, after two years in Alabama, my dad got a more challenging opportunity running a string of radio and television stations in Maryland. I had spent only a year at the University of Alabama, where most of my energies were devoted to enjoying myself. I then decided it was time to buckle down. Actually, my parents decided that. And so off I went to the University of Maryland at College Park. I had considered going back to Illinois, but for a variety of reasons I chose the University of Maryland. This turned out to be one of the most fateful choices of my life, because College Park was where I wound up meeting my wife and best friend, Nancy.

In my new buckled-down mode, I knew I had to figure out what I wanted to do with my life—or, at least, what I was going to major in. Having grown up in Chicago—which, among other things, was a major-league newspaper town—I'd always had a passing interest in journalism, so I took a few journalism courses. To my pleasant sur-prise, I found that I not only loved the subject, but without very much effort I excelled at it. Writing was something that came naturally to me, and I liked the way journalism forced you to organize your

▌ *Never* miss a newsper-son's deadline.

thoughts. (It was, happily, the way I normally organized my thoughts.)

I wish I could say journalism—or, at least, the media business—was a calling, but it wasn't. I decided to major in jour-nalism simply because I enjoyed it. I just said to myself, "Gee, this is something I'm good at, something I want to do." I was, of course, very lucky. Not only did I happen to have a marketable skill, but I'd also stumbled onto one of the secrets of a successful career. People often ask, "What's the key to success?" Well, I doubt there's any single key, but one of them surely is to do something you like. In any case, this sequence of events prefigured what was to occur years later when I started Sitrick and Company—which is to say, it just sort of happened. I saw an opportunity, and I took it.

As it turned out, the journalism department at the University of Maryland was in the business school, so I wound up earning a dual degree in journalism and business administration. In the end, of course, that proved to be the perfect educational background for the career I was ultimately to pursue. But at the time, I didn't have a clue where it would take me.

Needless to say, I learned a lot at the university. In terms of journalism, however, probably the most important lesson I acquired was something I picked up outside the classroom. I had just begun working on the college newspaper and was terribly excited about what I regarded as a truly devastating exposé I'd written about the fraternity system (of which I was a member). I handed the piece in, and the editor read it while I stood in front of her desk. When she was finished, she looked up at me and said, "This is probably the best article I've gotten since I became editor." Then she crumpled up my pages and threw them in the wastebasket. "It's five after three," she explained. "The deadline was three o'clock."

At the time, I was outraged, but she was right, and I never forgot the lesson. A lot of businesses involve deadlines, but nowhere are they more inviolable than in the news business. Too many people who deal with the press don't understand this. If a reporter calls you with a query and says his deadline is three o'clock, you'd better get back to him no later than three o'clock. Five minutes later, and it won't matter if you have the most fascinating answer imaginable—if his deadline has come and gone, there's nothing he can do with it. (And if you want to have a real impact on the story, you should get back to him sooner—before it's written.)

My first real job was working as a newsman for a local radio and television station. After that, I did some reporting for the *Baltimore News-American* and the *Washington Star*. Then, shortly after I graduated from college in 1969, while I was in discussions with the *Chicago Tribune* about a $125-a-week job as a reporter, fate intervened. Fate, in this case, took the form of the agricultural division of the University of Maryland. The division's public-relations office was looking for a public-information officer, and they were willing to pay me $160 a week. I had just gotten married, and that $35-a-week difference loomed awfully large. Thus, my entry into PR.

■   ■   ■

A big part of my new job involved traveling around the state meeting with local newspaper editors. What I learned from these visits proved invaluable. Time after time, the editors would tell me how frustrating it was to deal with most PR people—not because they objected to someone trying to push a story onto them, but because PR people so often seemed oblivious to their needs. "Why do they always send us press releases on things we have no interest in covering?" asked one exasperated editor.

> **A PR person must understand the wants and needs not only of his client, but also of the press.**

He then went on to answer his own question: "For the most part, they've never even read our newspaper, and they have no idea what we're looking for." As a result, he added, "we wind up taking most of the mail that comes from these people and throwing it in the garbage without even opening it."

This was a lesson I would carry with me for the rest of my career. Not only must a PR person understand the wants and needs of his client, he must also understand the wants and needs of the press. To put it plainly, you have to know your audience. That's a basic rule of journalism, and it's a basic rule of PR as well. What makes it tricky is that in PR, your audience is not simply the general public you're eventually hoping to reach, but also the reporters, editors, and producers on whom you must rely to get your message across.

As an ambitious young man, the challenge seemed clear to me. If I was going to be successful at public relations, I had to be able to figure out what made editors and reporters tick, what made them regard one bit of information as a potential story and another as a candidate for the circular file. At that moment, my real education as a spin doctor began.

∎ ∎ ∎

After about six months at the agricultural division press office, I realized that even though I was only twenty-two, I needed to be playing in a bigger pond—ideally, in a major metropolitan area. So I decided to go back to my hometown of Chicago. In 1970, I got a job as coordinator of press services at Western Electric's Hawthorne works. The following year, I went to work for Chicago's legendary Mayor Richard J. Daley.

Actually, I was hired as an information officer on the PR staff of the city's sprawling Department of Human Resources. But in fairly short order I found myself writing speeches and working on other projects as part of the mayor's office.

It was while I was working for the city that I really honed my placement skills—that is, my ability to come up with story ideas that major media outlets would use. My first step was to immerse myself in the operations of my department. By driving myself to learn every possible detail about what the agency was doing, I unearthed a variety of what struck me as newsworthy achievements. The fact was, we had some pretty innovative programs on the books—such as an enormously successful program to reduce recidivism among juvenile delinquents—that hadn't gotten nearly the attention they deserved. In fact, the recidivism program hadn't gotten any attention at all.

It occurred to me while working for the city that instead of writing the standard story-proposal letter to editors and producers, I might get better results if my pitch read more like a finished news or feature article. Editors, I knew, didn't have the luxury of mulling things over; if they didn't "see" a story immediately, they would invariably discard the proposal. By presenting them with the story itself—or, at least, one possible version of it—I minimized the chance that they wouldn't get the point. Equally important, I made sure that the first time they saw the story, it was from my point of view.

The results of this approach were nothing short of phenomenal. Suddenly, fabulously favorable pieces about Chicago's Department of Human Resources were appearing in *Time* magazine and *U.S. News & World Report,* and on the *CBS Evening News.* My bosses had never seen anything like it; the agency's profile had never been higher. As a result, at the tender age of twenty-four, I was promoted to deputy director of the human resources department's public-information office—the number two PR job at what was at the time the largest city agency in the nation's second-largest metropolis.

■　■　■

I was having a blast. I had not only the satisfaction of doing a demanding job really well, but also the thrill of the power of the office. (Remember, I was only twenty-four at the time.) But there was one problem. I was earning only about $12,500 a year, and my boss wasn't making too much more than that. Unfortunately, if I wanted to stay in PR, his was the best city job to which I could aspire. Clearly, I needed to think about moving on—preferably to the private sector.

After a few days of looking, I spotted an ad in the *Wall Street Journal* for a job as an assistant to the vice president of Chicago's oldest public-relations agency, Selz, Seabolt & Associates. That sounded pretty impressive to me, so I sent in my résumé. A few days later, Lee Seabolt phoned and invited me in for an interview. We talked for a while, during which he told me that he had received something on the order of 1,200 applications for the position.

Then he offered me the job. But what really impressed me was what he did after I accepted: "Well," he said, "now I've got to write all those other people and tell them the job's been filled." I thought that was pretty classy.

It was at Selz, Seabolt that I got my first experience with product publicity. I was working for Leo Floros, an experienced and extremely talented PR practitioner, as well as a very nice man, one of whose clients was Miracle White, a nonpolluting laundry detergent. Though it was manufactured by a division of giant Beatrice Foods, Miracle White was a pretty small player in the laundry detergent market—certainly in comparison to the Procter & Gamble giants like Tide. What that meant to me was that business as usual would get us nowhere. To publicize Miracle White, we'd have to do something out of the ordinary, something more than just talking about the benefits of clean water.

If you understand how the media think and work, you should be able to keep from being trampled.

One day I read a story about kids winning prizes by bobbing for apples. All of a sudden, it clicked: That's how we'd get publicity for Miracle White! We'd sponsor a fishing contest in the Chicago Park District lagoons. The thing about the lagoons was that they were terribly polluted; getting people to go fishing in them would force everyone to think about the importance of clean water—and, of course, a nonpolluting detergent like Miracle White.

Needless to say, it had been years since any live fish had been seen in the lagoons, so it was up to us to stock them. We got a bunch of carp—the only breed that could survive in those waters—which we tagged and let loose in the lagoons. Then we invited

Chicago-area anglers to try their luck. If you caught a tagged carp, you could win a U.S. savings bond.

The response was tremendous—from both the public and the press. Before long, Miracle White's chief executive Leo Singer and I were on a full-fledged media tour, going on television all over the country to talk about fishing, the need for clean water, and the carp we had put in the Chicago lagoons.

It was my next campaign, however, that really put Miracle White on the map. Leo was scheduled to give a speech before the Chicago Lion's Club, and he asked me to write it. He wanted to talk about the problems of pollution and how we all had to pitch in to do something about what was clearly a terrible situation. I remember thinking, "This is noble, but it's also boring. I need to come up with a way to make it news."

The night before he was supposed to give the speech, an idea occurred to me. I immediately picked up the phone and called Leo. "Did you see the article in the *Chicago Tribune* about a bunch of kids in Miami who imitated something they'd seen in a Burt Reynolds movie and doused a bum with gasoline and set him on fire?" I asked.

Leo hadn't, so I described it to him. Then I unveiled my idea. "If you really want to make a splash tomorrow," I said, "why don't you announce that you are declaring a war not just on water pollution but on mind pollution as well—and that as the opening shot in that war, you're going to be the first major advertiser to announce a policy of withdrawing all of your commercials from violent television programs."

A consummate marketer, Leo immediately saw the potential. "Brilliant, boy-chick! Have the speech ready for me by noon tomorrow," he said.

I wound up working through the night, but I met his deadline. Not only did I prepare the speech, but I also put together an accompanying press release. So armed, we went off to the Lion's Club to make history.

There were only two problems. One, no media showed up to cover his speech. And two, fewer than a dozen Lion's Club members turned up.

That didn't stop us, though. Leo delivered the speech as if he were on national television, we issued the press release, and I started calling the media. As I expected, once most editors and news producers heard what Leo had pledged to do, the story got terrific pickup. What really launched it was a major feature in *Newsday*, the highly regarded suburban New York newspaper. Suddenly, Leo's speech became a major national story. Scores of newspapers and radio and television stations picked up on the *Newsday* article, which was carried on the Associated Press wire, and reported this socially responsible executive's "selfless decision." Tens of thousands of letters applauding his action poured in from people all over the country. Leo was interviewed on radio and television stations across the country, including NBC's *Today* show, and more than two hundred newspapers published editorials lauding what he had done.

Clearly, Leo and Miracle White deserved the attention they got. The idea of pulling ads from violent television shows *was* a socially responsible—not to mention unusual—thing for a marketer to do. It was also a terrific story that no editor or news producer worth his salt could resist. I was learning the PR version of Newton's Law: that for every action there is an equal reaction. Do something predictable, and the press will yawn. Do something silly to get their attention, and they'll mock you mercilessly. Do something unexpected and meaningful, and you'll make the front pages.

The experience also reinforced the lesson I'd learned back in Maryland about the importance of knowing your audience. Put another way, I realized that every PR person always has *two* clients: the person who's paying the bills and the media. That isn't to say that PR people should subordinate the interests of their clients to those of the press. They clearly shouldn't. You can't do that and properly serve your clients. But smart PR practitioners do have to make sure they understand the press's interests. This is true of anyone dealing with the media on any level. Any time you can figure out a way simultaneously to excite the media *and* to promote your own (or your client's) agenda—as I managed to do with Leo Singer's television violence speech—I promise you: The results will invariably go careening off the chart.

■　■　■

I worked at Selz, Seabolt for about two years. Then, just after I turned twenty-seven, I decided that if I wanted to achieve my goal of continuing to learn and grow, it was time for me to move out of the agency business and into a corporate position. Turning once again to the *Wall Street Journal*, I discovered that National Can Corporation was looking for a manager of public relations and advertising. I applied, and got the job. Soon after I started, I found out that the company had gone through four PR managers in the previous five years. Undaunted, I dug in and, once again, I tried to learn everything I could about my new employer.

As had become my practice, I operated on the assumption that the best way to generate publicity was to look for things that would pique the interest of editors and reporters. Given their direct impact on the general public, I decided to focus on National

Can's many manufacturing plants. What makes a plant newsworthy? Well, for one thing, it provides jobs—and jobs, of course, are the key to local prosperity, especially in smaller towns. For another, a plant can be a pioneer in new production technologies or safety techniques or personnel policies—any one of which can have a profound impact on the local community, and thus be just the sort of thing an editor or reporter is looking for.

> **You can transform what looks to the outside world like a failure into something the press will report, accurately, as a success story.**

With all this in mind, I would go into a city where National Can operated a plant, find out what exactly it was that particular installation did that had the greatest impact on its community, and bring it to the attention of the local media. The result was invariably a favorable feature story or news broadcast that improved employee morale, fostered community relations, impressed customers, and ultimately boosted the company's overall image (not to mention its stock price).

In my six years at National Can, I managed in this way to generate a huge amount of favorable publicity for the company. But nothing succeeded as well as my suggestion that National Can should pledge publicly that it would not hire illegal aliens—and that our CEO Frank Considine should call upon other companies to follow our lead. Considine was not only a highly ethical man, he was also one of the smartest marketers and businessmen I've ever encountered, and it didn't take much to persuade him to take the point on this issue. But I think even he was surprised by the reaction it provoked.

For my part, I was then (and remain to this day) more than a little bemused that a CEO's announcement that he intended to obey the law would be considered breaking news. But public concerns about illegal immigration and employment had been building in intensity. It was generating a lot of media attention, and, as always, I studied the media's approach to the issue. What I found left me confident that our announcement would generate great coverage. In any case, I remember thinking, what did we have to lose? All we were saying was that we were committed to obeying the law and that other companies should do the same.

The result was Miracle White all over again—and then some. Mail poured in by the carload—from customers, from other business leaders, from ordinary folks of all kinds. We were buried, happily, under an avalanche of favorable publicity and laudatory editorials. Considine became a national figure, and National Can— which was only the third-largest company in its field—received far more and far better publicity than either of its two much larger competitors. The icing on the cake arrived when a book was published in which Considine, who was also a leader in civic, political, and philanthropic affairs, was named the second-most powerful businessman in Chicago—a well-deserved honor to which I would like to think our campaign contributed.

■   ■   ■

My success at National Can brought me a modicum of notoriety— and attracted the attention of executive recruiters. In 1981, after more than a year of prodding, I agreed to an interview with Wickes Companies, at the time a $4-billion-a-year, San Diego–based conglomerate. The offer was to run its PR operation as vice president of communications. I was only thirty-three years old, and the opportunity seemed too great to turn down.

At the time I was hired, all sorts of rumors were swirling around Wickes concerning the company's precarious financial predicament. Even a newcomer like me could see that the deepening national recession was bound to wreak havoc with the housing market, which was the basis of Wickes's business. Still, though I anticipated things might be a bit bumpy, I had no idea of the roller-coaster ride that was awaiting me.

At first, my challenge was to find a way to generate favorable publicity on a corporate level, without calling attention to the company's shaky financials. I did this by concentrating on what I called "the pieces of the whole"—that is, I pitched stories on the various divisions of the company that were performing well. Although there weren't all that many of them, there were enough to enable me to produce a steady stream of positive press. I also got a chance to exhibit my skills at keeping negative stories out of the press, or at least minimizing them.

The biggest challenge, however, came when Wickes filed for protection under the bankruptcy statutes in 1982, and I had to help convince the world that the company could survive even though it had just reported a loss of $400 million in the previous fifteen months, had a negative shareholders' equity of $250 million, and faced 250,000 angry creditors. If those facts weren't devastating enough, Wickes was forced to admit in its bankruptcy filing that it wasn't sure whether it had enough funds on hand to meet its payroll, let alone cover its debts and other cash needs.

The only way to overcome all this, I decided, was to try to get the media to focus on the future, not the past. My vehicle was Wickes's newly hired CEO, corporate turnaround expert Sanford Sigoloff. Sandy, a demanding and phenomenally brilliant former nuclear physicist who was nicknamed Ming the Merciless, had been brought in to rescue the company, and he was prepared to do whatever it took to get Wickes back on its feet. Starting the day of the bankruptcy filing and for months thereafter, I pitched profiles of Sandy and stories about his successes at other formerly troubled companies. Some months later, we featured him in a series of television spots for Wickes Furniture, Builders Emporium, and some of our other subsidiaries that made his a household name in Southern California, among other places, and also significantly contributed to the turnaround of those divisions. (As the *Los Angeles Times* later noted, "The commercials, featuring Sigoloff's piercing stare and the slogan, 'We got the message, Mr. Sigoloff,' helped boost Builders Emporium's sales and built up Sigoloff's image as the self-described 'toughest man in retailing.'")

Focusing on Sandy the way we did quickly restored customer, vendor, and employee confidence in Wickes, which in turn contributed significantly to the company's successful recovery (as well as to my promotion, in less than two years, to senior vice president—one of only five or six in the company). After countless eighteen-hour work days and seven-day work weeks, Sandy and his management team were able to bring Wickes out from Bankruptcy Court protection ahead of schedule in 1985—an accomplishment the bankruptcy judge characterized in open court as "a miracle."

From a PR point of view, the experience demonstrated how you can transform what looks to the outside world like an unmitigated failure into something the press will report, accurately, as a success story. The key is figuring out how to reshape the terms of reference and set a new tone—and doing it convincingly enough that the press eventually accepts it as a given. I'm not talking about smoke and mirrors. This sort of thing can't be conjured out of thin air. You need to be able to cite tangible evidence. In our case, we had the distinct advantage of Sandy Sigoloff's proven track record and impressive management skills to point to—plus a steadily lengthening list of solid accomplishments. Even so, it took a lot of plugging to get journalists to rethink their view of Wickes, to get them to take it out of their mental file drawer labeled "Bankrupt Failures" and put it in the one labeled "Impressive Comebacks."

In many ways, the techniques I employed at Wickes were no different from the ones I had learned and refined in my previous jobs. The major difference, of course, was that for the first few years at least we were operating in a crisis mode at Wickes—and in a crisis, everything becomes much more delicate. Normally, you pursue the media; in a crisis, the media are generally pursuing you. What's more, because a great deal tends to be at stake, you can't afford to trip. The fundamentals still apply: If you understand the psychology and dynamics of the media, chances are you'll be able to keep from being trampled in the rush.

■　■　■

Late in 1988, Sandy and his management team tried to buy Wickes, but the financing fell through and the company was put up for sale. In the end, a group of outside private investors gained control, and Sandy quit. I wasn't sure what I wanted to do, but I did know that whatever it was it wouldn't be at Wickes. When the new owners asked if I wanted to stay, I told them they didn't need me. That wasn't false modesty speaking; the reorganized Wickes was not going to be a publicly held company anymore, which meant that the role of the PR department was going to shrink considerably.

While I was mulling over my next step, Henry Sweetbaum, a friend in Europe who was unhappy with the PR firm working for his company, asked if I'd help him out with his annual report, media issues, and some other public-relations matters. When I said sure, he wrote a letter to his PR firm informing them that their services were no longer needed as he had just retained an outfit he called "Sitrick and Company." In fact, no such entity existed, nor was I sure that one ever would (though, I confess, I liked the name).

Not long after that, I got a call from another friend, this one a banker at the now defunct but then thriving investment firm of Drexel Burnham Lambert. He was working with Shamrock Holdings—the family investment vehicle of Hollywood mogul Roy Disney—in an attempt to take control of Polaroid. He wanted me to meet with Shamrock's president, Stanley Gold. "These guys are getting killed in the press," my banker friend told me. "They need your help."

Indeed, the newspapers in Boston, Polaroid's home town, were shredding Disney as a rapacious bandit ("Roy the Raider," they were calling him), and depicting Gold—a lawyer turned manager who had built one of the most impressive investment records in American industry—as an asset-stripper out to dismember a beloved corporate citizen. Disney and his wife were mortified, as was Gold. Clearly, something needed to be done.

"You know," I told my friend, "I really haven't decided what's next for me, and this Sunday I'm flying to London."

If my friend was put off by my diffidence, he didn't show it. "Well, how about meeting with us on your way to the airport?" he said.

What could I do? I agreed, and on my way to the airport that Sunday, I had the car wait for me outside the Drexel Burnham offices in Beverly Hills, while I went inside to meet with Stanley Gold and his bankers.

We talked for a while about how they were handling their press versus how I would handle their press, and before long we were debating. This struck me as ridiculous, so I turned to the group and said, "Look, maybe you can be successful with your approach, but I can't. If you want me to be involved, I only know one way to do this. I feel strongly mine is the approach we've got to take. If you disagree—well, that's okay, but I think you'll continue to get hammered."

The whole room was silent for a moment. Then Stanley nodded and said, "Okay."

"I'll take the responsibility," I added, "but I also have to have the authority."

Once again, Stanley nodded.

"Now tell me this," I continued, "are you really planning to strip Polaroid?"

"No," he replied. "But why do you ask?"

"Because if you are going to strip the company, we can't say you aren't. The press will eventually find out, and then they'll kill you."

"I'm not going to strip the company," Gold said. "I plan to run it and build it."

That was all I needed to hear. I told Stanley I'd be happy to help out.

My first order of business was to try to restore relations with the most important local newspaper—in this case, the *Boston Globe*. Some of Shamrock's advisors had been chuckling over how they had frozen out an overly critical *Globe* reporter—to the point at which her editor finally agreed to assign another reporter to the story, a decision that prompted the original reporter to burst into tears. I was appalled. Rather than regarding the incident as some sort of victory, I thought it was a terrible blunder by our side. "That particular reporter may be off the story," I told the advisors, "but that doesn't mean she's out of your life. At the very least, she's got to have some friends in the newsroom, and they're not going to be feeling very charitable toward you."

In an effort to get things back on track, I phoned the *Globe*'s business editor. He took my call, but he was (understandably) not very friendly. The paper had made a mistake pulling its original reporter off the Polaroid story, he told me curtly, and as of now, she was back on it. If I had anything to say, he added, I should say it to her.

Fair enough, I thought. I immediately phoned the reporter. No sooner had I finished introducing myself than she began ripping into me. "Your clients decided they weren't going to talk to me because they didn't like the way I was covering the story," she said. "Well, I'm serving notice on you now that that's not going to work. I'm going to write about this takeover whether or not you guys talk to me."

"Hey," I said, "I'm the new guy, and that's all history. Just tell me what you need."

"What I need," she shot back, "is access."

"Okay," I replied. "How about an exclusive interview with Stanley Gold, right in the *Globe*'s own offices?" The reporter was astounded—and she accepted the offer on the spot.

When I told him what I'd arranged, Stanley was a bit skeptical. "Look," I said, "no one can make your case better than you. And if you can win this reporter over, the rest of the press will be on your side before you know it."

So Stanley and I went to Boston, met with the reporter, and cleared the air. He was terrific. The result was a long, extremely favorable story in the *Globe* that accurately portrayed Shamrock's plans for Polaroid. A paid advertisement could not have said it half so well, nor have been remotely so credible.

Although we managed to turn the tide in the press, Shamrock

didn't get Polaroid. But it did make a reported $50 million on its Polaroid stock.

In any case, with that deal, Sitrick and Company's mergers-and-acquisition practice was launched. Today, with offices in Los Angeles and New York, and a staff of some thirty professionals (many of them former reporters and editors), we provide service to about 150 clients a year—mainly corporations, with a sprinkling of high-profile individuals, including sports and entertainment moguls like Marvin Davis, Kirk Kerkorian, and Don King, and Hollywood stars like Kim Basinger and Kelsey Grammer. We specialize in corporate, financial, transactional, and crisis communications, and for the past several years have been consistently rated as one of the top financial and crisis-management PR firms in the country.

Though we have a substantial practice in each of our areas, we're probably best known for our work in such sensitive situations as mergers and acquisitions, bankruptcies, court battles, and various other business and personal crises. Although every case we handle has its own peculiarities, the philosophy we employ with virtually all of them is basically the same. As I learned time and again throughout my career, whether you are a government agency that the public takes for granted, a private corporation under siege, or an individual whose good name is being dragged unfairly through the mud, the key to transforming the press from howling adversary to valuable ally is the ability to put yourself inside a reporter's head—which, as it happens, is just where we'll go in the next chapter.

CHAPTER 3

▌ Inside a Reporter's Head

"To a newspaperman, a human being is an item with the skin wrapped around it."
—Fred Allen

MOST CONTEMPORARY AMERICAN JOURNALISTS probably don't realize it, but their true spiritual father is not Woodward and Bernstein, or Edward R. Murrow, or even Brenda Starr. Rather, it's Finley Peter Dunne, a name not heard much these days. Dunne was a turn-of-the-century editor and newspaper columnist whose major (and well-deserved) claim to fame was a character he created and then featured in more than seven hundred newspaper pieces he wrote between 1893 and 1926. He called the character Martin Dooley, and speaking in his distinctive voice—an Irish brogue so thick you could cut it with a knife—Dunne was able to comment on a wide range of social and political topics with a candor and incisiveness that would have cost him his pulpit had he tried it on his own. An uneducated but sharp-witted Irish saloonkeeper *cum* philosopher, Dunne's Mr. Dooley offered acerbic observations on everything from electioneering ("Politics ain't beanbag") to human nature ("Thrust ivrybody but cut th' ca-ards"), painting in the process a clear-eyed if somewhat cynical portrait of a hypocritical culture that valued cunning and connections over virtue and merit.

In such a world—where, as Mr. Dooley once observed, "ivry man is th' equal of ivry other man befure th' law if he isn't careful"—there are few moral absolutes. But there are some, and one of them, according to Dunne, was the role of the press. It was, he wrote, to comfort the afflicted and afflict the comfortable.

Whether or not that is in fact the press's proper job, the line is a lovely one, and to this day editors and reporters quote it approvingly (though usually without knowing its provenance). More to the point, it reflects a mixture of cynicism and idealism, skepticism and naiveté, envy and compassion, that nearly a century later remains characteristic of more journalists than not.

What does this have to do with the art of spin? Pretty much everything. Though it may seem obvious, you'd be surprised how many otherwise intelligent people don't seem to realize (or at least acknowledge) that the key to successful spin—that is, getting your story told the way you'd like it to be told—is knowing how to get along with journalists. As skills go, this one is not all that hard to learn. But it does need to be learned, and the first lesson involves understanding what it comprises. To wit: Getting along with journalists doesn't necessarily mean being their friend, or providing them with all the information they ask for, or even laughing at their jokes. If it means any one thing, it means recognizing, if not always fully accommodating, the pressures under which they operate and the ambitions that drive them.

To outsiders, the press usually appears as one of two things:

a huge impersonal machine, propelled by obscure forces mere mortals can't even guess at, or a mindless pack of jackals bent on exploiting human misery and misfortune for its own venal ends. While neither of these images is entirely unjustified, the news business is really something else entirely—first and foremost, a very human enterprise carried out by a very

> **You must recognize the pressures under which newspeople operate and the ambitions that drive them.**

human group of individuals, each of whom possesses a particular set of attitudes, anxieties, affections, and aspirations.

Some of these concerns are professional, others are emotional; all are profoundly, sometimes painfully, personal. The point is that understanding just what they are and how to address them is crucial, for few things—not the inarguable facts of a particular situation, the subject's sterling reputation, or the phases of the moon—have a greater impact on how the press will treat someone than how that someone has treated the press. Which is to say, whether he has satisfied, ignored, or antagonized the motivations, desires, and needs of the individual reporters and editors assigned to his story. (While it's true that most journalists pride themselves on their professionalism, they are, after all, human—and as such bound to look more sympathetically at a subject who has treated them well than one who has not. This is not to say they'll overlook or ignore the facts, but how they have been treated can—and often does—impact the way they will interpret those facts.)

Needless to say, all journalists are hardly alike. But most do have some things in common. Not politics necessarily (more reporters may vote Democratic than Republican, but the myth that all journalists are reflexively liberal is just that—a myth), nor even a fondness for alcohol (the reality of the hard-drinking reporter began to fade around the same time as the businessman's three-martini lunch). The kind of people who choose journalism as a career tend to share something more fundamental than either of those things: They share a certain sort of temperament and a similar set of motivations. And in large measure, their distinctive temperament and motivations reflect the mixture of qualities (i.e., cynicism *and* idealism) that informed Finley Peter Dunne's notion of what a newspaperman should do, and be.

■ ■ ■

The first thing you need to understand about what makes journalists tick is that virtually all reporters, editors, and news producers believe in the notion of the "story." That is, they subscribe to the idea that there exists no better method of recounting events, trends, and developments than in the form of discrete stories, each with a beginning, middle, and end. This belief is so much at the core of their being (or, as the psychologists would say, it's so "internalized") that asking a journalist about it is likely to yield nothing so much as a bewildered stare. Nonetheless, the fact remains that this journalistic commonplace is merely a convention, and in the view of some, a rather arbitrary one at that. Indeed, it's been argued that reporting the news as a series of little mini-dramas is, at best, a highly stylized way of looking at the world; at worst, it may be an entirely inappropriate method that so distorts the nature of reality that it renders itself entirely useless, if not downright misleading.

The problem is that a good story requires drama, and drama requires conflict, not to mention a surprising or novel twist and a satisfying resolution. Alas, life (even business life) doesn't always provide these elements. Given the demands of their profession and the nature of their temperament, however, most journalists tend to interpret the information at hand in the way most likely to make it seem as if it did. Hence, what the professional athlete might regard as just a series of off days is reported by the

> **To get your message across to journalists, you must present it in the form of a story.**

sports columnist as perhaps the beginning of an ominous decline; what the tycoon will brush off as an innocent meeting with a competitor might be portrayed by the investigative reporter as a suspicious rendezvous, the genesis even of a potentially illegal conspiracy.

Outsiders often label this sort of thing as sensationalism, but it's really a process much more subtle than the tabloid practice of deliberately inflating innocuous events into something more likely to sell newspapers. When, for example, *New York* magazine reported that the so-called "Heaven's Gate" mass suicide near San Diego was a direct outgrowth of the wacky Southern California lifestyle, rather than an aberrant event that could have happened anywhere, it wasn't because the magazine's editors thought they could attract more readers that way; it was because they couldn't imagine interpreting the facts in any other fashion.

For the would-be spinmeister, the implications of this are clear. To get your message across, you must present it in the form of a story—that is, as a well-turned tale, complete with clearly drawn heroes and villains, exciting twists and turns, and all the other accoutrements of the storyteller's art. And the more taut and compelling your narrative, the better. Writers at *Newsweek* used to joke that there was one ultimate, all-purpose opening sentence that would work for any major story—whether it concerned an earth-quake, a *coup d'état*, or a Michael Jackson concert: "The dogs began barking at midnight." The idea, of course, was that to hook the reader every news story had to offer the kind of enticing atmosphere and addictive tension of a best-selling thriller.

Like all jokes, this one is built around a bit of an exaggeration—but not much of one. Just as an underwriter doesn't expect to sell a new issue on Wall Street without a good story to tell investors, a spin doctor can't hope to get anywhere with the media without an arresting yarn that includes compelling characters, an easily understood conflict, and a neat ending. As *Wall Street Journal* veteran Steve Sansweet observes: "Reporters don't like being spun, but if they get a good story, it doesn't matter."

■ ■ ■

On a more conscious level, journalists are driven by a familiar set of motivations—foremost among them, the desire to beat their rivals by producing one big exclusive after another. If money is the mother's milk of politics, as Jesse Unruh once observed, competition is the lifeblood of journalism. Every business involves competition, of course, but aside from the stock market and professional sports, it's hard to find one in which the results are posted as starkly or as often as they are in the news business. Every day—every hour, in some cases—a newsman must face up to the consequences of his work. Either he got the story or he didn't; either he made the deadline or he missed it; either he broke an exclusive or he had the same stuff as everyone else.

Rather than preying on them oppressively, this relentless comparing is what energizes most journalists. Instead of regarding it as a burden (the ordeal of having to prove yourself every day), they see it as a welcome opportunity (the inspiring challenge of *being able* to prove yourself every day). Indeed, it is the inescapable clarity of the news business's competitive arena—the fact that they are visibly on the line just about all the time—that more than anything else attracts many journalists to the profession (as opposed to some more ambiguous if better paying corporate venue in which who was responsible for what is rarely if ever evident). "People talk about reporters hoping eventually to make a big score—a book contract or a movie deal," notes the *Journal*'s Sansweet. "And in many cases, it's true. But what most reporters are working for isn't the big score, but the small score—the pat on the back from their bureau chief or editor, who calls the next day and says, 'You really beat the pants off the competition.' That's what reporters live for."

To this end, there is probably no more powerful motive at work in the journalistic personality than the desire to "own" a particular story—to have the story exclusively; or if not exclusively, then to have the interview no one else has; or if not the interview, then the quote; and if not the quote, the detail; and so on. Help a reporter accomplish this, and you'll have made, if not a friend for life, at least a grateful potential ally. As *Newsweek*'s Wall Street editor Allan Sloan puts it, "All I want is to be able to get someone on the phone who's willing to talk with me. Give me that, and I'll be a happy man."

∎   ∎   ∎

Journalists, of course, have egos, and for a variety of reasons (the intense competition, their constant proximity to the rich and/or famous), theirs tend to be both larger and more fragile than the average person's. "If you can't take it, you shouldn't dish it out" is not a maxim that has ever enjoyed much popularity among the fourth estate.

As practitioners of one of the few occupations whose impunity is specifically protected by the U.S. Constitution, newspeople have a healthy sense of professional entitlement, to put it mildly. This is odd in a way, for journalism isn't a profession like law or medicine with ancient precepts set down in stone and panels of venerable masters to decide who should be admitted to the practice. In fact, journalism isn't a profession at all, but rather a craft that involves what Walter Lippmann once defined as "an incredible medley of fact, propaganda, rumor, suspicion, and fears." Most reporters and editors take themselves quite seriously today, but it was not so long ago that the raffish irresponsibility epitomized by *The Front Page* was far more the rule than the meticulous double-checking glamorized in *All the President's Men*.

Experienced spin doctors know reporters want the inside scoop and never want to appear naive.

Though there have always been serious American newspapers committed to accurate, responsible reporting, U.S. journalism as a whole didn't really start to get respectable until the 1940s and 1950s. At that time, a better-educated breed of journalist began coming into the field; at the same time, news organizations and newspeople started to think of themselves as public servants of a sort.

Like so much else in America, the business was changed radically by Vietnam and Watergate. In Vietnam, journalists began to challenge their own government's statements on a scale and with an intensity neither side had ever previously even come close to experiencing. What began building in Southeast Asia in the mid-1960s came to a head a few years later in the Watergate scandals that brought down Richard Nixon; ultimately, the press and the government found themselves facing off as out-and-out adversaries.

The *Washington Post*'s tenacity in the Watergate chase at first embarrassed, then inspired the rest of the news media. It also transformed the image of journalists, both in their own eyes as well as the public's. To begin with, it turned reporters and editors into celebrities. With Robert Redford playing Bob Woodward and Dustin Hoffman portraying Carl Bernstein, newspeople couldn't help but seem glamorous. More significantly, the Watergate drama seemed to redefine the journalist's role in life: No longer a passive observer, he was now an active participant, a guardian of truth and morality in a corrupt society, a powerful force in the culture who could uncover wrongdoing and bring down a government—in short, a moral hero. As the Pulitzer Prize–winner (and former *New York Times* correspondent) David Halberstam observed a decade after Watergate, "The journalism I went into in the mid-1950s was a sort of dark corridor where only screw-ups went. Now we have a hot profession that attracts people viscerally interested in exercising power. Reporters are not that interested in issues, but in becoming stars."

∎ ∎ ∎

As Halberstam suggests, journalists are rarely content to labor in obscurity. Still, although most of them yearn for recognition—fame, even—that doesn't mean they're interested in becoming celebrities just so they can get a better table at the bistro of the moment. The recognition they seek is of a particular sort. Given the nature of their business, it shouldn't be surprising that the reputation most reporters covet more than any other is that of the insider, the guy (or gal) known for knowing everyone worth knowing, the "player" whose calls are always returned—even by those A-list types who *never* return journalists' calls.

In more than a few reporters, this desire is strong enough to overwhelm their professional judgment. Veteran entertainment-industry reporter Nikki Finke (who is herself considered one of the best-placed journalists in Hollywood) calls this the "big top" syndrome. "Even though he may give you nothing but pabulum, you find yourself going to the top person [in a company] for a quote," she says. "The reason is that he makes you look good. You can impress your editor with the fact that you can get him on the phone. In fact, the people you should talk to are the people who are sweeping up behind the elephants. After all, they usually have less of a stake in how the company looks, and as a result are more likely to be candid with you."

Reporters also want to be known as the sort of person who invariably knows the "inside" story—the "real" reason (as opposed to the "official" explanation) why the XYZ Corporation settled that lawsuit, or replaced that executive, or introduced that new line of crackers. The unspoken premise behind this sort of attitude, of course, is the belief not simply that things are not always what they seem to be, but that they are *virtually never* what they seem to be, and that anyone who accepts them as such is the opposite of a sophisticated insider—namely, an ingenuous patsy. This characterization may seem a bit harsh, and most reporters would probably claim to possess a more balanced view of the way the world works. But the fact is, to a greater or lesser degree, the simple but profound fear of appearing naïve colors a lot of journalistic thinking.

Among other reasons, this is why when someone announces

what might be regarded as good news, reporters will often react with suspicion. It's not that they are constitutionally incapable of accepting that sometimes things do turn out well. It's that they hate the idea that someone may be putting something over on them—so much so that any even vaguely positive announcement is often considered guilty (i.e., deceptive) until proven innocent (i.e., truthful). As a result, experienced spin doctors know that when they have good news to share, they often must be prepared to persuade the press that the story is not only accurate but that it also is *smart* (which is to say that it reflects the shrewd insider's understanding of what is really going on, and not simply what the client wants you to know).

▪ ▪ ▪

This shouldn't be interpreted to mean that reporters' true motives are vain and shallow. As Finley Peter Dunne recognized, there is in the news business a strong component of, if not morality, certainly idealism. Virtually no one goes into the news business for the money, and despite what many professional athletes and Hollywood types like to tell themselves, very few reporters are drawn to their craft solely for the opportunities it provides them to hurl mud at their betters. (This last notion—that a critical or skeptical journalist is really only expressing his envy of some gifted star lucky enough actually to lead the kind of life the reporter wishes he could have himself but is too stupid or untalented to achieve on his own—may provide some consolation, but it is rarely true.)

The fact is, a quarter-century after Richard Nixon resigned the presidency, the Watergate syndrome remains very much in evidence. That is, in addition to everything else, journalists still like to believe they are on the side of the angels—or as we used to say in the 1960s, that they are part of the solution, not part of the problem. It may sound simplistic or even (for all their horror of naiveté) jejune, but most reporters would insist that one of their basic jobs is to reveal the truth and expose bad guys for the public good. Or as the *Chicago Times* put it back in 1861, "to print the news and raise hell."

This belief in a higher purpose is why journalists tend to get so aggrieved when their motives are attacked. It's not that they feel guilty about anything; it's that they feel morally offended. They also sometimes feel embarrassed. After all, what professional cynic likes to admit that trapped inside his grizzled exterior the soul of an Eagle Scout is struggling to get out?

By the same token, there's generally more than standard human envy behind the disdain reporters so often display toward well-to-do business and political types, whom they tend to regard (occasionally for good reason) as being unconcerned with anything but their own advancement. The recipients of such scorn may think it's success *per se* that offends journalists, but that's rarely the case. As grubby as they may often seem, journalists are no less susceptible to the American dream than anyone else. Indeed, as publications like *Vanity Fair* and *People* consistently demonstrate, newspeople are capable of worshipping success with a fervor that would impress a fundamentalist snake handler. The problem journalists have with moguls of various sorts is what they see as the superficiality of their ambition, be it acquisitiveness for its own sake or mere personal vanity.

This moralistic side of the journalistic psyche is probably the most insufferable aspect of the reporter's personality; certainly, it's the most prickly. But it's not entirely unforgivable. For when it comes down to it, the idealistic yearnings of most newspeople are entirely honorable (if occasionally a bit grandiose): to epitomize journalism as an honest profession; to act as the true fourth estate, watchdog of the commonweal; to provide the countervailing force that keeps the oligarchs and plutocrats at bay. And if in the process a reporter can manage to make a name for himself—respected by his peers and honored by the Pulitzer committee—who's to say that's such a bad thing?

■ ■ ■

From this mixed bag of motives—some sensible and well-founded, others callow and superficial—comes the journalistic personality that everyone in and around the public arena must deal with. As *Newsweek* magazine noted back in 1981, in the aftermath of the Janet Cooke scandal (in which a *Washington Post* reporter's Pulitzer Prize–winning story turned out to be a fake): "The American media may well be the most accurate and unbiased in the world, but journalists are not acolytes at the altar of truth. They are fallible human beings, and the greater the skepticism with which the public regards them, the better off both press and public will be."

To which one might add, the more you consider what makes journalists tick, the more likely it is that you'll be able to meet both their personal and professional needs. And the more you can do that, the better your chances will be of getting your story told the way you want it to be told.

CHAPTER 4

▌ The Truth About Spin

"Some people think of the glass as half full. Some people think of the glass as half empty. I think of the glass as too big."

—George Carlin

TO MOST PEOPLE, THE WORD "spin" has an inherently negative connotation, and that's putting it mildly. They think of Michael Deaver choreographing camera shots of blacks and Latinos on the floor of the 1996 Republican National Convention in an effort to make the GOP seem multiculturally "inclusive." Or Dick Morris trying to polish Bill Clinton's "regular guy" image by persuading him to spend a vacation camping in the Grand Tetons rather than playing golf in Palm Springs. Or a company spokesman delicately describing a major chemical spill as a "minor industrial accident." Or Balkan warlords referring to genocide as "ethnic cleansing." They think of it, to borrow George Orwell's phrase, as something "designed to make lies sound truthful and murder respectable, and to give an appearance of solidity to pure wind."

To these people, spin is intrinsically and invariably deceptive; its sole purpose is to seduce us into believing something that clear-eyed analysis would reveal to be a lie or a sham. As former *New York Times* advertising columnist Randall Rothenberg put it in a scathing 1996 essay in *Esquire* magazine, it's "the burnishing of an irrelevancy until it appears to be germane, the redirection of a truth until it seems to be *the* truth"—in short, what we used to call "fiction, dissembling, fudging, lying."

> **It's not the facts that create people's viewpoints, but rather the way they are presented.**

Well, that's certainly one side of the story.

The closest thing to an authority on the subject, *Webster's New World Dictionary of Media and Communications*, defines spin in two ways. There's the old, innocent definition: "a new angle or fresh approach, as in to put a spin on a story or project." And there's the new, cynical definition: "language used to slant, twist, or manipulate a position, concept or event or an interpretation or modification designed to alter the public's perception of it." You pays your money, and you takes your choice.

Needless to say, hardly anyone uses the first definition anymore. To most people, the idea that you can spin a story without slanting or twisting it dishonestly seems ridiculous—at best, absurdly naive; at worst, a contradiction in terms. But is this really the case? Let's examine, for a moment, the logic behind the putatively self-evident proposition that spin is necessarily mendacious.

On one level, the scorn with which so many people regard the very concept of spin reflects the simple but intense human antipathy to anything that makes us feel that we've been manipulated or deceived. But it also reflects a deeper unease, one that derives from a widely held conviction most of us take for granted: namely, that there exists something journalists in particular like to refer to as the objective truth. The idea is that events exist independently of observers, and that there is one—and only one—account of any event that can properly be described as reflecting what "really happened." Or as the producers of the popular television series *The X Files* like to put it, "The truth is out there." The implication, of course, is that if we are sufficiently honest and diligent, we can discover and relate this uniquely accurate version of events, thereby adding to the sum total of human knowledge—while at the same time exposing all contrary versions as the deceptions and misrepresentations they must be. In this view, the truth is a wall built of bricks of fact, while spin is a whitewash designed to obscure the wall's real nature.

Even to question this notion is to open yourself to accusations of cynicism or worse. Of course, there is such a thing as objective truth. The tree falling in the forest makes a noise whether or not anyone is there to hear it. Certain things are just so, they are what they are, and all the fancy phrase-making in the world won't change them.

But is this the way the world really works? Up to a point, yes. That point, however, is more quickly arrived at than most people realize. Certainly, the common reality we all share seems to include a vast catalogue of indisputable, unalterable facts: George Bush succeeded Ronald Reagan as president of the United States, and was himself succeeded by Bill Clinton; the Florida Marlins won the 1997 World Series; the sky is blue; the earth is round (more or less); and the sun always seems to set in the west. Though epistemologists might quibble, for our purposes it's probably safe to say that these sorts of facts are objectively true—that only a sophist or a scam artist (or a member of the Flat Earth Society) would care to dispute them.

Such generally indisputable assertions cover a lot of ground, which is to say they usefully describe a good deal of the world we inhabit. But even putting aside pedantic quibbles (e.g., is the sky *really* blue?), they barely skim the surface of the huge ocean of discourse that fills our lives and occupies most of the media's time and effort. More typically, we find ourselves struggling to cope with incidents, events, and circumstances whose "true" nature is not so easily determined or defined. Take, for example, the major domestic political event of the mid-1990s—the reelection of President Clinton. On one level, it would seem to be a classic example of an indisputable reality: Clinton won the 1996 presidential election, while Bob Dole, Ross Perot, and a host of minor candidates lost. Certainly, if that was all the media had to say about what happened, they would have been on safe ground (epistemologically speaking, at least). But that wasn't all they had to say, nor should it have been. After all, the real significance of an election is not simply in the results *per se*, but in the implications of those results—what they reveal about the temper of the nation, and the extent to which they are likely to affect the government's future actions.

So what did Clinton's victory reveal about the temper of the nation? That the electorate was happy with his leadership? That it didn't trust Dole? That it had been bamboozled by a multimillion-dollar advertising campaign? That it was frightened by Republican extremism? That it was looking forward to the future? That it was afraid of the future?

And how was Clinton's victory likely to affect future government action? Everybody and his brother certainly had an opinion about that, but there was no way of knowing for sure, was there?

In his *Esquire* essay, Randall Rothenberg quotes *Washington Post* columnist E.J. Dionne, Jr., as musing about the "philosophical war going on between a theory that says there is no truth and another that says there is a truth and it's still worth pursuing." For his part, Rothenberg adds that he fears "the old school is losing that battle" (the old school presumably being the one that believes in the existence of a unique, identifiable truth).

Give any decent spin doctor (or reporter, for that matter) one set of facts, however, and he should be able to spin from it four different but equally accurate accounts of what happened, from the most negative version imaginable to the most positive rendition one could hope for. That's because it's not the facts

▌**Spin is deciding which facts are relevant, which are not, and how the facts relate to one another.**

that create people's viewpoints, but rather the way they are presented—how they are juxtaposed, which are emphasized and which are deemed irrelevant, where they are disclosed and by whom.

So what was the "true" story of the 1996 presidential election? Even limiting yourself to the most narrow of assertions—for instance, that Clinton won—begs a host of questions. (After all, he failed to capture a majority of the popular vote, and the Republicans continued to control both houses of Congress.) All you can really say is that Clinton captured a majority of the electoral college vote, as a result of which he was entitled to continue living in the White House for another four years. Which, as we noted above, is hardly the conclusion to any sort of meaningful story, but rather just a beginning.

In this light, it seems both smug and unrealistic to insist that there is only one "objective truth." Doesn't it make more sense to suggest there is no one "true" story, but instead a multiplicity of truths? To take this position is not, as Rothenberg and Dionne seem to imply, to throw up one's hands and surrender to cynicism or anarchy. Rather, it's to recognize that there is more than one way to stack those bricks of fact, and just because my wall winds up looking different from yours doesn't necessarily mean that I'm a liar or a fool.

So when we speak of spin, we are not speaking of whitewashing the wall of truth; nor are we speaking of distorting the facts or misrepresenting them. Rather, we are speaking of doing no more or less than what every conscientious journalist—indeed, every clear-eyed observer of any kind—does when confronted with the challenge of recounting some new event: namely, interpreting the known facts, deciding which are relevant and which are not, and making assumptions as to how one bit of information relates to another. In short, when we speak about the art of spin, we are speaking about the art of stacking those bricks.

PART II

The Rules of Spin

The art of spin employs equal parts common sense, strategic thinking, and specific knowledge of how the press works. It's not the sort of thing that should be undertaken lightly or by amateurs. But neither is it an arcane science or a black art. It is, rather, a rational discipline, and as such its "secrets" can be fully expressed in a series of completely straightforward, entirely comprehensible rules. The chapters that follow will discuss the rules of spin.

CHAPTER 5

News Media Abhor a Vacuum

If you don't tell your story, someone else will tell it for you.

"JOURNALISM," THE NOVELIST AND CRITIC Rebecca West once observed, involves nothing so much as "an ability to meet the challenge of filling the space." An erstwhile journalist herself, West understood her profession well. Indeed, this insight of hers cuts right to the heart of what makes the press tick—so incisively that it should be tattooed on the forehead of everyone who willingly or unwillingly gets caught up in, and hopes to survive, the unflattering glare of media attention. When the press is in full cry after a story, nothing matters more to the reporters covering it (and the editors and producers whipping them on) than having some fresh meat for the next edition or broadcast. The gaping hole in the upcoming issue, the yawning chasm that is tonight's half-hour news block—these demand to be filled. And no sooner will they be satisfied than a new cycle of holes and chasms will begin clamoring for attention.

"Feeding the beast," they call it. To the uninitiated, the process can be terrifying. As the deadline approaches—and in this era of multimedia synergy, the deadline is always approaching—newspeople begin to eye potential sources with the desperate stare of a starving wolf with hungry pups to feed. They must find someone to talk to them.

In this frenzied atmosphere, an object of press interest who decides to lie low (even for the most understandable of reasons) is adopting an extremely risky—not to mention potentially costly—posture. No doubt you've heard Abraham Lincoln's famous line, "Better to remain silent and thought a fool than to speak out and remove all doubt." Well, Lincoln fought his share of battles, to be sure, but in this media-dominated age, his advice just doesn't hold up. The fact is—and if there is one basic rule of spin, it is this—the news media abhor a vacuum. If you won't talk to them, they'll simply find someone else who will—which is to say, if you don't tell your story, someone else will tell it for you. And chances are, theirs won't be a version you like.

■   ■   ■

That, certainly, was the lesson Gene and Robert Pressman learned early in 1996, after they were forced to seek protection for their company under Chapter 11 of the U.S. Bankruptcy Code. The Pressman brothers were at the time co-chairmen and chief executives of the Barneys New York retail chain, and they ended up in bankruptcy court as a result of a dispute with Isetan, the Japanese company that had financed the transformation of their family-owned business "from a single store in an out-of-the-way Manhattan location," as one magazine put it, "to the ritziest specialty chain in America." Perhaps understandably, but definitely mistakenly, Bob and Gene thought they could get by with merely announcing the bankruptcy filing and then toughing it out. To call that a miscalculation is to put it mildly, indeed. Taking advantage of the Pressmans' silence, Isetan's representatives

> **Nothing matters more to reporters than fresh meat for the next edition or broadcast—"feeding the beast."**

were able to feed the media a decidedly jaundiced account of what was going on—and to persuade more than a few reporters that Barneys had lied to them, both in explaining why it had filed for bankruptcy protection, and in announcing its financial results over the previous years. As a result, the press turned on Barneys and the Pressmans like an angry beast. Not only did the Pressman side of the story remain untold, but the once-adored clothing chain and the family that owned it suddenly found themselves pilloried in the local and national media. Even worse, their silence was taken by vendors, creditors, and customers as tacit confirmation that the appalling accusations being spread by Isetan had to be true.

By the time Sitrick and Company got involved in the case nearly three months after the bankruptcy filing, the company's public image was in tatters. Only a year earlier, Barneys had been regarded as the smartest fashion retailer in the country. Now the business and retail trade press was holding it up as an example of everything that was wrong with trendy fashion marketing. And the mainstream press was piling it on. *Newsweek* accused Barneys of racism. The *New York Times* reproached it for hubris. *Vanity Fair* described the Pressman family as a latter-day House of Atreus.

How Barneys and the Pressmans got into this mess—and how we helped them get out of it—is a classic illustration of the importance of "feeding the beast," and the perils of starving it.

Through the 1980s the Barneys empire consisted of a single (though highly regarded) clothing emporium on the not-terribly-fashionable corner of Seventh Avenue and 17th Street in Manhattan's lower west side. Founded in 1923 by Barney Pressman as a no-frills men's haberdashery for bargain-hunters, Barneys became something of a New York institution after World War II, when the elder Pressman turned the business over to his son Fred. While retaining Barneys' emphasis on value, Fred Pressman took the store up-market, offering a wider range of more stylish clothing and accessories. Before long, it was *the* place to shop in New York for quality-conscious businessmen, not to mention several generations of bar-mitzvah boys.

Following his father's lead, Fred eventually brought his own two sons, Bob and Gene, into the business. In 1976 Gene convinced his father to expand into women's wear, and by the early 1980s Barneys had mushroomed into a seven-story, 70,000-square-foot temple of chic that was considered the trendiest clothing store in New York, and one of the most successful anywhere.

The logical next step, of course, was to expand Barneys beyond its downtown birthplace. To that end, in 1988 the Pressmans' bankers introduced them to Isetan, a $4-billion-a-year behemoth that was Japan's sixth-largest retailer. Though Isetan was publicly traded, it was (like Barneys) family run, and its president at the time, a cosmopolitan forty-three-year-old named Kuniyasu Kosuge, was every bit as brash and expansive as Bob and Gene Pressman.

Hitting it off, Kosuge and the Pressmans quickly sketched out an ambitious if somewhat intricate alliance whose aim was to link the two companies in what both parties agreed would be a "global retailing partnership." A new subsidiary, called Barneys America, was formed; 55 percent owned by Isetan, it proceeded to open Barneys mall outlets in nine upscale U.S. markets such as Manhasset, Long Island; Short Hills, New Jersey; and Dallas, Texas. Isetan also got the right

> **The way to get a complicated story fully and fairly told is to offer an exclusive to an established, respected news outlet.**

to open Barneys stores (20 percent owned by a Pressman family company) in Tokyo and Yokohama, a plum the Pressmans said would be worth more than $200 million over the next thirty years. (Indeed, the Japanese stores were hugely successful right out of the box; originally projected to take eleven years to become profitable, they were both making money within four.)

At the same time, Isetan agreed to finance the construction of three new full-size Barneys branches in Beverly Hills, Chicago, and midtown Manhattan. The terms of this part of the deal were particularly complicated; under the arrangement worked out by the partners, Isetan would pay all the land and construction costs for the three stores, in return for which it would receive a monthly rent based on a combination of the property value and sales volume at each location.

Amid champagne and sake toasts in New York and Tokyo, Barneys and Isetan sealed their pact in the spring of 1989. Both sides were so enthusiastic about the deal that the final agreement called for the partnership to endure for 499 years.

As things turned out, it lasted barely half a decade.

What happened was that, for a variety of reasons, the Beverly

Hills and midtown Manhattan stores turned out to be much larger—and hence more expensive—than first planned. As *New York* magazine later reported, "In Beverly Hills, the city unexpectedly required Barneys to build a five-story underground parking garage, and the store had to be built from the ground up rather than moved into an existing building." Similarly, the cost of the midtown Manhattan outlet wound up ballooning after Metropolitan Life, which was supposed to occupy the office space above the store, unexpectedly pulled out at the last minute.

As a result, what was initially to be a $250 million investment wound up soaring to $600 million. Quickly, it became clear that the original idea of Barneys paying Isetan a rent based on the value of the new stores no longer made sense. (Given the larger size of the stores, the rent would have been prohibitively high.) Thus, as early as 1991, Bob Pressman began suggesting that they renegotiate the alliance into a more straightforward equity partnership. Among other things, he offered to convert the original Barneys branch at Seventh Avenue and 17th Street into the "flagship store" of Barneys America, the chain of mall outlets that Isetan partly owned. The following year he wrote a letter to Isetan pointing out that "since the investment amount and corresponding store sizes, etc., are much different than originally contemplated," an "overall restructuring" of their alliance would seem to make eminent sense. To that end, he approvingly quoted an Isetan executive's suggestion that Barneys and the Japanese company "put all our interests into one big pot."

Unfortunately, by then the atmosphere at Isetan was no longer nearly as warm as it had been when the deal with Barneys was first struck. Battered by the Japanese recession, reeling from the effects of a currency-trading debacle and a raid on its stock, Isetan had changed. Among other things, the ebullient Kosuge was no longer in charge. Instead of being run by an entrepreneurial family, Isetan was now led by a cadre of bean-counters, accountable to the company's bankers, who were far less excited by the strategic potential of long-term growth—and far more concerned with the immediate burden of escalating short-term costs. By the end of 1993, the new management had cut off the flow of funds to Barneys. As a result, Barneys was forced to use its own money (some $63 million in all) to complete construction of the new stores and get them properly furnished. Strapped for cash, the Pressmans appealed to Isetan for help, and in March 1994, the Japanese company agreed to provide an emergency loan. But as a condition it insisted the Pressmans sign an agreement promising to work out a deal under which Isetan could convert the loan, along with the Barneys real estate it owned, into an equity stake in Barneys Incorporated. Since this was precisely what the Pressmans had been suggesting since 1991, they had no trouble accepting the provision.

The negotiations, however, went nowhere. Though the Pressmans were willing, Isetan dragged its feet. As a result, Barneys was soon running out of money once again. By the end of 1995, its cash on hand—which usually totaled around $25 million—had dwindled to barely $4 million. Ironically, the business itself was doing fine. The nine mall stores, along with the two big New York stores and their counterparts in Beverly Hills and Chicago, were all making money on an operating basis. It was the cost of seeing through the expansion without sufficient help from Isetan that had brought Barneys to the brink.

On January 11, 1996, after efforts to force Isetan to come around had failed, Barneys filed for Chapter 11 bankruptcy protection. The move stunned customers and competitors alike—no one more so than Barneys' seven thousand or so suppliers, who suddenly had no idea when, or if, they'd ever be paid for the goods they'd shipped to the chain. While refusing to speak publicly themselves, the Pressmans' PR people issued a press release insisting the bankruptcy was nothing for anyone to worry about, that the business was healthy and Barneys' debts would be paid. The filing, people were told, was merely a tactic in what was described as a "lease dispute" with a joint-venture partner.

> **Without hard evidence to back up your claims, even the best spin doctor can't help you.**

To outsiders, who knew little of Isetan and had no idea of the complicated story-behind-the-story, this cryptic explanation was of little use—all the more so because right up to the filing, the company had been reacting to complaints from vendors who were being paid slower than usual by insisting that business was better than ever. Now the tactic seemed to backfire. As one skeptical observer told the *Wall Street Journal*, "When a privately held company makes grandiose statements about how good business is and then suddenly goes into bankruptcy court, you begin to wonder what is truth and what is fiction."

To add to the growing suspicions, Isetan reacted to the bankruptcy filing by unleashing a barrage of PR that accused the Pressmans of playing fast and loose with both the facts and its money. The Pressmans, it insisted, were lying to the press when they claimed their business was healthy; on the contrary, the giant Japanese retailer insisted that Barneys was nearly insolvent—a predicament of its own making that the Pressmans were now trying to blame on the overly-trusting Japanese.

Isetan followed up its accusations with a lawsuit in which it claimed the Pressmans had failed to disclose that Barneys had been piling up "significant losses" even as Isetan was financing its ambitious expansion plans. Equally damaging, Isetan insisted that its involvement with Barneys was never "an open-ended... partnership," but merely consisted of some "limited real estate investments by Isetan."

Without any information to the contrary, the press accepted Isetan's version of events, and turned on Barneys and the Pressmans with a vengeance.

If there was ever a time for Barneys and the Pressmans to stand up and explain their side of the story, this was it. Unfortunately, with court papers flying back and forth, the Pressmans' advisors counseled silence, and the brothers took their advice. Thus unchallenged, Isetan's spokesmen were able to spin to their hearts' content without fear of interruption, distraction, or contradiction. Not only had the Pressmans misled their Japanese backers by concealing huge operating losses at Barneys, Isetan told the press, but they had lied to reporters as well. What's more, they had gone on a wild spending spree in building the new stores, outfitting them in the most extravagant and irresponsible manner imaginable—then concealing the massive budget overruns from Isetan until it was too late.

Now *that* was a story. The arrogant trendsetters of the 1980s overreach themselves in the 1990s, taking merciless advantage of the generous but naive Japanese, and when their dishonesty is exposed for what it is, they try to escape the consequences of their misdeeds by declaring bankruptcy, heedless of the impact on the thousands of small businesses that depend on them. Given that the Pressmans' only response to Isetan's lurid account was a series of easily discounted routine denials, who could blame the press for clutching such a wonderfully simplistic melodrama to its collective bosom and running with it?

In his witty memoir of government service, *Locked in the Cabinet*—itself an impressive effort at spin control—former labor secretary Robert B. Reich recounts a valuable lesson he learned about the media. "A retired newspaper editor," he writes, "once told me that there were just two stories in American life, told over and over again under many different headlines: *Oh, the wonder of it!* and *Oh, the shame of it!*, one following automatically upon the other with an intensity matched only by the intensity of its opposite, the depth of disillusionment proportional to the height of initial wonderment." So it has been, and so it continues to be. The same press that had celebrated the rise of Barneys through the 1970s and 1980s, cheering on the Pressmans' brash ambition and imaginative marketing skills, now turned with gusto to its dismemberment. And by holding their tongues, the Pressmans accelerated their own execution.

■ ■ ■

It was toward the end of March 1996 that the Pressmans brought in Sitrick and Company to try to turn the situation around. By then, Barneys was widely viewed as the villain of the story, and the press accounts of its woes were appropriately merciless. For the most part, the media had bought into Isetan's claim that not only had Barneys lied to its Japanese benefactors, but worse—*much* worse—it had lied to the press as well. Thus propelled as much by moral outrage as by the lust for a good story, virtually everyone from the smallest trade paper to the *Wall Street Journal* ran stories about how Barneys, for all its cool insolence and outward glossiness, was in fact a financial shambles—how the Pressmans' arrogance and self-regard was finally getting the comeuppance it deserved. *Newsweek* devoted a full page to an African American staffer's angry account of how, six years earlier, he had been unjustly accused of shoplifting at Barneys—and how he now hoped to "dance on its grave." *New York Times* op-ed colum-nist Maureen Dowd devoted

> **In public debate, reticence not only doesn't help, it also actively hurts.**

no fewer than three separate columns to savaging Barneys, which she seemed to regard as a symbol of everything that was wrong with contemporary popular culture.

The press was so bad that its dark predictions of Barneys imminent demise were in danger of becoming a self-fulfilling prophecy. After all, who would extend credit or ship goods to a company that everyone was saying not only might be going down the tubes, but *deserved* to go down the tubes?

In short, the situation was dire, and at my first meeting with the Pressmans and their senior management, I laid out the strategy I felt we needed to follow. "What we've got to do first," I said, "is get our side of the story told." That, of course, would be easier said than done. Still, we had a few things going for us. For one, the facts were on our side. Contrary to Isetan's assertions and the media's repetitions, Barneys was *not* losing money on an operating basis, nor had the Pressmans lied to the Japanese or anyone else. For another, the Pressmans had assured me there was plenty of hard evidence to back up their claims.

This last point was crucial, for as I told the Barneys team, "If we go to the media with our side of the story, we're going to have to be able to document it. Otherwise, they're going to say, 'You say this, while Isetan says that. Who do we believe?'"

To that end, I spent days with Bob Pressman (the number

cruncher of the two brothers) going through huge stacks of letters, memos, and financial reports, assembling our case like a lawyer preparing to go into court. Given the uniformly negative coverage from even the most usually reliable of media, what I found astonished me. There it all was in black and white: proof that Barneys' business *was* operating in the black, and that the Pressmans had not misrepresented the facts to Isetan (or anyone else, for that matter)—not their company's financial condition nor the fact that from the first it had been clear that the cost of their ambitious expansion project would be much higher than both they and their Japanese partners had originally anticipated.

Thus girded, I now had to figure out the best way to use this powerful ammunition. Clearly, it wouldn't make much sense to announce it in a press release. For one thing, no one would believe it. For another, even if someone did, chances are they wouldn't give it much play, and a story as complicated as ours desperately needed sufficient space if it was to be both coherent and persuasive. (Space was also important because the length of a story is generally taken as a measure of its importance. A long story is a major story, one that has impact. A small story about Barneys—even if it had somehow managed to tell the tale accurately and understandably—would have gotten lost in the tug-of-war of the publicity battle.)

No, the way to get a complicated story like the Barneys tale fully and fairly told was to offer it on an exclusive basis to an established, respected editor or reporter at an established, respected news outlet. As noted earlier, there are few motivations more powerful in the journalistic personality than the desire to score an exclusive—to "own" a story by coming up with information or access no rival can hope to match. In this case, what I had to offer was pretty potent stuff—an exclusive, inside look at one of the hottest business stories of the day: the Pressman brothers' own account, backed up by all the documentation a reporter could hope for, of what was really going on between Barneys and Isetan.

The question was, whom should I take it to? Ordinarily, I would have gone to the most prestigious and influential publications available—in this case, the *Wall Street Journal* or the *New York Times*. Unfortunately, the reporters covering the Barneys bankruptcy for both of those eminent newspapers already had equity in the other side's story—which is to say, what they'd written up to that point had pretty much reflected the Isetan party line. In order to present our account, they'd in effect have to tell their readers, "You know, for the last few weeks we've been reporting how Barneys fooled both us and Isetan. Well, now it turns out that Barneys was really telling the truth and it was Isetan that was lying to us." I doubted either of them would be willing to do that... and, even if they would, it would be a long, hard sell.

The thing to do, obviously, was to find a respected reporter and a respectable publication, neither of which had already staked out a position on Barneys. A little research quickly yielded the answer. *New York* magazine, I discovered, had yet to publish any major pieces on the controversy. I was delighted, for *New York* was the perfect vehicle for our story. Highly regarded by journalists, it was also widely read in both the financial and fashion communities. Adding to its allure, I happened to have worked with one of its senior editors, Rich Turner, whom I'd gotten to know when he was a reporter in the *Wall Street Journal*'s Los Angeles bureau.

For a story like this, you couldn't ask for a better journalist than Turner. To begin with, he was highly thought of, a tough reporter who was willing to consider all sides of a story. Beyond that, he had a business background (courtesy of the *Journal*) and he was very smart—which was crucial in this case.* We were, after all, dealing with a fairly complicated situation. Without an experienced financial reporter who knew how to read a balance sheet and could understand the intricacies of the Barneys–Isetan relationship, we would all be in trouble.

So I went to the Pressmans and recommended not only that they sit down with Turner but also that they open their files to him. I also gave them a speech that I often give clients in their situation. "Understand," I told them, "we are not talking about a puff piece here. Assuming Rich and *New York* decide to do the article, there's a very good chance—in fact, you can depend on it—that parts of it are going to make you wince. Not everything he says about you and your business is going to be complimentary. But you can't let that bother you. What we're concerned about is the overall tone, the overall message. If we do our job right, the story as a whole should completely change the views of both the media and the public."

The Pressmans agreed to give it a shot. With their okay in hand, I immediately phoned Turner. As expected, he was more than intrigued when I asked him if he thought his magazine might be interested in an exclusive interview with the Pressmans and the first account of their version of the inside story of the battle between Barneys and Isetan.

Over the next few weeks, Bob and Gene Pressman and I spent countless hours working with Turner, taking him through the numbers, explaining the history, laying out our case. We documented

---

* A lot of PR people say they prefer dealing with stupid reporters, because they're easier to spin. I've never believed that. After all, when a less-than-intelligent reporter is involved, there's a good chance he's going to make a mistake, and that mistake could wind up burning you as easily as anyone else. (Not that I myself have actually ever met a stupid reporter!)

everything. Each time Bob or Gene would mention a letter he'd sent Isetan, I'd insist that he go through his correspondence and dig out a copy to show Turner. "Here's the time-and-date stamp," he'd say. "See the telltale on top—it shows exactly when we faxed it." We presented our story to him precisely the way you would present a case to a judge and jury.

At the same time that we were working with Turner, Sandi Sternberg, one of my firm's managing directors, and I were looking for an opportunity to give our side of the story to the regular beat reporters at the newspapers that mattered most to Barneys—in particular, the *New York Times*, the *Wall Street Journal*, and *Women's Wear Daily*. We got our opportunity when Barneys was ready to announce its latest quarterly earnings. At that point, we invited each of the reporters in for a private briefing—in effect, a mini-version of what we were doing with Turner. Not that we were pitching anyone a story. All we wanted was the chance to walk each of the beat reporters through the numbers, to show them that Barneys was operating comfortably in the black and had been for some time. This fact invariably surprised them, which gave us the opportunity to explain how they'd been misled by Isetan.

Now, none of the reporters actually wound up writing that he or she had been deceived by Isetan. But overall the tone of their coverage began to change. Not only did they all report Barneys' positive quarterly results, they all noted that the company had been operating profitably for some time—in effect, putting the lie to Isetan's assertions without saying it in so many words. As a result, by the time Rich Turner's story came out in *New York* magazine early that May, the atmosphere was just right: Both the press and public were ready for a wholesale reevaluation of Barneys' situation.

Turner's story, which sprawled across seven full pages of the magazine, turned out to be everything we'd hoped for and more. Though it announced in an early paragraph that "we're not here to restore Barneys' trashed image," that's pretty much what it did. Making full use of the information we'd made available to him, plus the extensive reporting he did on his own, Turner (who's since left *New York* for *Newsweek*) produced a warts-and-all portrait of the Pressmans' frustrating relationship with Isetan that portrayed them not as amoral exploiters, but as sympathetic strivers, victimized in part by their own ambition, but more by Isetan's inconstancy.

The piece's impact was both immediate and profound. Combined with the background work we'd done with the beat reporters, it transformed Barneys' relationship with the media virtually overnight. Having once been held in high esteem, and then vehemently disdained, the Pressmans were regarded once again in a positive light. With their reputations largely restored, the brothers were not only able to manage the delicate business of operating a company under Chapter 11 protection without any major problems from suppliers or creditors, they were also able to put Barneys on the road back to solvency. As of this writing, the company is negotiating a new reorganization plan with the Hong Kong–based Dickson Concepts and the French-based DFS. Neither of these accomplishments would have been possible had they not followed the first rule of spin—and recognized the importance of making sure their story got told.

■   ■   ■

In one sense, of course, all Barneys and the Pressmans did was obey what British politician Denis Healey called "the first law of holes: If you are in one, stop digging." Reticence had gotten them in trouble (or at least exacerbated their other problems), so they opened up and started talking. End of trouble. (They may not exactly have lived happily ever after, but at least from then on their other problems were a lot more manageable.)

That doesn't mean, however, that "feeding the beast" should be regarded as being a purely defensive maneuver. Quite the contrary, as an offensive tool it can even the odds when you find yourself outgunned in the public arena by a much larger and richer adversary.

That's precisely what happened when Jess Jackson, the feisty owner of California's celebrated but relatively small Kendall-Jackson Winery, took on giant E. & J. Gallo in a bitter marketing dispute. Gallo had the money and the muscle, but by feeding the beast Jackson was able to level the playing field.

The battle began in the fall of 1995, when Gallo brought out an upscale chardonnay called Turning Leaf. Up until then, Gallo had enjoyed huge success with its screw-top jug wines and other downmarket brands, but it had never been able to crack the premium market. That was Jess Jackson's turf. Indeed, his Santa Rosa–based winery dominated the mass-market chardonnay business in the United States. With its distinctive tapered bottle, uncovered cork, and colorful label, Kendall-Jackson's Vintner's Reserve was both the best-reviewed and best-selling quality mass-market chardonnay in the country.

Not surprisingly, Jackson was less than pleased when he heard that Gallo was lumbering onto his turf. But his displeasure turned to outrage once he got a look at the new Gallo product.

What rankled Jackson wasn't the wine *per se*. He was used to competition and was confident of his chardonnay's superiority. No, what got him on the phone with his lawyers was Turning Leaf's appearance. For one thing, its label looked to Jackson (and to a lot of other people) like an out-and-out knockoff of his Vintner's Reserve label, right down to the autumnal colors and grape-leaf motif. For another, the Turning Leaf bottle was shaped and corked, he felt, exactly like the Vintner's Reserve bottle. In all, the resemblance between the two chardonnays' packaging—what the experts call their "trade dress"—was so striking that it seemed to Jackson that the Gallo people were deliberately trying to confuse shoppers into thinking that Turning Leaf came not from their winery but from his. (Indeed, the Gallo name was nowhere to be found on the Turning Leaf label.)

Whether or not the resemblance was deliberate, within six months of its debut, Turning Leaf had soared from 649th place in chardonnay sales to the number two spot just behind Kendall-Jackson's wine—hence Jess Jackson's outrage. As his lawyer later put it, "The act is so blatant, so obvious. But Gallo is like a huge elephant that thinks it can back up a busy highway and not bother anybody."

And there lay the problem. Gallo was so big. Sure, Jess Jackson could sue—and, indeed, early in April 1996 his lawyers marched into federal court in San Francisco and charged Gallo with trademark infringement. But such cases are notoriously difficult to win, and the Modesto-based jug-wine giant had the resources to overwhelm Kendall-Jackson completely if it chose. Then again, Jackson did have one advantage. As my associate Mike Kolbenschlag, another of our firm's managing directors, pointed out when we were brought in to help Kendall-Jackson, Gallo hated talking to the press. Jess Jackson, on the other hand, was more than willing to tell his story.

■　■　■

Huge, successful, and intensely private (the company doesn't even post signs on its vineyards), Gallo saw no reason to break with its traditional habit of sloughing off media inquiries when reporters began asking it about Kendall-Jackson's lawsuit. Perhaps it was confident of winning in court. Perhaps it thought no one would pay any attention to the case. Whatever the reason, its reaction to the suit was typically laconic: It issued a press release dismissing Kendall-Jackson's claims as "nonsense" and then retreated into its traditional silence.

Meanwhile, we were out telling our story to the press. Major pieces appeared in virtually every significant newspaper and magazine in the country (as well as on more than a few radio and television stations) about how giant Gallo was unfairly trying to steal tiny Kendall-Jackson's business. With secretive Gallo making only the most perfunctory response, it was our side of the story that got the prominent play. Obviously, it didn't hurt that given the enormous disparity in the size of the two combatants (Gallo ships well over fifty million cases of wine a year, to Kendall-Jackson's two million), there was a definite David-and-Goliath aspect to the dispute. (Not that we would point it out!) We were also able to line up plenty of sympathetic wine merchants and even some competing vintners who were willing to go on record endorsing Jess Jackson's complaints.

The press attention didn't change the outcome of the case in court, but that wasn't the point. The point was to "out" Gallo. And that we did. By the time the jury delivered its verdict in April 1997, ruling that the similarity in trade dress did not meet the legal standard for trademark infringement, there shouldn't have been an oenophile in the country who hadn't read, heard, or seen that Gallo had tried to pull a fast one—and that appearances to the contrary, Turning Leaf was not a Kendall-Jackson wine but a Gallo product.

Gallo may have carried the day in the court of law, but in the court of public opinion—which is where reputations are made and products are sold—it was Kendall-Jackson that prevailed. By feeding the beast, it was able to make the press its ally. As a result, the vast majority of stories written and broadcast about the case reflected Kendall-Jackson's point of view. And with the press on its side, public sympathy was bound to follow—which is precisely what happened. For all of Gallo's vast resources and marketing clout, it wasn't able to out-muscle Kendall-Jackson.

Certainly, there are times when discretion is definitely the better part of valor… but not when you're trying to create a public image, change a public attitude, or win a public debate. Indeed, in those circumstances, whether you are motivated by excessive modesty, supposed prudence, or outright fear, it's not merely that reticence doesn't help, it's that it actively hurts—especially when you're facing adversaries who don't feel similarly restrained.

"If I am not for myself, who will be?" asks the ancient verse. In the crowded, competitive arena that is public life today, it's a line worth remembering.

CHAPTER 6

Always Respond

*Never let a mistake or a misrepresentation
go unchallenged.*

A FEW YEARS AGO, AN EXECUTIVE at what was then one of the country's largest retail chains (not Barneys) received a phone call from a reporter at the *Wall Street Journal*. The reporter wanted the executive's comment on some disturbing rumors he'd heard. Apparently, word was going around that the company was experiencing financial difficulties and that vendors were no longer willing to ship it goods on credit, demanding cash up front, or at least on delivery.

Rumors like this can put a retailer out of business. Few companies—least of all, retail companies—have enough cash to pay for all their merchandise before it is delivered. But this particular rumor wasn't only dangerous, it was also false. Although the company did have financial problems, its vendors were still shipping on normal terms. The executive was thus understandably outraged (and somewhat panicked), and he brusquely dismissed the reporter's inquiry as nonsense. "I won't even dignify that with a response," he snapped, "except to say that it is patently untrue." Then he hung up.

> **You must find out the source of a reporter's mistaken impression; then refute it, point by point.**

The next day a story appeared in the *Wall Street Journal* recounting the rumors the reporter had heard, backed up by quotes from three of the company's vendors, all of whom said they would no longer ship their merchandise to the chain without payment in advance. The executive's one-sentence denial was included in the story.

As it happened, the three vendors quoted in the article were hardly representative of the chain's more than ten thousand suppliers. The reason they had stopped shipping merchandise was that they had been "cut off"—the result of a dispute with the chain over the quality and timely delivery of some previously contracted goods. Nonetheless, once reported by the *Journal*, their comments set off what is known in the trade as a vendor stampede.

Suppliers who had been previously shipping goods on normal credit terms suddenly began to get nervous—so nervous that many of them simply pulled the plug. The chain's headquarters were flooded with calls. "Look, I believe in you guys," company executives were told over and over again, "but I can't afford to be the only vendor still shipping on terms. After all, if something were to happen to you, I'd be screwed. I'm sorry, but I have to protect my interests. I still want to do business with you, but it will have to be on a C.O.D. or cash-up-front basis."

Determined to restore faith in his company, the chain's CEO

traveled to New York to meet with his bankers and personally reassure his most important suppliers. At the same time, his PR people contacted the *Journal* and convinced the newspaper to report on his efforts to calm vendor fears. But the resulting story only made matters worse.

While it noted what the CEO was doing, this second article also surveyed a wider array of the company's vendors. By now, nervousness had turned to panic, and many of them were refusing to ship. In the end, the story wound up exacerbating the situation.

Over the next few weeks, the situation continued to worsen— until finally what the *Journal* had reported became reality. The company's vendors stopped shipping on any but cash or C.O.D. terms. Eventually, the company had no choice but to file for Chapter 11 bankruptcy protection. Throughout the bankruptcy proceedings, its communications missteps continued. Today, it no longer exists.

■ ■ ■

It may come as a shock, but the press occasionally gets it wrong. Rarely with malice, usually under the pressure of deadlines, a reporter will take at face value a comment from someone with an ax to grind, misunderstand a statistic, extrapolate from an atypical situation, jump to the wrong conclusion. When that happens, the human tendency, especially when the mistake seems particularly boneheaded, is to want to brush it off just as one would brush off a pesky mosquito. Just as the retail executive brushed off the *Journal* reporter.

Big mistake.

Our impatient retail executive assumed, of course, that his flat denial was all that would be needed to correct the reporter's obviously erroneous impression. He believed that once he stated the rumors were false, the reporter would take his word for it and that would be that.

If only life were so simple.

The fact is, reporters—particularly reporters for major news organizations like the *Wall Street Journal*—require more than a simple denial to put the brakes on a story like this one. You might never lie to a reporter, but there are plenty of people who would, and have, particularly when their livelihood seems threatened. So it is that even the most knowledgeable source can find himself having to jump through hoops in order to persuade a reporter that he may be wrong about a story. This is especially true when the story in question (as in the case of the rumors about the retail chain) is clearly inimical to the source's interests. After all, no journalist expects anyone to do anything but deny a story that seems likely to hurt or embarrass him. A conscientious reporter will carefully write down your denial and will make sure to include it in his account. But that doesn't mean he necessarily believes you or that you have changed his mind about anything.

Hence, the second rule of spin: Always respond—and respond fully—to a press inquiry, no matter how off-base. Merely saying, "No, that's not true" isn't sufficient. You've got to do two things. First, you've got to find out what the reporter's mistaken impression is based on. Then, using that knowledge, you've got to refute it, point by point.

■ ■ ■

How then should that retail-chain executive have handled the call from the *Journal* reporter?

To begin with, he should have made sure he had the facts and the time to analyze them.

When Sitrick and Company gets that sort of call on behalf of a client, even if we know the answer to the reporter's questions, we try to take in as much information as we can before we give any out. That means asking the reporter if he wouldn't mind explaining the kind of story he's got in mind, and what got

> **The good spin doctor can both plant positive stories and kill unfairly negative ones.**

him started on it. We then find out what his deadline is and promise to get back to him with the information he's requested. Instead of having to ad lib, we now have time to assess the situation and, if necessary, develop a strategy.

As we noted earlier, the three vendors who told the *Journal* there were problems at the retail chain were hardly typical of the company's more than ten thousand suppliers. The fact was, the overwhelming majority of its vendors *were* continuing to support it. They *were* shipping on terms.

So instead of merely saying "That's ridiculous," when the *Journal* reporter asked about vendors refusing to ship, I first would have asked him how many vendors he had spoken to and who they were. It's true reporters often balk at identifying their sources, but in this case he probably would have told me, since he wound up quoting them by name in his story. In any event, he almost certainly wouldn't object to letting me know how many he'd interviewed.

Suppose he'd spoken to roughly half a dozen vendors. My response would have been polite but unapologetic. "Come on," I would have told him. "We have more than ten thousand vendors who sell to us. Are the people you spoke with major suppliers? We buy more than $1 billion worth of goods and services each year. Ask your sources how much business they do with us. What makes you think they're at all typical?"

Assuming that wasn't enough to get him to drop the story—and, frankly, I'd be surprised if it were—I'd then have asked him to give me a little time to pull together an official response. At that point, I'd get the company to assemble a list of names and phone numbers of fifty or one hundred—or two hundred—of its most supportive vendors. I'd give the names and numbers to the reporter and suggest he call any or all of them for a comment about the company.

Had the reporter revealed the identities of the disgruntled vendors he had interviewed, I'd have quickly ferreted out the details of each of their problems. In this particular case, it turned out that the outstanding balances in all three situations totaled less than $50,000 (out of the chain's *$1 billion* in annual purchases!), that in two of the three cases the reason payment had been held up was because the vendors had shipped inferior goods, and that the third case involved disputed payments of less than $10,000.

If, after being informed of all this, the reporter still insisted on proceeding with the story, I'd have asked if he had called any of the vendors on the list I'd given him. "Look," I'd tell him, "you have three vendors who say they are not willing to ship. I gave you the names of hundreds who say they are. It's only fair that if you print this story, you point that out and quote some of the vendors who are more representative of what's going on with this company."

I'd also have pointed out that publishing a story based on the negative comments of just three or four—or even a dozen—vendors out of more than ten thousand would be both irresponsible and damaging, not just to the company and its employees, but to its loyal vendors as well. Indeed, such a story wouldn't be reporting news but creating it. I'd then have gone off the record and informed the reporter that the company was very concerned that even though it wasn't true that its vendors had stopped shipping, an article in the *Wall Street Journal* saying otherwise could make it a reality.

Having actually been involved in such conversations more times than I'd like to remember, I can say with confidence that at the very least the *Journal* reporter would have phoned the other vendors for comment, as a result of which his story would have wound up much more balanced and accurate. Indeed, there's a good chance the story would have been killed altogether.

■ ■ ■

The strategy laid out above follows a simple logic. You elicit from the reporter the information on which he's based his tentative conclusions, you follow it back to its source, and you refute it point by point—or, rather, you create a situation in which he can do that for himself. This last point is key. Most responsible journalists do pride themselves on being open-minded. But like the rest of us, they generally find it easier to be open-minded on their own initiative than on someone else's—especially a spin doctor's.

That's not to say errant newspeople should always be treated with kid gloves. Spin is usually best applied gently, but every once in a while a bit more edge may be both necessary and appropriate.

Take, for instance, the time a major California newspaper was poised to report—prematurely, if not inaccurately—that the state attorney general's office was about to ask a grand jury to indict a client of ours. The reporter called our client and said an anonymous source had sent him a copy of a letter supposedly from the state attorney general's office indicating that he was soon to be indicted. Did our client care to make any comment? Our client did not. Instead, he promptly phoned me. I called the reporter, listened to what he had to say, asked about his deadline, and promised to get back to him.

The moment the reporter hung up, I dialed the client. Had he said anything to the reporter? No, he assured me.

I called the reporter back, and immediately took the offensive. How did he know the letter was for real? How could he be sure? Had the attorney general's office confirmed its assertions?

"No, they didn't," the reporter conceded. "But your client did. He was reading it right along with me." ("I only read the first sentence," my client stammered when I confronted him, as if that made him only a little bit pregnant.)

After having more than a few words with my client, I called the reporter back a third time. Whatever my client may or may not have said, I told him, it would be unconscionable for his newspaper to print that an indictment was on the way without some sort of official confirmation. For all he knew, the letter might be a forgery. Or if it was legitimate, crucial parts of it may have been altered.

The reporter knew I was right, and for three weeks he tried to find someone in the attorney general's office who would verify that our client would soon be named. Finally, he struck oil—or at least he thought he had. A low-level official told him on a not-for-attribution basis that, yes, our client was going to be indicted.

With that piece of information in hand, he called me for a comment.

At that point, I have to admit, I thought we were sunk. But I wasn't yet ready to throw in the towel. I drafted a short statement, which I sent to the paper. "We are surprised," it concluded, "that the method used to bring this matter [to the] public was a so-called anonymous leak."

Later that day, an editor at the paper phoned to let me know that they would not be publishing my statement as written. The reason, she maintained, was that it was inaccurate. "We got confirmation," she insisted. "We're not relying on the letter."

"Really?" I said. "Has the attorney general's office sent you a press release on the case?"

"No."

"Did they give you an official confirmation of the information you are about to print?"

"No."

"Are you psychic?" I asked. "Is that how you learned my client was allegedly a target?"

"No," the editor replied.

I pounced. "Then are you telling me now that your reporter misspoke—that he didn't learn about this supposed indictment through that anonymous letter?"

Unwilling to discuss the paper's unnamed source, the editor quickly ended the conversation.

I kept the pressure on. Over the next few days, I continued to question the reliability of the paper's information, challenging the editors to find a senior official willing to go on the record confirming that an indictment was indeed forthcoming. "A great deal of time has passed," I said. "How do you know that the information is correct? How do you know that the person who supposedly gave you the confirmation knows what he or she is talking about? How do you know things haven't changed?"

I knew, of course, that there was no way any senior official in the attorney general's office would provide the corroboration I was insisting upon. For one thing, I was pretty sure no definite decision had been made to indict my client. For another, even if one had been, it would be against the attorney general's policy to announce it prematurely.

Sure enough, the paper couldn't get confirmation. A few days later, the editor called me back. The story, she said, was on indefinite hold.

As it turned out, our client was indicted three months later. But that didn't mean we had done anything dishonest, for at the time the newspaper was originally planning to run its story, no decision had been made to charge our client with anything. Had we allowed this "news" to break prematurely, the resulting media coverage would have become a self-fulfilling prophecy. The attorney general's office is, after all, a political position. Reaction to a major news article might cause the prosecutors either to file a case that was otherwise marginal or to take more of a hard-line approach.

In any event, by the time the indictment came down, the reporter and his newspaper had moved onto something else. News is fungible: If one story doesn't pan out, journalists will go after another. As a result, the indictment didn't get much coverage, and the coverage it did get attracted relatively little attention—virtually none compared with what the original story would likely have generated. Even though the indictment was still news, it was now merely run-of-the-mill, official announcement news—as opposed to the eye-catching, "this reporter has learned exclusively" kind of news that might have provoked a media stampede or put pressure on the attorney general to come down particularly hard on our client.

So our somewhat aggressive response to the original inquiry paid off. By insisting that the newspaper be absolutely sure of its facts—which is no less than any of us should expect from the press, regardless of the circumstances—we were able to help our client dodge what might have been a truly destructive bullet.

■ ■ ■

Responding fully and appropriately to media inquiries involves more than simply adopting the correct tone and tactic. It also means understanding precisely to whom the response should be directed. Generally speaking, it's a good idea to dance with the person that brung you—which is to say, you should always try to avoid going over anyone's head. Reporters, in particular, just hate it when a source or a subject tries to short-circuit a story by leap-frogging over them to their editor—and as honorable as we know all journalists are, most of them are not above holding a grudge.

Then again, there are times when you have no choice.

A few years ago I got a telephone call from Marvin Davis's son, the producer John Davis. It was a Saturday afternoon, but John was all business. "Do you know the *Globe*?" he asked me.

"The *Boston Globe*?" I replied.

"No, no," he said, "the tabloid newspaper."

"Well, I'm not a reader," I said, "but I know it. What's the problem?"

John explained that the *Globe* was preparing to publish a story claiming that a good friend of his, a much admired movie star, had inoperable colon cancer. I didn't need to be a Hollywood insider to know the damage a report like that could do.

As always, my first response was to establish the facts. "Is it true?" I asked. "Does he have cancer? Because if he does, you don't want to lie about it. There are other ways to deal with something like this."

John assured me that his friend did not have cancer. The question then became how to persuade the *Globe* that its story was a nonstarter. Normally, I'd try to get in touch with the reporter who filed the item—or, failing that, his editor. In this case, however, we were right up against their deadline. What's more, following my normal procedure could end up doing more harm than good. The *Globe* was a tabloid, and tabloids have their own special way of doing things. Trying to talk the editorial folks out of publishing their story could cause them to dig in their heels. They obviously had a "source" willing to say that the movie star did indeed have cancer, and under the rules by which many of these publications play, that's all they needed to justify their decision to run the piece. (For some tabloid reporters, the fact that a "source" might not know what he's talking about is neither here nor there.)

> Spin is usually best applied gently, but occasionally a bit more edge may be appropriate—and necessary.

Then again, while the *Globe*'s journalistic standards might not compare with those of the *New York Times*, its legal standards were bound to be quite strict. (They had to be, otherwise the tabloid would have long since been put out of business by libel suits.) That suggested another avenue of approach—to the *Globe*'s general counsel, without whose approval no article could be published. What we should do, I told the movie star's people, was fax a letter to the general counsel detailing the truth about the star's condition, explaining the havoc that could be wreaked by an erroneous story such as the one the *Globe* was contemplating, and requesting that he look into the situation himself. I strongly recommended that the letter make no threats, legal or otherwise, but instead simply appeal to the *Globe* lawyer's conscience. ("It has to have the right tone," I said. "It has to be worded carefully. You don't want to get his back up. Treat him like a gentleman, and chances are he'll act like one.") The star's lawyers were skeptical; "I've tried this a number of times," one of the lawyers said, "and I have yet to be successful." In the end, however, they agreed to go along with my recommendation that we had nothing to lose and everything to gain.

So our missive went off. A few hours later, the *Globe* faxed a letter back to us. The story had been spiked.

This incident illustrates something crucial about the business of spin. Most people think the main task of PR professionals is to get the media to run upbeat stories about their clients. That's part of the job, to be sure, but it's hardly the most important part. No, what distinguishes a spin doctor from a press agent is not his ability to plant positive stories, but his ability to achieve a specific objective through the publication of those stories—and, equally important, his skill at mitigating or killing unfairly negative ones. It is particularly in this latter area that spinmeisters earn their stripes—and their fees.

What makes this part of the job so challenging is a fundamental aspect of human nature—few of us like to admit we're wrong. This happens to be particularly true of reporters, for whom both accuracy and understanding are primary values—and who, as a result, tend to take it quite personally when anyone dares to suggest they may be mistaken about something. It thus sometimes requires a lot more than merely rigorous logic and meticulous research to persuade a journalist to back off from an erroneous conclusion. As we have seen, it often also takes major dollops of psychology and diplomacy—and sometimes a certain amount of poker-table bluff.

Generally speaking, the most effective and efficient way to straighten out a mistaken reporter is to let him discover for himself the error of his ways. (This notion is implicit in the strategy I suggested for the imperiled retail chain, and I can assure you it works a lot better than trying to stuff the correct information down a reporter's throat.) Needless to say, this journalistic self-discovery doesn't just happen. It may be true that a good journalist will eventually come to see the light on his own, but when time is of the essence (as it usually is) a savvy spinmeister can accelerate the process by pointing the reporter in the right direction.

Occasionally, however, push comes to shove, and you have no choice but to respond to a misguided inquiry with a more combative stance. For instance, a reporter comes to you with an extremely negative story that you know is based on false or misleading premises, but no matter what you say or do, he simply refuses to back off. (Sometimes this can be the result of a genuine misunderstanding; occasionally, it's because the reporter is a crusader who, as the saying goes, doesn't like to let the facts get in the way of the truth.) At that point, you've got to start acting like a lawyer. That's not to say you threaten legal action. Rather, it means that like an aggressive defense attorney you must thoroughly analyze and meticulously dismantle the reporter's "case." The aim is to refute his allegations and evidence so completely that when it comes time for him to do his "summation"—whether it's to his editor, as he argues why his story deserves to run, or in the piece itself, where he must succinctly explain to readers just what he's got to tell them— his most potent assertions have been systematically defanged, and he finds himself with virtually nothing left to say.

■ ■ ■

My firm was involved in a classic example of this sort of thing in the fall of 1996. We were representing a financial services firm whose parent company had been at times among the most actively traded stocks on NASDAQ's Small-Cap market. One day, the parent company's chief executive officer phoned me with troubling news. A European-based investigative reporter for one of the major weekly news magazines had been asking questions of his largest stockholder, a Swiss financier. Though the reporter claimed to be doing a story about American financial services firms that were advertising in Europe, what he really seemed interested in was anything the financier might be able to tell him about the U.S. firm's relationship to a somewhat controversial Canadian investment mogul. Some two decades earlier, the mogul had pled guilty to a charge of stock fraud in Ontario—on what he insisted was the bad advice of his lawyer—and ever since he had been tarred with the label "convicted stock swindler." The news magazine reporter was now alleging that though the mogul was not formally listed as an officer, director, or stockholder of the U.S. firm, this former felon was secretly controlling and running the company. If this were true, both the mogul and the firm would be in big trouble.

The Canadian was, in fact, nothing more than a consultant to the company, but the reporter seemed convinced something far more nefarious was afoot. In part, this belief of his was based on two books that had been written about the mogul, both of which painted him as something close to the devil incarnate—and neither of which was particularly accurate.

The simplest thing to do, of course, would have been to sit the reporter down with the CEO, who could set the record straight about the Canadian's role. And for his part, the reporter was more than willing to come to the United States to do just such an interview. The CEO, however, was advised not to see him.

Normally, such reticence is a mistake, and if it hadn't been for some extenuating circumstances, I would have told my client that he was only hurting himself by refusing to meet with the reporter. But in this case he had a pretty good reason.

It seemed that a few weeks before the reporter had first contacted the Swiss stockholder, the stockholder had received a bizarre and threatening telephone call. Unless the stockholder paid him $6 million, the caller said, a series of stories would appear in a variety of news media, including CNN and the reporter's news magazine, smearing his company with the charge that it had an improper relationship with the Canadian "ex-felon." The stockholder promptly informed the Swiss authorities, who set up a sting operation and arrested the would-be extortionist.

No one was accusing the news magazine reporter of having any connection to or knowledge of the extortion attempt. Nonetheless, given the circumstances, the CEO felt distinctly queasy about being interviewed by anyone from his particular publication. The CEO's attitude wasn't helped by the fact that in trying to persuade him to grant an interview, the reporter had twice lied about the subject of his story. So the reporter was kept at arm's length.

Nevertheless, the CEO's reluctance to agree to a meeting only heightened the reporter's suspicions, and after a few weeks he told me that he was going to write his story with or without my client's input. At that point, I told the reporter that if he submitted a list of questions, I would do my best to get my client to answer them.

I did this for two reasons. First, when a reporter tells you he's going to do a story whether or not you agree to speak with him, all you accomplish by continuing to refuse to answer his questions is to guarantee that the article he ends up writing will be a hostile one. To be sure, reporters have been known to try to bluff recalcitrant sources into cooperating—to insist they are going to do the story even if they don't get an interview, when the truth is that without the source's cooperation they won't have anything worth publishing. But unless you have a lot of experience with this sort of thing—and know the reporter reasonably well—calling this particular bluff is an awfully chancy business that can all too easily blow up in your face.

The second reason I invited the reporter to submit a list of questions is that, in doing so, we had nothing to lose—and, potentially, a lot to gain. Yes, there are times when the most sensible response to a media inquiry is a polite "No comment." But such prudence invariably carries a price. As we noted earlier, while discretion may be the better part of valor, it rarely carries the day in a public debate. Or as Stephen Jones, the media-savvy defense attorney for Oklahoma City bomber Tim McVeigh, told a CBS News correspondent, "'No comment' gets you run over in the middle of the road."

Clamming up, in other words, is a tactic you want to avoid unless it's absolutely necessary. The problem is, how can you know if it's absolutely necessary unless you know what the reporter intends to ask you? Hence, the value of asking for a list of questions. At the very least, the list will give you a good idea of just what he's after, and on that basis you can make a much more informed decision as to whether you should comment. And who knows? The questions might well turn out to be quite answerable. Or if not all of them are, some of them might be, and a partial response is better than none at all. Even if you wind up not responding to any of them, you're still better off, since now at least you should have a much clearer sense of the kind of story the reporter has in mind.

In this case, the list of questions we received left no doubt that the reporter had a lot of misinformation about the Canadian and my client company. We were also able to glean that much of his story was based specifically on the two wildly inaccurate books that had been written about the Canadian investor. Armed with this knowledge, we informed the reporter and his editors—formally and in writing—that the books contained much false information, and that we assumed the news magazine would not rely upon either of them as a source. Predictably, the reporter responded by asking us to specify exactly what the books had gotten wrong—to which we retorted that it was not our job to tell him what was false, it was his and his magazine's job independently to verify everything they intended to claim as being true. Since the reporter didn't have the time or the resources to double-check all the information he wanted to use from the books, he wound up not being able to use much of it.

> **"'No comment' gets you run over in the middle of the road."**
>
> *—Stephen Jones, defense attorney*

That was the easy part. The tough part came after I finally persuaded my client to sit down with the reporter and personally deal with the rest of his misapprehensions. (Having seen the reporter's questions, the CEO was now eager to set the record straight.) We offered to pay the reporter's way to the United States for the interview, but journalistic ethics, he said, prevented him from accepting our hospitality, so the CEO and I wound up having to fly to Europe. Our meeting with the reporter lasted a grueling five hours, but in the end it proved to be more than worth the effort.

The news magazine did wind up running a story about my

client, the financial services company, late in 1996. As a result of our painstaking response to the inquiry, however, the reporter was unable to make his original charges stick—and his article wound up having no impact on the company whatsoever. By responding, and responding fully, we transformed a potential "Omigod!" into a big "So what?" That is what we call successful spin.

■   ■   ■

The process of refutation is invariably an exhausting one, as you go through the reporter's assertions point by point, fact by fact, questioning the reliability of his sources, pointing out the gaps in his logic, challenging him to prove each and every allegation. Obviously, to accomplish it successfully, you have to have done your homework, and the facts had better be on your side. But if you have and they are, the results are bound to justify the trouble. After all, a reporter who can't or won't go through this sort of inquisition is a reporter on shaky ground indeed. At the very least, his failure puts you in a position to contact his editors—or, if necessary, their lawyers—and point out exactly how much of his story is open to question, and how you assume they won't let any item get into print or go out on the air unless they are completely comfortable that every bit of it can be documented and confirmed.

The point here is that once you've done this, you're no longer on the defensive. Rather, it's now the reporter's turn. Instead of being the supposedly objective arbiter of the facts, he's suddenly just another partisan advocate, arguing an increasingly questionable case before a properly skeptical jury. The jury, of course, consists of his own editors and lawyers, whose personal attachment to the story in question is not likely to be very great—and whose natural fear of going out on a limb has, if anything, been heightened by your polite warnings.

In this sort of situation, under these sorts of pressures, the bar of proof tends to be set relatively high. Is a fact in dispute? Unless the reporter can cite chapter and verse (and if he's got it wrong, he won't be able to), chances are his editors or lawyers are going to insist that he cut it. Has the reporter depended heavily on an anonymous source? "Well," you can say to the people vetting his copy, "I know you can't tell me who the source is, but I assume you've got a procedure to satisfy yourselves that he really does exist, that he is reliable and knowledgeable, and that he did in fact say what your reporter quotes him as saying." If they don't, that part of the story is dropped. Reporters call this process "being nibbled to death by ducks," and they hate it, because little by little it chips away at their story until what may have begun as a mighty mountain of allegations has been reduced to a bland handful of dust.

There's only one way a story can survive this process, and that's if it was on firm ground to begin with—in which case what you really need is probably not a spin doctor but a priest.

❚　❚　❚

A postscript: Sometimes, despite your best efforts, a mistake or misinterpretation will make it into print. A common response, particularly among corporate people, is to ignore the error, the logic being that trying to get the record corrected—with a letter to the editor, say, or by asking for a retraction—will only call more attention to the original mistake. The problem is, if the error isn't dealt with, and dealt with promptly, the mistake will go into the archives uncorrected, and will likely be repeated by every journalist who looks up the clips as part of his research for some future piece on the same subject.

The controversial Canadian investment consultant, for example, always complained that most of the information printed about him wasn't true. Yet he never bothered to do anything about it. "Just let it lie," he would say. "I don't want to dredge it up again. Anyway, it doesn't do any good to write letters to the editor—the news is already out there." His attitude, unfortunately, was self-fulfilling. Every time a new journalist was assigned to write about something with which the Canadian was involved, he'd pull the old clips and repeat the same old mistakes. Before long, there were countless articles in the archives all saying the same erroneous things. Eventually, what was once a correctable error passed into the untouchable realm of conventional wisdom. Even the most conscientious of reporters is unlikely to question a "fact" that has appeared in dozens of different articles.

The lesson is clear. Never let a mistake go unchallenged. Always set the record straight—and do it as quickly as possible.

CHAPTER 7

▌Preempt the Situation

Seize the momentum and put the other guy on the defensive by getting your story out first and defining the issue.

TOM (NOT HIS REAL NAME) had a problem. A principal in one of the nation's largest venture-capital firms, he had in 1980 convinced his partners to put $100,000 into a fledgling (and nearly insolvent) company that made educational items, thereby rescuing the enterprise from ruin. In return for their investment, Tom and his partners got a 20 percent stake in the company, along with the fun of watching it not only manage to stay afloat but also prosper beyond anyone's expectations. The problem was, that's all they got out of it. By 1989, the company had grown to become one of the top-grossing outfits of its kind in the nation, fielding a small army of "educational consultants" who sold its products at home parties throughout North America and Japan. But though it was racking up annual revenues of nearly $70 million, and net earnings of more than $8.5 million a year, the company had yet to share even a penny of the proceeds with any of its backers—including the firm whose timely intervention had made its unlikely success story possible.

Adding to his frustration, Tom felt that the company's CEO, a former school teacher who had founded the business in her garage, was running it as if it were her own personal fiefdom. The CEO claimed, for example, that the company couldn't afford to pay out any dividends, yet she somehow managed to pay her-self more than $750,000 a year, while charging to her corporate expense account a variety of questionable items, including clothing, jewelry, a Rolls Royce, and trips to Bora Bora and Tahiti with an entourage that included her hairdresser, her manicurist, and a play-mate for her daughter.

> **The first major story invariably sets the tone for the media coverage that follows.**

Such excesses notwithstanding, the CEO had managed over the years to build up a formidable public image as a concerned mother turned businesswoman who cared more about kids and quality than profits and losses. Prompted by the efficient PR machine she had developed at the company, magazines like *Working Women* and *Inc.* had featured her innumerable times in stories that portrayed her as the very model of a modern female entrepreneur.

Tom was at his wit's end. Not only was the company refusing to pay out any dividends, but in response to his firm's complaints, it reorganized its board of directors, creating a new executive com-mittee that included every member except the representative of Tom's firm. What's more, it instituted a policy under which only executive-committee members would be covered by the company's liability insurance.

With his protests falling on deaf ears, Tom became convinced that his only recourse was to go to court.

Taking on the company and its well-publicized CEO, Tom knew, would not be easy—or pleasant. To complicate matters, Tom was understandably concerned about his own reputation. A veteran at the time of more than two decades in the venture-capital business, he and his firm had invested in some 135 separate companies over the years without ever feeling the need to sue any of them. That's not a streak one breaks lightly. Being a venture capitalist, after all, is not simply a matter of being willing (and able) to sign checks. You've also got to be able to persuade potential clients that you're the sort of person they wouldn't mind being in business with—something that tends to be difficult if you happen to be known for taking your partners to court.

With this in mind, Tom decided to come to me for advice before he unleashed his lawyers. "We plan to sue," he told me in the summer of 1989, "but I'm concerned because the CEO has one of the most successful PR operations I've ever seen, and I don't want bad publicity about how we treat our customers."

I nodded.

"So," he said, "do you think there's much risk?"

"Well," I replied, "let me tell you what I'd do if I were representing the company. I'd take out a little ad in the *Wall Street Journal* that said, 'If you want to see how Tom's firm treats its venture-capital partners, call this number and we'll send you a copy of the suit they served on us last week.'"

Tom went white. "And what would you do if you worked for us?" he asked.

"I'd preempt the situation," I said.

▪ ▪ ▪

In an argument or dispute, most of us tend to emphasize the importance of having the last word. But while that may be immensely
satisfying, having the last word doesn't necessarily mean you've
won the argument. As the eighteenth-century English satirist
Alexander Pope put it (rebuking the poet laureate Colley Cibber,
who made it a point of pride always to hurl the final retort, no matter how inane it might be):

> *Poor Colley, thy Reas'ning is none of the strongest.*
> *For know, the last Word is the Word that last longest.*

Pope had it right. What really matters is not having the last
word, but having the words people remember. So how do you max-
imize your chances of having your words "last longest"? Ironically
enough, in the public arena at least, the last word (in Pope's sense)
generally goes to whomever speaks first.

It's not hard to see why. Just as the fighter who throws the first
punch can determine the temper of the entire bout (particularly if
that first punch packs a wallop), the side that speaks first usually
gets to frame the debate—and defining the issue is often half the
battle. Are we talking about "youth services" or "midnight basket-
ball"? "Free-market incentives" or "welfare for the rich"? A
"courageous whistleblower" or a "disgruntled former employee"?
The first label thrown out for public consumption always enjoys a
powerful inherent advantage. Simply by virtue of its primacy, this
label (or slant on the situation) becomes the conventional wisdom,
the starting point for any intelligent discussion. Succeeding labels,
no matter how clever—or accurate—can't help but be viewed as

reactions to the first, and as such they are bound to be considered at least slightly suspect.

For the media, the first major story on a particular subject invariably sets the tone for the coverage that follows. Whatever impressions (or misimpressions), facts (or falsehoods), explanations (or confusions) that story contains are likely to be repeated over and over again. The reason is simple. When reporters are

> **Bring your situation to the media's attention so that you become the main source for the first story.**

assigned to a new story, one of the first things they do is check the "clips" (that is, the archives) to see what's already been written about the subject. For everyone working on succeeding pieces, the initial story becomes the common reference point, the mother lode of insight and information, with a mantle of authority that can be difficult to shake. Indeed, even if some aspects of the initial story are later decisively refuted, they may still continue to be cited in future stories, if only to give the authors of those stories the chance to knock them down again.

So it is that anyone poised on the brink of some sort of public controversy—whether it concerns a legal action, a political campaign, a lobbying effort, or a labor dispute—can give himself a considerable leg up on the opposition by arranging to be the main (if not the only) source behind the first story. Since there is no earlier story to which the reporter who's writing it can refer for guidance, the initial article or broadcast on a particular subject can't help but reflect the point of view of its main source—that is, the person who provides most of the information on which it's based. A savvy spin doctor will make sure that person is he, for whoever the source is, it will be his spin that becomes the conventional wisdom.

And how do you become the main source behind the first story? You accomplish that, not by waiting for the media to discover the story on their own (and then hopefully coming to you for comment), but by bringing the situation to their attention and persuading them it's worth covering. In other words, by preempting the situation.

■ ■ ■

This was precisely the tack I proposed Tom take in his battle with the educational-item manufacturer. The company's CEO may have constructed an impressive public image, but I believed the facts would show it was belied by her actions. Indeed, with her excessive salary (given the size of her company) and outrageous perks, she could easily (I felt) be portrayed as the Leona Helmsley of the west. As a result, in order to protect Tom's reputation and prevent the company from muddying the waters, all we really had to do was make sure that the first major press account of the dispute reflected what we knew to be the case—namely, that Tom and his firm were not some greedy pack of Wall Street vultures trying to "greenmail" a promising new company, as the CEO would later claim, but a much abused investor standing up for the rights of minority stockholders.

The only question was, whom should we approach with the story?

Normally, you start with the hometown press. But the company was not headquartered in a financial center like New York or Los Angeles. Rather, it was located in a small bedroom community. As a result, I was afraid Tom's lawsuit might be a bit too arcane for the local newspapers. (Even if they understood it, as crusades go, the rights of minority stockholders in closely held companies was not likely to be much of a barn-burner for their readers.) Clearly, the best venue for us would be the *Wall Street Journal*. For one thing, the *Journal* would understand the case's significance. For another, its influence cannot be overstated. Once the *Journal* gave its imprimatur to the story, the local media would be all over it.

So how could we get the *Journal* interested? And once we had the *Journal* interested, how could we make sure its first story reflected our point of view?

Actually, snagging the *Journal*'s attention turned out to be relatively easy. Though the company was hardly of Fortune 500 size, I knew the *Journal* was always on the lookout for interesting shareholder suits. It didn't hurt that the issue of minority-shareholder rights was a hot one, of far more than passing interest to many *Journal* readers, and that Tom's case had just the right mixture of substantive relevance and juicy details.

Tom's lawyers planned to file their lawsuit at ten minutes to four on a Friday afternoon, just before everything closed up for the weekend. To ensure that a reporter would be on the case—and, equally important, that there would be space for his story in the following Monday's paper—we tipped the *Journal*, off the record and confidentially, in advance to expect a copy of the suit as soon as it was filed. We also made sure our lawyers would be standing by to answer whatever questions the paper might have.

The moment we received word that the lawsuit had been filed, we messengered a copy to the *Journal*, where a reporter was waiting for it. Just as we had hoped, his story on the case ran the following Monday. Though it included comments from one of the company's attorneys, the article—which appeared under the headline "Investor Gripes He Ventured but Didn't Gain"—pretty much reflected our view of the situation. Indeed, not only did it detail

Tom's allegations at length, it quoted a respected law-school dean warning about the "opportunities for abuse" in companies like the one we were suing. Also, as we'd hoped, the *Journal* article provoked a wave of additional publicity, as the local media, including all the major regional newspapers, swarmed in, playing catch-up on the story. Predictably, they all followed the *Journal*'s lead, painting the company's CEO as an imperious and extravagant ingrate who'd taken poor Tom for a ride.

Needless to say, the coverage put the company and its management irrevocably on the defensive. Indeed, each time they tried to answer Tom's charges—or even offer up a few counter-charges of their own—the press would simply rehash everything we had said in the original filing. In the end, though the CEO had vowed never to pay Tom a nickel, she purchased his stock at an eminently fair price.

■ ■ ■

By acting preemptively in this case—that is, by aggressively lining up the coverage of Tom's suit against the company, rather than waiting for the media to come to us—we were able to frame the debate. As a result, the issue on the table was always the CEO's selfishness and abuse of minority shareholders, not Tom's alleged greenmail. In other words, we were able to fight the battle we wanted to fight.

This, in a nutshell, is what spin is all about. The ability to define the issue (to fight the battle you want to fight) may sound academic, but I assure you, it's enormously potent. As the great Chinese tactician Sun Tzu was fond of noting, most battles are won or lost long before either of the adversaries steps onto the field. That's because what ultimately counts in a conflict is not necessarily size or strength, but the character of the terrain and the nature of your objectives. Control those and no foe will be too formidable.

To be sure, preempting a situation doesn't always involve striking the first blow or firing the first salvo. Indeed, one of my favorite examples of the power of preemption is a case that had been going on for three years before we got involved. I am referring to the bitter legal and PR battle that erupted in November 1992 between the ABC-TV news magazine *PrimeTime Live* and the media-shy, North Carolina–based grocery chain Food Lion, Incorporated. On November 5, 1992, *PrimeTime Live* had broadcast a scurrilous "hidden camera" exposé that purported to reveal what one reporter described as "a range of stomach-turning food-handling practices in deli and meat departments" in Food Lion supermarkets. The twenty-five–minute segment seemed to show Food Lion employees rewrapping and reselling out-of-date meat and poultry, altering expiration dates on perishable dairy goods and deli salads, and using poorly or improperly cleaned equipment to prepare food for sale.

The report shocked the nation—and plunged Food Lion into turmoil. In its wake, the price of the company's stock dropped by 25 percent and the chain was forced to close eighty-eight of its stores as sales faltered and profits virtually disappeared over the next year.

Outraged by what it considered ABC's unethical tactics and misleading accusations, the company took the network to court. But, rather than suing ABC for libel or slander, Food Lion accused *PrimeTime Live* of fraud and trespassing. Specifically, it alleged that a *PrimeTime Live* producer and associate producer had lied about their identities and experience in order to get jobs at two Food Lion stores where they later used lipstick-sized cameras hidden under wigs to videotape their unsuspecting coworkers.

Food Lion's legal tactics were as novel as they were clever. The fact is, libel cases are extremely difficult to win in court. Journalists may not be held in very high esteem these days (a recent study by the University of Chicago's National Opinion Research Center found that only 11 percent of the public feels "a great deal of confidence in the press"), but juries still tend to favor them over big corporations. What's more, the law requires a libel plaintiff to prove that the defendant not only got the story wrong but that he did so with deliberate malice.

> **Spin is all about the ability to define the issue—fighting the battle you want to fight.**

Proving fraud, on the other hand, is a much more straightforward endeavor. And in this case, the charge seemed almost self-evidently true. Certainly, there was no question that the two ABC employees had falsified their résumés and arranged for phony references in order to get hired by Food Lion. ("I love meat wrapping," one of them wrote on her job application. "I would love to make a career with the company.") In the end, their only defense was to argue that as journalists they had some sort of special right to lie in pursuit of the truth.

But while Food Lion was on solid ground legally—and, indeed, it eventually won its case in court—it was badly outmatched in the court of public opinion. For one thing, as misleading as those hidden-camera videotapes broadcast by ABC may have been, to most people they looked like irrefutable evidence that the chain was brazenly selling spoiled food. For another, ABC made full use of the fact that Food Lion wasn't suing it for libel—and, hence, was not technically challenging the veracity of its report. Self-righteously seizing the moral high ground (and banking on the public's ignorance of the intricacies of libel law), the network was thus able to argue—persuasively—that

Food Lion's legal strategy amounted to a confession that the *PrimeTime Live* report had been accurate, and that the only way it could revenge itself on ABC's courageous and public-spirited muckrakers was with some fancy, and unfair, legal footwork. As *PrimeTime Live* senior producer Ira Rosen put it: "Who are the bad guys here? Food Lion was putting the out-of-date food out there. We were just covering the story. And for that, we get put on trial? That's the Bizarro world in Superman comic books. That's nuts."

■   ■   ■

Sitrick and Company got involved with Food Lion shortly before its case against ABC went to trial in December 1996. The chain had already hired the powerful Washington, D.C., law firm of Akin, Gump, Strauss, Hauer & Feld, and North Carolina's Womble, Carlyle, Sandridge & Rice, to handle the litigation. Recognizing that the publicity battle outside the courtroom would be every bit as important as the legal maneuvering inside, the Akin, Gump team asked us to help out. We had worked with them successfully once before, and they understood the importance of spin. "There's going to be a lot of coverage of this trial," Richard Wyatt, the lead Akin, Gump lawyer who developed Food Lion's winning legal strategy, told me, "and we need to take control of it."

Indeed, the press was all over the case—and no wonder. To hear ABC tell it, nothing less than the future of investigative reporting was at stake. The ability to work undercover was an essential element in journalism's arsenal, insisted the network's advocates. A victory by Food Lion, they added, would strip dedicated journalists of a vital weapon, making it impossible for them to protect the public by exposing powerful evildoers.

But was this really the central issue? I didn't think so. Then I saw the outtakes of the *Prime Time Live* report, and I *knew* it wasn't.

During the pre-trial discovery process, Food Lion had obtained from *Prime Time Live* much of the raw footage shot by the two tiny cameras hidden in its producers' wigs. Needless to say, ABC had objected furiously to the chain's request that it turn over this footage. When we finally got to see it, at least one of the reasons

> **Preemption is an effective way of dealing with virtually *any* kind of unpleasant news.**

for the network's reluctance became obvious. As Food Lion had maintained all along, the unedited videotape made it clear that the two undercover producers were hardly disinterested observers who merely recorded a series of awful things they happened to see going on around them. Rather, on numerous occasions, the tape showed them ignoring the instructions of supervisors to clean up a mess they'd made and swearing audibly when some other Food Lion employee corrected a problem. What's more, the raw footage exposed just how shamelessly selective the *Prime Time Live* producers had been in their editing, revealing several instances in which ABC's allegations were directly contradicted by tape relegated to the cutting-room floor. For example, the report broadcast on *Prime Time Live* included a clip of a Food Lion employee complaining about not wanting to sell a piece of chicken that didn't smell right. For some reason, the producers did not include the remainder of the employee's statement, in which she said that when she consulted her manager, he instructed her to throw out the suspect poultry, which she did.

As soon as I saw this material, I knew we'd win... at least in the court of public opinion. What the outtakes made clear, it seemed to me, was that the issue here wasn't investigative journalism, it was honesty in journalism. And despite what ABC might try to argue, there was no question that insisting upon honesty in journalism would not put investigative reporting—or anything else of value—at risk.

■ ■ ■

In terms of spin, the strategic implications of this realization were obvious. We would seize the momentum from ABC by redefining the issue. When the network insisted that Food Lion's lawsuit was an attack on all journalism, we'd simply ask reporters, "Hey, would your editor let you get away with the stuff those guys did?" Invariably, the answer was no.

Crucial to our effort was maintaining a continuous presence at the trial. My colleague Donna Walters, herself a veteran reporter and editor (and a member of a *Los Angeles Times* reporting team that won a Pulitzer), became a fixture in the federal courthouse in Greensboro, North Carolina, where the proceedings were held. After every session, she and an associate, Ann Djordjevic, would brief the press on the day's events, pointing out the significance of various pieces of evidence, explaining the meaning of this or that bit of testimony.

Before long, even some of ABC's staunchest supporters were beginning to wonder if *PrimeTime Live* hadn't crossed the line. As Marvin Kalb, the distinguished former NBC News correspondent who now teaches at Harvard's John F. Kennedy School of Government, noted in the *Washington Post*: "Central to the craft is the guiding principle that journalists should be the truth-tellers, which means they should not lie or concoct fanciful tales or identities or use hidden cameras or microphones. They should walk in the front door of a story, not sneak in the back and rationalize the deception by claiming it was the only way to get at the truth."

Increasingly desperate, ABC began enlisting its news division's biggest stars to argue on its behalf. *Prime Time Live* coanchors Diane Sawyer and Sam Donaldson got into the act, making personal appearances and insisting no one had done anything wrong. In a commentary on ABC Radio, Donaldson contended that all Food Lion had going for it was brilliant PR—a remark I probably should have had framed.

But the needle was moving. Public opinion was changing. From being viewed as the worst sort of scoundrel imaginable, Food Lion had come to be seen as more sinned against than sinning. By the time the verdict came in against ABC late in December—and the punitive damage award was announced a month later—most people (at least according to what we read, heard, or saw) were ready to agree that *Prime Time Live* had fudged the broadcast.

Regardless of what might eventually happen in the appeals process, Food Lion had its reputation back. By preempting the situation—specifically, by acting aggressively to change the nature of the debate—we had prevailed over a much more powerful opponent.

Acting preemptively is a potent strategy in just about any situation in which charges of some sort are about to be exchanged. Regardless of the merits or relative seriousness of either side's allegations, the rhetorical edge invariably goes to the antagonist who fires first. Indeed, the right kind of preemptive action can so undermine an adversary's credibility that a potentially damaging public slanging match can be short-circuited before it even gets started.

I once had a client who made the mistake of having an affair with a woman who worked for him. The relationship ended badly, as these things often do, and the next thing my client knew the woman was planning to sue him. The charges: sexual harassment and, of all things, rape.

In the course of conversation, my client mentioned to his lawyers and me that the woman had stolen a number of things from the office and, he later discovered, padded her expense account. Fine, the lawyers replied, if she files charges against you, we can file those charges against her.

To my way of thinking, that was exactly the wrong thing to do. "You can't wait for her to file before you do," I told them. "If you do, your action will look like a reaction. You've got to flip it. If you think she's going to file, you must preempt her by filing your case right away. We don't want to have to publicize your filing. In fact, we should do our best to make sure the filing gets no publicity. Then, when she gets to court, it will look as if she's filing her case against you as a reaction."

That's exactly what happened. When the woman filed her lawsuit, the press decided that it represented nothing more than malicious retribution for the action my client had brought against her earlier. Not wanting to get caught in the middle of what looked like a cat-fight (since both parties did not happen to be celebrities), the media took a pass. Not one word about the harassment and rape charges ever appeared in the press.

■ ■ ■

In general, preemption can be a tremendously effective way of dealing with virtually any kind of unpleasant news. There are few more efficient means of taking the wind out of a potentially damaging disclosure than redefining the significance of what is going on. For example, I once helped out an extremely wealthy individual with a huge family trust who had a number of real-estate investments go sour. Though there was no threat to his fundamental solvency, the fact that the banks had foreclosed on some of his properties was embarrassing, and he was eager to keep any mention of it out of the papers. (For the record, this individual does not appear on our client list, nor has he ever been identified as a client of ours.)

"Here's what we're going to do," I told him. "We'll just take the position that you're a centimillionaire, and what's going on is peanuts compared with what you're really worth."

This line had two advantages. One, it was true; and, two, it played to the journalistic antipathy to appearing naive. And it worked. When the press inquired, I brushed off the foreclosures as nothing more than a dispute my client was having with his bankers. "After all," I said, "what's a $200,000 mortgage—or even a $500,000 mortgage—to somebody who's worth several hundred million? He told his banks that if they would agree to his terms, they could take the properties." The reporters lost interest, and the foreclosures never got any publicity.

But the challenge became a bit more daunting when the bankers began threatening to take back two of his most well-known, high-profile signature properties. Clearly, if they went ahead and foreclosed, there was no way we could portray it as anything but a terrible failure on my client's part.

I thought about it for a while, then came up with a plan. We knew the bank had a group of Japanese investors lined up to buy the properties after it foreclosed on them. With that in mind, we told my client's bankers that we were prepared to forestall the foreclosure by declaring bankruptcy—unless they agreed to buy the properties from us for an extremely nominal amount. It didn't really matter how much they paid for the properties, we said, as long as the transaction was a sale and not a foreclosure. Naturally, the bank agreed.

Soon afterward, the news "somehow" leaked to a well-placed columnist that my client was selling his famous properties to a group of Japanese investors on undisclosed terms. After that, we just sat back and watched the story spread. When reporters would call me to find out what was going on, I'd decline to comment, though off the record I was able to confirm (accurately) that a sale had taken place.

As a result, when the Japanese took possession of my client's properties, it was portrayed in the press as the result of a sale, rather than a humiliating foreclosure. Such is the power of preemption.

■　■　■

Preemption can be particularly useful when, because of federal filing requirements and the like, the bad news is something you're obliged to disclose yourself. Let's say, for example, you're the CEO of a publicly held company that finds it necessary to renegotiate its long-term financing with its bondholders. Given the financial state of the company, it's clear that if you aren't able to come to terms with your lenders, there is a good chance you will have no choice but to file for reorganization under Chapter 11 of the federal bankruptcy code. If you're like most people, your instinct will be to downplay that possibility. Unfortunately, federal securities law requires you to include this information in your next quarterly 10-Q report.

How do you handle it?

One school of thought counsels against calling any attention to such awkward news. In other words, you don't say anything. You simply put out your 10-Q and hope nobody notices. If your company has a low enough profile and the stars are properly aligned, you might luck out. But the odds aren't good.

Twenty years ago, you might have gotten away with that sort of thing. But these days, what with the Internet, Federal Filings, the Dow Jones Newswire, Reuters, and Bloomberg, the chances are slim indeed that any even vaguely relevant piece of business or financial information will escape attention.

My feeling is that if you have something unpleasant to disclose, whether it's an embarrassing 10-Q or a disappointing earnings report, you're much better off bellying up to the microphones and owning up to it (metaphorically speaking, of course) than you are pulling the covers over your head and trying to pretend that everything will be just fine as long as no one makes a sound. By issuing a press release you get to characterize your news in your own words—which are bound to be considerably less inflammatory than those of a reporter who has come across your 10-Q on his own. (As we noted earlier, when left to their own devices, reporters tend to put the most dramatic spin they can on events, leaving you in the uncomfortable position of having to spin in response.)

Even better, if you put out your release before the 10-Q is actually filed, the only information the reporter will have to work with is what you provide—as a result of which, his account can't help but reflect your perspective.

That's not to say you should attempt to mischaracterize the filing, or absent-mindedly neglect to mention one or two of the more embarrassing items in it. As we noted earlier, dishonesty never pays.

We once had a client who tried that sort of thing. Predictably, it blew up in his face. He was about to file a 10-Q containing some embarrassing disclosures and had agreed to let us put out a release in advance of it. Unfortunately, he didn't tell us all the bad news. I guess he felt that by hiding it from us, it wouldn't get into the release, and if it didn't get into the release, it wouldn't get into the newspapers. What happened next is painful to recall. The release came out and worked perfectly, inspiring exactly the sort of coverage we had hoped for. Then the 10-Q came out. A few hours later, I got a call from an irate reporter. "What are you trying to pull here?" she demanded. When I professed ignorance, she said she'd just gotten a copy of the 10-Q off EDGAR (the Securities and Exchange Commission's online database of required corporate filings) and had discovered all sorts of terrible things that hadn't even been hinted at in our press release.

All I could say to her was, "I haven't even seen it"—which wasn't much of a response. (The client, it turned out, had withheld from us the pages containing the worst of the disclosures.) Not surprisingly, the reporter wound up writing a second story about the filing that just clobbered our client. For my part, I couldn't blame her. Indeed, after telling the client that my firm couldn't work this way, we resigned the account.

The point is, if you're going to try to preempt an unpleasant filing by proactively issuing a press release, you can't include only the information that you would prefer the press to focus on. It's everything or nothing. In many cases, that means making a difficult judgment call. There's always a chance that if you say nothing, your filing will go unnoticed—in which case, you get off scot-free. But you've got to weigh that unlikely possibility against the knowledge that a full disclosure will get coverage—but it will be coverage that probably reflects your perspective on the situation.

The same is true when you have disappointing financial results to report. If you're about to release a bad earnings report, rather than downplaying the news, you might want to consider doing a Dow Joneser—one of those short, explanatory interviews that runs on the Dow Jones news ticker—or a Q&A with Bloomberg or Reuters. Yes, more attention will thereby be directed toward your unfortunate numbers, but you'll also have more of an opportunity to explain them. As in so much of spin (and life), pre-empting the situation is a matter of risk and reward.

CHAPTER 8

The Facts Don't Speak for Themselves

Be accessible—and be prepared to educate the press.

NO TRUISM HAS GOTTEN MORE well-meaning people in more trouble than the time-honored but entirely bogus notion that the facts can speak for themselves. As practical-minded realists, we may like to believe that if the facts are on our side, we need do nothing more than invoke their authority for our view of things to prevail. Certainly, life would be a lot easier if that were the case. But there is no getting around it. Arguments do not make themselves; they must be made. Stories do not tell themselves; they must be told. As necessary as they may be to construct a good argument or create a good story, the facts alone are hardly sufficient. The mathematician Henri Poincaré once likened them to stones: enormously useful— but only when there is a guiding intelligence to organize them. ("Science," Poincaré noted, "is built up with facts, as a house is with stones. But a collection of facts is no more a science than a heap of stones is a house.") His insight is worth pondering.

In the context of spin, the salient point is this: You should never assume that the press will necessarily recognize the truth for what it is—or, certainly, what you perceive it to be. Just because *you* understand the implications of a certain set of facts doesn't mean anyone else will—least of all a reporter, who generally has neither the time nor the inclination to familiarize himself with the myriad subtleties that define your particular situation.

There are, to be sure, some diehards who insist that it's the media's job to get it right. To them, I say good luck.

Actually, that's not what I say. If truth be told, I sometimes get a bit abrupt when I'm in a strategy session with a client and his advisors, and one of the advisors argues that we don't need to talk to reporters because "our press release speaks for itself."

What I tend to say in such moments is, "Oh, I see—you don't care if the press gets it right."

"What do you mean?" the advisor invariably shoots back. "Of course I care if they get it right!"

"Well, it sure doesn't sound that way. Because when you say the release can speak for itself, what you're really doing is telling the press: 'Here are the facts. You interpret them. If you get it right, great. If not—well, too bad.'"

It's at this point that the advisor usually protests that it's the media's job to get it right. To which I generally respond that, no, it's the media's job to do the best they can. And it's our job to do everything in our power to make sure their best turns out to be good enough.

What that means in most cases is not just issuing a press release, then sitting back and crossing your fingers. It means making yourself available to explain (often over and over again) the meaning of the statement you've just put out. It means anticipating every likely misunderstanding and misapprehension, and moving quickly to correct them. It means being ready and willing, when necessary, to give reporters a crash course in the basics of your business (whether it involves explaining the logic of forward

> **All that counts in the end is whether the media accurately reflect your situation.**

interest arbitrage, the fine points of environmental law, or the rules of intercollegiate lacrosse).

You can fume all you want that a reporter who doesn't know the first thing about the world in which you operate should not presume to write about your affairs. Maybe so, but it happens all the time, and however unfair or unreasonable it may seem, if you don't provide an uninformed or inexperienced reporter with the background he needs in order to be able to understand your situation, he'll probably get it wrong—and if he does, it's not the press that will suffer, it's you.

That's the point to remember. Fairness has nothing to do with it. To someone caught in the glare of media attention, all that counts in the end is whether the stories that get written about him accurately reflect his situation. Complaining after the fact about mistakes or misunderstandings may win the sympathy of friends and relatives, but it won't do much to reassure all those spooked investors (or customers or creditors or voters) who know only what they read in the paper or saw on television.

One of our clients was once involved in a proxy fight to take over one of the best-known sports franchises in the country. Like most such struggles, it was a fairly complicated affair, filled with charges of managerial malfeasance, misappropriation of funds, and conflicts of interest, not to mention a host of arcane securities regulatory and accounting techniques. Our client prevailed, at least in part because we made sure he and his representatives were always available to explain to the press just what was going on.

Our client had first set his sights on this sports franchise in the mid-1980s, when he and a partner tried to buy it outright. Though the once glamorous franchise was in decline, he felt that with the right management its allure could be restored. Not surprisingly, the franchise's existing management saw things differently and spurned his offer. But our client wasn't about to be put off. In August 1990, he purchased just under 10 percent of the franchise's stock and announced his intention of mounting a proxy fight to wrest control from its longtime chairman and chief executive, a prominent local figure with a myriad of friends in both the entertainment and business communities—as well as a colorful and controversial background, the details of which were available to anyone willing to do a little digging through Lexis-Nexis and other public archives.

The facts were certainly on our client's side. For one thing, his credentials were impeccable. In addition to being the chairman of a major industrial company, he was also a major player in the sports world—the owner of successful sports franchises in two other states. For another, the numbers told a sorry—and inarguable—tale of deterioration and mismanagement at the target entity under its current leadership. As the *Wall Street Journal* noted, there had been a time when this particular franchise had been "the envy of the industry." Since 1980, however, attendance there had plummeted by 43 percent, and adjusted for inflation, revenues had fallen even further.

Nonetheless, the CEO of the target franchise was a formidable opponent. This individual had run the franchise for nearly two decades, and in the process had become something of an institution, amassing a cadre of loyal and well-connected supporters. They ranged from a former First Lady (who was an old friend) to a prominent entertainment mogul (who was a member of the franchise's board) to a well-known television star (who was also a board member—and who, in defense of the CEO, actually got into a brief wrestling match with a dissident board member in the directors' box). A determined if famously cantankerous individual, the CEO was not about to give up control without a fight.

That's not to say the incumbent CEO didn't have vulnerabilities. In addition to being responsible for the franchise's failing health, there was the matter of the CEO's own somewhat checkered past. The offspring of a sports mogul, this individual had first gotten involved in the business in another state—and as the *Wall Street Journal* later reported, in order to succeed professionally, had "doled out hefty political contributions and set aside stock… for prominent politicians." Though the CEO insisted that local sports officials gave franchise operators no choice but to sell stock to politicians at artificially low prices, the CEO was nonetheless named as an unindicted co-conspirator in an infamous 1971 corruption case in which a number of prominent government officials, including one former governor, were convicted of taking bribes.

That, of course, was all ancient history when our client mounted his challenge some twenty years later. What mattered most to him at the time was convincing a majority of the franchise's individual stockholders that he stood a far better chance than the existing management of being able to revive the beleaguered franchise's flagging fortunes. In response, the incumbent CEO argued that our client's previous experience was irrelevant. For his part, our client simply pointed to the franchise's continuing downhill slide under the current management ("It just makes you sick to look out and see this," he complained).

As the two adversaries went at each other, trading charges and countercharges, citing old court cases and obscure securities regulations, the press struggled earnestly—but not always suc-

Do your homework, and always take the time to educate the press.

cessfully—to sort it all out. The media's problem was simple: This was at heart a business story—yet because it involved a sports franchise, most of the journalists assigned to cover it were sports reporters. Now sports reporters may be as clever as the next fellow, but few of them know very much about business, and even less about the ins and outs of proxy fights and hostile takeovers. As a result, many of the statements and announcements put out by the two camps—not to mention the combatants' various legal and financial stratagems—left them baffled.

With so much of the press at such a loss, this was clearly a situation that cried out for hands-on PR. Certainly, no sensible person would simply issue a series of press releases and assume they could "speak for themselves." Yet that's essentially what the other camp did, even though they had a financial PR agency representing them. For some reason, their people didn't seem willing to invest the time and effort needed to make sure the media understood what they were talking about. As a result, every time they made an announcement or issued a release (which, to make matters worse, were generally written in indecipherable "lawyerese"), our side wound up being deluged with frantic phone calls from reporters desperate to find a friendly expert who might explain to them what it was that the other guys had just said.

Needless to say, we were happy to do what we could. Yes, explaining the situation to confused newspeople was time-consuming and often tedious. But it gave us a tremendous advantage in the ongoing public debate, since our explanations inevitably included our assessment of the accuracy and relevance of the other side's latest announcement. As a result, because they didn't make themselves sufficiently accessible, it was our perspective that prevailed in the vast majority of stories about the proxy fight. (The other side's perspective was generally conveyed in the form of an unilluminating "no comment." Or as one typical report in a major newspaper put it, "Officials at [the franchise] referred calls to a New York public relations firm. Officials there could not be reached for comment.")

The *coup de grâce*, if you will, came when we learned that the other side's representatives were trying to get the *Wall Street Journal* to do a major front-page story on their CEO. This struck me as surprising, since the public record was littered with numerous less-than-flattering incidents from the CEO's colorful past, but once again we were happy to help out. Though the *Journal* was at first a bit cool to the idea of devoting so much space to such a story, the newspaper's interest perked up considerably after we laid out, complete with documentation, what we had learned about the CEO from a survey of publicly available documents (such as 10-Ks, 10-Qs, and proxy statements) plus a Lexis-Nexis search.

The *Journal*'s profile of the incumbent CEO turned out to be devastating. In addition to cataloging the various brushes with the law that characterized the CEO's early years in the business, it detailed a series of more recent allegations, including misappropriation of funds at the target franchise. It also recounted a state court's reproach that under the incumbent CEO's leadership the franchise had attempted to "ingratiate itself" with state regulating officials in a manner that "is not acceptable in dealing with state agencies," and characterized the CEO's management style as bullying and overbearing.

Not long after the article appeared, the incumbent CEO threw in the towel, agreeing to resign from the franchise's board and signing off on a settlement under which our client took over as chairman and chief executive.

■ ■ ■

There are actually two lessons to be gleaned from this experience. One is the importance of doing your homework. If the other side's representatives had done their homework and thoroughly researched their client's background, they would never have pitched a story about the CEO to the *Journal*, because they'd have been aware of all the potentially embarrassing information so easily available from public sources like Lexis-Nexis and the Internet. (A simple rule of thumb: If you can find something in the archives, you can be sure a major news organization will too.)

The second—and more fundamental—lesson is the importance of being accessible. It was nice having the facts on our side in this proxy fight, but they wouldn't have done us any good if no one had understood them. By making sure we were always available to explain their significance, we ensured that the press got the story right.

It's impossible to overstate the value of access and explanation—particularly when you are in a fight. The fact is, you should no more expect the press to figure out a contentious, complicated story on its own than you would expect a trial jury to reach a verdict in your favor without having heard you present your case.

That's not to say the media are incapable of getting it right without the help of an outside advocate. But if your interests happen to be at stake, it's probably unwise to assume that justice will triumph without some effort on your part.

∎   ∎   ∎

For the most part, this process tends to be incremental—and not terribly glamorous. I sometimes refer to it as PR 101, because it involves the most basic aspects of press relations (or, as some call it, the care and feeding of the media): providing information to reporters, taking the time to make sure they understand it fully, treating newspeople with the consideration you'd like them to give you. It may sound simple, but don't be fooled. When executed properly, it can be awesomely effective. Take, for example, the time we helped a group of foreign investors beat out seven U.S.-based bidders in a fierce competition to acquire a failed—though still enormously valuable—life-insurance company. Or the time, a few years later, when we helped the very private Kirk Kerkorian prevail in a bitter and lengthy PR and legal battle with the giant French bank Credit Lyonnais. In both situations, as in the sports franchise proxy fight, the PR 101 fundamentals of access and explanation turned out to be the keys to success.

The insurance company campaign posed an interesting challenge, to say the least. Over the course of the go-go 1980s, this particular insurance company had come out of nowhere to become briefly one of the most significant players in the U.S. insurance industry. Its secret was junk bonds. Instead of putting its money in such traditionally conservative securities as Treasury notes and investment-grade corporate paper, the company loaded up on the high-yield, high-risk bonds pioneered by Drexel Burnham Lambert—so much so that the firm's maverick chief executive became known as Drexel's best customer. The outsized yields generated by Drexel's bonds allowed him to offer customers higher returns on life policies and annuities than any of his competitors, and by the late 1980s his sales force had managed to write nearly $50 billion worth of insurance.

> It's foolish to assume that justice will triumph without some effort on your part.

Unfortunately, when the junk-bond market collapsed in 1989, so did the value of the company's portfolio. And in April 1991, it was seized by state regulators in what was at the time the largest insurance failure in U.S. history.

Rather than breaking up the company and liquidating it piecemeal, the state insurance commissioner decided it would be better for everyone (especially the company's 350,000 policyholders) if the state could sell the firm as a whole. To that end, he froze its assets and put the company up for auction.

Over the next six months, eight groups wound up submitting bids for the seized company. The group we hooked up with was a consortium led by a giant European insurer and a subsidiary of a huge foreign bank. We got involved through the group's chief strategist, a brilliant American takeover expert who first made his name at Drexel. One of his partners was someone with whom I'd worked at Wickes, and one day he called me out of the blue to ask my help with a media problem. He and his colleagues had heard that *Business Week* was going ahead with a misinformed piece about their takeover bid. Could I find out whether such a story was in fact in the works?

Even though his firm was not yet a client, I assured my old

friend I would make a few phone calls and see what I could discover. Sure enough, what he and his partners had heard turned out to be true. *Business Week* was doing a story, and it had gotten a crucial fact wrong. I told my contact at *Business Week* that I could vouch for my friend's honesty and forthrightness. "If he tells me the information is inaccurate, you can take that to the bank," I said. My contact replied that the story was not yet closed, and could I put him in touch with my friend?

I could, and did, and the mistake was corrected before the story was published. The next thing I knew, my former colleague's firm had hired Sitrick and Company to work with its Washington PR counsel on the insurance company bid.

It was an interesting challenge. Of the eight groups seeking to acquire the seized insurance company, ours had clearly come up with the best bid. Unfortunately, we were also laboring under some major handicaps. Not to put too fine a point on it, we represented foreign interests that were seeking to take over a U.S. insurance company. What's more, some in the media were writing (incorrectly) that our takeover team's chief strategist was the very Drexel executive who had sold the ill-fated junk bonds to the insurance company.

And there was another problem. The bidding process was so terribly convoluted that there was no guarantee that even the experts—not to mention the press and the public—would recognize the superiority of our group's offer. What made it so complicated was that we weren't dealing with straight cash bids, in which the party offering the most dollars would win. Rather, each bid consisted of differently structured financing schemes that would deliver varying amounts of money to the company's policyholders. On top of that, there was the question of what each would-be buyer intended to do about the junk bonds in the company's portfolio. Under a new law, insurance firms doing business in the state were forbidden to invest more than 20 percent of their total assets in junk bonds.

In terms of spin, our mission was clear. We had to convince the media that our group wasn't the ogre they had been told it was—and at the same time, teach them enough about the insurance and investment businesses so they could understand why our bid deserved to win. Even with the facts on our side, it was as tall an order as they come.

Our first goal was to defuse the hostility directed at our chief strategist, the former Drexel acquisitions expert. Correcting the mistaken impression about him (specifically, that he stood to profit from a problem that he had somehow helped to create) took time. Basically, it involved sitting down with reporter after reporter and explaining that he was not responsible for the insurance company's junk-bond portfolio.

Once we had convinced reporters they had the wrong idea about our strategist, we concentrated on getting them to focus on what we regarded as the real story: namely, the nature of our group's bid and why it was superior. The key to evaluating the different bids, we explained, wasn't so much in the amount of money each group was promising to bring policyholders initially. Though our offer was as generous as anyone's, the fact was that, on this score at least, there wasn't a whole lot of difference in the field. Just about everyone was promising to pay policyholders somewhere between 80 cents and 90 cents on the dollar. No, what mattered, we emphasized, was what each of the various groups would do about the junk bonds in the company's portfolio. Or as one writer put it, after we'd briefed her, "It really sounds like everyone is missing the point. It's not about 85 or 87 or even 90 cents—it's about security and risk."*

On that score, happily, our bid was head and shoulders above the rest. Unlike any of the other bidders, we were proposing to buy all of the company's junk bonds for cash, thereby eliminating the risk that threatened the company's stability. (Specifically, the bank subsidiary in our consortium would take the junk-bond portfolio, while the surviving life-insurance company would be administered by the giant European insurer.)

As noted, PR 101 is incremental. It moves the press in little steps. But it does move it. And over time the coverage grew increasingly friendly. So much so that, by October 1991, when the state insurance commissioner endorsed our bid, it was a bit of an anti-climax.

The competition, however, wasn't over. The commissioner's recommendation had to be reviewed by a state-court judge. Though it was unlikely the judge would overrule the insurance commissioner, it was possible. Certainly, the other bidders weren't ready to admit they'd been beaten. In particular, one group was aggressively seeking to reverse the commissioner's decision.

In such an intensely political atmosphere, we needed to rally all the media support we could. What would really help, I realized, would be an outright endorsement from a major newspaper. So I called an editorial writer I knew at the largest daily in the state. With tens of thousands of the seized company's policyholders and investors scattered throughout the region, I told her, the disposition of its assets clearly mattered to a lot more people than just a few

* It's important to remember that during this period the junk-bond market was in the doldrums, and junk bonds were considered the symbol of all that was bad in the 1980s.

high-level financial types. Would she mind, I asked, if I brought in a few of my colleagues to discuss why we thought the state insurance commissioner had made the right decision in selecting our bid?

As soon as she agreed, I phoned the litigator who would be arguing the merits of our bid before the state-court judge. "What I want you to do," I told him, "is to recast your case in the simplest manner possible and explain to the paper's editorial board why it's in the best interest of their readers that our group buys this property."

The attorney, one of the top litigators in the state, was terrific. A week after he presented our case to the editorial board, the newspaper published an editorial in which it enthusiastically seconded the insurance commissioner's recommendation of our bid and called upon the judge to follow it.

We went through a similar process with the daily newspaper in the state capital, with a similar result. In the end, the judge upheld the commissioner's decision. Whether our efforts tipped the balance, I can't say, but our clients clearly thought so; certainly, they got the results they wanted.

∎ ∎ ∎

The Kerkorian case was even more contentious than the battle for the seized life-insurance firm. For Sitrick and Company, it began in December 1992, when Credit Lyonnais sued Kerkorian for $1.25 billion, claiming he had misrepresented the financial health of Metro-Goldwyn-Mayer, Incorporated (MGM), when he sold the film studio to Giancarlo Parretti two years earlier. Parretti was a shadowy Italian businessman and alleged swindler. Nonetheless, Credit Lyonnais had loaned him more than $1 billion to finance his acquisition of MGM. To no one's surprise (except, perhaps, the bank's), it wasn't long before Parretti had fallen behind on the payments, leaving Credit Lyonnais with no choice but to foreclose on its loans and take charge of the studio itself. From there, things went from ridiculous to absurd. With MGM hemorrhaging money, the bank decided to blame the debacle not on its own bad judgment in backing Parretti, but on Kerkorian.

> **Bad news needs to be explained; the worse the news, the more explanation is required.**

At the time, I was working with Kerkorian's top lieutenant, Alex Yemenidjian, a brilliant and talented accountant-turned-businessman who was in the process of taking Kerkorian's Las Vegas hotel, the MGM Grand, public. When I read about the Credit Lyonnais lawsuit, I immediately telephoned Alex. I told him that, in my opinion, unless Kerkorian made a concerted effort to get the word out, he was bound to be unfairly portrayed as the villain of this story. I pointed out that Credit Lyonnais had hired one of the top PR firms in New York, and I was certain they would do their best to make sure that goal was achieved. All one had to do was read their initial news release, which excoriated Kerkorian, to see what lay ahead.

After speaking with Kerkorian, Alex invited me to a strategy session that weekend at Kerkorian's house in Los Angeles with him, his boss, and a group of advisors that included Terry Christensen, Patty Glaser, and Steve Silbert—Kerkorian's longtime lawyers from Christensen, Miller, Fink, Jacobs, Glaser, Weil & Shapiro, one of LA's top litigation firms. Five days later, Kerkorian and his attorneys filed two $675 million countersuits that charged Credit Lyonnais with playing what was called a giant "shell game" in which the French bank had exaggerated Parretti's resources in order to push through his purchase of MGM. According to the suits, Credit Lyonnais feared that if the MGM deal stalled, Parretti's shaky empire would collapse, and the bank would be forced to write off hundreds of millions of dollars in questionable loans it had made to his companies.

It was a painfully complicated situation, and as events unfurled over the ensuing months, as more pleadings were filed, motions made, and information seeped out, it grew even more convoluted. Once again, however, we did our best to make sure the reporters covering the case understood every twist and turn. As I often explain to my clients, you don't have to give on-the-record interviews to help your cause; all you need to do is point reporters in the right direction.

In the end, the public record, as reported in the media, vindicated Kerkorian—it showed that he was the victim in this case, not the villain the initial press release had portrayed him to be. In 1994 a California judge threw out Credit Lyonnais's suit, and though the bank promptly refiled its complaint in federal court, the case was settled privately and confidentially a year later. Meanwhile, the international press, which was now paying closer attention to the bank, was reporting on a series of management scandals at Credit Lyonnais involving questionable lending policies and political favoritism. In one of the most outrageous cases, the bank was found to have bought out a cabinet minister's interest in a troubled company on exceptionally favorable terms. Ultimately, the scandals not only badly tarnished the bank's reputation but also helped drive the Socialist Party from power in France.

The bank finally sold MGM in 1996. The buyer was Kirk Kerkorian (or, more accurately, a management-led group backed by him). The eleventh-hour deal, in which Kerkorian's group beat out half a dozen other serious bidders, including the European entertainment giant PolyGram and media mogul Rupert Murdoch, stunned observers both in Hollywood and on Wall Street. Still, the press generally greeted Kerkorian's renewed involvement with MGM as an exciting and positive development for the studio—a sharp contrast to its earlier penchant (prompted in large part by his adversaries' spin) for portraying him as a ruthless wheeler-dealer.

■ ■ ■

It's one thing to persuade a protagonist to make himself or his representatives available to the media in basically positive situations like these. Things become a bit trickier when the news isn't so good. That's a problem, because that's often precisely when you should be most available. Bad news needs to be explained. And the worse the news, the more explanation is required.

One of the best recent examples of this was probably the stunning decision of the government of Orange County, California, to seek bankruptcy protection. If there was ever a case that illustrated clearly the importance of taking an active role in explaining the facts—rather than complacently letting them try to speak for themselves—this was it.

The first warning that Sitrick and Company was about to become involved in the Orange County mess came the morning of Tuesday, December 6, 1994, when a phone call came into our Century City offices from a lawyer at Stutman, Treister & Glatt, one of the nation's premier bankruptcy firms. I was traveling at the time, and returned the call from out of town.

"We have a major case on which we're going to need your help," the lawyer said.

"Well, I'm in New York until the end of the week," I replied. "But the head of our restructuring group, Sandi Sternberg, is in the office."

"I know Sandi," the lawyer said. "She's terrific. I'll call her."

A few minutes later, he phoned Sandi with a somewhat cryptic request. He wanted her to get in her car and head down the freeway to the Orange County administrative center in Santa Ana.

"What's going on?" Sandi inquired.

"Phone me from your car when you're on the freeway," the lawyer replied. "I'll explain it to you then."

Sandi didn't have to be asked twice. Clearly, something major was afoot. A few days earlier, the financial community had been jolted by the news that Orange County's previously much admired bond portfolio was in big trouble. According to a hastily conducted audit, questionable investment strategies had saddled the county— along with 184 other local government entities that had put money in its bond fund—with more than $1.5 billion in paper losses. As a result, longtime county treasurer Robert L. Citron had resigned, and Wall Street investors were balking at rolling over some $1.2 billion in short-term obligations that had just come due. As bizarre as it seemed, what the *Los Angeles Times* accurately described as "one of the nation's largest, wealthiest, and most politically conservative counties" was apparently headed for the financial rocks.

By the time Sandi arrived in Santa Ana, her suspicions had been confirmed. Orange County, she was told, was about to send its lawyers into federal court, where it would become the largest municipality in history to seek protection under the rarely invoked Chapter 9 of the U.S. bankruptcy code.

■ ■ ■

Declaring bankruptcy is not the end of the world, but it can sometimes seem that way. Certainly, it's never easy or painless. But whether it amounts to a tragic end or a new beginning depends almost entirely on how the individuals or institutions involved handle the situation.

Like any predicament that requires tough, complicated decisions, bankruptcy is especially difficult to carry out (and survive) in the public eye. It's not simply the embarrassment of having to admit that your affairs are on the brink of being overwhelmed by circumstance. That can happen to anyone. It's that with so many competing interests at stake—those of creditors, investors, customers, and employees, to name just a few—there's virtually no way to achieve any kind of workable consensus without a certain amount of table (and head) banging.

To complicate matters further, there is also the residue of mistrust that inevitably attaches to most bankruptcy filings—the entirely understandable though usually unfair suspicion that someone is trying to get away with something. Add to this the media's natural inclination toward cynicism—not to mention their discomfort with complexity—and you have a recipe for potential disaster. Or, at the very least, a situation that cries out for access and explanation.

■ ■ ■

As it happened, the Orange County fiscal crisis blindsided officials in more ways than one. In a particularly unfortunate bit of bad timing, the county had just made major cutbacks in its in-house press office, and those few PR professionals who remained on its payroll had absolutely no experience dealing with anything as sensitive and complicated as a bankruptcy proceeding. (In fact, very few PR professionals do.) As a result, the county was almost entirely unequipped to explain to either the press or the public the monumentally unsettling events that were about to unfold.

Hence the call to Sitrick and Company. At the request of the county and its lawyers, we mobilized a team of specialists to prepare for the avalanche of press inquiries the bankruptcy filing was sure to provoke. There were at least three aspects to our mission. First, we had to help the county explain—to its citizens, its employees, and its creditors—just what the Chapter 9 filing meant, and perhaps more important, what it didn't mean. In particular, we had to reassure a bewildered and increasingly anxious public that filing for bankruptcy protection didn't mean that the county was somehow "going out of business," that services were going to stop, or that police and firefighters would all have to be laid off. Second, we had to stabilize the situation and calm the investment community so the county's troubled bond portfolio could be liquidated on the best terms possible. And third, we had to train the county's own PR people so that eventually, once things stabilized, they would be able to represent the county's interests on their own.

By itself, the first task was overwhelming enough. The number of journalists who descended on Santa Ana was mind-boggling. The *Los Angeles Times* alone was said to have forty people on the story, while the *Orange County Register*, we were told, had assigned some twenty-five reporters. In addition, there were staffers from all the local radio and television stations, the three major networks and CNN, the wire services, the *New York Times*, the *Wall Street Journal* (which sent reporters from both its Los Angeles and New York offices), the three news weeklies, and most of the major business magazines—not to mention a crew from *60 Minutes*. In all, according to a Lexis-Nexis search we did, roughly 5,200 stories were published or broadcast about Orange County's bankruptcy in the first five weeks following the filing. That's an average of 145 stories a day, seven days a week.

To make things even more exciting, not all of the reporters on the story were financial writers. Indeed, a disconcerting number of them didn't know the difference between a balance sheet and a bed sheet. We thus found ourselves having to give what amounted to a course in Finance 101 to the lion's share of the press corps— explaining everything from the basics of bankruptcy law to the ins and outs of public borrowing. As a result, inquiries that should have taken us only five minutes to answer invariably ended up requiring a thirty- to forty-minute explanation.

How necessary was this sort of hand-holding? I'm not sure you can put a price tag on the value of keeping the public accurately informed in the midst of a major government crisis, and I won't try. Instead, I'll simply relate the circumstances surrounding just one misinformed inquiry we received at a critical moment—and the potential damage we averted by correcting it.

It was late on a Saturday evening just before the county was about to start liquidating its $5.5 billion bond portfolio, and a few of our people were hashing over strategy in Bruce Bennett's and Lou Bogdanoff's offices at Stutman, Treister. (Bennett has since left Stutman to form his own firm, Hennigan Mercer Bennett.) Around 10:30 PM, a reporter from one of the nation's leading newspapers called. His paper was preparing to publish a major story about alleged new "irregularities" in the county's record-keeping. According to the reporter, several hundred million dollars worth of bonds listed by the county as being among its holdings didn't actually exist. The newspaper suspected that Bob Citron, the disgraced former county treasurer, had tried to conceal his trading losses by creating a phantom portfolio.

When pressed for specifics, the reporter said he had found more than a dozen instances of "bogus" listings, in which the county claimed to own more of a bond than had actually been issued. For example, he told me, in one case the county said it owned $200 million worth of a particular bond, when in fact the records seemed to indicate that the entire original issue of that bond had totaled only $150 million. The reporter wanted us to comment on his findings.

If the newspaper's allegations were correct, we were all in big trouble. If the news didn't make a total shambles of the upcoming bond sale, it would at the very least badly hobble the county's ability to restructure its portfolio.

The first—and most important—thing to do, of course, was to determine the facts. To that end, we got the reporter to identify each of the suspect listings (which he did via fax), then called the paper's editor, whom we knew, and persuaded him to hold the story while we investigated the situation. Then we immediately began tracking down the so-called phantom bonds. Working through the weekend, we discovered that the reporter's would-be scoop was based on a fundamental misunderstanding. The bonds he had labeled as bogus were what are known as shelf-registration issues (so named because they "wait on the shelf," unregistered with the Securities and Exchange Commission, until investors commit to them). In such situations, the only entity that knows how much of a particular bond has actually been issued is the issuer itself. In fact, there were no phantom bonds. The newspaper simply had outdated figures, which is why its numbers didn't add up.

Presented with this information—along with a lengthy explanation—the reporter acknowledged it had all been much ado about nothing. As a result, he killed the story.

Had we been unwilling (or unable) to take the time and trouble to check out the supposedly bogus listings and to educate the reporter about the arcane intricacies of shelf-registration issues, chances are he would have published his allegations. (After all, he had no information to contradict what he had been told.) What the impact would have been on the upcoming portfolio sale—and, by extension, on the county's long-term fiscal future—is impossible to say with precision. But it wouldn't have been good. With potential buyers nervous enough to begin with, even if government spokesmen had put out an immediate denial, the mere fact that one of the most influential newspapers in the country was raising questions about the authenticity of the county's holdings would more than likely have rattled the market and depressed prices. Given the size of the portfolio, even a tiny decline would have had huge consequences. Indeed, if the story had wound up shaving 10 percent off the average sale price—a modest amount given the explosiveness of the allegations—that would have cost the county some $550 million; if it had reduced the average sale price by just 1 percent, that would have cost Orange County upwards of $55 million.

So is it worth the trouble to make sure you have an expert who not only understands the situation but also recognizes the value of taking an active role in explaining the facts? Considering the havoc that the "phantom portfolio" story could have wreaked—not to mention that it was just one of literally hundreds of equally misinformed pieces we wound up helping to kill or correct in similar fashion—I think the answer is self-evident.

CHAPTER 9

▌Think Strategically

*Understand your fundamental objectives and stay
focused on them.*

THE CALL CAME IN LATE on a Friday afternoon. A lawyer with whom
we had worked on a previous case was phoning from Denver to ask
us to help out with some damage control. "We're going to liquidate
the Purgatory Ski Resort," he explained bluntly. The shutdown, he
added, would throw several hundred people out of work and devastate the economy of the southwestern Colorado town of Durango.

"Why are you liquidating it?" I asked.

"The bank is refusing to renew their line of credit," he said.

"Why? Is Purgatory losing money?"

"Not at all. In fact, it's moderately profitable."

"So what's going on?"

With a discouraged sigh, the lawyer explained that the bank
that had been providing Purgatory with financing for more than a

decade had recently been sold to a larger, out-of-state bank. Though nothing about Purgatory's financial health had changed—indeed, it had just come off of one of its most successful seasons ever—the new management had abruptly decided to cut off the resort's credit line.

> **Media attention is never an end in itself; determine your objective and tailor your actions to it.**

Ski resorts generally depend on such lines to get them through the moribund summer months, when revenues are almost non-existent but expenses—which include advertising and marketing for the upcoming winter—are high. Purgatory was typical: Each summer it would meet its cash needs by drawing $2 million or so from its credit line, which it would pay back with interest when business picked up again at the end of the year. Without its credit line, there would be no way for Purgatory to meet its payroll, much less afford the promotional efforts necessary to make the next ski season a success.

"We're still talking to the bank, hoping to change its mind," the lawyer concluded, "but it doesn't look good."

I thought about all this for a moment. "How recently was the bank sold?" I asked.

"Not that long ago," the lawyer replied. "The deal was finalized within the last few weeks."

"In that case," I said, "I don't believe you're going to have to close the place after all."

"Why?" the lawyer asked with disbelief. "Do you know some arcane Colorado banking law that we don't?"

"No," I said, "but what is the governor of Colorado going to say when the *Denver Post* asks him about the impact on the state's most important industry—the ski industry—of the sale of Purgatory's bank to an out-of-state institution, a sale he approved? What is he going to say when they ask whether the bank promised to continue supporting businesses in Colorado? What is he going to say when they tell him the new owners of the bank have no interest in continuing to support the state's most important industry and as a result management has to close Purgatory and devastate an entire town? What do you think the state banking commissioner is going to say?"

There was dead silence on the other end of the line. After a long moment, the lawyer finally spoke up. "How soon can you guys be here?" he asked.

My colleague David McAdam was on a flight to Denver at 6:30 the next morning.

∎ ∎ ∎

If there is one characteristic that distinguishes the ordinary PR practitioner from the artful spinmeister it is that the spinner always thinks strategically. P.T. Barnum may have believed that there was no such thing as bad publicity, but to the spin doctor, media attention is never an end in itself. It is, rather, a means to some other objective. Determining just what that objective happens to be—and then tailoring your actions accordingly—is one of the most important keys to successful spin.

Business-school professors call this management by objective, and I happen to be a great believer in it. Whenever I take on a new client, the first thing I do is try to determine exactly what his objective is. More often than you might think, the client is as in the dark about his real aims as I am. He thinks he knows why he called me—to get his name in the papers, he might insist, or to keep it out—but after a bit of discussion he may come to realize that what he's actually seeking to achieve is something else entirely.

The lawyer for Purgatory, for example, thought he was calling Sitrick and Company in order to get some help containing the bad publicity he correctly assumed would accompany an announcement that the resort was going out of business. And had he phoned another public-relations firm there's a good chance that's precisely what he would have gotten. A traditional PR man would have gone promptly to work doing just what the lawyer had asked—drafting a press release, drawing up a list of media contacts, fashioning a damage-control plan. The liquidation of Purgatory would have proceeded apace, and within a few days or weeks the resort would have been history—along with all those jobs and a good-sized chunk of the local economy.

But that's not really what the lawyer was hoping to accomplish. What he really wanted more than anything else was to keep the resort open—to find a way to restore the credit line that the bank had canceled. By questioning him closely I uncovered this more fundamental objective and discerned the elements of a solution.

In the end, what I wound up doing was actually rather simple. Over the weekend, I phoned the business editor of the *Denver Post*. "I've got a story that will knock your socks off," I told him. "But before I say another word, here's the deal. My clients still think there's a chance they'll be able to negotiate their way out of this. So I'll give you this information on two conditions: one, that it's off the record until I say otherwise; and two, that if my clients are successful in their negotiations, this conversation never happened—meaning that nothing of what I'm going to tell you can ever appear in your paper."

The editor didn't hesitate. "Deal," he said.

"Oh, and one more thing," I added. "I'm going to give you this story exclusively, but in return I want major play."

"Mike," he responded, "you know I can't guarantee anything.

"**NEVER SAW ANYTHING** like it," said Mark Stevens, the captain of the *Cumberland*, as he docked with the *Jenkins*. He was referring to the omega. "Damned thing's got tentacles."

That was the illusion. Jack explained how the braking maneuver tended to throw it around a good bit, tossed giant plumes forward as it slowed down. And more plumes out to port as it continued a long slow turn. "Gives me the chills," said Stevens.

Jack Markover was a Kansas City product, middle-class parents, standard public school education, two siblings. He'd gotten engaged right after high school, an arrangement heartily discouraged by his parents, who had assumed all along that he'd go to medical school, succeeding where his father had failed.

Jack and the young woman, Myra Kolcheska, eventually ran off, sparking a battle between the families that ultimately erupted in full-blown lawsuits. Meantime, the subjects of the quarrel both lost their nerve at the altar. Let's give it some time. See how it plays out. Last he'd heard, she was married to a booking agent.

Jack never got close to medicine. For one thing, he had a weak stomach. For another his mother was a hypochondriac and he always felt sorry for the doctor who had to listen to her complaints. He suspected that doctors' offices were full of hypochondriacs. Not for him, he'd decided early on.

He'd gone to the University of Kansas, expecting to major in accounting, but had gotten bored, discovered an affinity for physics, and the rest, as they say, was history. No big prizes and no major awards. But he was a gifted teacher, good at getting the arcane out there on the table where students could either understand it or at least grasp why no human being anywhere could understand it. And now he'd acquired a place in history. He was the discoverer of the Goompahs. He could write his memoirs and toss down scotch and soda for the rest of his life if he wanted.

*　　*　　*

THE *CUMBERLAND* BROUGHT fuel, food, water, wine, all kinds of electronic pickups, some spare parts for the ship, and assorted trinkets that someone thought could be used as gifts to win over the natives. They consisted mostly of electronic toys that blinked and donged and walked around. Stevens smiled while he showed them to Jack. "Not exactly in the spirit of the Protocol," he said.

Jack nodded. "We won't be using them."

The big item in the shipment, other than the pickups, was a set of six lightbenders. "Did you bring one for the lander?" asked Kellie.

Stevens looked blank. "For the lander? No, I don't think so." He opened his notebook and flipped through. "Negative," he said. "Was there supposed to be one?"

"Yes," said Jack. "They assured us it would be here."

"Somebody screwed up. I'll look around in the hold. Maybe they loaded it without making an entry, but I doubt it."

He went back through the airlock while Jack and Digger grumbled about bureaucrats. It took less than five minutes before his voice sounded on the commlink. *"Nothing here."*

"Okay," said Jack.

"I'll let them know. Get them to send it out right away."

"Please."

"Right. No point in the individual units if you can't cover the lander."

Stevens finished unloading and announced that he'd be starting back to Broadside that evening. Schedule's tight, no time to screw around. And he laughed, implying that the same bureaucrats who hustled him back to Broadside in a mad rush would keep him waiting a week.

He had dinner with them, and irritated everybody by referring to the Goompahs as *Goonies*. Thought it was just impossibly funny. "That's what they're calling them back at Broadside," he said. And then, looking around at the others, "Who's going back with me?"

They'd talked about it at length. Two years was a long bite out of anyone's life. It apparently never occurred to Kellie to ask to be relieved. The *Jenkins* was her ship, and if it was staying, she was staying. Jack saw himself as mission director and, like Kellie, felt an obligation to remain. He also expected to go back eventually as a celebrity. Books would be written about Lookout, and biographies about him. "If we handle this right," he told Digger, "we can save a few of these critters and go back with our tickets punched."

And Digger could imagine no conditions under which he would abandon Kellie. Or, for that matter, Jack, whose opinion of him mattered.

So only Winnie was leaving. "Family obligations," she explained, not without a sense of guilt.

When the dinner ended, they said goodbye, companions of the past fifteen months. "Don't get caught in the storm," Winnie told them, as she delivered embraces to all and disappeared through the airlock.

Stevens was telling Kellie something about the hyperlink arrangements. He wished them luck, and he, too, made his exit. The hatches closed, and they heard the muffled clangs of the docking grapplers.

Then the *Cumberland* was drifting away. And they were alone.

TRANSMISSIONS FROM DAVID Collingdale ("Jahanigrams") had been arriving regularly, spelling out what the linguists didn't know, which was a lot, and what they needed Jack to do when the lightbenders arrived. More and better recordings. More pictures to provide context for the conversations. Recordings of the natives in various situations, at play, at worship, haggling over prices, and, trickiest of all, during courtship. The Jahanigrams became a major source of amusement.

They also received a transmission from the *Hawksbill*. A tall, dark-haired woman, just beginning to go gray, identified herself as Marge Conway. "*I'm bringing some equipment with me,*" she said, "*to try to create a cloud cover over the cities.*" She was wearing a baseball cap, which she tugged down over one eye. Digger suspected she'd been an athlete of some sort in her younger days. "*The equipment will be stealth technology stuff. The Goompahs won't be able to see it unless they get right on top of it.*"

"*I need a favor. I'd like you to scout the area for me. Find eight places where I can lock down my gear. These places need to have a few trees, at least. The more the better, actually. They should be as remote from populated areas as possible. And preferably four on either side of the isthmus, although that's not a necessity. They should be spread out, to the degree it's practical. I appreciate your help. By the way, I'd also be grateful if you could have Bill do some weather scans of the isthmus and offshore waters. Get me as much climate information as you can.*

"*Thanks. I'm looking forward to working with you on this. With a little bit of luck, we should be able to pull off a rescue.*"

"And I bet she will," said Jack.

IN THE MORNING they tried out the lightbenders. Jack was the only one of the three who had any experience with the devices. He opened the packages, took them out, and removed several pairs of goggles. "So we can see each other," he said, pointedly holding them up and then laying them on a table.

The lightbender consisted of a set of transparent coveralls and a wide belt. The belt buckle doubled as both control and power unit.

Jack pulled on the coveralls, added a wide-brimmed safari hat, smiled at them, and touched the buckle.

Digger watched with pleasure as Jack faded from sight. The process took about three seconds during which he became transparent, then vanished completely. Except for his eyes. They looked back at him from the middle of the chamber. More intensely blue and bigger than he'd ever noticed. And disembodied.

"My irises, to be precise," Jack said. "The system is selective. Has to be. If it blanked out your eyes, you wouldn't be able to see. So it isn't perfect."

"I'll be damned," Digger said. "You know, I've seen it in the sims, but actually standing in a room when it happens—" He started thinking about the possibilities of being invisible.

"That's why they don't sell them down at the mall," said Kellie, reading his expression.

She and Digger strapped on the gear. She faded away and Digger looked down at his body, found the appropriate stud on his belt, slid it sideways, and watched himself vanish. A wave of vertigo swept through him.

"It'll seem a little strange at first," said Jack's voice.

Kellie's dark eyes were full of mischief.

"Take a pair of goggles," said Jack, "so we can see each other." One of them rose from the table, apparently on its own, and went over the blue eyes. The goggles vanished and the eyes came back. "Ah," Jack said, "that's better." The other two pairs also levitated, and one was held out to Digger. He took it and put it on.

The light in the room dimmed, but two shimmering silhouettes appeared.

"You'll need to be careful about walking until you get used to things. You can see the ground, but you can't see your feet. At least not the way you're accustomed to seeing them. Sometimes they're not where you think they are. People have broken ankles. And worse."

Kellie popped back into the light. "I'm ready to go," she said.

"You know"—Digger smiled—"you could get into a lot of trouble with one of these things."

"Try your luck, cowboy," Kellie said.

The *Cumberland* had also brought a substantial supply of pickups. They looked like large coins. *Wilcox Comm. Corp.* was engraved on the head, with an eagle symbol, and a reproduction of their headquarters on the flip side. They were powered, like the e-suits, by vacuum energy, and consequently could be expected to perform for indefinite periods of time. The back side would adhere, according to the directions, to virtually any solid surface.

They put about thirty of them into a case and stored it in the lander. It was late evening on the *Jenkins*, late afternoon on the isthmus. "Let's try to get some sleep," said Jack. "We'll go down first thing tomorrow."

When everyone had retired, Digger stopped by the bridge, saw that Kellie wasn't there, and knocked gently on her compartment door.

"Who is it?" she said.

"Me."

The door opened slightly. She stood tying her robe. "Yes, Dig?"

"I love you, babe," he said.

"I love you, too." She made no move to open wider.

"You know," he said innocently, "you never know what might happen on these surface trips."

"They can be pretty dangerous," she agreed.

He reached in, touched her hair, pulled her forward. She complied, and their lips brushed softly. She came forward the rest of the way on her own, crushed her mouth against his, and held on to him. He was acutely aware of her heartbeat, her breasts, her tongue, her hair. His right hand pushed against the nape of her neck, sank down her back, cupped one buttock.

And she backed away. "Enough," she said.

"Kellie—"

"No." She put a hand on his shoulder, restraining him. "Once it starts, you can't get it stopped. Be patient."

"We have been," he said. "We just signed up for, what, another year or so out here?"

She looked at him a long moment, and he thought she was going to bring up Captain Bassett, which she often did when this topic arose. Captain Bassett had begun sleeping with one of his passengers on a run in from Pinnacle or some damned place. The other passengers had found out, the Academy had found out, and Bassett had been fired. Conduct unbecoming. Violation of policy. Once a captain engaged in that sort of behavior, he, or she, could no longer expect to be taken seriously by the other passengers.

But on this occasion, Captain Bassett didn't surface. Instead Kellie withdrew into her room and waited for him. He followed her in and closed the door. The bed was still made; a lamp burned over her desk. A book was open. She watched him for a long moment, as if still making up her mind. Then she smiled, her eyes narrowed, and she did something to the robe.

It fell to the deck.

KELLIE TOOK THEM back to the glade they'd used on their first landing, descending through a rainstorm and arriving shortly before dawn. They packed up a supply of water and rations and got ready to move out. After they were off the lander, Kellie would take it offshore to a safe place and

wait until called. Jack and Digger activated their e-suits but, at Jack's suggestion, not the lightbenders. "Let's wait until we're out of the woods," he
said.

"Why?" asked Digger. "Aren't we taking a chance on being seen?"

"It's still dark, Dig. All you'd do is make it more difficult to walk. It's
tricky in these things until you get used to them."

"You guys need anything," Kellie said, "just give me a yell."

They waved, turned on their wristlamps, and climbed out into the night.
The grass was wet and slippery. Jack led the way to the edge of the trees
and plunged in. Digger hesitated and looked back. The lander waited patiently in the middle of the clearing. The lights were off, of course, and the
sky was dark. More rain was coming.

He knew Kellie would stay put until her passengers were safely clear.
The east was beginning to brighten. Jack turned and waved him forward.
He was really enjoying his role as leader and lightbender expert. The lander
lifted, the treads retracted, and it rose silently into the sky.

Thirty minutes later they were out by the side of the road. Jack told him
it was time to "go under," which, it turned out, was the standard phrase for
switching on the lightbender. It had a disparate ring for Digger.

He touched his belt, felt a mild tingle as the field formed around him,
held out his arm, and watched it vanish. When he looked up, Jack was also
gone. He activated his goggles and his partner reappeared as a luminous
silhouette.

They turned south. Toward Athens.

THERE WERE ALREADY travelers abroad. Two Goompahs appeared riding
fat horses. They were gray, well muscled, with snouts, and ugly as bulldogs.
"Everything in this world," said Digger, "seems uglier than at home."

"Cultural bias?"

"No, they're ugly."

One of the Goompahs carried a lantern. They were engaged in a spirited
conversation, which included growls and thwacking their palms together
and jabbing fingers at the sky. They passed Jack and drew alongside Digger
and suddenly grew quiet. To Digger's horror, the closer of the two had raised
his lantern and was looking in his direction. Staring at him.

The animals sniffed the morning breeze, but they wouldn't be able to
detect any unusual scents because the e-suits locked everything in. Still, it
was a trifle unsettling, especially when one of the beasts turned its head
and also looked at Digger.

"Your eyes, Dig," said Jack. "Close your eyes."

He put his hand in front of them and began backing away. The riders exchanged remarks, and Digger was sorry he didn't have a recorder running because he could guess the meaning. Harry, did you see that? You mean that pair of little blue eyes over there?

Harry rode to where he'd been standing and looked in all directions. They exchanged a few more comments and the one without the lantern detached a switch from his saddle. Just in case something had to be beaten off.

Digger had to restrain a laugh at the weapon. But he actually did hear a word repeated by the second rider: *Telio*. The name of his companion?

Digger was tempted. *Challa, Telio.* But he could guess how the pair of them would react to a voice coming out of the air. He compromised by trying to memorize the features of the one who might be Telio. It was difficult because they all looked alike. But he marked down the creature's nervous smile, a battered left ear, and the shape of nose and jaws. *Maybe we'll have a more opportune moment.*

OVER THE NEXT hour, they encountered several groups and a few lone pedestrians. There were both males and females on the road, and Digger noted that one of the females was alone on foot. The area was apparently safe.

They began to see scattered dwellings. The forest gradually died away and was replaced by farms and open fields. They stopped to watch a female working just outside a small building on a mechanical device that might have been a spinning wheel. An animal, a two-legged creature that looked like a goose with an extraordinarily long bill and protruding ears, waddled out the door, looked in their direction, got its neck stroked, and nibbled at something on the ground.

Digger backed off a few steps. "You sure we're invisible to the animals?" he asked.

The creature's ears came up.

"Yes. But it's not deaf. Stay still."

He'd learned to cover his eyes with his hand and peek through his fingers.

They passed a building that might have been a school. Inside, young ones scribbled on stiff gray sheets.

The room was decorated with drawings of trees and animals. Thick sheets, covered with characters they could not read, were posted around the walls. He could imagine the messages. *Square Roots Are Fun* and *Wash Your Hands after Going to the Bathroom.*

THERE WAS NEVER a moment when you could say that you were entering the city. The fields contracted into parks, buildings became more frequent, and traffic picked up.

They were approaching a stream. It ran crosswise to the road, which narrowed and became a bridge. Jack examined the construction and took some pictures. Planks, crosspieces, bolts, beams, and a handrail. It looked sturdy. A wagon rumbled across, coming out of the city, and the bridge barely trembled.

A lone female was approaching. Jack and Dig always stopped when traffic of any kind was in the vicinity and they did so now. But she looked in their direction, and her lips formed an 'o' the way humans do when they're puzzled. She was looking curiously down at Jack's legs.

And Digger saw that he'd pushed against a melon bush. The melons were bright yellow and big as balloons and maybe a trifle ripe. The problem was that Jack had backed against them and lifted one so that it seemed to be defying gravity.

"Watch the melon," he told Jack, who eased away from it.

The melon slowly descended, the branch picked up its weight, and the plant sagged.

"Doesn't look as if this being invisible," said Digger, "is all it's cracked up to be."

The female wore wide blue leggings, a green pullover blouse, and a round hat with a feather jutting off to one side. She looked dumbfounded.

Something moved behind him. Wings flapped, and Digger turned to see a turkey-sized bird charging out of a purple bush. It raced clumsily across the ground, stumbled once or twice, and launched itself into the air.

The female watched it go and moved her lips. It wasn't quite a smile but Jack knew it had to be. Smiles seemed to be universal among intelligent creatures. Noks did it. The Angels on Paradise did it. He'd heard somewhere that even whales did it.

She advanced on the melon, studied it, touched it, lifted it. After a moment she let it swing back down. Jaw muscles twitched. Then she casually turned and continued on her way.

"Better be more careful," said Digger.

"How bad was it?" asked Jack.

"It was afloat."

Ahead, the road passed through farmland, rolling fields filled with crops, plants and trees in long rows, green stalks and something that looked like bamboo. Other fields lay fallow. Occasional buildings with a slapdash appearance were scattered across the landscape. Some were barns. Others were the huge, sprawling structures in which large numbers of Goompahs lived. They appeared sometimes singly, sometimes in clusters of three and four.

It was clear that they were home to communal groups, although what divided them from other groups or bound the individuals together remained a mystery. As they continued on, this type of structure became more frequent, but occupied smaller segments of land. And there were individual homes as well. Parks began to appear. The road became busy, and eventually expanded into a thoroughfare. Shops lined both sides.

Some public buildings possessed a level of elegance almost rivaling that of the temple. But most were of a more pedestrian nature, austere and practical. All were filled with the creatures, who leaned out windows and exchanged comments with the crowds outside. Young ones played in doorways, others frolicked on rooftops. Everybody seemed to be having a good time.

"Partyville," said Jack.

Most of the shops were flimsy structures, plaster or wood with awnings hung over them. A few were brick. The shelves were well-stocked with fabrics, fish, wine, clothing, jewelry, cushions, animal skins, and every other conceivable kind of product.

"They have money," whispered Jack. "Coins. A medium of exchange."

It was a chaotic scene. Merchants hawked products, customers pushed and shoved to get close to the counters. A quarrel broke out in front of what appeared to be a weapons shop. Everywhere Goompahs haggled over prices and commodities.

The coins Jack had seen were spread across the counter of a fabric shop. Hadn't been picked up yet by a careless proprietor. Behind him were displayed woven spreads and shirts and trousers and even a few decorative wall hangings.

It occurred to Digger that a coin would make a dazzling souvenir.

He hesitated. Everybody was so tightly packed together. But therein lay safety, right? In this crowd, who'd notice getting bumped by an invisible man?

"Jack," he said. "Wait here."

"Wait, Dig. Where are you going?"

"I'll be right back."

The battle at the weapons shop had not gotten past a lot of screaming and yelling. But it had cleared an area for him to pass through. The weapons shop had bows, arrows, knives, and javelins on display. They looked mostly ornamental, something gawdy to hang on the wall and maybe claim you'd taken from a fallen enemy.

His path to the coins took him directly past the squabbling Goompahs, who were hurling threats and making gestures at each other. Digger got jostled by one of the combatants, who turned in surprise and looked for the offender. *"Kay-lo,"* he growled, or something very much like it.

The largest of the coins was about the size of a silver ten-dollar piece. It looked like bronze. A plant or tree was engraved on it, and a series of characters around the edge. In God We Trust. It was roughly made, the product of a primitive die, but it would be a priceless artifact to take home.

"*Don't do it, Digger.*" Jack's voice was stern.

"It won't hurt anything."

"*No.*"

"It'll help the translators."

Silence. Jack was thinking it over.

Digger would have liked to leave something in exchange, another coin, preferably, but he had nothing like that available. He'd think of something later. Come back tomorrow. Behind him, the combatants were drifting apart, issuing a few final threats before calling the whole thing off.

He scooped up the ten-dollar piece and turned quickly away.

The shopkeeper screeched. The sound stopped Digger cold because he thought he'd been too quick to be observed, thought the shopkeeper had been distracted by the dispute.

But he was staring directly at Digger. And beginning to babble. Others turned his way and moaned.

"Digger," said Jack. "Your hand."

To the Goompahs the coin must have been afloat in the air. Part of it, the part covered by his hand, would have been missing altogether. He tried to adjust his grip, but it was too big. He was about to slip it into his vest when a large green paw tried to close over it. The thing held on and he couldn't let go. One of the creatures growled, and another barged into him. Somehow one got hold of his belt. They went down struggling and suddenly the one with his belt let go, drew back with a terrified expression, and howled. The coin got knocked away.

They were shrieking and squealing and scrambling desperately to get away from him. He realized to his horror that he was visible. They were screaming "*Zhoka!*" over and over, and the pitch was going high. He didn't know what it meant but it was obviously not good.

He got his hands on his belt, turned the lightbender field back on, and was relieved to see that it still worked. He tried to scramble away from the mob. But the Goompahs were running for their lives. Jack cried out and damned him for an idiot. Digger was knocked sideways and trampled. He went down with his hands over his head, thinking how there's no safe harbor in a stampede for an invisible man. He took kicks in the ribs and head, and something that felt like a pile of lumber fell on him.

When it was over, he staggered to his feet. The street was empty, save for a few injured Goompahs trying to drag themselves away. And Jack's ghostly form lying quite still.

Digger hurried over to him and killed the e-suits. Jack's head lolled to one side. He tried mouth-to-mouth. Pounded on his chest.

Nothing.

A last lingering Goompah blundered into them, fell, moaned, and got up running.

LIBRARY ENTRY

. . . Other people have families. I have only my work. The only thing that I really ask of this life is that I do something at some point that my colleagues consider worth remembering. If I can be reasonably assured of that, I will face my own exit, however it may come, with serenity.

—Jack Markover
Diary, March 4, 2234
(Written shortly after discovering the Goompahs)

chapter 19

OTHER THAN REACTIVATE the lightbenders, Digger didn't know what to do. He told Kellie that Jack was dead, but she didn't have to ask him how it happened because he poured it out. Damned coin. *All I did was pick up a coin and they all went crazy. My fault. He's dead, and it's my fault.*

"*Take it easy, Digger,*" she said. "*Sometimes things just go wrong.*" A long pause. "*Are you sure?*"

"Yes I'm sure!"

"*Okay.*"

"He told me not to do it." He was sitting in the middle of the street. It was dusty and bleak. There was still a crowd of the things, and every time he moved, the dust moved, and the Goompahs groaned and pointed and backed away.

"*Where is he now?*"

"Right where he fell." In broad daylight. On the street. A couple of the Goompahs had been hurt, and others were creeping cautiously closer, trying to help, probably asking what happened.

"*We have to get him out of there.*"

"He's a little heavy." Even in the slightly reduced gravity, Digger couldn't have gone very far with him. Jack's face was pale. The features, which had been twisted with agony when Digger first got to him, were at rest now. There was no heartbeat and his neck appeared to be broken. "I've tried everything I can, Kellie."

"*Okay, Digger. You have to keep calm.*"

"Kellie, don't start on me."

She ignored the comment. "*You want me to come?*"

"No. Stay with the lander."

"*I mean, with the lander.*"

"No. My God, you'll panic the town."

"*Can you commandeer a cart maybe? Get him to a place where I can get to you?*"

"You're talking about a cart with no driver going down the street?"

"You're right. I don't guess that would work."

"Not hardly." The crowd was closing in again. He hoisted the body onto his back and staggered off with it toward an alley.

"Digger, I feel helpless."

"Me too." Digger was crushed by guilt. Actually, he told himself, *they* killed him. The stupid Goompahs. Who would have thought they'd react the way they did? Damned things were dumber than bricks.

The alley ran between the backs of private homes on one side and what looked like shops on the other. It was empty. He stumbled on and told Kellie what he was doing. "I'll stay here with him until it gets dark," he added. "Then we'll do what we can."

HE SET JACK down but saw immediately there was going to be too much traffic. Goompahs coming from the far end, and a couple angling off the street he'd just left. There were some fenced spaces behind the shops, and he chose one and hauled Jack inside.

"I'm okay," he told Kellie.

He settled down to wait. Kellie would have stayed on the circuit with him, but he was in no mood for small talk, and she got the message and signed off. Digger sat wishing he could go back and change what he'd done. It was a horrible price to pay for a moment's stupidity.

He could see past a chained door into an area that contained a couple of urns and shelves filled with pottery. Goompahs thumped around inside, but no one ever came out into the yard. For which he was grateful.

The sun crossed the midpoint overhead and slipped into the western sky. Voices drifted down the alley. Doors opened and closed, animals brayed and slurped, and once he heard someone apparently beating a rug.

Jack's body began to stiffen.

He talked to Jack during the course of the afternoon, but quickly broke off when he found himself apologizing. No point to that. Instead he promised to do what he could to make the mission successful. That's what Jack would have wanted, and Digger would make it happen. It was the only way he could think to ease his conscience.

The rain clouds that had been threatening the area off and on all day grew dark and ominous, but in the end there were only a few sprinkles, and they blew away.

The streets became noisier as darkness fell. The relatively subdued crowds haggling over prices were replaced by Goompahs out to enjoy the evening. Traffic in the alley stopped. For a while oil lamps burned in the shop, but they went out as the first stars appeared. Doors closed and bolts rattled home.

Kellie checked with him occasionally. He'd calmed down during the course of the day, had gone back and forth between blaming the Goompahs and himself, would have liked to pass off responsibility, but kept coming back to the warning from Jack. *Don't do it.* Jack had known what would happen.

It was almost midnight before he decided the attempt could be made in relative safety. Even then a few Goompahs were still hanging about in cafés. "*On my way,*" said Kellie.

They caught a break. She came in from the sea, and as far as Digger could tell, no one saw the lander descend over the rooftops. The Goompahs in the cafés were singing and laughing and having a good time, and they stayed in the cafés. Kellie hovered high, above rooftop level, and threw down a line. Digger looped it around his harness and secured it beneath Jack's arms. When he was ready, he took a deep breath. Dangling from a lander wasn't his idea of a good time. "Okay," he said. "Ready to go."

SHE FOUND A deserted beach and took it back down. When they were all on the ground she climbed out, embraced him, looked sadly at Jack, and embraced him again. "I'm sorry, Dig," she said.

They returned him to the *Jenkins* and conducted a memorial service. Jack had not been affiliated, but he'd occasionally commented that he would have liked to believe in the idea of a God who so loved the world—so they read a few appropriate passages out of the Bible. And they said good-bye to him.

When it was finished Kellie told him to get a drink, and she would take care of putting the body in storage. In the light onboard gravity, that wouldn't be a problem, so he gratefully accepted the offer.

While she was below, he opened one of the bottles that Mark had brought in the day before—it seemed like a different age now—and poured two glasses, setting one aside.

It occurred to him that he had his wish—that he was finally alone with Kellie.

HE FILED A report in the morning, accepting full responsibility. But he kept the statement general, not mentioning the coin, merely stipulating that he'd been momentarily careless and been consequently detected, and that the crowd had panicked. He added that he understood they would probably want to pull him out. If that was their decision, he would comply. But he asked that he be allowed to stay on, to finish the mission.

Meantime, there were pickups to be distributed around the isthmus. They returned to the glade, but when Digger started to leave, Kellie announced her intention to go with him.

"Too dangerous," he said.

"That's exactly why you need someone else along."

They argued about it, but Digger's heart was never in it, and after he felt he'd convinced her of his basic willingness to go it alone, he agreed, and they started out.

By midday they were back at the scene of the riot. The garment district. Life had returned to normal, and if the Goompahs were talking about the previous day's events, it was impossible to know. The merchant from whom he'd tried to pilfer the coin was still at his stand, and seemed immersed in hawking his wares.

"Let's get some recordings," said Kellie, all business, and probably determined not to let him think about yesterday.

A couple of blocks west of the shopping district lay an area dominated by parks and public buildings. One of the structures had signboards outside, rather like the ones you might still see near small country churches in the southern NAU. They took pictures and went inside.

A broad hallway with a high, curving roof ran to the rear of the building. There were large doors on both sides, and a few Goompahs wandering about, lost in the sheer space. Goompah voices came from one of the side rooms.

Digger looked in and saw several gathered around a table. They might have been debating something, but it was hard to tell. Goompahs seemed to put more energy into speaking than humans did. The laughter was louder, the points were made more vociferously, the negotiately was more demonstrative. In this group, voices were raised, and tempers seemed frayed.

"Fight coming," said Kellie.

Digger doubted it. "I think they just like to argue."

"They don't hide their feelings, do they?"

"Not much." Digger walked quietly into the room and planted a pickup on a shelf that was crowded with scrolls, aiming it so it got a decent view of the table. Then they went back out into the hall.

"Bill," Digger said. "First unit's up. How's reception?"

"Loud and clear. Picture's five by. What's the argument about?"

"One of them was cheating at poker."

"Really? Do they play poker here?"

Digger grinned. "Bill has no sense of humor."

Kellie squeezed his arm. "Sure he does. He did that last line deadpan."

*   *   *

THEY WENT INTO other buildings and placed more pickups. They set a few around some of the shops and hid others in the parks.

The parks were everywhere. They were furnished with gorgeous purple blooming trees and cobblestone walkways and flowering plants in a stirring array of colors. There were benches, low and wide, impossible for either Digger or Kellie to use, but perfect for the locals. And there were statues, usually of Goompahs, sometimes of animals. One, depicting several winged Goompahs, formed the centerpiece among a group of walkways. The subjects were displayed in licentious poses. They wore no clothes, although genitals were discreetly hidden. The females, they could now confirm, *did* have breasts on the order of human mammaries.

"Incredible," said Digger, just before a cub—what did you call a young Goompah?—crashed into him and sent them both sprawling. But none of the adults noticed anything unusual. The pup squalled and pointed at the spot where Digger had been standing and looked puzzled. A female helped him to his feet and chattered at him. Watch where you're going, Jason.

Two teams of seven players engaged in a game that looked remarkably like soccer. On another field, riders on the fat horses careered about, chasing a ball and apparently trying to unseat each other, using paddles as swatters. Small crowds gathered to watch both events. At the swatting-match, it was hard to tell whether it was an individual sport or teams were competing. If the latter, Digger could see no way to distinguish the players. But the crowd got involved, jumped up and down, stomped their feet, and cheered loudly whenever someone fell out of his saddle.

KELLIE WAS MOVING too quickly for him. Digger had not entirely adjusted to using the lightbender. Not being able to see his own body, but only a luminous silhouette, still threw him off-balance. He hadn't been aware that he watched his feet so much when he walked.

"You all right, Dig?" Kellie asked.

"Sure," he said. "I'm fine."

They were walking near the north end of the park, an area lined with fruit trees. In fact, Athens almost seemed to have been built within a huge grove. Greenery was everywhere, and edibles just hung out there waiting for someone with an appetite. No wonder these creatures seemed to have so much time for leisure.

"This place might be like some of the South Sea islands," said Digger. "Everything you need grows on the vine, so nobody has to work."

*   *   *

THEY SPENT THE afternoon trying to analyze how the city functioned. *This* looks like a public building, probably the seat of government. And *that* is maybe a courthouse or police station. (Digger had seen a uniformed functionary going in.) I'd say that's a library over there. And look at this, a Grand Square of some sort, where the citizens probably gather to vote on issues proposed by the town council. "You think they vote here, Digger?"

"Actually," he said, "I doubt it. Place like this will probably turn out to be run by a strongman of some sort." Around him, the shops seemed prosperous, the Goompahs content. Other than the one uniform, there was no sign of armed guards. "Still, you never know."

They peeked through the windows of a two-story building and saw rows of Goompahs sitting on stools, copying manuscripts.

They visited a blacksmith, watched an artisan crafting a bracelet, and got stranded in a physician's quarters when someone unexpectedly closed a door. They tried to abide by Jack's dictum that the natives not be allowed to see unexplainable events. So they sat down in the presence of the physician and his patient, and waited for their opportunity.

The patient was a male with a bright blue shirt. He was apparently suffering from a digestive problem. It was then that Digger first noticed the ability of the natives to bend their ears forward. While the patient answered questions, his doctor did precisely that. They left a pickup.

Later, they wandered through the markets near the waterfront. This was the same area that Digger had visited on that first night, when he'd placed the original set of pickups. The shops were decorated with brightly colored linens and tapestries. Pennants flew from rooftops. There were quarrels, beggars, some pushing and shoving, and once they saw a thief get away with what looked like a side of beef. So maybe Athens needed some policing after all.

Barter was in effect, as well as the monetary system.

Several times, Digger brushed up against the creatures. It was hard to avoid. What was significant was that the Goompahs, after they'd bounced off empty space, stared at it in surprise, moved their jaws up and down and muttered the same word. It was always the same. *Kay-lo.* The same thing the Goompah in the quarrel had said. He filed it away as an expletive, or as *strange*.

Two buildings on opposite sides of an avenue each contained a raised platform, centered among rising rows of benches. Concert halls? Places for political debate? Theaters in the round? They were empty at the moment.

"I'd like to see the show," he told Kellie.

"We can come back this evening," she said, "and take a look."

*   *   *

IT WAS TIME to go see the temple.

It stood atop a crest of hills on the southern edge of the city, gold now in the approaching sunset. They climbed a road and finally a wide wooden staircase to get to it.

It was bigger up close than Digger had expected, round and polished, without ornamentation other than an inscription over the front entrance. Doric columns. A winged deity guarding the approaches, and watching over an ornate and lovely sundial, as though she were keeper of the seasons.

Walkways curved around the building and arced out to the highest point of the promontory, overlooking the sea. There were a goodly number of Goompahs, some simply strolling along the paths, others wandering among the columns and through the temple itself. There was no mistaking the sacred tone of the place. Voices were lowered, heads bowed, eyes distant. It was there that Digger first felt a serious kinship with the Goompahs.

A young one was being taken to task by a parent for breaking into a run and making a loud noise. A pair, male and female, approached the front entrance hand in hand, drawing closer together. Digger saw one bent with age struggle to kneel on the grass, lift a hinged piece of stone (by a ring installed for the purpose), and put something beneath it. *Money*, Digger thought.

An offering?

Moments later, a child who'd been with him retrieved the object. Or retrieved part of it.

"What do you think?" Digger asked.

Kellie's hand was on his arm. "Don't know. Passing the torch, maybe. Bury in sacred ground and recover. Pass it on beneath the eyes of the gods. Probably leave part of it for the religious establishment."

The winged deity was about three-times life-size, and, unlike the ones in the park, this one was clothed. The wings were larger, sweeping, regal. She—there was no question it was female—carried a torch which she held straight out from her body. Save the wings, the figure shared all the physical characteristics of the natives, but Digger would never have considered calling her a Goompah.

They mounted the steps. Digger counted twelve. And he thought immediately of twelve months, twelve Olympians, twelve Apostles. Was all this stuff hardwired into sentient creatures everywhere?

The columns were wide, maybe twice as far around as he could have reached. The stone felt like marble.

The interior was a single space, a rotunda. The ceiling was high, possibly three stories, and vaulted. A stone platform, perhaps an altar, stood in the central section. Other statues gazed down at them. None had wings, but all shared a sublime majesty. They wore the same leggings and pullovers and sandals as the locals, but in the hands of the sculptors they'd become divine effects. One male divinity looked past Digger with a quiet smile, a female watched him with studied compassion. Another, more matronly, female cradled a child; a large warrior type was in the act of drawing a sword.

Not entirely without conflict, were they?

An older deity, with a lined face and weary eyes, bent over a scroll. A girl played a stringed instrument. And a male, overweight even for a Goompah, was transfixed in the act of laughing. He seemed somehow most dominant of all, and he set the mood for the place.

"Are you thinking what I am?" Kellie whispered.

That all this was going to be destroyed? That the circular shape of the temple was unlikely to save it because it was much too close to the city? "You know," he said, "I'm beginning to get annoyed."

The floor was constructed from ornately carved tiles. There were geometric designs, but he could also see depictions of the rays of the sun and images of branches and leaves. There were more columns in the interior. These were narrower, and they were decorated by the now-familiar symbols of the Goompah language. They moved through the temple, taking pictures of everything.

The worshipers walked quietly. No one spoke; the only sounds came from the wind and the sea and the periodic scream of a seabird. In the west, the sun was sinking toward the horizon.

An attendant passed through, lighting oil lamps. "It's getting late," she said. "You ready to go back?"

Digger nodded. He removed a pickup from his vest, kept it carefully hidden in his hands, until he'd inserted it in the shadows between a column and a wall. "Last one," he said.

"You think there's much point, Dig? I don't think anybody here says anything."

"It's okay. The atmosphere of this place is worth recording and sending back."

But he knew they wouldn't capture the atmosphere on disk. Hutchins, sitting in her office three thousand light-years away, would never understand what this place felt like.

They stood a moment between two columns and watched a ship pass. Digger tried to remember what the ocean looked like to the east. How far was the next major landfall?

"Traffic must all be up and down the isthmus," said Kellie. "North and south."

Not east and west. There was no evidence the Goompahs had been around the world. Strictly terra incognita out there.

The visitors to the temple were filing away; Digger and Kellie were almost alone. The lamps burned cheerfully, but their locations seemed primarily designed to accent the statuary.

Digger looked at the flickering lights, at the figure of the woman and child. What was the story behind that? The images were aspects, he knew, of the local mythology. Of the things that the Goompahs thought important. This was information that Collingdale would want to have.

The place was different in some ineffable way from houses of worship at home. Or even from pagan temples.

They paused again before the winged figure at the entrance. "Somebody here studied under Phidias," said Kellie.

Digger nodded. Creature from another world that he was, he could still read dignity and power and compassion in those features. And the torch that she held spoke to him.

He looked back into the rotunda. At the laughing god.

THE ISTHMUS ROAD seemed unduly long on the return, and Digger was weary by the time they reached the lander. Night had fallen, and he was glad to shut off the lightbender and the e-suit and collapse into his seat.

Kellie gave a destination to Bill, and they lifted off and turned seaward. "How we doing?" she asked, reminding him that his bleak mood was still showing.

"Good," he said. "We're doing fine."

For a long moment he could hear only the power flow. "You going to be all right?" she asked.

He looked out at scudding clouds, bright in the double moonlight. "Sure." *Don't do it, Digger.* He was okay. A little down, but he was okay. "Where are we going?"

"There's an island. Safe place to spend the night."

"Alone with Collier on an island," he said. "Sounds like a dream."

"You don't sound as if you mean it."

"I'm all right," he insisted. "This island. Does it have a name?"

She thought a moment. "Utopia," she said.

LIBRARY ENTRY

The great tragedy confronting us here is not that the Goompahs,
to use the common terminology, face massive destruction, although

that is surely cause enough for sorrow. But what makes me sad is that they may pass from existence without ever having understood the supreme joy that accompanies the life of the spirit. They have lived their lives, and they have missed the heart of the matter.

—Rev. George Christopher
The Monica Albright Show
Wednesday, May 7

PART THREE

molly kalottuls

chapter 20

THE NEWS OF Markover's death had delivered a jolt, reminding everyone
on board that the operation on which they were embarked had its unique
dangers.

A few members of the research team had known him. Peggy Malachy
had worked with him years earlier, and Jason Holder recollected signing a
petition that Markover had sent around, though he could not recall the
issue. Jean Dionne remembered him from a joint mission years before.
"Good man," she told Collingdale. "A bit stuffy, but you could depend on
him."

Collingdale had been on a weeklong flight with him once. He remembered Markover as aggressive, arrogant, irritating. Although he wouldn't
have admitted it even to himself, he was relieved he wouldn't have to deal
with him at Lookout.

THE LINGUISTS WERE getting torrents of raw data from the *Jenkins*. They'd
broken into the language, and were in the process of constructing a vocabulary that by then numbered several hundred nouns and verbs. They understood the syntactical structure, which resembled Latin, verb first, noun/
subject deeper in the sentence. They had the numeric system and most of
its terms down. (Base twelve, undoubtedly a reflection of the fact that
Goompahs had twelve digits.) They knew the names of about forty individuals.

The city that Markover had called Athens was *Brackel* in the language of
its inhabitants.

Brackel.

Whatever else you could say for the Goompahs, they had tin ears.

The residents of *Brackel* were *Brackum*. Well, Collingdale thought, there
you are.

Two other cities for which they had names were *Roka* and *Sakmarung*.
The planet, their word for Earth, was *Korbikkan*, which (as at home) also

meant *ground*. They lived *in* it, and not *on* it, implying they had no sense of the structure of things. Their name for the sea was *bakka*, which also meant *that which is without limit*.

They had a complex conjugal system of shared spouses, which Collingdale and his team of specialists hadn't quite figured out yet. *Brackel* seemed to be home to approximately twenty-eight community groups. Spouses within a group had free access to each other, although it appeared they settled on a favorite or two, and only had relations with others to keep up appearances or morale or some such thing. It wasn't an area in which Collingdale was interested, but some of his experts were already making lascivious jokes.

Offspring from one group could, on maturity, become a member by marriage of specified other groups. But the choices were limited to prevent genetic damage. It was a cumbersome system, which would, he suspected, eventually give way to monogamy. Holder wasn't so sure, pointing out that similar systems were still in use in remote places at home.

They had not established whether the same system was in use in the other cities, although preliminary evidence suggested it was.

Life among the Goompahs seemed to be pretty good. Apparently, the crops all but grew themselves. Digger Dunn was still dithering about getting a reliable climate analysis, but it looked as if the temperatures ranged from cool to balmy.

The Goompahs talked a lot about politics, leading Holder to conclude that the general population participated in government. Whether the city was an aristocracy or a democracy, or some variant, was still impossible to say. Although some of Collingdale's people were entranced at the prospect of finding out, it was not a detail that particularly concerned the director.

And that fact puzzled him. He'd thought that his reason for coming, aside from managing a rescue, was to learn about the Goompahs. But he'd lost interest. In fact, he'd begun to suspect that he'd never really cared all that much. He gradually began to realize that he'd come because of the cloud.

His xenologists had insisted from the beginning that he warn the *Jenkins* people not to establish contact with the natives under any circumstances. They all seemed to think nobody else should say hello, but that it was okay for them to do it because only they knew how to do it correctly.

He'd warned them that policy had not changed to the degree that they should expect to sit down over dinner with the natives. (They still hadn't agreed on an appropriate term of reference for the aliens. *Goompahs* set his teeth on edge. *Brackum* was limited to the inhabitants of *Brackel*. Peggy Malachy liked to call them Wobblies. Collingdale began trying to encourage the use of *Korbs*.)

Shelley Baker invariably looked amused when they talked about limiting or barring communication. She said nothing in front of the others, but she'd told him privately that the omega made all the difference. "We're going to have to talk with them," she said. "If nothing else, we have to be able to tell them to get out of the cities."

MARY SENT A message every couple of days. She kept them short, well within Academy guidelines. She'd tell him about a show she'd seen, or how she'd run into some old school friends downtown. Or how she still went to Chubby's, but the sandwiches had tasted better when he was there.

He replied in kind. He was busy, and sometimes couldn't think what he wanted to say. But he enjoyed switching on the system and imagining she was in the room with him. He told her about the work they were doing, how he'd been tweaking the visuals they were going to use to get rid of the cloud. And that he was trying to learn the Goompah language. "We can make the sounds," he said. "Judy says we got lucky. Now it's just a matter of doing the work."

Seeing her, listening to her voice, sometimes happy, sometimes wistful, fed his hatred for the omega. He took to spending time in the VR tank, where he conjured up the view from Lookout, as it would be in late November, when the cloud would be prominent in the skies. Vast and ugly, torn by its own gee forces, it would be coming in over the western ocean, visible only at night, rising shortly after the sun went down, growing larger and more terrifying with the passage of time.

It was obvious Judy was worrying about him. She occasionally joined him in the tank, when she thought he was getting too moody. "The clouds aren't personal," she insisted. "Whoever, whatever, did this, it happened a long time ago. Who knows what the purpose was? But I'll bet, when we find out, if we ever find out, we'll discover it's more stupidity than venom."

"You're kidding," he told her, as they stood together on the shore near *Brackel* and looked up at the omega. He saw it as pure malice. And while he was not a violent man by nature, he would happily have taken the lives of the engineers that had put these things together.

But she was serious. "Whatever it was, it's long dead. The machinery keeps working, keeps pumping them out, but the intelligence behind them is gone. And it couldn't have hated us. It didn't know us. It just—" She stopped. "I'm not sure I'm making sense."

He gazed up at the cloud, quietly unfolding across the star fields. "Judy," he said, "I don't know how else to explain these things other than as an act of pure evil."

"Well," she said. "Maybe." She shrugged and looked out to sea, and he thought how attractive she was. More so there on the beach than in the confines of the ship. He wondered at the capability of women to take on part of the beauty of their surroundings.

But he could not keep his eyes long off the cloud. He yearned to be able to reach up and strike the thing out of the sky.

JUDY WAS BARELY out of her twenties. She had a Ph.D. in anthropology, specializing in primitive religions, from the University of Jerusalem. Her reputation for linguistic capabilities had brought her to Hutch's attention. Collingdale had heard she was also a pretty good equestrienne.

Her parents, she told him, had been horrified when she volunteered for the mission. Nobody else crazy enough to go. Get yourself killed. There'd been a pretty big blow-up, apparently.

At her worksite she'd mounted pictures of several of the Goompahs for which they had names. Goompahs used a string of names, of which two defined the conjugal group and the region of birth. The others appeared to be individual and arbitrary.

To Collingdale they all looked alike. But Judy laughed and said there were clear differences. This one had a large chin, that one a weak mouth. She even claimed she could distinguish personality traits and moods: Kolgar was gruff, while Bruk was amiable.

She'd mastered enough of the language to be able to carry on a respectable conversation, though not with Collingdale, who'd fallen far behind. He could commit some of the words to memory, and knew how to say *hello*, *fish*, *cold*, *night*, *home*, and another dozen or so terms. If he were stranded he might even have been able to ask for the local equivalent of coffee, which was a brewed hot drink called *basho*. Sounded Japanese to his ears.

But she encouraged him and told him he was doing fine. And he took pride in the fact he was light-years ahead of his peers. Bergen, Wally Glassner, and the others couldn't have gotten the time of day.

They were still having trouble with the syntax. But there was plenty of time, and Judy was more than satisfied with their progress, so Collingdale was pleased.

They were at a point at which most of the data coming in from the *Jenkins* was repetitious, but Judy's team was becoming more practiced at setting it aside, at finding the constructions that helped them solve the inner workings of the language.

There were all kinds of sites where they'd have liked to see pickups. But the quantity of units was limited. And they were all in *Brackel*. They had only verbal descriptions of the other cities.

Requests to Digger not only indicated target sites, but also designated which surveillance units could be moved elsewhere. A transmission still took several days to reach the *Jenkins*, and moving the pickups around took more time. It was cumbersome, but they were making progress.

There was no information yet about local religions. Collingdale had no idea how old the civilization on the isthmus was. Had it been preceded by something else? What did the Goompahs know about the rest of their world?

Digger wanted to know whether he should use his own judgment about the pickups. Plant them, let them sit for a bit, and then move them around rather than wait for instructions.

Yes, you nit. Do whatever you can to get as much coverage as possible.

But that didn't work out either. A feed that had become interesting suddenly went dark and by the time they could direct him to get it back up and working, the line of inquiry had dried up.

Most of the cities seemed to have a library. They were getting pictures of Goompahs sitting down to read, but Collingdale and Judy couldn't see the materials. Invade one of those places, they told Digger. We need to find out what they're reading. Send pictures of the scrolls. Sometimes he wondered whether Digger had any imagination at all.

Judy made suggestions where the surveillance units might be placed for maximum effect. She pointed out that they'd gotten next to nothing whatever from the interior of the temple. Nothing ever happened on the main platform, the altar, whatever it was, except that one of the worshipers occasionally got up and stood on it in a pious manner and looked around.

Inevitably they ended back on Collingdale's beach, where he stared out at the dark sea—the wine-dark sea—while she stood by to ensure he wasn't alone.

A few cities along a seacoast. Widespread literacy. Sailing vessels. A peaceful society. Probably participatory government. Apparently universal education. Not bad, actually.

He wondered whether the human race had just encountered its first serious competitor. The *Korbs* would need an industrial revolution and all that. But if they could skip the Dark Ages, and the assorted other imbecilities that people had come up with, they might leapfrog ahead pretty quickly.

And the omega. They'd have to get past that too.

"They've got a lockup," Judy announced without warning.

"A jail? How do you know?"

"Somebody got tossed in."

"Do you know why?"

"No. I think he was trying to steal some fish. Got caught, the shopkeeper

chased him down, and somebody came and took him away. So there *is* a
police presence of some sort."

They also had a series of terms for what seemed to be political leaders.
There was a *kurda*, and a *krump*, and a *squant*. But they were unable to get
equivalences for them. They were in charge, but whether a *kurda* was a
king, a representative, a ward boss, or a judge, there was simply no way to
know.

WITH SO MANY young people on board, social life on the *al-Jahani* was
active. It didn't usually get rowdy, but there was a fair amount of partying
and VR games. The older members of the mission, anxious to get away from
the noise, took to congregating in a storage area on C Deck, near the shuttle
bay, where they talked about the mission, their careers, and the omegas.
They worried about whether they'd get to Lookout in time, and reminisced
about the old days.

Collingdale had traveled with most of them before. And if they'd become
cranky over the decades, they were nonetheless good people. They'd en-
dured months and sometimes years digging on Quraqua and Pinnacle, or
cataloging the systems within a couple of hundred light-years of Earth until
we knew the diameter, weather, and mass of every world in the neighborhood. A couple had been at Deepsix when it had blooped into the gas giant
Morgan. They had a history of getting results. Melinda Park, for example,
had served four years on Serenity, a space station assignment that would
have driven Collingdale completely around the bend. But she'd directed
efforts to determine the laws of planetary formation and had won an Amer-
icus for her efforts.

Ava MacAvoy, who'd been with him at Moonlight, was there. And Jean
Dionne, with whom he'd once conducted a romance that had been a kind
of shooting star, lots of flash and then an eruption and nothing left. Except
regrets. Nevertheless, or possibly because of that fact, they'd remained
friends. Their captain was Alexandra Kyznetsov, who had also been at
Moonlight, lobbing nukes from this very ship. She'd been embarrassed at
the way things had turned out and assured Collingdale immediately after
departure that she'd brought no bombs this time.

It would not have been correct to say that during the passing months
they'd become a tightly knit group. In fact they didn't agree on much. Some
thought the basic mission was to study the society on Lookout (before it got
obliterated?) while others thought the intent of the mission was to get ready
to set up a rescue effort. Although how the latter was to be done was unclear.

Some argued that, under the circumstances, they should forget the Protocol and make contact with the Goompahs, while others maintained it would do far too much harm. There was disagreement over how the basic research should be handled, who should be allowed down on the surface, what the priorities were, and how best to make decent coffee using the onboard equipment.

"*Basho,*" said Collingdale.

"I'm sorry?" said Elizabeth Madden, who'd been complaining about the coffee in Alexandra's presence, but who had no idea what Collingdale was talking about.

"*Basho.* Coffee. You'll have to get the language right if you want to prosper on the surface."

Madden was the most outspoken of those who wanted to maintain the isolation policy. She was a small woman who always spoke in a level tone, never got excited, and seemed to have a mountain of facts to support any position. There was a quality in her manner that implied, without her saying so, that her opponents merely needed to hear the reality of a situation to see the foolishness of their position. She occupied the Arnold Toynbee chair at King's College, London. Her husband Jerry, also a xenologist of considerable reputation, had accompanied her, and usually led the opposition.

She was alarmed when she first heard that Judy Sternberg was having the pickups moved around.

"Unconscionable risk," she maintained. "We were lucky the first time. It would have been prudent to wait until *we* were on the scene."

Judy shrugged. "I can't see that any harm might be done."

She closed her eyes and sighed. "If the *Korbs* so much as become aware that we exist," she said, "their entire worldview will change." Their natural development would be set aside, she argued, and they would become dependent, at least in their philosophy and probably in their development of technology.

"Ridiculous," said Judy.

"They'll wind up on reservations! There has never been an exception to the general law."

Madden didn't explain which law, but there was no need to do so. Somebody-or-other had laid down a manifesto that a civilization could not survive collision or integration with, or even a bit of jostling by, a more advanced culture.

"If we don't intervene directly," said Judy, "there won't be enough of them left for a reservation."

"That's an exaggeration, Judy. You know it and I know it. We've survived at least one of these things at home, and other worlds have survived God knows how many. It kills off *individuals*, and that's regrettable. But it will not kill off the culture." They were sitting in the area they'd fixed up in cargo, which someone had nicknamed the Oxford Room. "Our obligation is to save the culture. To give them their chance to evolve."

Well, maybe she was right. But Lookout was not a global civilization. It was a handful of cities, positioned on a narrow strip of land between major oceans. The cloud was coming and when the destruction was over, maybe the archeologists could go in and look at what was left of the culture. And the xenologists could go home.

RAW DATA POURED in. Collingdale sent his analyses on to Hutchins, with information copies to the *Jenkins.*

The package went out daily at the close of day. They were, he thought, making excellent progress.

He had just finished sending off a message to Mary, exulting over how well the effort was going, when Judy asked him to come by the workroom.

He hurried up to the B Deck conference room that the linguists had taken over. Judy was there with a couple of her people, Terry MacAndrew from the Loch Ness area, and Ginko Amagawa from Yokohama.

She handed him a printout. "We just found this," she said. "Thought you might be interested. It's from a conversation on a park bench."

It was in Goompah, but using English letters. Nobody tried to translate it for him, and Collingdale felt the force of the compliment. He had to translate it however word by word:

"*ROM, HAVE YOU NOTICED THAT* HARKA *AND* KOLAJ *ARE MISSING?*"

"*YES. THREE NIGHTS NOW. WHAT DO YOU THINK?*"

"*I DON'T KNOW WHAT TO THINK. I HAVE NEVER HEARD OF ANYTHING LIKE THIS.*"

"*IT SCARES ME.*"

"*IT SCARES ME TOO, ROM.*"

Collingdale's first thought was that two of the young ones had been kidnapped. Or two lovers had eloped. Did Goompahs elope?

"We're not sure what *Harka* and *Kolaj* refer to. But we think they may be stars."

"Stars?"

Judy glanced at Ginko. Ginko's eyes were dark and worried. "We think they've just seen the cloud, Dr. Collingdale."

ARCHIVE

Nobody here can understand how it happens that a race virtually confined to a limited land area, sealed off both north and south by natural impediments, has managed to maintain what is clearly a peaceful existence. There are no armies, no walls, no battle fleets. No indication that anyone even carries weapons other than what might be expected for hunting purposes.

We are not yet certain, but early indications suggest the cities are independent, that there is no formal political framework, but that somehow they coexist peaceably.

This framework is difficult to understand in light of the fact that the Goompahs are clearly carnivores. Hunters. They do not appear to have a history extensive enough to explain the amity in which they live. We would also like to understand why they find Digger such a fearsome creature.

We share the sense of loss at Jack's death. But I would be remiss not to commend Digger and Kellie, without whom we'd be flying blind.

> —David Collingdale
> Hyperlight Transmission
> June 9

chapter 21

...INVADE ONE OF the libraries. *We need to find out what they're reading. Get access to the scrolls.*

The *Frances Moorhead* arrived in the middle of the night with the industrial-size lightbender, which would hide the lander. Kellie and Digger thanked the captain, and transferred Jack's body. That was an ordeal that reopened wounds and left Digger wandering aimlessly through the ship after the *Moorhead* had gone.

He'd received a sympathetic message from Hutchins shortly after the incident. She was sorry, shared their grief, don't blame yourself, bad things happen. But she didn't know everything, didn't know Jack had warned him to stop, didn't know Digger was going to lift the coin.

"She never really asked for the details," he told Kellie. "She must know I left stuff out."

"I'm sure she does. But the Academy needs heroes." She looked at the lightbender and looked at him. "She's giving you a chance, Dig."

Kellie saw to it there was no time for him to sit around feeling sorry for himself. They tied the unit into the lander's systems, connected field belts around the hull, ran a successful test and headed for the surface.

KELLIE TRUSTED HIM. Had it been someone else, she might have been frightened. The prospect of being caught out there alone, weeks away from the nearest base, with a guy who was coming emotionally apart, would have been unnerving for anyone. But she'd known Digger a long time.

This wasn't their first flight together, and though she'd been aware from the beginning of his interest in her, she hadn't taken him seriously until the beginning of this mission. She wasn't sure what had changed. Maybe she'd gotten to know him better. Maybe it was that he hadn't embarrassed her by becoming persistent. Maybe it was that she'd simply realized that he was a good guy. In the end, she'd come to enjoy just being with him.

But the way in which Jack had died was a nightmare. And the ironic aspect of the event was that she wasn't sure she wouldn't have made a grab for the coin herself. Mistakes happen. And if you get unlucky, there's a price to be paid. It doesn't make you culpable, she told herself, and occasionally, when it seemed necessary, Digger.

She was glad to see the library request come through. It provided a challenge and gave him something else to think about.

THE MOST ACCESSIBLE means of entry into the center of *Brackel* was through the harbor. But she couldn't simply set down in the water, even with the lightbender field protecting the lander. Its treads would create twin depressions in the water, an effect that would startle any witnesses. So they waited until the sun went down. When it was reasonably dark, Kellie came in over the harbor, past a vessel anchored just offshore (there was a light in a forward cabin but no other sign of life), and descended a few meters away from a deserted pier.

Digger was beginning to feel like an old hand. He slipped into the gear, turned on the Flickinger field, switched on his converter, put his laser cutter into a pocket, and activated the lightbender. Kellie climbed into her own gear and followed him out the airlock onto the pier.

He looked back at the lander. Its ghostly silhouette rose and fell in the incoming tide. Kellie directed Bill to move it well out into the harbor. They watched it go, then turned toward the city.

It was a bright, clear night. The big moon was overhead; the smaller one was rising in the west. It wasn't much more than a bright star.

Digger led the way through the harbor area. Lights were going on, cafés filling up, crowds roaming the streets. They took down four pickups, two for the library, and two, as Digger said, "for a target of opportunity."

The target of opportunity showed up when they passed the two structures they'd thought of as theaters-in-the-round. Both were busy. Oil lamps burned out front, signs were prominently displayed, and the locals were pushing their way in.

"Care to stop at the theater first, my dear?" asked Digger.

"By all means," she said. "We can do the library in the morning."

They chose one and took pictures of the signs, several of which featured a female Goompah with a knife, her eyes turned up. (When a Goompah turns those saucer eyes to the heavens, one knew that great emotions were wracking his, or her, soul.)

They waited until most of the patrons were inside before they joined the crowd.

The circular hall was three-quarters filled. Most of the patrons were in their seats; a few stood in the aisles holding conversations. Most Goompah conversations were animated, and these were no exception. That they kept looking toward the stage indicated that they were discussing the show. Stragglers continued to wander in for several minutes. Kellie and Digger stayed near the entrance, where they had room to maneuver.

Oil lamps burned at the entrances, along the walls, and at the foot of the stage.

"What do you think?" asked Kellie, pressing a finger against the pickups, which were in his vest.

"I think Collingdale would *kill* to have a record of whatever's about to happen."

"My feelings exactly."

They waited until everyone seemed to be settled, then picked an aisle, moved in close, and squatted. An attendant went through the auditorium extinguishing some of the lamps. There was no reasonable place to attach a pickup, so Digger simply aimed it manually.

THE SHOW WAS a bloodbath.

At first Digger thought they were going to see a love story, and there was indeed a romance at the heart of the proceedings. But all the characters other than the principals seemed angry with everyone else for reasons neither of the visitors could make out. An early knife fight ended with two dead. Swords were drawn later and several more perished. One character was hit in the head and thrown off the stage to universal approval.

The action was accompanied by much music. There were musicians down front, manning wind and string instruments and a pair of drums. Onstage, the characters danced and sang and quarreled and made love. (Much to Digger's shock, there was open copulation about midway through. The audience, obviously moved, cheered.) Later there was what appeared to be a rape. With Goompahs it was hard to be sure.

The music jangled in Digger's ears. It was all off-key. It banged and rattled and bonked, and he realized there was more to it than the instruments he'd seen. There was something like a cowbell in there somewhere, and noisemakers clanked and clattered.

About forty minutes into the show, the female love interest gave in to temptation a second time, either with a different character, or with the same character wearing different clothes. Digger couldn't make it out until the end, when three apparently happy lovers strode off arm in arm. Hardly anyone else was left standing. The audience pounded enthusiastically on any flat surface they could find.

"*Romeo and Juliet* with a happy ending," said Kellie.

Romeo, Frank, and Juliet, Digger thought. Nevertheless, in his view, a distinct improvement. Digger liked happy endings.

The crowd drifted out. Some headed for cafés, others strolled into connecting streets. Everyone was on foot. No carriages rolled up, no horses.

It had gotten late. There was a sundial in front of the theater, but that obviously wouldn't work at night. He wondered how the locals scheduled a show. When the moon touched the sea? Sunset plus time for dinner plus time to walk in from a half kilometer away?

Anyhow, he had gotten it all on the pickup. They returned to the lander and sent it off to the *al-Jahani,* wondering how it would be received there.

THEY STAYED IN the lander, in the harbor, overnight. It was hard to sleep, because it was the middle of the afternoon their time.

Despite everything, despite his culpability in Jack's death and his sympathy for the Goompahs, he had never felt more alive. Kellie had fallen into his arms like ripe fruit, and he knew beyond any doubt that whatever happened out here he would take her home with him.

She lay dozing inside a blanket while he considered how well things were turning out and fought off attacks of guilt over the fact that he felt so good. It was possible his career might be over; he might be sued by Jack's family and possibly barred from future missions by the Academy. But whatever happened, he was going to come out ahead.

After a while he gave up trying to sleep and opened a reader. He scanned some of the more recent issues of *Archeology Today,* then tossed it aside for a political thriller. Mad genius tries to orchestrate a coup to take over the NAU. But he couldn't stay with it and eventually ran part of the show they'd watched that evening. The Goompahs seemed less childlike now.

"The audience loved it." Kellie's voice came out of nowhere.

"I thought you were asleep."

"More or less."

"It was all pretty matter-of-fact," he said. "Nobody seemed shocked."

She shrugged. "Different rules here."

"I guess."

She rearranged herself, trying to get comfortable. "But you know, if I was reading the story line right—it's hard to be sure of anything—but I thought they reacted pretty much the same way we would have. You could pick out the villain, and they didn't like him. They approved of the young lovers. Even if there were three of them. They were silent during the killings. Holding their breath, it seemed to me."

Digger had had the same reaction.

"What did you think of the score?"

He laughed. "Not like anything I've heard before."

THEY WENT TO the library next day. It was a battered L-shaped gray stone building set along two sides of one of the smaller parks just a block from the theater. They found a signboard posted inside the heavy front doors. Several pieces of parchment were displayed, on which someone had listed about two hundred items. "Maybe it's an inventory of the holdings," suggested Kellie.

They took a picture and drifted into a large room given over to reading. Nine or ten Goompahs sat at tables, poring over scrolls. A couple more were standing before boards to which notes were attached. (Looking for a ride home?) Another examined a map at the back of the room. A couple of the readers were making notes. To do that, it was necessary to go to the librarian, secure a pot of ink and a pen, and do it right there at his station, where he could watch, presumably to ensure you didn't have any sloppy habits. You used your own parchment, which was sometimes attached to a piece of wood and resembled a clipboard, and sometimes rolled inside a cylinder.

Digger noticed that the windows were screened with metal crosspieces and supported heavy shutters. Unlike many of the public buildings he'd seen, this one could be locked and bolted at night.

There were two librarians, both male. Both wore black blouses and purple leggings. Otherwise, they were not at all alike. One was older, obviously in charge. He moved with deliberation, but clearly enjoyed his work. He was constantly engaged in whispered conversation with his patrons, helping them find things, consulting a wooden box in which he kept sheaves of notes. None of the material seemed to be in any kind of order, but he kept dipping into it, rummaging, and apparently coming up with the desired item, which he would wave in the air with satisfaction before showing it to those he was assisting.

His name, or perhaps his title, was Parsy.

His aide was equally energetic, eternally hustling around the room adjusting chairs, rearranging furniture, flattening the map, talking with clients. He had something to say to everyone who came or went.

Between them they kept a close watch on the readers. Their primary function, Digger suspected, was to make sure no one got away with a scroll.

Kellie wanted to look at the map. "Back in a minute," she said. "Don't go away." He followed. The map was of the isthmus, and it looked reasonably accurate. The cities were marked and labeled, and he noted the symbols that represented *Brackel*. The map ended beyond the most northern and southern cities. *Terra Incognita*. A few islands were included. Digger remembered one, a big one to the west. Utopia, which they were using as a base for the lander, was not on the map, although it should have been. Beyond the big western island, he thought, lay the edge of the world.

He took more pictures, then resumed wandering through the room, looking over the rounded shoulders of the readers. The texts were, of course, hand-written.

The scrolls were not laid out on shelves, as printed books might have been. They were kept in a back room, secure from potential thieves. A visitor consulted the list at the front door, filled out a card, and submitted it to one of the two librarians, who then retreated into the sanctum sanctorum. Moments later, he emerged with the desired work. Judging by labels, many of the books required multiple scrolls, but it appeared only one scroll at a time could be had. And, of course, nobody checked one out and took it home.

The inner stack was closed off. It was a small room, located immediately behind Parsy's desk, and sealed off by furniture so that no one could get near it without being seen by him. It had no windows and no other exit, save into a private washroom. Its walls were lined with cubicles, in which lay the scrolls. The cubicles were marked with a few characters. *Biography*, Digger thought. *Northern Isthmus Travel. Literature. Mystery.* There were altogether approximately two hundred labeled volumes, comprised of roughly three times as many scrolls.

Digger, maybe for the first time since he'd been a child, took a moment to reflect on the pure simple wonder of a collection of books. Throughout his life he had always had immediate access to whatever book he cared to look at, to whatever body of knowledge he wished to explore. Everything humans knew about the world they lived in was within fingertip reach.

Two hundred books.

Literacy appeared to be widespread. The readers did not seem, in any way he could determine, to belong to a higher class than the Goompahs strolling the streets. He recalled the school he and Jack had come across outside *Brackel.* Outside *Athens.*

THEY WERE PLANNING to wait until the place closed, and then begin the recording session. It was late afternoon, they'd been away from the lander for ten hours, and Digger discovered a need to relieve himself. It would have been easy enough had it been dark. Just find a remote street corner, shut the systems off, and go. But it was still daylight. They'd not been using the sacks that allowed one to dispose of waste inside the suit because then it became necessary to haul it around, and neither of them cared to do that.

Just organize things properly, Jack had always maintained, and you won't need it.

Right.

Digger was thinking how he'd like to grab some of the scrolls and run. He entertained an image of a group of scrolls apparently leaping into the air and streaking for the exit on their own.

"You okay?" asked Kellie.

"Looking for a washroom."

"Good luck."

He found it at the rear of the building. There was only one for the general public, apparently intended for both sexes. He pushed through the door and entered a small room, equipped with a floor-level drain and some wide benches. No commode. You sat on a bench, if need be. The room was occupied, but only by one individual. Digger waited until it was empty, killed the e-suit, did the deed (listening anxiously for footsteps outside, trying to plan what he'd do if he got caught, knowing he couldn't just reactivate the unit without making a mess of himself).

But he got through it okay. Just in time, though. The door was opening as he hit the switch. Flickinger field on. Lightbender on. Goompah in the room, standing uncertainly in the doorway, as if he had just seen something out of the corner of his eye.

All kinds of firsts were being set here. First person to watch an alien theatrical production. First to visit a library. First to use a washroom.

He smiled and walked out into the corridor, forgetting that, to an observer, the door opened of its own volition. He realized what he'd done just as he started to close it behind him. Two more Goompahs were coming, one of each sex. The door caught their attention and he moved away from it, leaving it ajar. They looked at it, looked at each other, did the Goompah equivalent of a pair of shrugs, and went in.

Digger returned to the reading room, found a chair toward the rear, and sat down to wait.

CLOSING TIME. THE last of the readers was waddling toward the door. When she was gone, the librarians took a quick look around, straightened chairs, picked up some loose pieces of the hard crackly material that passed for notepaper, and arranged their own stations. Parsy went into the back room, counted the scrolls, opened a logbook, and signed it. His colleague, whose name seemed to be Tupelo, put out the oil lamps, closed and bolted the shutters, and retrieved a wooden padlock from his desk.

Kellie was visibly impressed by it. "They're not entirely without technology," she said.

"No big deal," said Digger. "The Egyptians had them four thousand years ago."

Tupelo closed the stack room door and lowered a bar across it. Digger had feared they might padlock the room, and he was primed to try to lift the key. But it didn't happen, and he was feeling that he was home free when someone knocked at the front door. The librarians opened up and a small, evil-looking beast was led in on a leash. The creature looked like an undersized pig, except that it had fangs, fur along its jaws and across its skull, and a line of quills down its back. It snorted and showed everyone a healthy double row of incisors. Its master, a brightly-ribboned female, moved in with it while the two librarians finished checking around to be sure everything was attended to.

"That what I think it is?" asked Kellie.

The animal's red eyes came to rest directly on Digger, and it commenced to pull at its leash. Its master spoke to it and the thing looked away momentarily and growled. Then its head swung back.

"As soon as she turns it loose," said Kellie, "things are going to get tense."

The librarians filed out through the front door. The female looked around the darkened room, apparently puzzled by the beast's behavior. Digger watched her kneel beside the animal and stroke its neck.

"Our chance," he told Kellie. He edged toward the stack room, raised the bar, and signaled Kellie to get inside. When she'd gone through, he followed and pulled the door shut.

Simultaneously he heard a shout. Then, unmistakably, the beast was galloping across the reading room. They heard it slam into the stack room door, which Digger was holding shut.

More voices outside. Howling and scraping.

Then someone was tugging on the door. Digger backed away from it, looking around for a weapon, seeing nothing except the scrolls. The commotion outside continued until finally he heard the female's voice. Kellie produced a pistol and was about to thumb it on when the door opened. But the animal was tethered again.

Parsy held up a lamp and stepped into the room. Tupelo was speaking, probably trying to explain how the bar happened to be in the raised position.

The animal, fortunately, was being held back.

They looked in all directions. Obviously, no one was hiding there. When the animal continued to growl and show its teeth, its master kicked it. The thing whined but quieted. They dragged it clear, the door swung shut and the bar banged down.

"I guess we're in here for the duration," said Digger.

"We can cut our way out if we have to," said Kellie.

They listened to receding voices. Then came the familiar charge across the room by the little pig, and lots of snuffling outside their door. But the thing wasn't trying to tear it down this time.

Digger heard the front door open and close.

"What was the plan again?" asked Kellie.

The animal whined.

"No problem," he said. "When they come tomorrow to secure the doggie and open up, we'll just stroll out."

The lightbender field faded, and she was standing before him. "Have you considered the possibility," she asked, "that tomorrow may be Sunday?"

THERE WERE, IN fact, 587 scrolls. They were tagged and divided into fourteen cubicles. Digger set up a lamp and worked one cubicle at a time, taking them out singly, logging the marking on the cubicle and on the tag for each scroll. When they were ready to start, one held the pickup, the other handled the scroll. And they began to record the Complete Available Works of the Goompahs.

Digger once again wished he had command of the language, and promised himself he would learn it, promised himself he'd read at least one of the texts in its original form before he went home.

They were surprised to discover some illustrations: animals and plants, buildings, Goompahs, maps. Other segments might have been mathematical, but since they didn't know what the local numbering system looked like, or the mathematical signs, they couldn't be sure (other than some sections devoted to geometry).

The paper used in the scrolls was of a textured quality, appealing to touch, but thick enough to limit the length of the work that could be placed on a single dowel.

The dowels were made of wood or copper. A few of the scrolls were contained within protective tubes that had to be removed before the parchment could be unrolled. The printing itself was simple and unadorned. Like the architecture, Digger observed.

They worked through the night. There was a brief rain storm around midnight. The creature at the door whined once in a while, scratched occasionally, but never went away.

They watched the time, and when they knew the sun had been up for a half hour or so, and could hear the unmistakable sounds of traffic outside, they decided they were pushing their luck, shut down the effort, and put everything back.

In time they heard noises at the front, heard the doors open, and someone took the beast away. It protested, the caretaker protested, and there was much pawing and scratching at the wooden floor. And then everything went quiet for a while. Eventually the stack door opened, courtesy of the younger Goompah, and they passed out into the musty, sunlit reading room.

"I feel as if we owe this guy a good turn," said Digger.

Kellie was a glowing wraith in his goggles, gliding between chairs and tables. "If we can figure out a way to turn that cloud aside," she said, "you'll have done that. And more." The library was empty save for the aide. "What did you have in mind?"

"When this is over—"

"Yes?"

"—And we know how things stand, I'd like to leave something for him. He'd never know where it came from. A gift from the gods."

"Leave what, Dig?"

"I don't know. I'm still thinking about it. These folks like drama."

"Oh."

"Maybe something from Sophocles. Translated into Goompah."

LIBRARY ENTRY

"Are books important, Boomer?"

"Reading them is important."

"Why?"

"Because they take us places we can't get to otherwise."

"Like where, for instance?"

"Like China, when they were building the Great Wall. Or Italy, when they were discovering that the world could be explained rationally. Or Mars when McCovey and Epstein first walked out the door."

"That sounds pretty exciting, Boomer."

"There's someplace else too, that's especially important."

"Where's that? Ohio?"

"Ohio, too. But I was thinking that it's the only way you have of getting behind someone else's eyes. It's the way we found out that we're really all the same."

—*The Goompah Show*
All-Kids Network
May 21

chapter 22

IT WAS THE first day of full-time basic Goompah. The change came easier than anyone would have dreamed. Of the entire group of trainees, only two seemed to be struggling with the spoken languages, and even they could order food, ask directions and understand the bulk of the response, comment that it was going to rain, and inquire whether Gormir would be home in time for dinner.

They'd been speaking Goompah almost exclusively in the workroom since mid-May. And now Judy and her *Shironi Kulp*, her Elegant Eleven, were ready to excise all English from their vocabularies for the balance of the outbound flight, save when they had something that had to be passed on to the *makla*. The word meant *outsider*, she confided to Collingdale. It was the closest they could get to *barbarian* in Goompah.

They were permitted one sim per day. But teams had been assigned to translate the English so that even the entertainment was offered in the target language. An honor code was in effect, and violators were expected to turn themselves in.

Collingdale was present when Juan Gomez admitted to an infraction within an hour of converting to the new system. Juan explained himself in Goompah, and Collingdale couldn't follow. Something to do with Shelley. The penalty was mild, a requirement to do an extra translation from one of the *Brackel* Library texts. A heroic poem, Judy explained.

Collingdale tried to restrict himself to Goompah in the presence of the *Kulp*. He was making progress, and he enjoyed impressing his young wards. They never ceased looking surprised, and he began to suspect they didn't have a high opinion of his intellectual abilities, or, for that matter, of those of the Upper Strata in general. "Too locked in to their mental habits to be taken seriously," Judy said with a perfectly straight face. "Except you of course."

"Of course."

"It is a problem," she said. "People live longer all the time, but they still freeze up pretty early. Flexibility goes at thirty."

"You really think so?"

"Lost mine last month."

However that might have been, they called him in on that first full Goompah day and bestowed on him the *Kordikai* Award, named for an ancient Goompah philosopher famed for constructing what humans would have called the scientific method.

Had his support for them been tentative, that act alone would have won him over. They were the best people he'd ever worked with, young, enthusiastic, quick learners, and, perhaps, most important of all, they believed in what they were doing, saw themselves as the cavalry riding in to help an otherwise-doomed people. When the time came, when the cloud darkened the skies and frightened the wits out of the Goompahs, the *Kulp* would arrive, one for each of the eleven cities (by then they knew that the southernmost pair were a single political unit), their alienness hidden within Judy Sternberg's exquisite disguises. They would go in, do a few high-tech magic tricks, claim the gods had sent them to warn of approaching disaster, and urge the inhabitants to clear out. Head for the high ground.

What could go wrong?

"*Challa*, Dr. Collingdale." They shook his hand and told him they intended the *Kordikai* to become an annual award.

BUT SPEAKING GOOMPAH more or less full-time was one thing to talk about and something else to do. The breakfast is good. There's a fruit bowl on the table. I am reading an interesting book. They had the lines down. And all quite effectively, except, of course, that they really needed to engage with native speakers. As things were, the conversation remained hopelessly superficial. It is nice out. Your shoes are untied. I am a little red pencil box.

"*Pay-los*, Dr. Collingdale." Good-bye. See you around. Until next time.

And *that's* what could go wrong. There would be all kinds of nuances that they were not going to pick up because there was no one to tell them where they were getting it wrong.

At dinnertime, he went into the dining room. Five of the *Kulp* were at a corner table. He wandered over and, in his measured Goompah, asked them how it was going.

It was going well.

Had they encountered any problems?

Boka, *Ska* Collingdale. *Friend* Collingdale. *Mr.* Collingdale. *Acquaintance* Collingdale. Who really knew?

*   *   *

BUT THEY'D LEARNED much since Digger and Kellie had penetrated the library.

The cities were significantly older than anyone had assumed. Their roots went back at least five thousand years. If that were so, how did one explain that they were still sitting on the isthmus? Why had they never expanded into the rest of their world? What had happened to them?

Prior to the foundation of the first city, which the Goompahs believed to be *Sakmarung*, the world had belonged to the gods. But they had retreated to the skies, and had left the isthmus, the *Intigo*, which was also their word for *world*, to the mortal beings, created by a mating between the sun and the two moons; between Taris, who warms the day; Zonia, who brightens the night; and the elusive Holen, who flees and laughs among the stars.

The Goompahs had started with a ménage à trois, and several of the experts suspected there was a connection with the tradition of multiple husbands and wives in each connubial group. Collingdale knew that mythology inevitably comes to reflect the aspirations and ideals of any society.

They'd acquired illustrations of eleven gods and goddesses, and it had not been hard to match them with the sculptured figures in the temple at *Brackel*. There were deities charged with providing food and wine, laughter and music, the seasons and the crops. They maintained the sea, saw to the tides, controlled the winds, maintained the cycle of the seasons. They blessed the births of new arrivals and eased the final pains of the dying.

Jason Holder pointed out to him that, although their duties were similar to those of earth-born deities, there was a subtle difference. The gods at home had given their bounty as a gift, and might withdraw it if they were miffed, or out of town, or jealous of another deity. The *Intigo*'s gods seemed to have a responsibility to make provision. It was not quixotic, but rather an obligation. It almost seemed as if the Goompahs were in charge.

Also significant, Holder continued, there was no god of war. And none of pestilence. "All of the deities represent positive forces," Jason said. But he admitted he didn't know what to make of that fact, except that the Goompahs seemed remarkably well adjusted.

The artwork from the library texts revealed much about how the Goompahs saw their gods. They did indeed embody majesty and power; but there was also a strong suggestion of compassion. One of the deities, Lykonda, daughter of the divine trio, had wings. And she always carried a torch. So they knew who welcomed mortals at the entrance to the temple. There was as yet no indication that the natives believed in an afterlife, but Jason predicted that, if they did, Lykonda would be on hand to welcome them to their reward.

The cities formed a league whose political outline was vague. But they had a common currency. And neither Judy's people nor Hutch's analysts back home found any mention of defense needs. Nor did the available Goompah history, sketchy though it may have been, indicate any kind of conflict that humans would have described as war. *Ever.*

Well, some intercity disagreements had sent mobs from one town to the outskirts of another, where they threw rocks or, in one celebrated incident, animal bladders filled with dyed water. There had been occasional fatalities, but nowhere was there a trace of the kind of mass organized violence that so marred human history.

There had even been a handful of armed encounters. But they'd been rare, and the numbers involved had been small. Collingdale could by no means claim to have a complete history of the *Intigo*. Still, this seemed to be a remarkably peaceful race. And a reading of their philosophers revealed a subtle and extraordinary code of ethics that compared favorably with the admonitions of the New Testament.

The Goompah world appeared to be limited to the isthmus and the areas immediately north and south. Their sailing vessels stayed in sight of land. There was no indication whether they'd developed the compass. They had apparently not penetrated more than a few thousand kilometers in any direction from home. They had not established colonies. They showed no expansionist tendencies whatever.

The Goompahs possessed some scientific and engineering ability. Judy's team had found a book devoted to climatology. Most of its assertions were wrong, but it revealed an underlying assumption that climatic fluctuations had natural causes, and if one could assemble the correct equations and make valid observations, weather prediction would become possible.

Some among them suspected they lived on a sphere. No one knew how they'd figured that out, but a number of references to the *Intigo* described it as a globe. Occasionally the adjective *world-circling* was attached to *ocean*.

The team had recovered and partially translated thirty-six books from the *Brackel* Library. Of the thirty-six, thirteen could be described as poetry or drama. There was nothing one might call a novel, or even fiction. The rest were history, political science—their governments were republics of one form or another—and philosophy, which had been separated from the natural sciences, itself no small achievement.

THE UPPER STRATA made an effort to join in the spirit of things. They prepared lines and committed them to memory, so the common room filled up with Goompah chatter.

Challa this and *Challa* that.

Frank Bergen wished everyone *mokar kappa*. Good luck. Literally, *happy stars.* They could find no Goompah word for luck or fortune, so they'd improvised. Dangerous, but unavoidable.

When Wally offered a chocolate brownie to Ava, she had the opportunity to deliver her line: *"Ocho baranara Si-kee." I am in your debt.*

Ava smiled, and Wally, fumbling pronunciation, replied that her blouse looked delicious.

Jerry Madden told Judy that he hoped she found success in all her endeavors, delivering the line from memory. And getting it right.

She replied that things were going quite well, thank you very much, and that his diction was excellent, rendering the last word in both Goompah and English.

Jerry beamed.

Elsewhere, Peggy got a suggestion from Harry Chin: "When stuck," Harry told her, "you can fall back on *karamoka tola kappa.*"

Peggy tried it, beat it up a bit, and finally got it right.

"Excellent, Peg," he said. "We may draft you into the unit."

"Of course. And what does it mean?"

" 'May the stars always shine for you.' "

DINNER WAS SERVED with a Goompah menu, although the food was strictly terrestrial. While they ate, Alexandra, trying to use the language, told Collingdale something. But she butchered it, tried again, and threw up her hands. "You have a message from the DO," she said, finally.

It was simply a status report. Hutchins had rounded up the assistance of a few more experts in a half dozen fields, and shown them the recordings and the texts from Lookout, and she was forwarding their comments. Her own covering remarks were short and to the point. *You might especially want to pay attention to Childs's observations on the arrangement of the statuary in the temple. Billings has interesting things to say about the recurrence of the number eleven, although there's probably nothing to it. Pierce thinks he's isolated a new referent for the dative case. Hope all's well.*

What struck him was that she said it all in Goompah. And got most of it right. Not bad for a bureaucrat. "Alexandra," he told the captain, "the woman has something going for her."

Much the same thing happened when the daily transmission came in from the *Jenkins.*

"David, we got another show for you last evening." Digger did it in Goompah. Collingdale hadn't known anybody on the *Jenkins* was making the effort.

Digger went on to explain they'd recorded a drama for which the *al-Jahani* already had the script. He smiled out of the screen, signaling that he understood quite well the value of *that*. An unparalleled chance to tie together the written and spoken versions of the language.

Magnificent, Digger, thought Collingdale.

"We've also relocated some of the pickups to Saniusar. *They're all designated, so you won't have any problem sorting them out. Raw data is included with this package.*

"One more thing. I'm trying to translate Antigone *into Goompah. But we don't seem to have the vocabulary. I don't know how to say* glorious, forbidden, fate, brooding, *and a bunch more. I've included the words. If any of your people have time, I'd appreciate the help."*

Antigone?

Alexandra looked over at him, her forehead creased. "Why?" she asked.

He shook his head. "I've no idea, but it sounds like a decent exercise."

COLLINGDALE WAS IN the shower, preparing to call it a day, when Alexandra's voice broke in with a general announcement: *"Attention, please. This is the captain. We are going to jump back into sublight for a few hours. There is no problem, and no reason to be concerned. But we'll be performing the maneuver in two minutes. Please get to a restraint."*

Two minutes? What the hell was going on? She sounded calm and reassuring, but that was what most alarmed Collingdale. This was an unscheduled stop, so obviously something was wrong.

"Everyone please find a harness and settle in."

It struck him that it was probably almost the first back-to-back English sentences he'd heard all day.

"It's nothing serious," she said when he called.

"It's an unscheduled jump, Alex. That sounds serious to me."

"We're only doing it as a precaution. Bill picked up an anomaly in the engines."

"Which engines?"

"The Hazeltines. That's why we're making the jump. It's routine. Anytime they so much as burp, we go back to sublight."

"In case—"

"—In case there's a problem. We don't want to get stuck where no one can find us."

"What kind of anomaly?"

"Rise in temperature. Power balances."

He had no idea what that implied. "I thought the engines were shut off while we were in hyperspace."

"Not really. They go into an inactive mode. And we run periodic systems checks." She paused. *"Actually, we've been getting some numbers we don't like for the last week."*

"That doesn't sound good."

"It may not be a problem. On the other hand, we rushed the al-Jahani into service. Maybe before it was ready."

"We going to be okay?"

"Oh, sure. There's no danger to anybody."

"You're sure?"

"Dave, if there were any risk whatever to the passengers, any risk, I'd shut her down and call for help. Now, get into your bunk. I have work to do."

HYPERFLIGHT IS A disquieting experience, an apparently slow passage, at about ten knots, through unending fogbanks. For reasons he didn't entirely understand, he had begun to think of his relationship with Mary in much the same way.

His communications with her had dropped off somewhat. His fault, really. Nothing new ever happened on the *al-Jahani*, other than the progress they were making understanding the Goompahs. At first he'd told her about that, but her replies suggested the stories about *zhokas* and temples and Goompah revels were not exactly at the center of her interests.

So now, at least, he had some real news to report. We are back out under the stars, he told her, and they look good. You don't appreciate them when you see them every night.

He'd been cooped up for more than three months. It was already the longest nonstop flight he'd made, and it would be another half year before they arrived at Lookout. "All sense of movement is gone, though," he said. "We're at almost 1 percent of lightspeed, but we seem to be frozen in space."

Becalmed in an endless sea.

One-third of the way to Lookout. He tried to say it aloud in Goompah, but he didn't know how to express fractions. Or percentages. Did Goompahs have decimal points?

They must if they'd designed and built the temple.

And his mind ran on: How would you say *jump engines* in Goompah? *Molly* was *jump*. No reason he couldn't use it as an adjective. And a machine, a mechanism, like the hand-cranked pump they used to get water into their plumbing system, was a *kalottul*. Hence *molly kalottuls*, literally *jump machines*. Without their *molly kalottuls*, how long would it take to get to *Brackel*?

It occurred to him that he was putting all this into the transmission. But it would scare her, even though he'd assured her there was no danger. Still, he went back and deleted it. He finished up, telling her they would be on their way again shortly. And that he missed her.

He didn't tell her that he thought he was losing her. That he felt every mile of the void between them. Not the void as it was counted in light-years. But as in *distant, remote, hidden*.

The laughter was gone.

When he'd completed the transmission and sent it off, he went back to the problem he'd set himself. How long to travel to Lookout at current velocity?

They were still about eighteen hundred light-years away. At one light-year per century.

Better have a good book ready.

Alexandra came back on-line: *"Dave, you can tell your people we're okay. Just running some tests now. We'll be getting under way again within an hour."*

"We're clear?"

"Well," she said, *"we've got some worn valves and a feeder line, and the clocks have gotten out of sync. We've checked the maintenance reports, and they never got to them in port."*

His first reaction was that heads would roll. And it must have shown when he told her that he hoped they'd be able to get to Lookout without any more problems.

"You can't really blame the engineers, Dave. Everything was being rushed to get us out of there. Actually, it should have been okay for a couple more runs. But you can never really be sure. I'm talking about the valves and the feeder line now. The clocks we've already taken care of. And I'm replacing the line. The valves, though, are something else. Heavy work, in-port stuff. We can't do much about them, except take it easy on them the rest of the way."

"How do you take it easy on a jump engine?" he asked.

"You say nice things to it."

"Alex, let me ask you again—"

"There's no risk to the ship, David. These things are engineered so that at the first hint of a serious problem it jumps back into sublight and shuts itself down. Just as it did this morning." Her voice changed, became subdued. *"Whether we get to Lookout or not, that's another story."*

LIBRARY ENTRY

"How far is the sky, Boomer?"
"It's close enough to touch, Shalla."
"Really? Marigold said it's very far."
"Only if you open your eyes."

—*The Goompah Show*
Summer Special, All-Kids Network
June 21

chapter 23

"ELECTRICAL ACTIVITY PICKING up inside the omega," said Sky. It was getting close to the hedgehog.

"*Estimated time fifty minutes,*" said Bill. The rate of closure was just over 30 kph.

The *Heffernan* had backed away to 80 million klicks, the minimum range set by Hutchins. They were watching by way of a half dozen probes running with the omega, and they were maintaining jump status so they could leave in a hurry if the need arose. That used a substantial quantity of fuel and would require all kinds of refitting when they got back to Serenity. But that was the point: They were making sure they would get back.

"I don't know how big this is going to be," Sky told Em, "but they've got my attention."

The overhead monitor carried a picture of the omega as seen from the monitors, a wall of churning mist streaked with bursts of incandescence. The cloud was usually dark and untroubled, but now it almost seemed as if the thing was reacting to the chase. Sky was glad to be well away from it.

Other displays provided views of the hedgehog and the forward section of the omega. He watched the range between them growing shorter. Watched the flow of black mist across the face of the cloud, the electricity rippling through its depths.

Emma refused to commit herself about what would happen. "Large bang," she said. Beyond that, the data were insufficient. It was all guess-work. That was why they were out here doing this, to find out.

The cloud seemed almost to have a defined surface. Like a body of water rather than mist. Sky had looked at some of the visuals from researchers who had snuggled up against omegas and even on a couple of occasions penetrated them. The clouds looked thick enough to walk on.

A flash of lightning, reflected through the monitors, lit up the bridge. The pictures broke up and came back. "Big one," he said.

The hedgehog had seemed enormous when the thruster packages had closed in on it two months before. Six and a half kilometers wide. Skyscraper-sized spines. Seen against the enormous span of the omega, it might have been only a floating spore.

More heavy lightning.

"Bill," said Sky, "let's buckle in."

The AI acknowledged, and the harnesses descended around them.

"You know," said Emma, "about twenty years ago they towed an old freighter up to one of these things and pushed it inside. One of the Babcock models. Looked like a big box."

"What happened?"

"It got within about twenty klicks before a bolt of lightning took it out. All but blew it apart."

"At twenty klicks."

"Yep."

"Won't be long for our guy." He tried to relax. Theirs was an unsettling assignment. God knew they were far enough away to have plenty of warning, and they could jump out of danger. But Hutch had explained there was a risk, they just didn't know, she would understand if they'd just as soon pass on the assignment. In case the worst did happen, they were maintaining a moment-to-moment on-line feed to Serenity.

The range shortened to twenty kilometers, the range of the freighter, and then to fifteen. The cloud flickered, and Sky could have sworn he heard a rumble, but that was, of course, impossible, so he didn't say anything but just watched the gap continue to close.

At twelve klicks Bill reported that electrical activity inside the cloud had increased by a factor of two over its normal state.

At ten, a lightning bolt leaped out of the roiling mist and touched the hedgehog. Embraced it.

One of the imagers went out. "I think it hit the package, too," said Emma.

The hedgehog was by then so close that none of their angles showed separation. It was almost into the cloud.

A second bolt flickered around the hedgehog, licked at it, seemed to draw it forward. The mists churned. And the hedgehog slipped inside.

The pictures coming from the probes showed nothing but cloud. He checked the time. Sixteen forty-eight hours. Adjust for signal lag and make it 1644.

They waited.

Ragged bolts ripped through the cloud. It brightened. And then it began to fade.

"Well, Em," said Sky, "that was something of a bust. Do we go around the other side to see if the hedgehog comes out?"

Emma was still watching the screens. "Not so fast," she said.

For several minutes the omega grew alternately brighter and darker. Lightning flowed along its surface like liquid fire. Then it began to shine.

And it went incandescent.

One by one, the feeds from the accompanying probes died.

Emma's eyes looked very blue.

"Bill," said Sky, "be ready to go."

"*Say the word, Sky.*" The engines changed tone.

It was becoming a sun.

"What's happening to it, Em?"

"I have no idea," she said.

"Bill, has it exploded?"

"*I don't think so. The sensors are gone, but the remotes haven't detected a shock wave.*"

"That's good."

"Readings are off the scale," said Em.

He shut down the monitors.

"*Sky, do you wish to leave the area?*"

"This is goofy," said Em. "How can we not be getting a shock wave?"

"I have no idea."

"It shouldn't be happening. I can't be sure because everything we have is blown out. But the way it was going, I'd guess it's putting out the light-equivalent of a small nova. Without the explosion. Without the blast."

"Is that possible?"

"We'll see what the measurements look like. Meantime, yes, I'd say we're watching it happen."

"I don't think I understand."

"Think flashbulb," she said. "And tell Bill we should go."

LIBRARY ENTRY

. . . And then there are those who say there is no evidence of the existence of God.

Think about the universe. To understand how it works, one must grasp the significance of light. It is the speed limit, the boundary, the measure of physical reality. We use it as a metaphor for knowledge, for intelligence, for reason. We speak of the forces of light. It is so bound up in our souls that we think of it as the very essence of existence. And yet there is no definable necessity for a physical force that can be observed by sense organs. By eyes. If there is proof anywhere of an involved God, it is the existence of light.

—Conan Magruder,
Time and Tide

chapter 24

Woodbridge, Virginia.
Sunday, June 29.

HUTCH SAT ON a rocker on the front deck watching Maureen and Tor tossing a beach ball back and forth. Maureen's tactic, when she had the ball, was to charge her father, giggling wildly, while he ran for cover. But she inevitably lost control of the ball, popping it in the air or squirting it sideways or kicking it into the rosebushes.

It was an early-summer day, filled with the sounds of a ball game a couple of blocks over, and the barking of Max, their neighbors' golden retriever, who wanted to get out to play with Maureen, but they weren't home and nobody was there to unlatch the screen door. So Max whined and barked and snuffled.

The warning from Alex, from the *al-Jahani*, had come in only moments ago. *If you have an alternate plan, you might want to implement.*

Yes, indeed. Send in the second team.

Alex was citing a fifty-fifty chance that she could make it to Lookout. But Hutch knew she didn't really believe that. Captains were expected to be both accurate and optimistic. It was a tradition that probably went back to Odysseus. But it didn't take much insight to see how she really felt.

The problem was that, other than the *Hawksbill*, there was no alternate plan. If the *al-Jahani* broke down, she'd have nothing left but the kite.

Maureen was charging her daddy again, trying to raise the ball over her head. Max was barking. Somebody must have just belted a long one at the ballpark because the crowd was roaring. Maureen tripped over her own feet and went rear end over beach ball. She came up screaming, rubbing her eyes. Tor hurried to her side and scooped her up and returned her to the deck, where Hutch soothed her and checked her for scratches and handed her a glass of lemonade.

"You all right?" Tor asked.

It took a moment before she realized he was talking to her and not to Maureen. "Sure. Why do you ask?"

He sat down beside her and looked at her in a way that said she was wearing all her emotions.

She shrugged. "Maybe it'll get there. Sometimes I tend to assume the worst."

Tor nodded. "That's what I've always heard about you."

Maureen was trying to gulp her lemonade. "Take your time, sweetie," said Hutch.

Cathie Blaylock came out of her house across the way, waved, picked up something on her deck, and went back inside. Maureen put the lemonade down, said, "Daddy, again," and started tugging at her father's knee. Ready to go another round.

"You don't have anybody you could send after them?" he asked. "Pick them up if they get in trouble?"

"No," she said quietly, "nobody who could do that and get them to Lookout on time."

"So what are we going to do?"

"Only one thing we can do."

"And what's that?"

"Hope our luck holds. And alert Digger that he might have to get inventive."

WHILE SHE WAS on the circuit, the watch officer told her that the results from the *Heffernan* had just come in.

Hutch held her breath. "What happened?"

"It lit up," he said. *"The cloud became a torch."*

"Is it a tewk?"

"Too soon to tell. The lab just got it. But they're pretty excited."

Two hours later she had confirmation from Charlie. *"No question,"* he said. *"It's the same spectrogram."*

ARCHIVE

COSMIC MARKER. It now appears that the omega clouds, which have mystified scientists for thirty years, and have spawned a whole new branch of research, may be only an experimental device themselves. Although their purpose remains unclear, according to Dr. Lee MacElroy of the International Research Center in Edinburgh, they may well be part of an experiment gone awry.

—*Science News*,
June 30

LIBRARY ENTRY

Priscilla Hutchins's Diary
(Reaction to above)

MacElroy never got anything right in his life.

—July 3

chapter 25

DIGGER HAD BECOME fascinated by the Goompahs, had learned to enjoy the shows, would have gone down every day to mingle with the crowds, to visit the temple, to stand outside the cafés, wishing he could take a place at one of the tables and join in the conversation.

Kellie told him he had cabin fever. But it was more than that. He had never been anywhere before where the inhabitants seemed to enjoy themselves so thoroughly. The nights were filled with laughter and music, and the downtown area played host each evening to happy crowds.

So they took the lander down regularly, and, to the extent they were able, mixed with the locals. Some nights they strolled along the beaches. Others, they went to concerts and visited sporting events, and sometimes they just sat in one of the parks.

Had they been able to set aside the coming storm, and the haunting memory of Jack's death, it would have been a golden time. Kellie was bright and upbeat. She shared his fascination, had picked up enough of the language to understand much of what was going on around her. And he knew that the day would come when he'd look back on these evenings with a sense of wistfulness and loss.

The omega had by then become visible in the sense that a small patch of stars had gone missing. Occasionally Digger overheard conversations about it, conversations that grew more frequent as the weeks passed and more stars blinked out. The Goompahs admitted to each other that they'd never seen anything like it. There was no record of any such occurrence in the histories, and Digger could see they were getting nervous. He wondered how they'd be when it filled the sky.

The thing rose at night a few hours after sunset, and dropped into the sea just before dawn. And the Goompahs watched.

Where was *Melakar*?

Where was *Hazhurpol*?

Behind the cloud, he was tempted to tell them. They're there, and if you folks know what's good for you, you'll start thinking about packing up and heading for the hills.

It might have been the sense that Athens, *Brackel,* with its theaters and its parks and its scrolls, was approaching its demise: It might have been this realization that drove him through its streets like a ghost, savoring its life and its fragile beauty.

Kellie tried to slow him down. She told him he was becoming obsessed. Maybe, she said, he should think about going back. Going home. Get away from there.

But he would not do that. Wouldn't consider it.

Kellie thought the kite might work. She knew Hutchins well and had a lot of confidence in her. Digger didn't point out that Hutchins hadn't hidden her feeling that the *al-Jahani/Hawksbill* mission was a long shot.

Now that they could wrap a lightbender field around the lander, it was much easier getting in and out of *Brackel.* Kellie usually brought them in among the orchards and open ground on the north side of the city. One day, she picked instead a glade a short distance off the isthmus road. "Breaks the monotony," she said, as the invisible craft descended.

Digger looked at the woods, hunting for Goompahs, but Kellie reassured him. "Bill can't see anybody down there," she said. "It's okay."

Any*body.*

It was, as far as he could recall, the first time.

HE EXPECTED THIS to be an interesting evening. Even more popular among the Goompahs than the theater was an event that was part lecture, part free-for-all. A speaker, usually a visiting authority of one kind or another, attempted to present a point of view on a given topic while the paying customers engaged him in open debate. (Or agreed with him, as the case might be, though, in Digger's experience, it seldom was.) The visitor might be discussing the health benefits of sunlight, an abstract ethical issue of one kind or another, the merits of a drama that had recently been hooted out of town, or a supernatural visitation she had undergone and which had led to a spiritual awakening and the sure and certain knowledge that the members of her audience were groping through moral darkness and needed to get their act in order. It was all great fun, and Digger was often left in doubt whether any of the Goompahs on either side of the issue were serious. The attendees paid for the privilege, the speakers looked for subjects that would provoke outrage, and everybody had a good time.

They were called *sloshen,* for which there is no completely accurate En glish translation. Call it a felicitous quarrel, a happy argument, a glorious difference of opinion.

That evening's guest speaker, according to notices that had been posted for several days, would be Macao Carista, who was described as a cartographer. Macao was from *Kulnar*, a city immediately northwest of *Brackel*. According to the displays, she was widely known throughout the *Intigo*.

While lingering several days earlier in the lobby of the building that would be used for the presentation, Digger had overheard enthusiastic patrons commenting that she always brought maps of places to which no one had ever journeyed, or sometimes of which no one had even heard.

She used the evenings, apparently, to talk about her travels, describing various kinds of fantastic creatures she'd seen, armored *terps* as tall as she was, *bandars* that spat venom at a range exceeding the diameter of the hall (which was considerable), flying *solwegs*, talking *bolliclubs*. Last time out, she was reported to have described two-headed Goompahs, which she'd seen on an island in the eastern ocean. One head, she'd said, always spoke the truth, and the other always lied. But you never knew which was which.

And there was *Yara-di*, the city of gold.

And the bridge across the bottomless *Carridan* Gap, built by unknown hands, using engineering principles beyond the grasp of any alive today. The bridge was so long that, when she crossed on the back of a *berba*, it had taken three days.

She'd spoken of the *Boravay*, the carnivorous forest, from which no traveler, save Macao, had ever returned.

"Sounds like a hell of a woman," said Kellie.

Goompah, thought Digger. *She's a Goompah. Not a woman.*

A strict and formal decorum was observed during the *slosh*. No hooting, no raised voices. "If the honored speaker would pause for a moment," one might say, "before we wander farther into confusion—"

It was a cool night. A brisk wind blew off the sea, and management needed several fires to warm the hall to a comfortable level. Macao was obviously popular because Goompahs filled the building, and sat talking quietly to one another while they waited for her to appear.

The audience, about two hundred strong, were seated above the stage, amphitheater style, but restricted to three sides. Kellie and Digger, who had long since planted a pickup near the stage, lurked in the roped-off section, well out of the way. At the appointed hour, two workers pulled a large armchair into view, made a great deal of fuss getting it aimed in the proper direction, and returned with a frame on which Digger assumed Macao would put her maps. Then they brought out a roll of animal skin and leaned it against the side of the chair. They added a table and a lighted oil lamp, and when they had everything arranged to their satisfaction, they scurried off. A bell tinkled, the audience quieted, and a Goompah in red and gold entered from the side. He placed his palms together, the equivalent of bowing to the audience. Digger missed part of his comments, but it came down to, Welcome, ladies and gentlemen, please give a hand to our world-traveling guest, Macao Carista.

The audience rapped politely on any available flat surface, and Macao made her entrance. To Digger's eyes she was pretty much indistinguishable from the other females. She wore a bright yellow blouse with fluffy sleeves. Green leggings. And animal-hide boots. A gold medallion hung on a purple ribbon about her neck.

"Well," she said, "this looks like a desperate bunch." And they were off and running. Macao, it seemed, had just returned from a long overland journey to the north. Through the desert and beyond the jungle where, she claimed, it grew cooler again. She regaled her audience with tales of the mystical *Lyndaia*, where the gods had placed the first Goompahs; of attack *bobbos* and the flying *groppe*, and a giant *falloon*, which had half a dozen slithery tentacles, and "only last year, as we all know, dragged a full-masted ship to the bottom." And finally she spoke of *Brissie*, the city on the edge of forever. "From its towers," she said, "one can see the past and the future." She recognized a hand in the audience. "Please give us your name," she said.

"Telio. And what did *you* see, Macao?"

"Do you really wish to know, Telio?"

The questioner had a smashed ear. It was the same Telio he'd seen on the isthmus road what now seemed a long time ago.

"Yes," he said. "Tell us."

"Be aware first that I looked to the west, to the past. What's past is done, Telio. There's no point gazing that way."

"So what did you see?"

"Well." Feigning reluctance. "I saw a world filled with gleaming cities. Where our ships crossed the seas, and no part of the *Intigo* was hidden from us. Where travelers could find (something) wherever they went."

Digger and Kellie were off to one side, but at the edge of the stage. They were getting everything—Macao, Telio, and the audience reaction. Dave Collingdale's people would love this.

"Orky," said someone in the audience. A female. "Crossed the seas to *where*?"

"Oh, yes," Macao said. "That *is* the question, isn't it?" She hadn't sat down yet in the chair. She was using it instead as a prop. She circled it, gazed at her audience from behind it, leaned on its arm. Played to the expectant silence. "What do you think is on the other side of the sea?"

"There is no other side," the questioner said. "The sea goes on forever. There may be other islands out there somewhere, but the sea itself has no end."

"How many believe that?"

About half the hands went up. Maybe a bit more than half.

Macao fastened her gaze on the questioner. "The sea is (something)," she said. "It never stops. That sounds like a lot of water."

Orky made the rippling sound that passed for laughter among Goompahs. A few pounded on chair arms. "If the sea has an end, what kind of end is it? Does the water simply stop? Is there a place where you can fall off, as Taygla says?" Macao, obviously enjoying herself, *flowed* across the stage. "It's really an interesting question, isn't it? It almost seems there is no satisfactory answer to these things." She got up, opened the roll of animal skin, and withdrew a map, which she put on the frame. This was an attempt at cartography on a much larger scale than anything they'd seen at the library, which had been limited to the area in and around the isthmus. Her map showed icy regions in the south and deserts to the north, both correct. But it showed a western continent much closer than it actually was, and the big pole-to-pole continent a few thousand klicks east was missing altogether.

But the map contained a shock. "Wait here," he told Kellie.

"What?" she whispered. "Where are you going?"

He was already up on the stage, moving behind Macao, until he stood directly in front of the map. It reminded him of those sixteenth-century charts that showed personified clouds blowing in different directions, or whales spouting. There were no whales or animated winds on this one. But it *did* have what appeared to be a graphic of a human being. A male.

It was at the bottom of the chart, riding a winged rhino.

It wasn't done in sufficient detail to know for sure that it was human. But it was close. Eyes, mouth, and ears were all smaller than a Goompah's. It had pale brown skin, and it looked a lot better than the natives. Its clothing was standard, a loose-fitting shirt and leggings. And it carried something that looked like a harpoon.

"The sad thing is," Macao was saying, "we really don't know whether Orky is right or wrong. We don't know whether this map is right or wrong." She advanced without warning in Digger's direction and he had to scramble clear. Damned things were quicker than they looked.

"It's one of us," Digger told Kellie.

"What is?"

"On the chart."

She paused in front of the map, pretending to study it, but they could see her eyes look away while she considered what came next. "In fact, we don't even know what lies beyond the *Skatbrones*." Digger had heard the term before and believed it referred to the mountain range that sealed off the northern continent from the *Intigo*.

"We come here and talk about all manner of curious beasts, some of which I've actually seen, and some of which not. But not one of you knows which is true and which an imagining. And I put it to you that that is not a supportable state of affairs."

"It's not a perfect representation," Digger continued. "Arms are too long. Feet are too much like their own. But it's close."

A cup of water and an oil lamp stood on a table beside Macao. Digger decided she looked good in the glow of the lamp. Large malleable ears. Supple arms. Cute in the way, maybe, that a giraffe was cute. If her features were less than classic, they were nonetheless congenial and warm. Her eyes swept across him and seemed for a heart-stopping moment to linger. As if she *knew*.

More hands were going up. She recognized one.

"I'm Koller. It's true we can't see far, Macao; but it's impious to talk the way you do. The gods (something, something) these things for a reason."

"And what is the reason, Koller?"

"I don't know. But we should (something) the will of the gods. You come here and make up these wild tales, and I wonder whether the gods laugh to hear what you say. I'm not sure I want to be sitting this close to you when we all know that a bolt could come through the roof at any moment."

She smiled at him. "Koller, I think we're safe."

"Really? Have you looked at the sky recently?" And with that Koller got up, made his way into the aisle, and left the building.

"Well," Macao said. "I hope nobody gets (something, but probably 'singed') when it happens."

The audience was silent, except for a couple of nervous laughs.

"The thing is," said Digger, "it looks like us, but not quite. And it's sitting on one of those rhinos. But the rhino has wings."

She had to go look for herself. When she came back she touched his arm. "Never see the day one of those things could get off the ground," she said.

"That's what I'm wondering about."

"How do you mean?"

"It's obviously a mythological beast."

"So you think—"

"—The guy that looks like us is a mythological beast, too."

"Hey," she said, "he looks like you, not me."

So the next question was, what sort of mythological beast? Considering the way everyone had panicked whenever they'd caught a glimpse of Digger, he thought he could guess.

"I actually *have* done a fair amount of far traveling," Macao was saying. "There are a lot of strange things out there. Some strange things in here, too." She said it lightly, and they pounded their appreciation. "If you go out the front door of this place and turn left, and walk a few hundred paces, there's a park. It's called *Binlo*, or *Boplo*—"

"*Barlo*," someone said from the third row.

Digger suspected she'd known all along. "*Barlo*." She tasted the word on her tongue, rolled it around in her mouth, smiled, and took a coin out of her sleeve. "Later this evening, when we're finished here, if your way home leads through *Barlo* Park, stop a minute, and consider that *this* is the world that we know." She held the coin so it flashed in the lamplight. "*This* small piece of metal encompasses the entire known world. Where we live. It's the isthmus, and the land up to the *Skatbrones*, and the Sunrise Islands, and the Seawards, and the Windemeres, and the shoreline as far as we can see. And south to the Skybreakers. Every place where we've walked." She gazed curiously at it. "And the park is the world beyond. The great darkness into which we've cast no light.

"We boast of our maps, and we call ourselves (something). We pretend to much knowledge. But the truth is that we are gathered around a fire"— she lifted the lamp, and watched shadows move across the room—"in a very large and very dark forest." She turned the stem and the light flickered and died. "I can't bring myself to believe there's an infinite amount of water in the world. But maybe I'm wrong." Someone was trying to get her attention. "No," she said, "let me finish my thought. We live on an island of light. What extends beyond us in all directions is not the sea, but our own ignorance." The lamp blinked back on, as if by magic. "Persons like me can come before you with the most preposterous stories, and no one really knows what is true and what is not. In fact, despite everyone's (something), there really *is* a *falloon*. It doesn't actually gulp down ships." She moved to the edge of the stage, gazing out over her audience. "As far as I know."

Digger and Kellie moved cautiously around the stage so they could see better.

"I've seen it with my own eyes," she continued. "Yet when I tell you about it, you assume that I make it up. Why? Is it because you have evidence to the contrary? Or because you *expect* me to invent such tales?

"Each year, in the spring, the citizens of *Brackel* celebrate the founding of their city. *Kulnar*, which is, of course, older by several hundred years, celebrates in midwinter."

Several of the audience stood to repudiate her remark. Someone flung a scarf into the air. The question of which city was older was obviously a matter in dispute, and advocates were present for both claims.

Macao let it go on for a bit, then waved them to order. "The truth is, nobody really knows which city is older. But it's of no consequence." Her audience quieted. "However—" She drew the word out. "—That we have been here so long, and know so little, even about our own history, is to our discredit." Digger could hear a cart passing outside.

She held up a scroll. "This is Bijjio's *Atlas of the Known World*. It's accurate, as far as anyone knows. But it is really no more than a few introductory remarks and a lot of speculation." She paused and took a sip of the water. "We all know the story of Moro, who sailed east and returned from the west."

An arm went up in back. "My name is Groffel." The speaker swelled with the significance of what he was about to say. "You're not going to tell us the world is round, I hope?"

"Groffel," she said, "it's time we found out. Found out if there really are lands over the horizon. If there really are two-headed Goompahs. But we need support. We need *you* to help."

There were shouts. "The Krolley mission," someone said. And: "They're lunatics." And: "My honored friend should open his mind."

A voice on the far side, near the wall: "I assume, Macao, we're talking about contributions."

She waited until her audience had subsided. "We are talking about an *investment*," she said. "We are talking about our future, about whether we will still be wondering about these issues a hundred or six hundred years from now." She seemed to grow taller. "I don't say who's right and who's wrong. But I do say we should settle the matter. We should find out.

"Three ships will make the voyage. Like Moro, they will travel east, into the sunrise. They will record whatever islands they encounter, and eventually they will return over *there*." She pointed toward the back of the auditorium. West. A murmur ran through the audience.

"But why now? When the signs are bad?"

Kellie stirred. "Signs?" she asked. "Does he mean the cloud?"

Another voice: "How long will it take?"

"We estimate three years," she said.

"And on what is the estimate based?"

"The size of the world."

"You know the size of the world?"

Another smile. "Oh, yes."

"And how big is it?"

"It is a sphere, 90,652 *gruden* around the outside."

"Really?" This was Orky again. "Not 653?"

"Round it off a bit, if you like."

Someone in back stood up. "You've measured it?"

"In a manner of speaking. I have seen it measured." She waited for the laughter, got it, let it die away, and added: "I am quite serious."

"And was it done with a measuring rod?"

"Yes," she said. "Actually it was done with *two* measuring rods." She was completely in control. "Scholars placed rods of identical lengths at *Brackel* and at *T'Mingletep*. Who knows how far *T'Mingletep* is from here?"

"A long walk," said someone in back. But he didn't get the laughter he expected, and he sat down.

"That's right. Although it's on the western sea, it's almost directly south of *Brackel*. And the distance has been measured. North to south, it is precisely 346 *gruden*." Digger had seen the term *gruden* before, but until that moment he had no idea whether it was the length of someone's arm or a half dozen klicks.

"The shadows cast by the rods were measured through the course of the day. The shadows are longer in *T'Mingletep*. And the difference in lengths between *T'Mingletep* and here makes it possible to calculate the size of the world."

"It's too much for me," said Orky.

Whether 90,000 *gruden* seemed outrageously big or too small to the audience, Digger couldn't tell. But he knew the experiment, of course. It was similar to the one performed by Eratosthenes, who got very close to the size of the Earth in 240 B.C.

They were silent for a time, and she recognized a big Goompah in the front row. "Klabit," he said. "Macao, I don't know whether it's round or not. But if it really *is* round, wouldn't the water run off? Wouldn't the ships themselves fall off when they got far enough around the curve?"

Macao let them see the question had stopped her. "I don't know the answer to that, Klabit. But the ground between here and *T'Mingletep* is curved. That's established beyond doubt." She looked out over her audience. "So the truth is, nobody really knows why the water doesn't run off. Obviously, it doesn't happen, or there'd be no tide tonight." (Laughter.) "I admit I don't understand how the world can be round, but it seems that it *is*. I say, let's find out. Once and for all. Let's send the ships east over the ocean and watch to see from which direction they return."

Her audience had become restive. Macao left the stage and went out among them. "The mission will cost a great deal of money. The funds from this evening, after I've taken my expenses—"

"—of course—" said a voice on the far side.

"—of course. After that, I will contribute the proceeds to the effort. This is your opportunity to become part of the most significant (something) expedition ever attempted by our two cities.

"But they need something more than money. They need volunteers. Sailors." She paused and looked down at Telio. "It will be a dangerous voyage. Not something for the faint of heart. Not something for the unskilled."

"I fish for a living," said Telio.

"Just what they need. I'll send your name over."

The audience laughed. Someone commented that Telio was lucky to have gotten such an opportunity.

Macao was back on her stage. She held up her hands. "Velascus talks about the defect each of us has, implanted by Taris, to prevent our being perfect. For *you*—" she looked at one of the Goompahs off to her left—"it is perhaps too great an affection for money. And for Telio over there, it may be a (something) toward jealousy. For me, perhaps, it is that I have no sense of humor." (Laughter.) "But for each of us it is there. The *individual* defect. But there is another flaw that we all share, that we share as a community.

"You remember *Haster*?"

Yes. They all did.

"What's *Haster*?" asked Kellie.

"No idea."

"The colony failed within three years. As did the several attempts that preceded it. Why do you suppose that is? Why have so many efforts to move abroad been abandoned?"

There were several older children seated in the rear. One of them stood to be recognized. "It is wild country beyond the known lands," she said. "Who would want to live there?"

"Who indeed?" echoed Macao. "And I put it to you that herein lies our fatal defect. Our common flaw. The characteristic that deters us. We love our homeland too much."

WHEN THE LAST of the lights had gone out, and the cafés had emptied, Kellie and Digger wandered the lonely walkways that bordered the sea at the southern edge of the city. They were wet, and the Flickinger field produced by the e-suits was notoriously slippery underfoot, especially in such conditions. It didn't seem to matter what sort of shoes he wore. He turned it off, and gasped in the sudden rush of cold salt air.

Kellie heard his reaction and guessed what he had done. She followed his lead. "It's lovely out here," she said.

The sea was rough. It roared against the rocks and threw spray into the air. A sailing ship, squat and heavy, lay at anchor. Lights poured out of the after cabin, and Digger could see a figure moving about inside.

"Do the Goompahs have the compass?" asked Digger.

"Don't know."

"Does Lookout have a magnetic north?"

"Yes, Dig. About twelve degrees off the pole. Why? Does it matter?"

"If they don't have a compass, how will they navigate on that round-the-world jaunt they're talking about?"

"Sun by day, stars by night. Shouldn't be all that difficult. Except I don't know how they'll get past the eastern continent. They'll have the same problem Columbus did."

It was too dark to be able to make out where the horizon met the sky. Digger tried to visualize the sea east of Athens. He remembered a couple of big islands out there, and a few smaller chunks of land beyond. Then it was open ocean for several thousand kilometers.

He understood why the Goompahs had never crossed their oceans. How long had it taken before Leif Eriksson and the longboats made the run across the Atlantic? But it seemed odd that there'd been no serious effort to explore the continent on which they lived. It was true there were natural barriers, but they had sail, and they had easy access by water. They weren't in the classic Greek situation of being penned in an inland sea.

They wandered out onto a wooden pier, and Kellie's hand lay gently on his hip. It was a floating pier, and some of the planks were loose or missing. They kept going until they reached the far end, where they stood listening to the ocean. A few gulls were in the air. The universal creature. Any world that produced oceans and living things eventually produced gulls. Swamps gave you crocodiles. Forests always had wolves. Living worlds were exceedingly rare, but their creatures were remarkably alike. Which after all made sense. How many different ways are there to make a fish? The variations were almost always limited to details.

A lantern moved across the deck of the ship.

He liked this place. It felt a bit like an island lost in time. "You know, Kellie," he said, "I wish there were a way we could talk with her."

"With whom?"

"With Macao."

"Forget it," she said. "You'd scare the devil out of her."

LIBRARY ENTRY

The oddest thing about the entire evening was the image on the

map. Except that his skin color was a bit light, the guy on the winged
rhino looked like my uncle Frank.

—*Jenkins*, log
Captain's entry

chapter 26

MORE SURVEILLANCE DEVICES had arrived, and Kellie and Jack had spread them throughout the isthmus this time, instead of confining them to *Brackel*. *Saniusar*, the northernmost Goompah outpost, was the last of the cities to receive its allotment.

It occupied the shores of a bay and was surrounded by a ring of picturesque hills, which grew progressively higher until they ascended finally into towering mountains.

Beyond the mountains lay dense jungle, and beyond the jungle lay a broad desert, extending for thousands of kilometers, well north of the equator. Digger was beginning to understand why the Goompah world ended on the north at *Saniusar*.

"But they have ships," protested Kellie. "I can understand why they haven't crossed the seas. But running up and down the coast shouldn't have been a problem."

"Don't be so sure. How far did the Greeks go?"

"But they were hemmed in. Couldn't get beyond the Mediterranean."

They'd been wandering the streets of Goompah cities like the wind, unseen, irrelevant. He missed Jack, and he missed being able to sit down with friends, and he missed being able to party.

He had been relatively isolated before. But it had always been in some desolate spot, remote from everything, with maybe a couple of technicians who spent all their time talking about the local grade of sandstone, or the level of humidity at a given latitude. But here, with Kellie, he was surrounded by a vibrant community whose energy crackled through the cities every day and lit up the night, and he was cut off from it all.

He touched her luminous form, her arm, her shoulder. The mild vibration projected by the external surface of the e-suit was reassuring. She moved beneath his fingers and folded herself into him. Everything was accessible through the field except her lips, which were shielded behind the hard bubble that covered her face.

They were standing outside a double-domed building on the edge of the city, looking north toward a tangle of river and valley and granite. A few of the natives were wandering about, some working, some playing with young ones, some just walking. To the west, over a few hilltops, the sea was bright and cool.

"I love you, Kellie," he said.

Her body moved against him. She was laughing.

"What's funny?"

"At the moment," she said, "your choices are limited."

"I don't know." He switched his e-suit off. The smell of salt air swept in. Lovely stuff. "I saw some pretty good-looking females at the park yesterday."

The tingle blinked off with her suit. "I love you, too, Digby," she said.

"I wish I could see you."

"Maybe tonight, if you behave."

He found her lips, and they stood quietly for several moments, enjoying each other. "Kellie," he said, "I'd like very much if you would be my wife."

She stiffened, simultaneously pulling him forward and pushing him away.

He wondered if anyone else had ever proposed to an invisible woman.

"Digger," she said, "I'm honored."

That didn't sound good.

"I'm not sure it would work."

He switched off his goggles, and the spectral form vanished. Only those dark eyes remained. "You wouldn't have to quit," he said. "It wouldn't mean your career. We could work something out."

The wind off the sea was cold. "It's not that."

"What's the problem?" he asked.

Her eyes narrowed. He'd long since become accustomed to disembodied eyes, and had discovered that they did actually reflect mood and emotion. He'd always assumed that only happened in the context of a complete facial expression. "Digger, I'd like very much to marry you—"

"—But—?"

"I'm not interested in any short-term arrangement. I don't want to commit myself to you and discover that a few years from now everything's changed and we head our own ways."

He pulled her back into his arms. All resistance was gone, and he was surprised to notice her cheeks were damp. "You want me to sign an agreement that I'd renew?"

She thought it over. "No," she said. "I wouldn't ask that. Wouldn't do any good anyhow. I just—" She trembled. It seemed out of character. "In my family, we don't believe in doing things halfway. You commit, or you don't. If you commit, don't expect that if you change your mind in five years, I'm going to shake hands and say let's be friends."

He was holding her tight by then. And he wanted very much to see her, but there were too many Goompahs drifting around. "It would never happen, Kellie. I love you. I want you to be my wife. Forever. No time off. No letting the lease run out."

"You're sure?"

"Yes."

"And you'll feel the same way when we get home?"

"Of course." He pressed his lips against hers. "You're a hard sell."

"Yes I am. And if you don't mean any of this, the price'll be high."

ASIDE FROM DISTRIBUTING pickups, they'd also roamed through the cities recording engraved symbols, statuary, architecture, whatever seemed of interest. They'd found a museum in *Mandigol*, filled with artifacts excavated from beneath existing cities. So there were Goompah archeologists.

They'd found several academies, or colleges, the most extensive of which was located in *Kulnar*, the home of Macao. *Mirakap*, an island city that was actually part of *T'Mingletep*, hosted concerts almost nightly. They'd recorded several, some purely instrumental, others employing singers. The Goompahs, by the way, conceded nothing to humans in the range of their voices. On the *al-Jahani*, Collingdale and his people seemed to have a higher estimation of native music than did Digger and Kellie.

They watched sailboat races at *Hopgop*, on the northeastern shore, and track events at *Sakmarung*. In all these places, the café was king. Everyone retired at the end of the day to the assorted bistros and taverns, and the evenings slipped away in laughter and conversation.

Life was good on the isthmus. The land was fertile, the sea full of fish, and it didn't look as if anyone had to work very hard.

"They've been around as long as we have," Digger commented on one of the reports to the *al-Jahani*. "But technologically, they've gone nowhere. Does anybody have any kind of explanation at all?"

They didn't. There were a couple of people with Collingdale, Elizabeth Madden and Jason Holder, who thought that Goompahs simply weren't very smart. The fact that they could use tools and build cities, they argued, didn't mean they could manage an industrial revolution.

But if they hadn't progressed technologically, they were doing well politically. All the cities had representative governments, although the machinery was different from place to place. *Sakmarung* had a single executive, chosen by a parliamentary body from among its number. He (or she) served for two local years and could not under any circumstances reassume the post. The parliamentary body was elected by a free vote of the citizenry. Collingdale thought everyone was granted the franchise, but that question was still open.

Mandigol took the classical Spartan approach: It had two executives, with equal power, who apparently kept an eye on each other. *Brackel* elected a parliament and an executive council, not unlike the world government at home. There was no indication of political unrest, no inclination to make war, no poverty-stricken Goompahs in the streets.

On the whole, thought Digger, *they've done pretty well. Of course, it helps when you can pick your food off the trees on the way home.*

"Maybe it's the Toynbee idea," said Digger.

"Who's Toynbee?"

"Twentieth-century historian. He thought that, for a civilization to develop, the environment has to be right. It has to offer a challenge, but not so much of a challenge that it overwhelms everybody. That's why you get progress in China and Europe but not in Micronesia or Siberia."

But Goompahs were not humans. And who knew what rules applied? Yet the shows, the parks, the temples, the late nights on the town: The Goompahs *seemed* human in so many ways. *They were,* he thought, *what we might have chosen to be, if we could.*

But what was the secret?

They were capable of quarrels and scuffles. He'd seen a few. They had thieves. The locked doors at the libraries and other places that held objects of value demonstrated that. But their females thought nothing of walking the streets at night. And there were no armies.

"Their society's not perfect," said Kellie. "But they're getting a lot of it right."

"Could it be the DNA?" he asked.

"You mean a peace gene?" She shrugged. "I have no idea."

"I mean an *intelligence* gene. Technology or not, I'm beginning to wonder if they're smarter than we are."

Two statues stood atop the twin domes. They appeared to be representations of two of the deities they'd seen at the temple in *Brackel*: the elderly god, the one who'd had the scroll; and the young female with the musical instrument. "Mind and passion," suggested Kellie.

All the temples they'd seen—each city seemed to have one, and there'd been a few out in the countryside—were roofed, but were otherwise left open to the elements. It was always possible, at any time of day or night, to enter a temple.

A few visitors wandered among the columns that supported the twin domes. The gods seemed to have been assigned separate quarters there. They were seated or standing or, in a couple of cases, reclining on benches. The effect created was less distant and majestic than they'd encountered elsewhere. These were the gods at home, informal, casual, come on in and have a drink.

Along the walls, they were depicted helping children ford a river, calming a stormy sea, holding a torch high for travelers lost in a forest. That was Lykonda, her wings spread wide to keep the chill of the night from her charges. From the scrolls, they knew a little about her. She was described as the defender of the celestial realm, although they did not know why she held that exalted title. She was the guardian of knowledge, champion of the weak, protector of the traveler. Mistreat a stranger and answer to Lykonda. Elsewhere they found the laughing god, who was apparently in the middle of delivering a punch line to a group of convulsed Goompahs.

"When a god tells a joke," whispered Kellie, "who's not going to laugh?"

ANOTHER DEITY, WHOSE name they did not know, wielded a sword.

"*Look!*" Kellie stopped in front of the frieze. He wore a war helmet, held a staff with a fluttering pennant in one hand, and raised his weapon in the other. He looked enraged, with demonic creatures swarming toward him. The attackers were armed with spears and cudgels. Brute weapons.

Digger caught his breath.

The demonic creatures—

—Looked reasonably human. Like the figure on the winged rhino.

"Their noses are a little long," said Kellie, speaking into a sudden silence.

As were their limbs. And they had claws rather than fingernails. Their hair was straggly, trailing down their backs. Their expressions breathed malevolence and treachery. They were male and female, and they very much resembled the demons one found in fifteenth-century art.

"We been here before?" asked Digger.

A group of birds scattered out of a tree, regrouped, and fluttered off to the west.

"Well," said Kellie, "I guess we know why they went screaming into the night when you showed up."

THE LAND BEYOND the temple rose through broken country toward the *Skatbrones*, the Goompah name, not for a single range, but for the vast mountainous north. A few homes dotted the lower slopes, and there were a couple of orchards. The lander had been left on a remote crag.

Kellie summoned it, and they boarded it from the temple grounds, taking a chance. But she kept the starboard side toward the sea so that no one could see the airlock open.

They climbed in and closed the hatch. Kellie took them up and headed back to the crag. Digger shut his systems down, and when they landed he happily grabbed a hot shower, changed clothes, and collapsed into his chair. After Kellie had her turn in the washroom, Bill served dinner. To her delight, Digger produced candles and a bottle of red wine from the *Jenkins's* store. "Whatever made me think," she said, "that you weren't very romantic?"

"I majored in romance," he said. "It's why women have chased me so persistently all these years."

"I understand completely. Pour the wine."

He'd have preferred champagne, but their small store was long since gone. And he'd have liked something a bit more elegant for the occasion than meat loaf, but the lander had its limits. He filled their glasses, lit the candles, proposed a toast to his lovely fiancée. They closed the viewports so that no light would leak out, and enjoyed an evening that Digger knew he would remember forever.

THE FOLLOWING NIGHT, they flew over the city.

Digger loved riding in an invisible aircraft. They kept the lights doused inside, and when he looked out, there were no stubby wings and no hull. It reminded him of his early boyhood, when he'd ridden the glide trains from Philadelphia to Wildwood, New Jersey. They'd crossed the Delaware River en route, on a bridge whose span and girders and trusses weren't visible from inside the train. Sitting in his seat with his parents across from him, Digger (who had been *Digby* then, and no nonsense about it) had loved to look out at the sky and the river, and pretend the car wasn't there, pretend he was an eagle. It had been a long time, and he hadn't thought about those rides, those *flights*, for thirty years.

The city lights were dim by human standards. Oil lamps here and there. Candles. A couple of open fires. Yet they were warm and inviting, illuminating a place of magic. A place he'd want to come back to one day, when the crisis was over.

Romeo and Juliet was playing that night, would play for the next three evenings. The actual title was *Baranka*, and it was indeed a tale of lovers from feuding families. Baranka was the girl's father, portrayed as an essentially decent but strong-willed character who cannot get past his own anger at his perceived enemies.

Reading it in a language he hadn't begun to master, Digger couldn't make a judgment as to its quality, but he was struck by the degree to which it dealt with familiar issues. When he'd mentioned it to Kellie, she'd commented that they'd been talking about a sense of humor as a universal among intelligent creatures, and she suggested the most characteristic universal could turn out to be programmed stupidity.

He wondered whether a translation might not play one day in New York and Berlin.

"How do you feel?" she asked, breaking a long silence.

"Good." He thought she was referring to their new status.

"Really?" She seemed surprised.

"What are we talking about, Kel?"

She grinned. "How's it feel to be the enemy of the gods?"

"Oh." He produced an image of the frieze. The resemblance to humans was uncanny. "Not so good, actually." He raised his voice a notch. "If you're listening out there, whatever I did, I didn't mean it."

Kellie's eyes glowed. "You think there are human-style critters around here somewhere?" she asked.

He thought about it. "Don't know."

"It occurs to me," she said, "that if there are, the cloud could be a godsend for them."

"In what way?"

"If it were to wipe out the Goompahs, it might clear the boards for the second wave."

"The monkeys."

"Yes. Maybe."

"From the look of things," he said, "I don't think it would be an improvement."

They landed and strolled among the crowds, and even went into a Goompah café, turned off the e-suits, and sang with the customers. It was great fun, and Digger yearned to shut down the lightbender as well and tell them he and Kellie were there and they liked a good time as much as anybody. Despite the isolation, they made it a special evening. At the end, with the omega back in the sky, and the lights going out, they returned to the lander and flew back to the crag. It overlooked the temple, a jagged piece of rock with sheer walls dropping away on all sides. And it was glorious in the light of the big moon. Farther north, the hills and ridges gave way to dark forest. The city was quiet, little more than a few smoldering lights in the night.

They got out of the lander. There was a stiff wind out of the west, and Bill was predicting rain sometime during the early-morning hours. But when you're tucked safely inside a Flickinger field it doesn't matter much. They were still out there when the storm came. It was an exhilarating feeling, to be caught up in the wind and the rain, with the temple below and

Kellie holding tight. But when the first lightning flickered across the sky they decided the situation called for prudence. They lingered momentarily in each other's arms, and Digger turned off her field. Before she could react she was drenched.

She pushed him away and ran for the lander.

He followed happily, using his remote to switch on the navigation lights. Her clothes had become transparent.

IT WAS STILL dark when he came fully awake. He listened and heard a distant sound. Felt it in the lander.

Voices.

Chanting.

Kellie was asleep beside him. He lifted himself carefully out of the blankets, but couldn't see anything from inside. He pulled on his e-suit and went out into the night. It was coming from the temple grounds.

He walked to the edge of the crag and looked down. There were torches and movement. And the chant.

But it was impossible to see what was happening.

His experience with the Goompahs told him that they weren't big early-morning risers.

He went back inside and woke Kellie.

THERE WAS A pair of Goompahs wearing black hoods and robes and carrying torches, led by another in white. It immediately felt like *déjà vu*, here they come again, where's the javelin? And sure enough, there it was, hauled along by a bearer.

The crowd had grown. Someone was playing a set of pipes, and the marchers were chanting, although Digger could catch only an occasional word. *"Darkness." "Righteousness." "Your glory." "Help."*

Help.

Help us put a new roof on the temple?

Help us in our hour of need?

They were crowded together. Digger and Kellie kept a cautious distance.

The three robed figures moved along one of the walkways, staying in step, not military precision, but practiced nevertheless. The crowd fell in behind. He estimated it at several hundred, and they were joining in the chant and becoming more enthusiastic.

The rain had cleared off, and the stars were bright and hard.

The procession moved through a patch of woods and issued finally onto a beach. When Digger got there, well in the rear, the three leaders had thrown off their sandals and advanced a few paces into the surf. They spread out into a semicircle. The one in white looked older than the others, and he wore a wide-brimmed white hat.

"*Creature of—*"

The onlookers had gone quiet. They all stayed back out of the water.

"*—the night—*"

Digger suddenly realized he hadn't brought a pickup. He had no way of recording this.

"*—Depart—*"

They got as close as they could, moving down into the wet sand, leaving footprints. But it was too dark for anyone to notice.

The marchers were looking out over the sea—

No, in fact they were looking *up*. At the black patch, which was sinking toward the northwestern horizon.

"*—Hour of need—*"

A large wave rolled in, and the one in the white robe floated over the top of it.

He raised his arms and the night fell silent. He stood several moments, and it seemed to Digger he was hesitating. Then he went a step or two farther out. The bearer appeared alongside him and offered the javelin. He took it and held it aloft. His lips moved. Trembled.

More Goompahs were arriving at every moment, some coming from the temple area, others arriving from the far end of the beach. But they were all silent.

He aimed the javelin in the direction of the omega, jabbed at it a few times, and handed the weapon off to one of the others. And as Digger watched in growing horror, he strode out into the waves, his robes floating, until at last *he* was floating. Then he was swimming, struggling to move forward against the tide. The sea tried to push him back, but he kept going and at last he got beyond the breaking waves.

He continued swimming for several minutes.

And he disappeared.

The one who had received the javelin stripped off his outer garment to reveal a white hood and robe. He raised the weapon over his head, and called out to Taris, the defender of the world.

"We beg you accept our (something). And protect us from *T'Klot*." The hole. The omega. "Malio takes our plea to your divine presence. Hear him, we beg you, and extend your hand in this our time of need."

LIBRARY ENTRY

Religion is like having children, or taking medicine, or eating, or any of a thousand other perfectly rational human activities: Taken in small doses, it has much to recommend it. One need only avoid going overboard.

—Gregory MacAllister,
"Slippery Slope,"
Editor-at-Large, 2227

chapter 27

SIX MONTHS AND three days out. Collingdale had expected his people would be climbing the walls by then. But they were doing okay. It was true that some of the early enthusiasm had worn thin, but that might have been because there was less to be gleaned from the stream of data coming in from the *Jenkins*. By and large, they had recovered an extensive vocabulary, and they understood the syntax. From there on, mastering the language would be largely a matter of pronunciation and nuance.

Once they'd gotten on top of things, Judy had cut back on the Goompah-only requirement. They'd derived some serious benefits from the restriction, but it had lost its charm quickly and, despite the early compromises, it had begun to strain relations between the *Shironi Kulp* and the other passengers. In a nonstop voyage of record-breaking duration, it just wasn't a good idea. So the linguists continued to limit themselves to Goompah in the workshop, but they had long ago become free to use whatever language they liked, with the provision that they were to regard Goompah as their native tongue, and to resort to it as the language of choice.

It had worked well.

The brief tensions that had appeared subsided, the Goompah jokes lost their edge, and Collingdale noted a decrease in the resentment that *everyone* on board had developed toward him and Judy.

Well. There you were. But, as he'd explained to Alex, and to several others, Judy had had a job to do, and the language policy had been the best way of getting it done.

They'd extracted a series of Goompah aphorisms from the library material, which were posted on a bulkhead in the workroom. *Deal justly with your neighbor.*

Assist the weak.

Be kind to all.

Everyone was invited to add to the collection, and Collingdale stopped to scribble one that he'd come across in a treatise of the teachings of Omar

Koom. (That first name brought a smile. Were there also Goompahs somewhere named Frank? Or Harriet?)

The principle that he'd added to the collection: Accept no claim without
evidence.

He liked that. Where's the proof? I'm from Missouri.

How peaceful would the history of his own world have been if that idea
were universally accepted? Yet these were the same creatures who exor-
cised demons and had allowed one of their own to walk into the sea in an
effort to head off the cloud. It hadn't taken much analysis to confirm that
was what it had been about, the idiot ceremony that Digger had watched.

Well, humans weren't very consistent either.

He stood a few moments studying the list. Enjoy your life because it is
not forever. Whatever gives pleasure without injuring another is to be
sought, but let no pleasure become so ingrained that it overcomes reason.
Beware addictions; the essence of the good life is a free exercise of the will,
directed by reason.

Beware addictions.

Judy was talking about eventual publication. *Goompah Wit and Wisdom.*
Might be a best-seller one day.

He admired their utilitarian approach to life. Beauty equated to a kind of
simplicity. Suiting the form to the purpose. No frills. They'd never have
approved of Renaissance cathedrals or Main Line mansions. Keep a clear
eye on what is important and do not get caught up in the frivolous.

It was, he thought, mundane stuff. But it had a ringing clarity and lacked
the Puritanical sense of guilt that this sort of code would have had back
home. If you get something wrong, fix it and move on. Do not weep for
that which is beyond your control.

*Accept responsibility. Bring no one into the world whom you are not prepared to
love and nourish.*

He wondered how a society that seemed to put no limits on sex managed
that?

ONE OF THE linguists had become romantically involved with Ed Paxton, a
mathematician, and the captain had performed the wedding. Collingdale
had always found mathematicians dull, methodical, and unimaginative.
Why anybody would marry one, he could not understand. He'd wondered
why evolutionary forces hadn't wiped the breed out.

Paxton had seemed typical of the tribe, but he had conquered the heart
of Marilyn McGee, an attractive blonde who had shown a penchant for
winning the shipwide chess tournaments.

Another wedding was in the works, this time between two of the linguists. There was talk of doing a Goompah ceremony. Digger had captured a couple of isthmus weddings for the record, so they had models. And Judy was already designing a costume for the captain. Everybody involved would need an appropriately styled hat, and the only projected change would be a substitution of the Judeo/Christian God for Taris, Zonia, and Holen.

They'd also done a few Goompah sing-alongs. Those had become popular with everyone. And they'd staged two native dramas.

Judy had collected eight Goompah dramas from the scrolls, and two more that Digger had recorded. Two were tragedies in the classic sense; the others were like something out of the Baines Brothers, with lots of slapstick, characters running into walls, getting caught *en flagrante*, and constantly falling down.

The shows frequently involved the audience. In one, a staged brawl spilled over into the front rows, where the patrons got caught up in the battle. Characters chased each other through the aisles. One comedy was apparently interrupted midway when bandits, fleeing from authorities, raced down a center aisle with bags of coins. One of the bandits tossed his loot to a patron, who was then set on and dragged off by the authorities. The audience loved it, and the human observers needed time to recognize that it was all rehearsed.

Another show stationed a medical unit at the rear of the theater. Periodically, when someone fell down onstage, or walked into a chair, the actors called out "*Gwalla timbo,*" which translated roughly to *medical team*. The *gwalla timbo* would then gallop forward, bearing stretchers and splints, collect the injured party, plunk him unceremoniously onto the stretcher, and charge back out, usually dropping the patient en route. It was hilarious.

He would have liked to spend an evening in a Goompah theater with Mary.

THEY ALSO WATCHED three funerals. The dead were wrapped in sheets and interred in the ground in the presence of family and friends. The mourners did not give in to weeping or other signs of hysteria, although several had to be helped away, and two collapsed altogether.

Collingdale and the linguists listened closely to the ceremonies. The blessings of the gods were invoked in two, and religious references did not show up at all in the third. There was no talk at any of them of a hereafter or suggestions that the deceased had gone to a better world, leading the humans to suspect that the Goompahs did not believe in an afterlife. He suggested to Judy that she advise her people not to mention the fact in personal messages home. "No point stirring up the missionary society," he said.

They also were able to interpret the signs that Jack and Digger had seen on the schoolroom wall on their first visit. It had been somewhat difficult because the characters were stylized. But they read THINK FOR YOURSELF and SHOW ME THE EVIDENCE.

They had a record of one class in which the students were learning basic arithmetic. They were operating off a base twelve. Which meant that 14 + 15 = 29, but there are actually 33 items in the result. Ed explained it to him, but it gave Collingdale a headache, and he simply nodded yes when asked if he understood. It didn't really matter anyhow.

He was impressed by the fact that widespread literacy seemed to exist. That was no small accomplishment when one considered the paucity of reading materials.

There was a priest class, whose actions Digger had recorded on several occasions.

Think for yourself.

There was no visual record of the sacrifice made at *Saniusar.* Digger had said there were several hundred locals in attendance. Pretty sparse crowd when you think of it, in a town with a population they'd estimated at around thirty thousand.

That was 1 percent for a service intended to invoke salvation for the city. "It tells me," Frank Bergen said, "that these critters don't take their religious obligations very seriously."

THE ONE ASPECT of life on Lookout that Collingdale found unsettling was the open sexuality. That struck him as stranger even than the cleric who had gone into the ocean. Scheduled orgies could be found most nights in most cities. With signs inviting participants to pop by. The Goompahs no longer looked like the happy innocents of the early days.

Hutch had also been surprised and had told him she would have liked to bury it for the time being, but the news had already gotten out. A number of politicians and religious leaders had expressed their shock. If you could do orgies at city hall, what kind of society were you running? No wonder they didn't have time to conduct wars.

The general public, Hutch thought, seemed to be taking it in stride.

He was still in the workroom looking at the Goompah aphorisms when Bill broke in. *"Incoming for you, David,"* he said. *"From the* Hawksbill.*"*

Julie Carson was about an hour and a half away via hyperlight transmission.

One of the screens lit up with the *Hawksbill* seal, then Julie appeared. *"Dave,"* she said, *"I wanted to say thanks for the material on the Goompahs. We're getting an education. Whit, by the way, is trying to learn the language, but I don't think he's having much luck."*

Collingdale felt a sudden bump and heard the steady thrum of power in the bulkhead change tones. It grew louder. And became erratic.

"He thinks they're more advanced than we are." Julie smiled. At least he thought she had. Her image disintegrated, came back, and began to roll over. *"He says they're less violent and less hung up about sex. I've watched them pop one another in the street, and they don't seem less violent to me. They just look funnier when they fall down."*

The screen went blank. The captain's voice broke in: *"Everybody please get to a harness. We'll be making a jump in less than one minute. I say again . . . "*

Collingdale's heart sank. They were still ten weeks from Lookout.

ARCHIVE

We now know that the creatures the media have been so blithely referring to as *Goompahs*, with all the innocence and unsophistication that term implies, in fact worship pagan gods, practice an equivalent of human sacrifice, and engage in unrestrained sex. Margaret, this is shocking behavior, utterly beyond belief. It demonstrates the absolute depravity of the Nonintervention Protocol. Do these unfortunate creatures possess souls? Of course they do, or they wouldn't be seeking their Creator. But they're being misled, and they need to be shown the truth. I urge everyone who's out there watching today to get in touch with their congressman, to write to the Council, to demand that the Protocol be declared null and void.

When you think about it, Margaret, it's already too late for a lot of them. A disaster of major proportions is about to overtake them, and large numbers of them are going to their judgment utterly unprepared. We have an obligation to act, and it seems to me if we fail to do so, we will share their guilt.

—Rev. George Christopher,
The Tabernacle Hour

chapter 28

THEY WERE OUT under the stars again.

"No chance?" he asked Alexandra, pleading with her, *demanding* that she come up with *something*.

"I'm sorry, David," she said. "It's *kaput*."

They were moving at 20,000 kph. Crawling. "How about if we just try it? Just make the jump back? See what happens."

Alexandra was about average size, came up maybe to Collingdale's shoulder. She lacked the presence of some of the other female captains he'd known, did not have the knack of putting iron into her voice when she needed to, did not have Priscilla Hutchins's blue gaze that warned you to back off. Nevertheless she said no, and he understood that she would not risk the ship.

She was blond, with good features, not beautiful, but the kind of woman you knew you could trust if you were in trouble. Under normal circumstances she was congenial, easygoing, flexible. "Overriding," she said, "would pose a severe risk to the ship and the passengers, and we will not do it."

There wasn't much jiggle room that he could see. He argued for a couple of minutes before reluctantly conceding. "I'd better let Julie know."

"I've already sent a message to the *Hawksbill*. They should be getting it in about—" she checked the time, "an hour."

"How about Hutch?"

"I thought you'd want to do that."

Yes. The crash-and-burn transmission.

First he needed to inform the passengers. He did it from the bridge, telling them what they'd undoubtedly already guessed, that they were stranded, that help would be coming, but that all possibility of moving on to Lookout was gone. "I'm sorry," he said. "We took our chances, and it looks as if we lost." He paused and shrugged helplessly. "I'm not sure yet how long we'll be here. Broadside has been notified. They'll send over a relief mission, but the captain tells me it's going to take a few weeks to get to us, at best. So everybody make themselves comfortable.

"I should add, by the way, that there's no danger."

He sent the bad news to Hutch from his quarters, keeping it short, nothing but the facts. Engine burnout. Going nowhere. We've let Broadside know. Everybody's safe. We have plenty of air and food. He tried to sound upbeat, knowing the news would hit her hard. There was nothing she could do, of course. She was too far. There'd be no rabbits out of the hat this time, like the ones at Deepsix and on the *chindi*.

The next message went to the *Jenkins*. "Digger, we won't be coming. Jump engines blown. I'm going to try to arrange transportation for myself on the *Hawksbill*. But you better assume everything's up to you. You need to figure out a way to get the Goompahs to evacuate the cities prior to the hit."

Then he considered what he wanted to tell Julie. He started by calling Alexandra, who was back on the bridge. "If we ask them to come here, to us, do they lose enough time that we endanger their mission?"

Alex looked tired. *"Hard to say, Dave. If they get lucky and find us right away, it shouldn't be a problem. But the jumps are imprecise. You know that as well as I do. And especially under these conditions."*

"What conditions do you mean?"

"They're already in hyperspace. They're going to have to jump out, figure out where they are, set a new course, and come get us."

Damn. He looked out his portal at the stars. He could see the Tyrolean Cloud that, according to Melinda Park, was a hundred light-years across, filled with burning gas and young stars. At their present speed, the *al-Jahani* would need five million years just to go from one end of the cloud to the other. "Thanks, Alex," he said.

He switched over to the AI. "Bill, message for the *Hawksbill*."

"Ready to record, David."

The *Hawksbill* was a cargo hauler with a total passenger capacity of two. They already had two. They'd need Marge, so Whitlock would have to come aboard the *al-Jahani*, trade places with Collingdale.

How the hell could he say that? Julie, it looks as if the *al-Jahani* is out of action. I need you to pick me up. I know there's a space problem, but we don't really need the poet.

No, best not insult Whitlock. Julie seemed to like him.

He wrote his ideas down, made a few adjustments, activated the system, and read it to her, trying to look spontaneous. Then he told Bill to send it.

Next he tracked down Judy. "Let's get everybody together," he said. "We need to talk."

The mood on the ship was bleak. The frustration was fed not only by the perceived importance of the mission, but by the depth of individual commitment. These were people who'd invested a year and a half of their lives. His group of linguists, his *Goompahs*, had spent seven months working to acquire the language, had done so, had actually believed they were going to go into the *Intigo* and rescue tens of thousands of the natives. The others, the senior personnel, the Upper Strata, were watching an unparalleled opportunity, a chance to observe a functioning alien civilization, go south.

"What are you going to tell them?"

Before he could answer, his link vibrated against his wrist. "Collingdale," he said.

"*Dave.*" Alexandra's voice. "*I've got a delegation of your people up here.*"

He looked at Judy. "You know about this?"

She shook her head. "No."

The bridge was off-limits except to a few specified persons, or by invitation. It was supposed to be the one place in the ship to which the captain could retreat from social obligations. When Collingdale and Judy got there, all eleven of their linguists were either crowded inside or standing around the open door.

Harry Chin tried to take Judy aside.

"After we clear the bridge," she snapped.

But Harry showed no inclination to be put off. "Listen, we've got too much invested in this to just sit here."

Collingdale had never been a good disciplinarian. In fact he had relatively little experience with difficult cases. The people he'd led on past missions had always been mature professionals. Tell them what you needed and they produced. They might question authority on occasion, but the tone was subtle. *This* felt like mutiny.

But Judy never hesitated. "Listen," she said, raising her voice so they could all hear. "The decision's been made. Everyone go back to the workroom. We'll talk there."

Mike Metzger had been standing beside Harry, lending support. He was tall and reedy, usually the epitome of courtesy. A muscle in his neck was twitching, and his expression was a mixture of anger, regret, nervousness. He turned and looked at David. "Can't you do something?" he asked.

It wasn't clear whether he was talking about remaining stalled in the middle of nowhere, or returning to the workroom. But he was close to tears.

Terry MacAndrew put an arm around his shoulders to calm him. "Judy," Terry said, lapsing into the Scottish burr that David had only heard previously when Terry drank too much, "we've talked it over. We're all willing to take the chance. And we know *you* are."

"You've all agreed to this."

"Right. We say we should move ahead. Take our chances."

"Really."

"The stakes are too high just to sit here."

" 'The stakes are too high'? You've been reading too many novels."

Terry glanced back at Alex, who was out of her seat, standing by one of the navigation panels, looking bored and annoyed. "We're too close to quit now. Bill thinks we'd be okay if we tried it." He turned toward Alex. "Isn't that right, Captain?"

She dismissed him and spoke to Collingdale. "As I told you earlier, David, if we go back in and the system breaks down, which it is threatening to do, we'll stay in there." She looked around at the others. "Permanently. That's not going to happen to my ship. Or to my passengers. Bill has nothing to say about it." Her eyes came back to Collingdale. "Please get your people off my bridge."

THE REPLY FROM the *Hawksbill* arrived shortly after midnight. Julie's message was simple and direct: *"On our way. We can make room for one more."*

ARCHIVE

Alex, sorry to hear about the problem. I'm sending the *Vignon*. They'll do a temporary fix to get you running again. But everybody, including you, will be evacuated to the *Vignon* before attempting transit. Let Bill bring it in.

Good luck. Frank.

—Broadside transmission
September 18

PART FOUR

chimneys

chapter 29

THEY WERE SITTING on the docks watching the Goompahs get ready to launch their round-the-world mission. Three ships stood in the harbor, flags flying, masts filled with bunting. A band was banging away. The sailors were saying good-bye, it seemed, to the entire population of the *Intigo*. Small boats waited alongside the piers to ferry them out to the ships. Bouquets were being tossed, and on at least two occasions celebrants fell off the piers and had to be rescued. Various dignitaries, including Macao, were making speeches. In the midst of all this a message came in from Dave Collingdale.

" . . . *You better assume everything's up to you. You need to figure out a way to get the Goompahs to evacuate the cities prior to the hit."*

Up to me? Digger listened to a more detailed report from Alex to Kellie, describing how the *al-Jahani* was stranded in the middle of nowhere, of how they were safe and not to worry, but that they wouldn't be going anywhere for a while.

"Well," said Digger, "at least they're okay."

"Dig," she said, "what are we going to do?"

Somehow or other, Digger had half expected something like this would happen. Hutch had warned him, and he remembered the old line that anything that can go wrong will go wrong. It had been on his mind for weeks, a dark possibility that he kept trying to push away. But the sad reality was that his options were limited.

"We can't work miracles," she said. "And when they have a few minutes to think about it, they'll realize that."

Digger watched something splashing out in the harbor.

"We should ask for specific instructions, Dig. Don't let him lay this on your back."

"The *Hawksbill* is still coming," he said.

"Yes."

"Maybe they can decoy it. If they can do that, there's no problem." He listened to the murmur of the sea. The band was starting up again, and more flowers were flung into the air.

Kellie's silhouette was seated a couple of meters higher up on a grassy slope. They were well out of the way of the crowds. "I'm sorry, Digger," she said.

The night before, they'd listened to Goompahs talking about *T'Klot*. The hole in the sky.

"There's a rational explanation," some were saying. And others, that it was the work of *zhokas*. Devils.

"I don't like it."

"I don't care as long as it stays in the sky."

"They were saying down at Korva's that the priests think it's coming here. That the gods are angry."

"Is that possible?"

"I don't know. Not too long ago I'd have thought a hole in the sky couldn't happen."

"I wonder whether it's not because of all the immorality."

"What immorality?"

"Well, you know, children don't have much respect for their elders anymore. And a lot of people say there are no gods."

"Are there gods?"

"I'm beginning to think not."

The omega was located in a constellation the Goompahs called *T'Gayla*, the Reaver. It consisted of an arc of six stars that they thought looked like a scythe.

SEVERAL OF THE departing sailors broke away from the crowd, wobbled out onto the pier, and climbed into the boats that would take them to the waiting ships. There was much waving of colored filigrees and throwing of seeds, not unlike the custom of tossing rice at newlyweds. The band picked it up a notch.

Digger felt sorry for them. Like Columbus, they were attempting an impossible journey. Columbus had thought the planet considerably smaller than it actually was. Isabella's retainers knew better, and that was the reason they'd resisted underwriting the voyage. Had North America not been there, the great mariner would probably have disappeared somewhere at sea and become a different kind of legend.

The Goompahs had the dimensions down, even if many of their well-wishers refused to believe the world was round. But once again there was a major continent blocking the way. Two, in fact. There *was* an east–west passage through each, long chains of rivers and lakes, but finding their way would be an impossible task for the voyagers.

He watched, suspecting none of the sailors would see home again. His old friend Telio was among them, with his smashed left ear and his lopsided smile. He was hefting a bag made of animal skins, ready to go on his great adventure.

By midafternoon the sailors were all aboard. The ships were the *Hasker*, the *Regunto*, and the *Benventa*. The *Charger*, the *Spirit*, and the *Courageous*. They hoisted anchor, put up sail, and, accompanied by cheers and drums, started toward the mouth of the harbor. There was a ridge several hundred meters north of the piers, and another crowd had gathered there, where they could get a better view as the ships stood out to sea.

"We shouldn't be doing this," said Digger.

"Letting them go?" asked Kellie.

He nodded. "They're going to die out there."

She looked at him a long moment. "It's what noninterference means."

"You know, we have authorization to intervene."

"Not for something like this. Listen, Dig, you want to jump in and figure out a way to turn them around, I'm with you. But I think they should be left to find their own way. Build their own legends. One day this'll be part of their history. Something they can be proud of. They don't need us involved in it."

He gazed sadly after them. "The day will come when the crews on the ships will be praying for someone to step in."

She had gotten closer to him, and her hand rubbed his shoulder. "This is why I love you, Dig. But it's not our call. Even if it was, what would you do? Give them a map of their world? Maybe throw in the compass? Where do you stop?"

Digger had no idea. He wondered what human history would have been like had someone arrived to shut down, say, the Persian Wars. Handed us a printing press and some lenses and spiked the gunpowder. Would we really be worse off? There was no definitive answer, but he knew that, in this time, at this moment, he wanted to reach out to the three ships, now rounding the spit of land at the north end of the harbor.

They were silent for a time. The wind blew across them. The crowd began to break up. "Look at it this way," she said. "As the situation is right now, the ships probably have a better chance of surviving than the people left behind. They'll be well away when the cloud gets here."

"That's a consolation."

"Well, what do you want me to say?"

"I still think we should warn them," said Digger.

"God's position."

"How do you mean?"

"You can intervene for a short-term benefit. But it might not be advantageous over the long haul."

"We're not going to get metaphysical, are we?"

She lay back on the soil, and her irises stared up at the sky.

Digger got to his feet and looked toward the city, spread out across a range of hills behind them. And at the mountains beyond. "I think we have to make another attempt to talk to them."

He heard her sigh. "Instead of just waylaying somebody on the road," she said, "how about we select a likely candidate this time?"

"Macao," he said.

She nodded.

THEY HAD LOST her in the crowd. How did you go about finding someone in a nontech city? You couldn't look in the directory, and there was no way to ask without scaring the citizens half to death.

They tried scouting the lecture circuit. But they found no advertising, no placards, nothing that suggested Macao was on the schedule.

"We don't even know for certain that she lives here," grumbled Digger. "She might just have been here for the launch."

"No," said Kellie. "In *Brackel,* she was listed as Macao of *Kulnar.* This is her home."

"Or maybe where she was born. But okay. Let's assume you're right. How do we find her?"

"There has to be a way to communicate with people. To pass messages around."

Digger thought about it. How did you get a message to Cicero? You wrote it out on a piece of parchment and sent it by messenger, right? But where could they get a messenger?

They called it a night and took the lander out to Utopia, where they were safely alone.

In the morning, as they were getting ready to return to *Kulnar,* he asked Kellie whether he could have the silver chain she wore as a necklace.

"May I ask why?"

"I want to give it to another woman."

She canted her head and regarded him with a combination of amusement and suspicion. "The nearest other woman is a long walk, Digger."

"I'm serious," he said. "It's important. And when we get home, I'll replace it."

"It has sentimental value."

"Kellie, it would really help. And maybe we can figure out a way to get it back."

"I'm sure," she said.

On the way into the city, he retrieved one of the pickups and attached it to the chain. "How's it look?"

"Like a pickup on a chain."

Actually, he thought it looked pretty good. If you didn't look too closely, the pickup might have been a polished, dark, disk-shaped jewel. It was the way a Goompah would see it.

They found the local equivalent of a stationery store. It carried ink, quill-style pens, parchment of various thicknesses, and document cylinders. Because the weather had gotten cool, a fire had been built in a small metal grate in the middle of the floor. Its smoke drifted out through an opening in the roof. It wasn't Segal's, but it was adequate to their needs.

"So where do we get a messenger?" asked Kellie.

"Macao's an entertainer," he said. "They should know her at the public halls." He disliked stealing merchandise, but he put the store in his mental file beside the *Brackel* Library, for future recompense. He lifted two cylinders, a pen, a pot of ink, and some paper that could be rolled and placed inside. Then they went next door to a shop that sold carpets, and made off with some coins.

The public buildings that hosted *sloshen*, shows, and other public events, were lightly occupied at that time of day. They picked one and looked in. Except for a couple of workers wiping down the walls, it seemed empty.

They found a room with a table, closed the door, and sat down to write to Macao.

The cylinders, which were made of bronze, were about a third of a meter long. They were painted black with white caps at either end. A tree branch with leaves for decoration on one, birds in flight on the other. What would one of these be worth at home?

"What do we want to say?" asked Digger. "Keep in mind that I can't write the language very well."

"I don't see why we should write anything," said Kellie. "All we want to do is find out where she lives."

Sounded reasonable to him. He twisted the caps and opened both cylinders, but stopped to wonder whether the messenger might look inside. "Better put something in there," he said. He sat down at the table, pulled one of the sheets toward him, and opened his ink pot. *Challa, Macao,* he wrote. And, continuing in Goompah: *We've enjoyed your work.* He signed it *Kellie* and *Digger.*

She smiled and shook her head. "First written interstellar communication turns out to be a piece of fan mail."

He inserted the message, twisted the cylinder shut, put the caps on, and reached for a second sheet. *Please deliver to Macao Carista*, he wrote.

They found an inner office occupied by a Goompah who seemed to have some authority. He was installed behind a table, talking earnestly to an aide, describing how he wanted the auditorium set up for that evening's performance. They were staging a show titled *Wamba*, which rang no bells for Digger.

Shutters were closed against the cool air. A pile of rugs was pushed against one wall, and a fire burned cheerfully in a stove. A pipe took the smoke out of the building.

While the Goompahs were engaged in their conversation, Digger moved to the side of the table, keeping the cylinder inside his vest, where it remained invisible.

"Up there, Grogan," said the Goompah behind the desk.

Grogan? Another peculiar name for a native. Kellie snickered. The sound was loud enough to escape the damping effect of the suit and attract the attention of the Goompahs. Puzzled, they looked around while she held one hand over her mouth, trying to suppress a further onset. *Grogan*. Digger, watching her, felt a convulsion of his own coming on. He fought it down and took advantage of the distraction to slip the tube onto the table, along with three of the coins he'd taken. With luck, it would look like a piece of outgoing mail.

"It must have been the fire," said Grogan.

The one behind the table scratched his right ear. "Sounded like a *chakul*," he said.

That brought a second round of snorts and giggles from the corridor, where Kellie had retreated. Digger barely made it out of the office himself before exploding with laughter. They hurried through the nearest doorway into the street, and let go. A few passersby looked curiously in their direction.

"This being invisible," said Digger, when he could calm down, "isn't as easy as it's supposed to be."

WITH JACK'S DEATH, they'd shed the policy of not splitting up. Their increasing familiarity with the cities of the *Intigo* might have caused them to become careless, but Kellie had pointed out that they had commlinks, that if either of them got into trouble, help was always nearby.

So they divided forces. Digger would stay near the office, watching to see what happened to the message they'd left, while Kellie would post another one at a second likely location. Eventually, they hoped, one or the other would get delivered.

But the prospect of hanging around the nearly empty building all day did nothing for his state of mind.

When she'd left, and he'd gone back inside, he saw that the coins had vanished and the message had been moved to the edge of the table. That was encouraging. But the cylinder remained untouched through the balance of the morning, and he began to wonder whether he should have marked it URGENT.

There were several other visitors, including a female who exchanged sexual signals with the office occupant and then, to Digger's horror, closed the door and proceeded to engage him in a sexual liaison. All this occurred despite the fact there were others immediately outside who could not possibly have misunderstood what was happening.

Digger, unhappily, was forced to watch.

There was much gasping, clutching, and slobbering. Clothes went every which way, and the combatants moaned and laughed and sighed. There were protestations of affection, and when, midway through the proceedings, somebody knocked, the manager politely told him to come back later.

When it was over, and the female gone, the message remained. The occupant of the office, whose name Digger now knew to be Kali—unless *Kali* was a derivative of *lover* or *darling*—threw some wood on the fire and settled back to his paperwork.

Digger opened a channel to Kellie and told her what had happened. *"Valor above and beyond,"* she said.

She had planted her message, she told him, only to see it get tossed aside. She'd recovered it, and the coins, and had gone to a third location.

Kali left several times to wander through the building. Digger stayed with the cylinder, and was leaning against the wall, bored, when Kellie called to say her message was on the move.

"I'll let you know what happens," she reported. *"Meantime I think you should stay put."*

Kali came back and went out again. Kellie was by then following the messenger, who'd been given one of the three coins. *"I guess we overtipped,"* she said.

"Crossing the park. Headed north.

"Messenger's a female. Really moves along. I'm having all I can do to stay up with her.

"Threatening rain.

"Uh-oh."

Digger was watching Kali trying to stay awake. "What do you mean 'uh-oh'?"

"She's gone into a stable. Talking to somebody."

One of the workers came in and began straightening up the office, working around Kali. Digger waited in the corridor, but he kept an eye on the cylinder.

"Digger, they're bringing out a berba. *One of those fat horses.*

"She's getting on."

"The messenger?"

"Yes. And there she goes, trotting off into the park. Bye-bye."

"How about grabbing one of the critters for yourself?"

"You think anybody would notice?"

Digger had a vision of a riderless *berba* galloping through the park. "I don't know."

"Believe me, it wouldn't be pretty."

"If you can keep the animal in sight, Kellie, I'll try to have Bill follow her."

"The park is the one immediately west of where you are. She's headed north."

"Okay. Hang on. I've got a channel open to Bill now."

Bill acknowledged his instructions. Meanwhile, the cleaning person finished up and left. It was a perfunctory effort. Kali never stirred.

Bill was on the circuit to Kellie: *"Can you describe the animal?"*

"It's got big jaws. It waddles when it runs. And it looks like all the rest of them."

"Color. What color is it? There are a lot of Goompahs down there riding around."

"Green. It was green. With a big white splash across its rear end."

"Wait one."

Kali shook himself awake, wandered outside, looked at the sundial that dominated the area in front of the main entrance, and came back in.

"I can't find the animal," said Bill.

"Damn."

"I need more information. Several of them look like the one you describe. How about the messenger? Any distinguishing characteristics?"

"She's a Goompah."

"Good. Anything else? What color's her jacket? Her leggings?"

"White. White jacket. No, wait. Yellow. I think it was yellow."

"Leggings?"

"White."

"You sure?"

"Yes." But she'd hesitated.

*   *   *

BILL INSISTED THERE was no rider wearing yellow and white atop a beast of the description Kellie had given. But it didn't matter. Near the end of the afternoon, Kali bundled up the cylinder with some other papers, glanced curiously at it, shrugged, picked up a bell to summon an assistant, and handed him everything. The assistant made a further distribution. The cylinder and a couple of other items ended in the hands of a young Goompah with a bright red hat.

Digger, having learned from Kellie's mistake, noted his clothing, noted also that Kali kept the three coins, and followed the creature out of the building.

"Mine's on the way," he reported. The big items in the description were the red hat and a violently clashing purple scarf, a combination that should be easily visible to the naked eye from orbit.

The messenger stopped for a cup of the heated brew that passed locally for tea. He engaged in a loud conversation with a couple of others. He wasn't anxious to go home, he told them. His mate, wife, *zilfa*, was still angry. They laughed and took turns offering advice on how he should handle it. One of the comments translated roughly to "Show her who's boss." When he'd finished, they agreed to meet tomorrow, and he picked up his deliveries and headed across the street into a stable. Minutes later, he saddled up and headed north.

"*I've got him,*" said Bill.

MACAO LIVED IN a brick cottage on the northern side of the city. It was a long walk, mostly uphill, and they were exhausted when they arrived. By then, Bill reported, both cylinders had been delivered.

The cottage was one of several set at the edge of a dense forest. There was a small barn in the rear, and a modest garden probably given over to raising vegetables. The sun was down, and the first stars were in the sky. An oil lamp flickered through closed, but imperfectly fitted, shutters. Black smoke rose out of a chimney.

Something yowled as they approached, but nothing challenged them. A gentle wind moved against the trees. They heard voices farther along the crest, sporadic, sometimes laughing or shouting. Digger could make out only part of it. "Kids," he said.

Goompah kids.

They paused under a tree facing the house. Something moved against the light.

"I think it should be just one of us," said Digger.

Kellie agreed. "Has to be you," she added.

"My personality?"

"Right. Also your language skills." He felt her hand on his wrist, restraining him. "Maybe you should kill the lightbender."

Digger took a deep breath and thought of the demonic, foul creatures
being dispatched by the god with the sword. They all looked like him and
Kellie. So how best approach her? Demon or disembodied voice?

He turned off the device. "I don't look so terrible, do I?"

"You look ravishing, love."

"All right. Let's try it this way. She is, after all, enlightened."

"Yes. Absolutely."

"Can't go wrong." He walked up to the front door, which was a bit low
for him. It was constructed of planks laid side by side, painted white, and
polished with a gum of some sort. "First contact," he told Kellie. And he
knocked.

"Who's there?" He recognized Macao's voice.

Footsteps approached the door.

"Digger Dunn," he said.

"Who?"

"I was at your *slosh* in *Brackel,* and I listened to you speak at the launch.
Could I ask a question, please?"

A bolt was thrown, and the door swung out. Her eyes locked on him.
He'd expected a screech in those first moments, screams followed by bed-
lam, neighbors on the way, animals howling, torches in the night, God
knew what. He was prepared at the first indication of panic to hit the switch
and wrap himself again in the lightbender.

But she laughed. And when he stayed where he was, half-shrouded in
darkness, she reached back and produced an oil lamp. She held it up to
inspect his face. And the laughter died.

"Is that *real?*" she asked, staring and beginning to breathe irregularly. She
was gripping the door, hanging on to it for support.

"*Roblay culasta.*" I'm a friend. He didn't budge. Did nothing she could
interpret as threatening. "Macao," he said. "I know my appearance is
strange. Frightening. I'm sorry. I come from very far."

She stared. Her mouth worked but nothing came out.

"From beyond the sea," he said. "It's important that we speak."

She sighed and staggered back into the room. She wore a bright yellow
blouse with rolled-up sleeves and a pair of red shorts that hung to her knees.
Digger hesitated, edged forward, saw that she was on the verge of collapse,
and reached for her arm.

She did not react.

He took hold of it and eased her into a chair.

"*Still got the old charm,*" said Kellie.

Macao needed a couple of minutes. She opened her eyes, looked at Digger, and instinctively turned her face aside as though he were too horrible to behold. He tried his most winning smile. "I won't harm you, Macao," he said softly. "And I'm not a *zhoka*, even though I look like one."

She quailed in his presence. "Don't hurt me," she said, in a tiny voice.

"I would never do that." He eased the door shut, found cups and a flagon of wine on a table, and poured some for her. She shook her head no. He was tempted to try it himself. "No," she said. Her voice was barely audible. "Lykonda, protect me."

"I, too, have great affection for Lykonda," he said.

She simply sat there, limp as a wet towel, staring at him, as if she'd retreated into some far corner of her mind.

"Macao, I'm sorry to frighten you. But it's important that we talk. About *T'Klot*."

Her jaw muscles tightened, and he again thought she was going to pass out.

"I've come to try to help you."

It was a pleasant home. Fireplace, several chairs, plank floor, a looking glass, a table, and a shelf with several scrolls. The shutters were flanked by thick blue curtains. A second room, opening off the back, was dark. "I will leave in a few minutes, Macao. Because I know that is what you wish. But first I need you to listen to me."

She tried to speak, but the words wouldn't come.

"It's all right," he said. "I'm a friend."

She got her breathing under control. And finally looked directly at him. "I did not see you," she said, "at the *slosh*." And she laughed. The sound touched a few notes that sounded hysterical, but she held on. "Why have you come?"

"The hole in the sky," he said, forgetting himself and using English. "*T'Klot*."

"Yes." She glanced past him at the door. It was supposed to be furtive, he thought, but maybe Goompahs weren't good at that sort of thing. "Is it the creation of Shol?"

"Who's Shol?"

"*You* are Shol."

"No. No, Macao. I am Digger, and Shol didn't create the hole. But it is very dangerous."

"If you are not Shol, not a *zhoka*, what are you?"

"I'm somebody who's come a long way to help you, Macao. Let me tell you first that, in *Brackel*, you were right. The world *is* round."

"Is that *true*?" A light came into her eyes. And she seemed to recover herself. "Is that *really* true?"

"Yes," he said. "It's really so. But it's not why I'm here."

She started to ask the obvious question but, probably fearful of the answer, stopped.

The chairs were made from interwoven strips of hide on a wooden frame. They were a bit low for Digger, but they were more than sufficiently wide. "May I?" he asked, glancing at a chair facing her.

She made no move to say no, so he lowered himself into it. "The Hole presents a serious hazard. To everyone in the *Intigo*."

She glanced at the cup of wine and he passed it to her. She took it, gazed into it as if assuring herself that it would not snatch away her soul, and put it to her lips. "You may have some," she said, "if you wish."

The universal. Share a drink with someone and bond. Would it prove to be true in all cultures? He poured a few drops into a second cup and raised it to her. "To your courage, Macao," he said.

She managed a smile.

He held the cup to his lips and tasted the brew. It was bitter. "It's actually a cloud," he said, "a vast storm. It will arrive in ninety-three days, and it's going to wreck the eleven cities."

Ninety-three of the shortened days at the *Intigo*. Eighty-six standard days on board the *Jenkins*. The target date was December 13.

It was the most painful conversation of Digger's life. Macao was terrified, and the news wasn't helping. "It'll bring tornadoes and lightning and high water and rocks falling from the sky and we don't know what else."

In spite of everything, she managed a half smile. *If you don't know, who would?*

She was struggling to control her emotions. And he found his respect for her growing. How many of the women back home could have sat more or less calmly conducting a conversation with a demon?

"Rocks cannot fall from the sky," she said.

"Believe me, they can."

"Then why can I not see them?"

"I don't understand the question."

"There are no rocks in the sky. If there were, surely we would see them."

"The rocks are very far away. And hidden in the cloud."

"How far?"

How to translate 30 million or so kilometers into a number she could understand? "*Very* far," he said.

"The sky is only a shell. What you are telling me is incomprehensible."

"Macao," he said, "what are the stars?"

"Some say they are the light from the celestial realm, which we can see through holes in the shell."

"But you don't believe it?"

"No."

"Why not?"

"It does not seem to me to make sense."

"Good for you. What do *you* think the stars are?"

"I do not know."

"Okay," he said. "I want you to take my word that the hole in the sky is dangerous. That, when it comes, it will bring great suffering. Your people, the people across the *Intigo*, must get away from the cities, must get to higher ground. If they cannot do this, they will die."

Her eyes cut into him. "Despite your words, you are, after all, a manifestation of evil."

"I am not."

"If you are not, then stop this thing that you say is coming. Surely you are able to control a hole. Or a cloud. Or whatever it is."

"It's a cloud."

"Only a cloud? And you, with all your power, cannot brush it aside?"

"If I could do that, do you think I would be here asking for help?"

She looked at him and shuddered. "I don't understand any of this. Who are you, really?"

"Macao," he said, "in *Brackel* you talked about lands beyond the seas. And about giant *falloons* and attack *groppes* and flying *bobbos*—"

"*Bobbos* that attack and *groppes* that fly—"

"Pardon?"

"You had it backward."

"Sorry. Memory fails."

"*Bobbos do* fly."

"Oh."

"Ordinary *bobbos* fly all the time. They are in the trees outside at this very moment." She injected an adjective after *ordinary* that he did not understand. Probably something like *run-of-the-mill*. "How could you not know?"

"That *bobbos* fly? Because I'm not from around here." He gazed intently at her. "I wouldn't know a *bobbo* from a seashell." He put the cup down. "You talked, in *Brackel*, about the city from which people can see the past and the future."

"*Brissie*," she said.

"Yes. *Brissie*." He leaned forward, watched her push back in her chair, and immediately retreated. "Macao, we are looking at two possible futures now. If you are willing to trust me, you can save your people. Or, if you cling to the superstition that brands me as something out of the dark, then you and all that the *Korbikkans* have built, will be destroyed."

"In ninety-three days, you say?" Her voice shook.

"Yes."

More wine. "And I am to do what?"

"Warn them."

"They will not believe me."

"Who will not?"

"Everyone. People are afraid of *T'Klot*, but they would not believe that a supernatural messenger has come to me with this news." She looked at him carefully. "Of all persons here, me especially."

"And why is that?"

"Because I am a professional storyteller. An exaggerator of considerable reputation." A bit of pride leaked into her voice.

"I will go with you."

"No!" It was almost a shriek. "That would be the worst thing you could do."

Time for another tack. "Do you know the mayor?" The *booglik*.

"I've met him once."

"Can you get in to see him?"

"Possibly."

"Do so. Tell him what I've told you. Tell him, when the time gets close, he has to get his people out of *Kulnar*. Have them take several days' supply of food and clothes. And blankets. Go to high ground. Any who fail to do so will almost certainly be lost."

She folded her hands in the manner of one praying. "It's no use," she said. "He won't listen to me. It's ridiculous." A tear ran down her cheek. It surprised him to realize she had tear ducts.

"Digger Dunn," she said. "Is that really your name?"

"Yes."

"It is a strange name."

He fumbled in his jacket, and found Kellie's necklace. "I have something for you." He held it out to her. "It will bring you good luck."

She looked at it uncertainly, as if it might bite. Gift from a *zhoka*. But at last she took it, and while she drew the necklace over her head, Digger tried the most harmless smile of which he was capable. "It looks lovely," he said. "Like you."

"Thank you." She pressed her fingertips against the pickup. "I have never seen anything like this. What is it?"

"There is only one in the world." In a sense, it was true. "It was made especially for you."

Macao gazed at herself in the looking glass. She turned back toward him, pleased, frightened, uncertain. "Thank you," she said. "Digger Dunn."

He nodded.

"For everything," she added.

LIBRARY ENTRY

The general public seems surprised that the Goompahs are so much like us. They had expected aliens to be, well, *alien*. As if their mathematics should be incomprehensible, as if they would develop from something other than a hunter-gatherer society, as if they would not need shelter from the storm, as if they would not love their children.

Indeed, they have all these things, and a great deal more. They have selfish politicians, they have squabbles, they even enjoy ball games.

There are, of course, some differences. To our eyes, they look odd. They do not seem interested in traveling far from home, to the extent that they hardly know what lies a few hundred kilometers beyond their seacoasts and their borders. They have primitive religious notions. And they seem to have some ideas about sex that most of us would frown on. At least, if anyone's looking.

Maybe it's time to recognize them for what they are, spiritual siblings. If one could sweep the differences in appearance and technology aside, who could doubt that many of us would feel quite comfortable in *Brackel*, the city that our researchers still insist on calling Athens? And it's probable that these creatures of a far world would enjoy themselves thoroughly in Georgetown, or out on the Mall.

The Goompahs, the *Korbikkans*, as they call themselves, join us and the Noks as the only known living civilizations. The Noks quarrel constantly. The Korbikkans seem to have found a way to live in peace. How can we look at either of them and not see ourselves?

—C. W. Chrissinger
Staying the Course

chapter 30

THE IMAGER ON Macao's necklace was apparently facing her skin, so they got no picture. It seemed likely that she lived alone. They heard no conversation during the evening, just the sounds of someone moving around, pouring water, playing one of the stringed instruments. The wind blew against the side of the cottage, and forest creatures hooted and twirped. Doors opened and closed, the bolt rattled, and occasionally someone sighed.

It was the rattles that got Digger. How many times could she check the lock? And the sighs. Well, he could understand that. She'd just had a visit from a *zhoka*, and if the Goompahs shared the standard earthly tradition, that the devil could be very smooth, all Digger's charm might not have helped.

Most surprising, they both thought, was that, when he'd left, she had not run screaming into the night. Had not gone to a friend or neighbor to describe what had happened.

They were listening from Utopia. Digger was emotionally exhausted. Almost as if *he* had just gone through an unexpected meeting with a demon. He'd gotten a shower as soon as they arrived, and sat wrapped in a robe, listening to Macao move around her cottage.

"If it were me," said Kellie, "I'd be out of there and headed for my mother's. Or something. Anything to get with other people."

The omega was rising. It was approaching too slowly to make out any real change in its appearance from night to night. But when he compared images from a couple of weeks earlier, he could see the difference. And the Goompahs, more attuned to watching the night sky than he was, knew it was growing.

He pushed his seat back and drifted off. Digger usually woke two or three times during the night, but this time he slept straight through until Bill woke him shortly after dawn. *"Macao is up,"* he said.

The imager was facing out now, so they watched while she stoked the fire, tossed in a log or two, washed, and got dressed. Then the necklace went inside her blouse, and the visuals were gone again. But they could hear, and that should be sufficient. She left the cottage for a few minutes, exchanged pleasantries with a neighbor, looks like rain, how's your boy?

Then she was back, and water was pouring again. They heard wet sounds they couldn't identify. Dishes moved around. Cabinet doors closed. Utensils clinked.

"When did we get knives and forks?" asked Kellie.

"The wealthy had them in the Middle Ages."

Kellie got bored and made for the washroom. He listened to her splashing around in the shower. When she returned, wearing a *Jenkins* jumpsuit, nothing had changed. They could hear the rhythmic sound of Macao's breathing. And her heartbeat.

Kellie looked out at a gray ocean. "What do you think?" she asked. "Did you convince her?"

Yes, he thought he had. He was *sure* he had.

Kellie brought him a plate of toast. He smeared strawberry jelly on it.

They heard boards creek. And more sounds at the fireplace. The visual, which had simply been a field of yellow, the color of her blouse, changed. Became the interior of a room he hadn't seen before. The back room. Then they were looking up at a ceiling, with no movement detectable. "She's taken it off and laid it down," said Digger.

A bolt lifted, and a door opened and closed. "Front door," said Kellie.

"Well, that's not so good."

"She might just be headed for the barn. Off to feed the animals."

MACAO WAS GONE several hours. When finally she came back another female was with her.

"*Where?*" asked the other female.

"*Here.*" They saw a movement between the lens and the ceiling. An arm, maybe?

"*Right there.*"

"*And you stayed here all night?*"

"*Ora, I believe him.*"

"*That's why they're so dangerous, Mac.*" Mac? Mac? "*Shol is the king of liars.*"

"*Look,*" Macao said. "*He gave me this.*"

The picture blurred, and they were looking at Ora. She was wearing a red blouse and a violet neckerchief. One green eye grew very large and peered out of the screen at them. "*It's quite nice,*" she said. "*Lovely.*" And then: "*What's wrong?*"

A long pause. "*I was wondering if he might be here now.*"

"It's daylight. They can't stand the daylight."

"Are you sure? There was talk of a zhoka *out on the highway last spring. In the middle of the day."* The eye pulled away. They saw walls, then they were looking at the ceiling again.

"Mac, you're giving me chills." That wasn't precisely what she said. It was more like causing her lungs to work harder. But Digger understood the meaning.

"Why did it come to me? Ora, I don't even believe in zhokas. *Or at least I didn't until last night."*

"I warned you something like this would happen. Walking around laughing at the gods. What did you expect?"

"I never laughed at the gods."

"Worse than that. You denied them."

"Ora," she said, *"I don't know what to do."*

The debate continued. Macao denied the charges, argued that she'd only maintained the gods did not run day-to-day operations. Did not make the sun move. Or the tides roll in.

Ora seemed nervous about being in the cottage, went on about apparitions, and suggested Macao might like to stay with her a while. Whatever devilry Digger might have imposed, it didn't stop the two females from eating. And then they were gone, with no indication what step Macao would take next.

The pickup still provided a clear picture of the ceiling.

NOT KNOWING WHAT else they could try, they simply waited it out. A large insect buzzed the pickup. The shutters were apparently open because there was plenty of daylight. After a while, the light became dimmer, and they heard rain on the roof.

"She's gone to see somebody about it," said Kellie.

It was possible she'd gone to the governance building, *T'Kalla*. The chief executive in *Kulnar* was the *booglik*. I'm on my way to *T'Kalla* to talk to the *booglik*. It sounded almost normal.

He was still sitting, staring morosely at Macao's overhead, at *Mac's* overhead, when he heard the door open. By then the rain seemed to have stopped.

"Did you get it?" Ora's voice.

"Right here."

Footsteps moved across the planks. *"No sign of him?"*

"No. We're alone."

"Good. Listen, save some of the kessel *for me, Mac."*

He heard sounds like a knife cutting through onions.

"I thought you didn't believe it would work."

"No. I said I don't trust it to work. But there's nothing to lose by trying it."

The cutting continued. Then: *"There, that should be enough."*

"Where do you want to put it?"

"In the doorway. Just block the threshold with it."

"All right. You're putting it in the windows too, right?"

"And in the fireplace. Just in case."

Bill broke in: *"I have a reference to kessel."*

"Let's hear it," said Kellie.

"It's a common herb, found throughout the Intigo. *Sometimes ground into grains and used as a seasoning. It's also thought to provide a bar against demons and other spirits of the night."*

"A bar?" said Kellie.

"That's why they're putting it in all the entrances. Keep the demon out."

"What good's a sliced vegetable going to do?"

Digger was tired of it all. He was tempted to go back to the *Jenkins* and just sit tight until help arrived. Let somebody else deal with these loonies. "Think garlic," he said.

"**WHAT DO WE** do now?"

Digger was ready to call it off. "Only thing I can think of, other than conceding we are not going to get through to these yahoos, is to go directly to the head guy. There must be somebody in this town who isn't afraid of goblins."

"I'm sure there is. But I doubt it's the *gloobik*."

"Booglik," he said. "So who do you recommend?"

"Don't know. Maybe the captain on the round-the-world voyage. What was his name?"

"Krolley."

"Maybe we could get to him. He's got to have *some* sense."

"He'd have to be willing to turn around."

"You don't think he'd do that?"

"I don't know him. But I suspect we'd have a better chance with somebody local."

Kellie looked discouraged. Digger was beginning to realize she'd thought, as he had, that they'd won Macao over. "Even if we'd succeeded with Macao," she said, "she'd still have had the problem of convincing the authorities. Macao didn't think she could do it. And, despite the way things turned out, I don't believe she was playacting." She closed her eyes. "I think we need a different approach."

"What do you think will happen with her?"

She thought about it, and smiled sadly. "When the cloud closes in, I think she'll fix herself some sandwiches, grab a tent, and head for the high ground."

"Taking no chances."

"That's right. Maybe she'll take a few friends with her."

Digger saw no way out. Other than going directly to the *booglik* and trying to persuade him. "We need some of Collingdale's costumes. If we could at least fix ourselves up to look like the locals, we might have a chance."

Kellie looked discouraged. "Face it, Dig," she said, "What we need is some divine intervention."

They had returned to the *Jenkins* and were on the night side of Lookout. Clouds below were thick, so he couldn't tell whether they were over land or sea. He was becoming familiar with the constellations, and had even made an effort to learn them by their Goompah names. *Tow Bokol Kar*, the Wagonmaker, floated just over the rim of the world. And there was *T'Kleppa*, the Pitcher. And just beside it, *T'Monga*, a bird that had probably never existed. Its closest cousin in terrestrial mythology was probably the roc. It was reputed to be able to carry off Goompahs.

"How about," said Kellie, trying to shrug off her mood, "staying inside the lightbender when we talk to them?"

"You think that'll scare them less than the *zhoka*?"

"Can it scare them any more?"

He shook his head. It wouldn't work. Disembodied voices never work. It's a rule.

"Maybe there's another possibility," she said.

"I'm listening."

"Why don't we try using an avatar again?"

He shook his head. "Can't synchronize their lips to match the dialogue. It's okay if the avatar goes down with a prepared speech, delivers it, and clears out. But the first question somebody tosses at him, like, where did you say you were from, and we're dead."

"It's a shot," she persisted.

"Won't work." He could imagine himself in the *booglik's* quarters, playing a recording to match the previously prepared lip movements of the Goompah avatar. And the *booglik* breaking in, hey, wait a minute, while the avatar either galloped on, or stopped dead and picked up again where he left off no matter what question got asked.

They were catching up with the sun. The long arc of the world was brightening.

His circadian rhythms had been scrambled. Moving constantly between the shorter days and nights of the *Intigo* and the standard twenty-four-hour

GMT on the ship had left them both uncertain what time of day or night it was. But even if dawn was coming, he was hungry. "How about some dinner?" she suggested.

TWO HOURS LATER they sat in the long stillness of the *Jenkins*. There were times when Digger thought that if he put on the infrared goggles, he'd see Jack's ghost drifting through the corridors. He heard echoes that hadn't been there before, and whispers in the bulkheads. When he mentioned it to Kellie, she commented that now he might understand a little of what Macao had felt.

"The noises," she added, "are made by Bill. Sometimes he talks to himself."

"You're kidding."

"No. Really. He holds conversations."

"What about?"

"I don't know."

"Haven't you ever asked him?"

"Yes."

"What did he say?"

"Ask him yourself."

Digger was reluctant. It seemed intrusive. But that was silly. You couldn't offend an AI. "Bill," he said. "Got a minute?"

A literary version appeared, world-weary with high cheekbones and a white beard. He was seated in the chair that Jack used to favor. *"Yes, Digger. How may I be of assistance?"*

"Bill, sometimes I hear voices. In the systems."

"Yes. I do, too."

"What are they?"

"The systems communicate all the time."

"They do it by talking?"

"Sometimes."

"But don't you control the systems?"

"Oh, yes. But they're separate from me. They have their own priorities."

"Okay," he said. "Let it go."

Bill vanished.

"Satisfied?" asked Kellie.

"I don't think he told me anything."

"The voices are his." She was browsing through the ship's systems. Or maybe gameplaying. He couldn't tell.

"I have a question for you," Digger said.

"Another one."

"Yes." He straightened himself. "We haven't set a date yet."

"Ah. No, we haven't." She narrowed her eyes, appraising him. "We won't be home for a long time."

"We don't have to wait until we get home."

"You're sweet, Digby."

"I'm serious."

She was framed in the soft glow of the computer screen. "What do you suggest?" she said.

"A ship's captain can perform a wedding."

She allowed herself to look shocked. "Surely not her own."

"I had Julie Carson in mind. When the *Hawksbill* gets here."

She thought about it. "All right," she said finally. "If you're determined, how can I stand in the way? We'll have to send for a license."

"We've plenty of time."

"Okay, Digger." She grinned. "Seeing how you affect the other females around here, though, maybe I should rethink this."

THE AVATAR IDEA was not entirely without merit. Provided it was possible to produce one that could deliver the message and clear out. Here's the deal and no questions asked.

"But how would you do that?"

"You suggested we could use divine intervention."

"Can you arrange it?"

"I have an idea, Watson," he said, doing his best Oxford accent. "We'd need some projectors, though. A lot of projectors."

"Tell me what you have in mind."

"Bill, let's see some Goompahs."

"*Any in particular?*"

"Yes. A female. Macao would be good. Give us a picture of Macao."

She blinked on. It was Macao as she'd looked during the *slosh* at *Brackel*. Bright yellow blouse with fluffy sleeves. Green leggings and animal-hide boots. And the medallion on the purple ribbon.

"Okay. Bill, have her say something."

Macao smiled at him. "*Challa,* Digger," she said, in a perfect imitation of Kellie's voice. "*You are a little* zhoka, *aren't you?*"

He grinned. "The lip sync is okay. Not perfect, but okay."

"*It wouldn't fool anybody. Unless you give her a fan and have her hold it in front of her mouth. To get it right, I need to have a little warning in advance what she's going to say.*"

"I don't get it," said Kellie. "If we're agreed the real Macao probably couldn't accomplish anything, what can her avatar do?"

"We need to make some adjustments. Then, maybe, quite a lot."

ARCHIVE

From the Goompah Recordings
(Tyree of *Roka* at a *slosh* in *Brackel*)
(Translated by Ginko Amagawa)

Strange things are happening. There have been reports of *zhokas* on the highways, and of voices speaking in an unknown tongue in empty places. And a huge hole has opened in our skies and grows larger every night. Those of you who know me know that I have always believed that everything has a rational explanation. That the world is governed by immutable law and not by the whims of spirits and demons.

There are some who argue that these are all portents of approaching catastrophe. Let me say first that I cannot offer explanations for these events. But I have not yet become so desperate that I've started believing there is such a thing as a portent. It may be that the demons on the highway are figments of overheated imaginations. That the voices in the night are really nothing more than the wind. And that the hole in the sky, which has begun to look like a cloud, will prove to be a new kind of storm. But that like any other storm, it will blow for a while, and then it will exhaust itself, and the sun will rise in the morning.

Meantime, I'll remind you that if catastrophe of a previously unknown nature is indeed on the way, that there is nothing to be done about it. Except enjoy the time we have left with family and friends. But this is extremely unlikely. We have a tendency to assume the worst, to give way to fear whenever something we do not understand presents itself.

Since no plausible action can be taken against demons, disembodied voices, or the thing in the sky, I suggest that we put it all aside, that we refuse to allow these phenomena to upset our daily routine. That we in no case give way to panic.

Now that we all recognize that I don't know what's going on any more than you do, we'll open the floor for comments or questions.

—September 19

chapter 31

THEY GOT LUCKY. The search for the *al-Jahani* could have taken as long as a week. Establishing a position when one was adrift in interstellar space was less than a precise science. Furthermore, hyperlight signals did not lend themselves to tracking. So a searcher was dependent on radio transmissions, which were desperately slow. Julie could only guarantee that she would put the *Hawksbill* reasonably close to the damaged ship. And, when Marge asked how she defined *reasonably*, she admitted she was talking about 80 billion kilometers or so.

Julie had expected to spend a minimum of two days in a fruitless search, then be directed to forget it and go on without Collingdale. But in fact they came out of hyperspace within range of the *al-Jahani*'s radio signals. Julie got her fix and jumped a second time. They emerged within a few hours of the stricken ship.

In fact she didn't see the point of all the hassle. The *Hawksbill* couldn't accommodate the linguists; couldn't even take on Frank Bergen, who was to have ridden shotgun with the decoys. Only Collingdale would be making the rest of the flight, and she didn't see why he was needed.

Collingdale hadn't taken the time to explain it to her, and he was in charge, so she said nothing. Not even to Marge and Whit. Although they weren't above wondering why they were going to so much trouble for somebody who was just going to Lookout to watch.

"Well," said Marge, "don't anybody take this the wrong way, but it will be nice to see a fresh face on board."

Julie got blankets and pillows out of her supplies and tried to make her storage room into a sleeping accommodation. There was no bed; Collingdale would have to make do on the deck.

At 1942 hours they picked up the *al-Jahani* in their telescopes, and three hours later they slipped alongside. Marge and Whit had both asked whether they could take some time to go aboard the other ship, just to say hello. Look around someplace different. Marge had an old friend aboard the *al-*

Jahani. Julie would also have liked to get away from the narrow living space of the *Hawksbill* for a few hours, so she'd proposed it to Collingdale.

"*Don't have time,*" he said over the link. "*We need to get going forthwith.*" *Forthwith.* She didn't know anybody else who talked like that.

"My passengers could stand the break," she'd said. "They've been cooped up in here for six months."

"*Wish we could. But every hour puts that thing closer to Lookout. It's just impossible.*"

"Okay," she said.

"*Sorry,*" he added.

Marge settled for saying hello to her friend, the planetologist Melinda Park, by commlink. But she wasn't happy, and Julie thought that Collingdale might be in for a long ride.

He was on his way through the airlock within thirty seconds after the green lights went on. "Thank God," he told Julie. "It's been a nightmare." And he added more apologies. "But there's just too much at stake."

"It's okay," she said. "But you're leaving Bergen. Who's going out with the decoys?"

"I am," he said.

There was a quick exchange with the *al-Jahani's* captain. Were there any injuries? Did she have sufficient supplies to last until the relief vessel came? Could Julie provide any assistance?

"*We're fine,*" said Alexandra. And it might have been Julie's imagination, but she sensed an unspoken *now*.

Collingdale stood behind her, looking at the time, suggesting that they really should get moving, assuring her everything was satisfactory on the other ship.

Eight minutes after they'd arrived, the *Hawksbill* edged away, fired its thrusters, and began to accelerate toward jump status.

Julie had expected to feel apologetic about the storeroom quarters she was giving him, but as things turned out she felt a degree of satisfaction showing him the blankets on the deck and the two cramped washrooms.

COLLINGDALE WAS SO pleased to be aboard a functioning ship, on his way to Lookout, that he didn't really care about spartan conditions. During acceleration, he belted in on the couch in the equipment locker, the only one they had available.

He watched the *al-Jahani* diminish with distance, and he felt a tinge of regret for Judy and Nick and Ginko and the others, who had worked so hard and accomplished so much. He thought about calling Judy, delivering a final farewell, but he'd done that before leaving. Any more along those lines would be maudlin.

What he had to do now was to see that the cloud got sidetracked, so that what had happened to Judy's team wouldn't matter in the long run.

He waited in his harness, looking around the bare-bones room, grateful that he was moving again. He closed his eyes and tried to relax, but he kept seeing the omega that had swept down on Moonlight. And he wished he had a bomb big enough to blow the damned thing to hell.

That was the problem with Hutch's decoy idea. It was good, and it might work. But it only deflected the cloud. It didn't *kill* it. That was what Collingdale wanted. Go to the next step and kill it.

After forty minutes' acceleration they still had not jumped. Every flight he'd ever been on had been able to do it in thirty minutes or so. He called the bridge to ask.

"Big ship, David," she said. *"It takes a while."* Her tone was mildly hostile. He tried to remember if he'd said or done anything to offend her. Probably upset that she didn't get a chance to visit. But time was too valuable. The hour that they squandered now might make all the difference. "Okay," he said. "I didn't know."

He *did* know that if she tried to make the jump before the Hazeltines were ready, the *Hawksbill* would go boom. "Take your time," he said.

HE WAS PLEASED to be on the ship that housed the decoys, that would actually be used to frustrate the omega. He spent hours on the bridge, explained to Julie that he'd commanded a superluminal at the beginning of his career, and wanted to know everything. He talked at length with Bill, was allowed to sit in the captain's chair, enjoyed calling up status reports, running maintenance routines, putting the AI through his paces.

Julie, pleased that he showed such interest, showed him through the ship. Here were the comm circuits; there was life support; here's the power mode complex. They toured the engine room, the shuttle launch area in the lower cargo bay, and main storage, where the antigrav generator was located.

He wasn't sure why he was so interested in the ship. He hadn't particularly cared about the *al-Jahani*. It must have been because he knew *this* would be the vessel. Bergen was out of the game now, and Collingdale would be taking the *Hawksbill* into battle.

It made him feel young again. As if all the world waited for him to show up and set things right. "Julie," he said, "tell me about the jump engines. Has the technology improved?"

"I doubt it," she said. "I don't think anything basic has changed in thirty years."

HE HADN'T HEARD from Mary in two weeks, other than a short expression of her regret that the mission had broken down. It wasn't *short*, actually. She'd gone on for ten minutes. Everything was fine at home. Some of her new students had little sense and no ethics. *"They're studying law for all the wrong reasons."*

He'd begun to wonder whether he should let her go. God knew when he'd get home, and it seemed unreasonable to keep her waiting all that time. His deepest fear, even more than losing her, was that she would come to resent him.

On the other hand, where would she find somebody else like David Collingdale? It was a private joke he told himself. But there was some truth to it.

Avery Whitlock's Notebooks

The mood on the ship has changed. It may be a momentary thing, but I doubt it.

David Collingdale seems to be decent enough. He speaks kindly to everyone, and he apologized to us all for the delay involved in rescuing him from the al-Jahani. Still, we were quieter this evening than we have been at any time on the flight. The chemistry has changed in some subtle, or maybe not-so-subtle, way. The easy camaraderie of the past months is gone, as abruptly as though it had never existed. We are formal now, and tentative, watchful of what we say. And though it seems logical to conclude that with the passage of time the former atmosphere will return, I do not think it will happen.

—September 18

chapter 32

Arlington, Virginia.
Tuesday, September 23.

SHE HATED THE chime that came in the middle of the night. Priscilla Hutchins was not a hands-on manager. Her technique was to frame the objectives, provide the resources, find the right people to get the job done, and stay out of the way. That meant that when a call came in at 3:00 A.M., whether it was personal or professional, it was inevitably bad news.

She picked up the link and held it to her ear. Tor rolled over and looked at the time.

"*Hutch.*" It was Debbie Willis, the Academy watch officer. "*The engines went.*"

Damn. After the first incident back in June she'd been half-expecting it. But there'd been nothing she could do. Everything was just too far away. "Anybody hurt?" she asked.

"*No. They're all okay.*" She thought she heard a cry from Maureen's room, but when she listened there was only silence.

"Okay," she said. "Julie and Digger have been informed?"

"*Yes. We have a transmission from Alexandra. You want me to relay it?*"

"Does it say she can effect repairs and get to Lookout before the cloud does?"

"*I haven't looked at it. But Broadside reports they're unable to proceed with the mission.*"

"Help on the way?"

"*Yes, ma'am.*"

"Okay. Thanks, Deb. Forward the stuff from Alex."

Tor was watching her. "The *al-Jahani*?"

"Yes."

"I'm sorry, babe."

"Me too."

She heard the sound again. Maureen having a bad dream, maybe.

"I'll get it," said Tor.

"No." She headed for the door. "It's okay."

While she sat with Maureen she heard Tor leave the bedroom and go downstairs. Nights like this, when he knew things weren't going well for her, he got restless. When the child was quiet, she followed and found him dozing in his chair, a book open on his lap, the lamp on behind him. She put the book on the coffee table, turned off the light, and settled onto the sofa. "Nothing you could do," he said, without opening his eyes.

"I could have held them up another week. Completed the routine maintenance. They'd've found the problem if I'd done that."

"Why didn't you?"

"Didn't have a week to spare. But at least they'd have gotten there."

He made a noise deep in his throat. "You're second-guessing yourself," he said. "If you'd gone that route, and they'd gotten there too late to intervene, you'd have been blaming yourself for that. Should have taken a chance and let them go a week earlier."

"Well," she said, "maybe the kite'll work."

IN THE MORNING she sent off messages to Collingdale, to Vadim at Broadside, and to Digger. Collingdale had informed her of his intention to continue his journey on the *Hawksbill*. She wished him luck and told him she knew he would do what he could. She instructed Vadim to give priority to whatever requests might come in from the other two. If Digger could see any way to get the Goompahs to high ground, he was to proceed and damn the consequences.

WHEN SHE GOT to the Academy in the morning, there was a message from Broadside, informing her that Jack's body would be coming back on the *Winckelmann*. The Academy had a formatted letter to be sent out on such occasions to next of kin, but it seemed cold, so she settled in to write her own.

She left word with Asquith's secretary that she wanted to see the commissioner when he came in. When he hadn't appeared by ten, she called him on his link. He discouraged that sort of behavior. Emergencies only, he insisted. He didn't like to feel tied to the Academy, enjoyed telling others that he ran a shop in which it didn't matter whether his subordinates could talk to him or not. It was the mark of a good manager that decisions were made and action taken even when he couldn't be reached.

On the other hand, if he got blindsided by somebody on Capitol Hill, he'd complain for days about his staff not keeping him informed.

"*Yes?*" he demanded irritably.

"I don't know whether you've heard yet or not. The *al-Jahani* blew its engines. It's adrift."

There was a long pause, and she heard him sigh. *"Any casualties?"*

"No."

"Well, thank God for that, at least. Whose fault is it?"

"I don't know. Probably mine."

"How'd it happen?"

"It just went. We took a chance, and it didn't work out."

"Okay. Look, relax. We'll get through this."

AN HOUR LATER Eric was at her door. "We've got serious problems," he said. "How am I supposed to explain this?"

Eric Samuels was an imposing man, tall, well dressed, with an articulated voice that one instinctively trusted. Until it became clear that he lived in a world of images and mirrors. Perception is everything, he was fond of saying. In a glorious sally a few weeks earlier he'd told a group of particle physicists that the underlying lesson to be learned from quantum theory was that reality and image were identical. "If we don't see it," he'd said, "it's not there."

"Explain what?" she asked.

"The *al-Jahani*. What the hell else would I be talking about?" He looked frantic.

"Sit, Eric," she said.

He stayed on his feet. "What do I tell them?"

"You have a press conference today?"

"I do *now*." Eric was good with the media when things were going well. And that was usually the case at the Academy. Most problems and setbacks could be buried because the general public simply wasn't that interested in the work the Academy did. A recent study by UNN had shown that 50 percent of Americans had no idea whether Alpha Centauri was a planet, a star, a constellation, or a country in west Asia.

But the public *loved* the Goompahs.

She broke out the decanter and offered him a glass. Eric was a straight arrow whom she had never known to touch alcohol on the job. But this would be an exception. Yes. Please. "The commissioner insisted we issue a statement," he said. "Get out ahead of the curve. Make ourselves available."

"What are you going to tell them?"

"That one-half of the rescue mission broke down. What else can I say?"

"You're not going to put it like that, I hope?"

"No. Of course not." He looked puzzled. How else could one put it?

"Just attribute it to insufficient resources to meet an emergency of this magnitude."

"Of course."

"It's true," she said. "We did the best we could with what we had."

"You think they'll buy that?"

"It's *true*, Eric."

"That doesn't always guarantee that we can get by with something." He tried his drink and made a face. "Anyhow, if we go that route, it might offend the Senate committee, or maybe even the Council. See, that's the problem. It sounds as if we're trying to blame somebody."

"And you'd rather blame—"

"—A technician. Somebody who can always get another job with somebody else." He smiled weakly. "Not you, Hutch. I'd never think of blaming *you*."

"Good." She'd been wondering about that all day, whether in the end, needing to point a finger at somebody, Asquith wouldn't find it expedient to target her. *Admitting to the media he should have kept an eye on things himself. Hutchins tried to get it right, but I should have stayed on top of it. Not really her fault though. Bad luck.* She wondered what Sylvia was doing these days.

"Just tell the truth," she said. "It'll come out in the end anyway." She had to bite down on that line, knowing the truth that came out would depend on the way the media perceived what Eric had to say, and what they wanted to stress. Generally, they were inclined to go after people in high places. Which meant that they would probably bite the Senate committee and the commissioner.

She was becoming cynical. A few years back, she'd have considered her present job more than she could possibly have hoped for. But here she was, the director of operations, eminently successful in her career by any reasonable measure. And she wondered why she was doing it.

The job had turned out to be not what she'd expected. She'd thought it would be operational, with some politics mixed in. Truth was, all her critical functions were political. The rest of it could have been handled by anybody who could count. She'd discovered a talent for politics, and didn't mind jollying people along provided she didn't have to compromise herself. Asquith didn't altogether approve of her. He thought she was something of a crank. But she *was* good at her job, and she thought he'd be reluctant to let her go. Although not so reluctant he'd be willing to face fire from the Hill.

"I hate days like this," Eric said.

She nodded. "Don't worry about it. It's not the end of the world." At least not for us.

*   *   *

EARLY THAT AFTERNOON she got a call from Charlie, who'd been serving as director pro tem of the astrophysics lab. *"I've been debating whether to bother you with this, Hutch,"* he said. She came to full alert. *"Can you stop by the lab either today or tomorrow?"*

It didn't sound like a breakthrough. "I'll be over in an hour or so, Charlie."

It was more like three hours, and by then a rainstorm had moved in and turned into a downpour. In dry weather she'd have gone outside, strolled past the pool, and tossed some popcorn to the ducks. But she descended instead to the tunnel that connected the Academy's complex of buildings.

The walls were concrete, painted a hideous ocher, the long monotony broken only by pictures of the Academy's ships and stations, and some astronomical shots, galaxies and nebulas and planetary rings. Somebody had added one of the omegas. It was dark and menacing, sections of it illuminated by interior power surges. Long tendrils of cloud reached forward, threatening the observer, and an escorting asteroid was front and center.

She wondered what the Goompahs would think when they saw it up close.

There were three other known races who had ventured into interstellar space: the unknown architects of the *chindi*, who were apparently a race bent on preserving everything of value, who had found their own unique way to defeat time. The Monument-Makers, who had obviously gone to a lot of trouble for the civilizations at Quraqua and Nok. And, finally, the Hawks, who had performed a rescue when Deepsix went into a long-term ice age several thousand years ago.

And now her own species, trying to help where it could. They were in good company. And she felt a modicum of pride. If Darwin ruled on planetary surfaces, it appeared that a concern for one's neighbor was a working principle at higher levels.

Unless, of course, one counted the agency behind the omegas.

She'd have liked to talk with representatives of those three races, but nobody knew where the *chindi* had originated, the Hawks were lost in time, and the few remaining members of the race that had spawned the Monument-Makers were savages on a backward world with no knowledge of their former greatness.

Charlie Wilson must have been alerted she was coming. He met her in the corridor and escorted her into the lab. "Now understand," he said, "I don't really know what any of this means."

"What any of *what* means?"

Charlie was still filling in as acting lab director. He was doing a good job, but eventually she'd have to bring in somebody with an established reputation.

He took her into the tank, which was a small amphitheater. Thirty-two seats circled a chamber. Like so much of the Academy, it had been designed with public relations in mind. But it had turned out the general public wasn't all that interested. Usually, it was used by only one or two people at a time, but it occasionally served visiting groups of schoolchildren.

They sat down, and Charlie produced a remote. The lights faded to black, the stars came on, vast dust clouds lit up, and they were adrift somewhere in the night. The sensation that they were actually afloat among the stars, the two of them and their chairs, was broken only by the presence of gravity and a flow of cool air.

"We now have forty-seven tewks on record. You know that."

"Yes."

"All forty-seven are in places where we would have expected to find omegas. So we can assume they are all the same phenomenon."

He shifted in his chair, turning so he could face her. "Some of the Weathermen were close enough to the events to allow us to look for purpose. That is, what was the explosion supposed to accomplish? All of them took place in interstellar space. No worlds nearby. So it's not an attempt to cause general havoc. It's not somebody being vindictive."

"Tell that to Quraqua."

He nodded, conceding the point. Civilization on Quraqua had been obliterated. "All the clouds we've checked, each one is programmed to follow the hedgehog at a slightly higher velocity. When it overtakes the thing, it attacks the hedgehog, which then explodes, triggering the cloud, and you get the tewk."

"Okay. But why?"

"Who knows? Anyhow, it puts out as much light as a small nova. Somebody else will have to figure out why. We just know it happens."

"So what's the point? Why has someone gone to all this trouble?"

"I can't answer *that* question. But I can tell you that these things happen in bunches. Harold saw that from the first. Even when we only had a handful to look at. There's a pattern. There are six distinct areas where we've had events. But that's not to say we won't find others as Weatherman proceeds.

"The yellow star on your right is the supergiant R Coronae Borealis. Seven thousand light-years from here." He touched the remote. A hand's width to one side of the supergiant, a new star sizzled into existence. "Coronae 14," he said. "The fourteenth recorded event."

And a second new star, a few degrees away. "Coronae 15." And, a few degrees farther on, a third. Sixteen.

If there were to be a fourth, she could have guessed where it would be. But there wasn't.

"They're all this way," he said. "We get five here, six there. All within a relatively short time span. Maybe a thousand years or so. And each series is confined to a given region."

"Which means what?"

He looked frustrated. "Hutch, it's a research project of some sort. Has to be."

"What are they researching?"

"I don't know. It must have to do with light. Some of our people have made some guesses, but we don't have anything yet that makes sense. But you understand that would be the case if they were on a level sufficiently beyond us."

"Like Kepler trying to understand gravity fluctuations."

"Yes. Exactly."

LIBRARY ENTRY

NEWSCOPE
(Extract from Eric Samuels Press Conference)

New York On-line:	Eric, can you tell us precisely what happened to the *al-Jahani*?
Samuels:	There was a problem with the engines. With the jump engines. Uh, Bill?
Cosmo:	A mission as important as this, with so much hanging on it: Weren't they inspected before it left port?
Samuels:	We always do an inspection before ships leave the Wheel. In fact, this one was due for routine maintenance, but there wasn't time to finish. Jennifer.
Cosmo:	Wait. Follow-up, please. Are you saying it was sent out in a defective condition?
Samuels:	No. I'm not saying that at all. Had we known there was a problem, we would have corrected it, no matter how much time it took. In this case, we didn't see a problem, we were pressed for time, so we went ahead. We just

	got unlucky. Jennifer, did you want to try again?
Weekend Roundup:	Yes. If there was a question about this one, why didn't you send another ship?
Samuels:	We didn't have another ship. Not one with the carrying capacity we needed. Harvey, did you have something?
London Times:	You're saying the *Academy* didn't have another ship?
Samuels:	That's correct.
London Times:	How is that possible? The Council and the White House both claim they're doing everything they can to support this effort.
Samuels:	Well, there are limits to what can be done on short notice. Lookout is extremely far. Janet.
UNN:	Eric, what is the prognosis for the Goompahs?
Samuels:	We're still hopeful.

In the morning she hauled Charlie out of the lab for a walk along the Morning Pool.

The forty-seven events, he said, were concentrated in a half dozen widely separated areas. None of the areas was even remotely close to the bubble of space through which humanity had been traveling for the past half century. "Which is why," he told her, "we haven't seen these things in our own sky. But a few thousand years from now, when the light has had time to get here, there'll be some fireworks."

Two of the areas were out on the rim, one near the core, and three scattered haphazardly. "And none anywhere else?" she asked.

"Not yet. But the Weathermen are still arriving on station in a lot of places. We'll probably find more."

There was something solid about Charlie. He wasn't going to get caught up in wild speculations, and in his presence Hutch always felt things were under control. It was a valuable quality in a man so young. Charlie lacked his former boss's genius, but everybody did. And you don't need genius to have a bright future. You need common sense, persistence, and the ability to inspire others. And she could under no circumstances imagine him telling her he understood what the omegas were, then leaving her to wait while he gathered more evidence. He wouldn't even have set it up as a big announcement. He'd have simply told her what he knew. Or suspected.

She looked at the sky and wondered who would be there when the light show began.

Harold had been at the Georgetown Gallery, he'd said, when the epiphany came. When he decided he knew what was happening. But if Charlie were right, if they were doing advanced research, research on areas currently beyond human understanding, how could that have happened?

Was it possible he'd seen something at the gallery?

She called them, something she should have done long ago.

An automated voice asked how the Georgetown Gallery could be of service.

"Have you anything currently on display, or anything that's been sold over the past six months, that has as its subject matter the omega clouds?"

"One moment please."

A human voice picked up the conversation. *"This is Eugene Hamilton. I understand you're interested in* Omega.*"*

"I'm interested in anything you have, or may have had over the past six months, that uses the omegas as its subject."

"That would be René Guilbert's Storm Center. *You're familiar with it, of course."*

"Of course." In fact, Tor had mentioned it, but she couldn't remember the context. "May I take a look at it, please?"

"If you wish. You understand, of course, that the power and elegance of this piece, even more than most, cannot begin to be adequately conveyed electronically."

"Yes, I understand."

"Perhaps you would prefer to come by the gallery? Ms.—" He hesitated, inviting her to introduce herself.

"Hutchins," she said. "I'd prefer for the moment to see it here."

"Of course. One moment, please."

Moments later the work materialized on-screen. Guilbert had captured all the gloom and foreboding of the objects, had caught the immensity and overwhelming power. The malevolence, however, was not there. This was not an object that was out to kill; it just didn't give a damn. Don't get in its way and you'll be fine. Pretty much like *Moby-Dick*.

She made a copy and thanked Hamilton, assuring him she would run by to take a look.

Had Harold seen it?

She showed the copy to Charlie and he shrugged. "It's an omega, all right." He produced a disk. "I thought you might like to have this."

"What is it?"

"A history of what we've tried to do with the tewks. If anything occurs to you, I'd love to hear about it."

*   *   *

SHE SAT IN the tank for more than an hour watching the results of Charlie's efforts to find a rationale for the tewks. He and his team had tried to establish a real-time sequence, depicting what the events would look like if light traveled instantaneously. That took them nowhere. They had looked at energy yields, at electromagnetic variations, at the ranges to nearby objects that might be affected by the events.

It was a hodgepodge.

For all she knew, it could be a code.

She smiled at the thought while a cloud lit up on the far side of the room, near the emergency exit. And went out. A minute later, fifty years in real time, another, a hand's width away, flared and blinked off. They were like fireflies.

She increased the pace, the flow of time, and saw seven consecutive events coming down from the top of the chamber on her left, then six behind her. She had to take Charlie's word that they were not occurring at precise intervals. She really couldn't tell, just looking at a watch. But it was close enough. A series here, a series there.

They knew now that the events had a range of anywhere from twenty-seven to sixty-one days. And there were different spectra, which is to say the lights came on in different colors.

And that was another strange thing: A series was always the same color. Blue overhead, white at the back of the chamber, red on her left. What the hell was going on?

SHE HAD A conference that afternoon, attended a planning session with the commissioner's staff, and got out well after seven o'clock. Between meetings she resolved a dispute between department heads, arranged a visit to Serenity for a senator, and signed a special award for Emma, Sky, and the *Heffernan*, to be presented when they arrived back at their home station.

It cooled down considerably when the sun set, and she strolled into the roof transport complex thinking that she should have dressed more warmly.

"Where to, please, Ms. Hutchins?" the cab asked after she'd wiped her card.

On a whim, she said, "Georgetown," and gave the address of the art gallery on Wisconsin Avenue.

"Very good," said the cab as it lifted away.

They turned north over the Potomac, much swollen since the days of the Roosevelts. Constitution Island, with its cluster of public buildings, glowed in the encroaching night. The Lincoln, Jefferson, Roosevelt, and Brockman memorials watched serenely from their embankments. And the Old White

House, with its fifty-two-star U.S. flag spotlighted, stood behind its dikes. A cruise ship, brightly illuminated, moved steadily upriver.

The night was filled with traffic. A shuttle lifted off from Reagan, headed for the Wheel. Glidetrains were everywhere. She called Tor, warned him she'd be late.

"What's in Georgetown?" he asked.

"I'm headed to the gallery." Tor was, of course, familiar with the place. Years ago, they'd handled much of his work.

"Why?"

"Not sure. I want to get a look at Guilbert's *Storm Center.*"

He seemed satisfied. She almost thought he'd been expecting something like this to happen.

The flight needed only a couple of minutes. They descended into Wisconsin Park, and the cab asked whether she wanted it to wait.

"No," she said. "That won't be necessary, thank you."

"Very good, Ms. Hutchins."

She smiled. The AI had a British accent.

The gallery was located on the east side of Wisconsin Avenue, which had been designed originally for carriage traffic and horses, given over later to motorized ground vehicles, and was now restricted to pedestrians and, once again, horse-drawn coaches. She touched her commlink to the reader and climbed out.

Every night was date night in Georgetown. The restaurants were full. Shoppers and tourists wandered the streets, music and laughter drifted out of a dozen cafés, and in the park a mime was entertaining a group of children.

The Georgetown Art Gallery was located between a furniture store and an antique shop. The entire block of buildings had a dilapidated, run-down look. The architecture suggested these were the kinds of shops where you could get quality merchandise with the sheen rubbed off, but at bargain prices. The front door of the gallery was open, and she could see two men talking. As she watched, the conversation moved inside, and the door closed.

THE ESTABLISHMENT OPERATED on two floors, connected by a rickety staircase. The interior smelled of furniture polish and cedar, and the lighting was dimmed. Thick drapes covered the windows, and heavy carpets the floors. The decor was stilted, formal, uncompromising. She had stepped back in time into the twenty-second century.

Despite the fact she was married to an artist, she didn't know much about the various schools, or even the prominent masters. So she wandered among landscapes and portraits of people dressed in the styles of another age. There were a few paintings of a more esoteric sort, geometric designs really, intended to stir the blood in ways she did not understand. Tor had attempted to explain some of the techniques to her, but she'd let him see that she was a Philistine in these matters and he'd let it go.

Except the two men, she saw no one else. Their conversation broke up, one left, and the other came her way, smiling politely. "Good evening," he said, and she recognized Eugene Hamilton's voice. "May I be of service?"

"Mr. Hamilton," she said. "My name's Hutchins. I spoke with you earlier."

He beamed. "Ah, yes. The Deshaies."

"No," she said. "Actually we were talking about a Guilbert."

"*Storm Center*."

"Yes."

"It's right over here." He took her toward the rear and turned into a side room. Here was *Storm Center* immediately on her left. And he was right: The monitor had not done it justice.

The cloud was alive and churning and illuminated by internal power, and it was coming her way. Not after *her*, she understood. Nothing personal. She was too insignificant to warrant notice. But she had best stay clear.

"Mr. Hamilton," she said, "did you by any chance know Harold Tewksbury?"

His brow furrowed, and he repeated the name to himself. "Rings a bell," he said, uncertainly.

But no, he had no idea. Couldn't tell her if he'd ever seen him in the shop. He hoped there wasn't a problem.

She was wondering if he'd bought any paintings here. "He's recently deceased," she said.

"I'm so sorry."

"As are we all, Mr. Hamilton. I'd wanted to get something appropriate in his memory. The sort of thing he might have liked."

"Ah, yes. I see."

"He'd spoken occasionally of the gallery. In glowing terms, I should add."

Hamilton bowed modestly.

"I thought if I could get a sense of the sort of paintings he'd purchased in the past, I might be able to make a better choice."

"Yes. Of course." Hamilton wandered behind a counter and consulted his listings. "How did you spell his name?"

HE'D BOUGHT A Chapdelaine. *Frolic.* Hamilton showed it to her. A young woman reading on a park bench amidst a swarm of squirrels, cardinals, and bluejays. Storm clouds coming.

Purchase date was March 10. That would have been the week he died. But she saw no connection between the squirrels or even the approaching storm and the omega.

She went back and looked at the Guilbert again.

"I can see," he observed, "that you're taken with *Storm Center*. It's quite nice. I suspect it would make a remarkable addition to your home."

Yes, it would. It was of course a trifle pricey. As was everything in here. "I agree," she said. "But my husband's taste is so hard to gauge. You do understand?" She sighed. "Let me think it over. And if you don't mind, I think I'll look around a bit more."

She embarked on a tour through the place. Hamilton excused himself to look after another customer.

She thought maybe there'd be something in the more abstract paintings, the perceptual exercises of VanHokken or the exaggerated landscapes of Entwistle. But in the end she became convinced that whatever insight Harold might have entertained, she was not going to find it in Georgetown.

"IT BEATS ME," she told Tor over salmon and potatoes. Maureen had already eaten and was playing in the living room.

"Did you bring Charlie's disk home?" asked Tor.

She reached behind her, picked it up from the server, and laid it beside his plate. He poked at it with his fork, as if it might bite. "They can't make out anything at all?"

"Only what I've told you."

"Mind if I take a look?"

"Be my guest." Tor was bright, but he was strictly an arty type. No mathematical skills, no science to speak of. He'd watch, shake his head a few times, and at the end tell her that it beat the devil out of him.

They finished up and took their wine into the den. Maureen eyed the disk. "Sim, Mommy?"

"Not exactly, love," said Hutch. "Pictures of stars."

"Good." She collected one of her dolls, seated in its chair, and sat down on the floor beside it and told it to enjoy the show.

Tor put the disk in the reader, and they settled on the sofa.

It was the same show Hutch had watched earlier in the day. Tor paid close attention, occasionally making sounds deep in his throat as the brief lights blinked on and off. Hutch sipped her wine and let her mind wander. And Maureen mostly talked to the doll. "Up straight, Lizabeth." And "Cake, Mommy?"

When it was over, Tor sat silently for several minutes. Finally, he turned to her. "You say Harold only had *eight* of these things to work with?"

"Something like that. They were just beginning to find them."

"And he figured it out?"

"Well, no. I never really said that." She tried to recall what Harold had actually told her. That he thought he knew what was happening. That he needed more data. That he'd get back to her.

"All I see is a lot of lights."

"Well, thanks, Tor. That's very helpful."

"I don't think he knew any more than we do."

"They're pretty," Maureen said.

NEWSDESK

ASTEROID BARELY MISSES EARTH
Passes Within Eighty Thousand Kilometers
Nobody Noticed Until Danger Was Over
3 Km-Wide Rock Would Have Killed Millions
Investigation Promised

MOTHER CHARGED IN MURDER OF HUSBAND, FOUR CHILDREN
Only Survivor When Flyer Goes Down
Police: Victims Were Dead Before Crash

CHURCH OF REVELATION SAYS OMEGAS ARE EVIDENCE OF DIVINE WRATH
"Modern World Is in the Last Days"
Christopher Says Time Is Running Out

BOLTER WINS HISTORY PRIZE
National Book Award for The Lost Crusade

JURY SELECTION COMPLETE IN "HELLFIRE" CASE
Patterson Claims Personality Warped by Church Dogma
"Programming Started at St. Michael's"
Could Open Floodgates

WORLD POPULATION UNDER TWELVE BILLION
Decreases Sixty-third Straight Year
"Still Too Many"

HURRICANE EMMA FLATTENS GEORGIA COAST
Six Hundred Dead; Billions in Damage
"People Wouldn't Leave"

BRITAIN MAY BRING BACK MONARCHY
Tourism Takes a Beating

AFTER THE CHINDI HEADS FOR NEW YORK
Alyx Ballinger Brings London Hit to Broadway

PRE-QUAKE EVACUATIONS UNDER WAY IN AFGHANISTAN
7.1 Expected within Days
Center to Be 50 Km West of Kabul

COUNCIL GIVES ASSURANCE ON GOOMPAHS
"We're Doing Everything Possible"

ROCKETS CLINCH TITLE
Arky Hits Ninetieth

WOULD-BE ROBBER SUES LIQUOR STORE
Fall through Skylight "Caused Permanent Damage"
"Should Have Been Marked As Unsafe"

NFL VOTES TO EXTEND REGULAR SEASON IN '35
Teams to Play Twenty-six Games

chapter 33

THEY HAD NOT stopped speaking Goompah. Two ships were on the way, were due in fact at any time now, to take the passengers off, and to prepare the *al-Jahani* for a flight to Broadside, where they'd repair the vessel. Or junk it.

But if they still complained about the *molly kalottuls* that had betrayed them, if they still said *Challa, Judy* to her in the morning, the spirit had gone out of it.

Six of them were going on to Lookout. They'd get there a few weeks after the cloud and put on their Goompah gear and help hand out blankets and sandwiches to the survivors.

Of the other passengers, who had come specifically to see the Event, all but Frank Bergen would be going back.

They'd been adrift for six weeks, and the level of frustration had gotten pretty high. They'd all be glad to get off the *al-Jahani*. Snake-bitten ship. They'd blamed her, blamed Collingdale, blamed Hutchins, blamed the president of the NAU. It hadn't helped, of course, that Collingdale had gotten off and was now only a few weeks from the target, while here the rest of them sat. Things had gotten so bad that Alexandra had called a meeting and told them to relax, to accept the fact that there was always a degree of uncertainty in a flight like this one, that they had taken their chances and it hadn't worked out and they should be satisfied to know they tried. As good as the efficiency record was in superluminals, they had to realize there were a lot of moving parts, and redundancy for everything wasn't feasible. Things break down. Especially if you're going to run out of port in a rush, without attending to routine maintenance. "You wanted to get there by early December, and that meant we had to pull the trigger sooner than we'd have wished. We took a chance, and we lost. Accept it."

They didn't like being lectured by the captain, but it gave them a new focus for their dissatisfaction, and maybe that was all that was needed.

Judy liked Alexandra. She offered no apologies, never allowed Frank or any of the others to intimidate her, never backed down. Took no nonsense.

SHE HAD LOST all patience with the complainers around her, with Melinda Park, who kept talking about how valuable her time was and how it was being wasted; with Wally Glassner, who was prepared to tell anyone who would listen how he would have done things had he been in charge; with Jerry Madden, who'd been there now for seven months and what did he have to show for it?

Even among her own people, some had not been able to come to terms with the situation. And *they* were all young, convinced they would rise to the top of their respective professions, would keep control of their lives, and would one day retire after many years of success and joy.

At midmorning, Alexandra got on the allcom to inform her passengers that one of the rescue vessels had made the jump out of hyper and would be within visual range by late afternoon. That was the *Vignon*, which would be taking off everyone who was going back. The *Vignon* would deliver them to Broadside, where they'd embark on another ship for the flight home. It would be an eight-month run altogether, putting them back in Arlington by summer. Keeping her voice carefully neutral, the captain thanked them for their patience and understanding.

The *Vignon* would also be carrying engineers. They would do whatever had to be done to get the jump engines running again. The *Westover* was due within a few days. It would pick up Frank and Judy and the six members of her team who were going on to Lookout. When they were safely on their way, Bill would take the *al-Jahani* to Broadside. And if something went wrong en route and the ship disappeared into the mists, well, no one would be lost with it.

The people who were going back on the *Vignon* began clearing out their quarters. When Judy wandered into the common room after lunch, Melinda Park and Charlie Harding were already sitting there with their bags packed. "I'll miss you, Judy," Charlie said, and Melinda used a smile to indicate she felt the same way. The gesture also suggested that Melinda couldn't believe that Judy hadn't had enough. Next time Melinda rode one of these things, she said, people would read about it in the *New York Times*.

Several of the linguists came in, also ready to go. Rochelle was leaving, and Terry MacAndrew. Judy wasn't certain, but she thought *he* was leaving because *she* was.

Despite the circumstances, it wasn't a good career move for the linguists to bail out on the mission. It would get around, and people had long memories. When future positions came open, they'd go to the ones deemed loyal and dedicated. Judy had mentioned that to the group shortly after they'd bobbed to the surface out here, advising them to do what they thought best, but underscoring how important reputation was.

On the other hand, they were linguists rather than researchers, and maybe the people hiring them wouldn't care the way she would.

During the next half hour, the rest of those who were leaving showed up, Malachy looking tired and dispirited, Jason Holder frowning as if everything that had happened out here had been personally directed at him. Elizabeth Madden held up pretty well, and Ava MacAvoy. Jean Dionne was visibly relieved to be turning around. Of them all, Judy was going to miss John Price, tall and quiet and good-looking, a guy she could have fallen in love with, until she discovered he always took care of himself first. And Mickie Haverson, an anthropologist who spoke the best Goompah outside her people, and who had talked about putting on one of the disguises, and wandering around the cafés trading stories with the natives.

Valentino and Mike Metzger were packed and ready to go. And Marilyn McGee and Ed Paxton. Judy wondered how that marriage would fare when they got back into a normal situation. She was convinced that romances formed under unusual circumstances had little chance to prosper. But maybe she was wrong.

One by one, they shook her hand and kissed her. Thanks, Judy. I wish it could have worked out better. Appreciate the opportunity. Good luck. I hope there are some left when you get there. Sorry it turned out this way.

Alexandra came by, expressed her regrets, and gave them their compartment numbers on the *Vignon*. Twenty minutes later, the ship moved within visual range. It was that star over there, the one that kept getting brighter, that broke apart finally into a cluster of lights. Then it was alongside, sleek and gray, a dwarf compared with the *Hawksbill*. But big enough. And with working engines.

The engineers were the first ones through the airlock. Judy, who somehow felt it her duty to be on hand, stood to one side while Alexandra greeted them as they came in. There were two of them, both males, carrying cases and gauges, with instruments dangling from their belts and cables looped over their shoulders. Both very businesslike. Alexandra took them below.

THE ENGINEERS MADE several trips back to the *Vignon*. At one point, in front of Judy and several others, one of them told the captain that the engines would not have survived another jump. When Judy asked Alexandra what that would have meant she said that they would either have exploded or, more likely, stranded them in hyperspace. It was a reflection of the mood in the ship that Judy wondered whether the conversation had been staged to rebuff those who'd grumbled at the captain's insistence on going no farther.

Ah, well. She had no reason to doubt Alexandra, but she would have considered doing that herself had she been in the captain's place.

Meantime, the doors opened on the *Vignon*, and there was a final round of handshakes and farewells as people headed across. When the exodus had ended, the *al-Jahani* felt empty. Subdued. Only Frank remained, and six of her *Shironi Kulp*.

Charlie Harding, who had never stopped talking about how he looked forward to watching the cloud sweep in over Lookout, raining down meteors and then lightning bolts (although he felt sorry for the inhabitants, yes, pity we can't do more for them) got bored waiting for the *Vignon* to depart and came back to complain. Judy hoped they wouldn't leave without him.

She strolled down to her workroom and found Ahmed and Ginko engaged in a role-playing game, while Harry Chin watched. It had something to do with trying to move supplies down a mountain slope with a limited number of pack animals, all of whom could not be watched at once, in the presence of lions that attacked wherever they saw an opening.

Nick Harcourt was in the tank leading the Boston Philharmonic in a rendition of the *1812* Overture. Guns roared, the strings and horns delivered "La Marseillaise," and the drums rolled. Shelley and Juan were with him, so caught up in the performance that they didn't see Judy come in. She closed the door and found a seat.

They were inside a symphony hall, although Judy had no idea if it was a specific site or simply something made up by Bill. Nevertheless, there was the illusion of a packed house. She closed her eyes and saw tattered flags and cannons and cavalry charges. She knew Napoleon was involved—it was hard to miss—but she wasn't sure about the other details. Was it Brits on the other side? Or Russians? Well, it didn't matter. She let the music overwhelm her, carry her along. Once more unto the breach, dear friends. And finally she was participating in a thunderous ovation while Nick bowed and pointed his baton to various sections of his orchestra, which responded with a few fresh chords, thereby provoking another round of applause.

Alexandra came in and passed her a message marked PERSONAL. It was from Digger, and it outlined a plan to induce the Goompahs, when the time came, to evacuate their cities. He wanted her opinion.

It was as good as anything she'd been able to think of. Might even work. She scribbled off a short reply: *Try it. Good luck. Will join you in the new year.*

Hell, he might have something. Maybe they'd pull it off yet.

After dinner, the captain of the *Vignon* offered a tour of his ship. Everybody went. The kids went because they thought superluminals were exciting. Wally Glassner went because it provided a chance to pontificate on how much better the appointments were compared with what they'd had to live with for the past seven months. Jason Holder went so that he could make sure no one had accommodations superior to his. The other members of the general staff went so they could express their relief at getting away from the *al-Jahani*.

Judy went so she could be one more time with the eleven linguists and her shattered dream of riding to the rescue.

The captain of the *Vignon*, whose name was Miller, or Maller, or something like that, was an unassuming man of modest proportions, shorter even than she was, but who was obviously proud of his ship. He enjoyed showing her off. And, in fact, the *Vignon* was the most recent addition to the Academy's fleet. It had briefly belonged to the late Paul Vignon, a banking magnate, who had willed it to the Academy. "It was originally named *Angelique*," the captain explained, "after a girlfriend." At the family's request, the ship was renamed for the donor, who had never actually been aboard her. (Whether the personal pronoun referred to the ship or the girlfriend was not clarified.)

The tour ended in the common room, where the captain had arranged to have drinks and snacks laid out. Judy wandered from one conversation to the next, aware that she was having trouble getting the thundering beat of the *1812* out of her mind. She could not resist smiling, standing with MacAvoy and Holder, while the latter went on about the stupidity of administrators at the University of Toronto, where he'd punished their incompetence by leaving his position as leading light in the Sociology Department. As Holder described his vengeance, cannons went off in her head, banners rose through the gun smoke, and saber-wielding cavalry units drove into the flanks of the infantry.

"Why are you smiling?" Holder asked, stopping in midsentence to stare suspiciously at her.

"I was just thinking how difficult it will be for the U.T. to make up for the loss."

"Well," he said, not entirely certain whether he had been mocked, "I didn't really want to do any damage, but at some point they have to come to realize . . ." and so on.

When the opportunity offered, she excused herself and went back to the *al-Jahani*. Despite what they'd been through, she wasn't anxious to leave the broken ship. They'd accomplished a lot here, had broken into the language of the Goompahs, had mastered it, had read their literature, absorbed some of their philosophy and their ethics.

She sat down and paged through her notebook of Goompah wisdom.

Enjoy life because it is not forever.

There was no indication they believed in an afterlife, or in any kind of balancing of the scales. No judgment. No Elysian fields. They seemed to see the world, the *Intigo*, as an unpredictable place. But it was their home, as opposed to the idea it was a place through which they were just passing en route to somewhere else.

Therefore, pleasure was a good unto itself.

Regrets usually arise from things we failed to do that we should have, rather than things we have done that we should not.

Accept responsibility.

Enjoy the *moraka*, which didn't translate, but which seemed to imply a combination of love, passion, the exotic, intimacy, friendship.

Beware addictions. The essence of the good life is a free exercise of the will, directed by reason.

Beware addictions.

But wasn't *moraka* an addiction?

"Bill," she said, "I want to record a message. For transmission."

"*To?*"

"David."

"*When you're ready, Judy.*"

She thought about it a long time. Smiled into the imager, tried to look casual.

"Dave," she said, "the relief ship got here today. Some of our people are bailing out. Rest of us are headed in your direction. When you get where you're going, keep in mind things may not work out. If that happens, don't blame yourself." She almost thought she could see him, sitting in his cabin on the *Hawksbill*. Thinking about nothing except the omega. "Have a good flight. I'll see you in January."

"*Transmit?*" asked Bill.

Somewhere, far off, she heard the thundering hoofbeats of Cossacks.

"Send it."

"*Done,*" said Bill.

ARCHIVE

(Excerpts from *The Book of the Goompahs*)
(Translated by various members of the *Shironi Kulp*)

We exist for the sole purpose of making one another happy.

It is said, with pride, that we are the only creature that looks at the stars. But who knows what the galloon contemplates in the dead of night?

Every advance, every benefit, is the gift of an individual mind. No group, no crowd, no city has ever contributed anything to anyone.

Whatever you have to say, make it brief.

Good advice is always irritating.

Defend your opinion only if it can be shown to be true, not because it is your opinion.

Authors love to be petted.

Integrity means doing the right thing even when no one is looking.

Every good jest contains an element of truth.

The queen of virtues is the recognition of one's own flaws.

Snatch a kiss and embrace the consequences.

chapter 34

MOST OF THE projectors were micros, units ranging from the size of a pen up to a full-scale Harding monitor that came complete with a tripod. Four hundred of them had been collected at Broadside, the majority from their own supply, a few from one of the corporate development groups and independent researchers. They'd been shipped in four containers on the *Cumberland*. Mark Stevens also brought the two gold rings ordered by Digger. And a cartload of congratulations.

While the *Cumberland* unloaded its cargo, the *Hawksbill* arrived insystem. Stevens announced he'd stand by in case needed, which meant he wasn't anxious to forgo some human company after the long run out from the station.

The micros would be placed at strategic sites, then could be activated from the *Jenkins*, and would relay whatever visual image, and spoken message, was fed into the system. All that remained was to get them in place. And prepare the message.

The omega dominated the night sky. It was a great black thundercloud twice the size of the bigger moon. And it grew visibly larger each evening. The Goompahs saw it clearly as an approaching storm, one that refused to behave like ordinary storms. They were terrified. The talk in the streets was that when it came they would all hide indoors, with the shutters drawn. But they were still thinking exclusively of heavy rains and a few lightning bolts. Maybe over an extended time. Several days or so. There was no sense of the enormity of the thing, or of the damage that hurricane-force winds might do. Digger wondered whether the Goompahs had any experience with tornadoes or hurricanes.

They were approaching a part of the operation that Digger didn't like. He had known the plan for months, that when the *Hawksbill* got there, Kellie and Julie Carson would switch places. Julie would take over the *Jenkins*, and Kellie would switch to the *Hawksbill*, which she would command during the decoy operation. That was happening because she wasn't licensed to pilot the AV3, the heavyweight lander that would be used during the cloud-making effort.

It hadn't seemed like anything to worry about several months earlier but as time passed, and the cloud grew bigger, and somehow more unnerving, he found himself increasingly unhappy. They'd talked about it, he and Kellie, and she had explained there was no alternative, and not to worry because she'd be careful, and nothing was going to happen. So he let it go and said no more.

THEY'D PATROLLED EACH of the cities, making charts, watching to see where the crowds were, where the show would be most effective. It was late autumn in the southern hemisphere, and the nights were getting long. The weather wasn't cold, by Digger's standards. It never got below fifteen Celsius, and rarely below twenty-five. Kellie commented that you could tell when it got really cold in the *Intigo* because they had to move the drinks indoors.

Picking the public sites for the projectors had been easy enough. They'd concentrate on areas close to the cafés and meeting halls. And the temples would be good. They weren't crowded at night (when the performance would be most effective), but there were inevitably a few individuals enjoying the sacred atmosphere.

The Goompahs seemed not much given to organized religious ceremony. The only ones Digger had seen were the exorcisms, and the prayer for assistance, which had been followed by the sacrifice of the prelate. The temples drew reasonably sized crowds every day. But they were subdued crowds. They wandered separately among the figures of the gods, and if they prayed, they did it quietly. There would have been no chanting or weeping or collapsing in the aisles in a Goompah temple.

THE *HAWKSBILL* WAS about three hours behind the *Cumberland*. It was a big, boxy vehicle, with eight cylinders lashed to its hull.

The ship itself was a series of progressively longer oblongs, just the sort of thing the clouds seemed to like. There'd been a couple of experiments years ago in which derelicts that looked not too different from the *Hawksbill* had been allowed to sink into omegas. Unlike rounded vehicles, which had simply dipped into the clouds and come back, the derelicts had inevitably ignited fierce electrical storms, and on one occasion, a ship had been blasted apart on approach.

The entry locks of the *Jenkins* and the *Hawksbill* weren't compatible, so Collingdale and his people had to come over in go-packs. As much as Digger liked having Kellie to himself, it was nice to see somebody new. There'd been no one other than Stevens for months.

Unless you counted Macao.

He still felt discouraged about his evening with her, and wished there were a way to hold a normal conversation with her. Wished he could do so without scaring her. Hi, Macao. I'm from South Boston. Long way from home. How's it going?

For all the talk about opening their minds and not jumping to unwarranted conclusions, *Think for yourself*, the Goompahs weren't as bright as he'd hoped.

He'd seen Judy's translations, segments of the *Book of the Goompahs*, and he wished he could find those who had been writing the maxims. They were the people he needed to talk to.

Judy had told him the work was attributed by name and by epoch, although they hadn't figured out the system of dating yet or, for that matter, where the epochs all fit. "They're probably all dead," she'd added cheerfully.

He watched the *Hawksbill*'s airlock open, a tiny hatch up on A Deck, just behind the bridge. They came out one at a time and got ferried across by Julie. When they were all in the airlock, Kellie closed the outer hatch, pressurized, and opened up.

There's no real way to describe the sense of camaraderie, and of tribal linkage, under such circumstances. Digger had never been so happy to see visitors in his life. As an added bonus, his sense of responsibility for the lives of several hundred thousand Goompahs faded a bit. Collingdale was here now. He was the senior guy, and consequently in charge.

"Good to meet you, Digby," he said, extending his hand. "And this must be the bride." Kellie looked uncomfortable but accepted the comment in good spirits. "We're glad to be here." He jerked his thumb in the direction of the omega. "Doesn't look good, does it?"

"No," Digger said quietly.

"Goompahs must be scared half out of their minds."

He introduced Marge Conway, a tall, middle-aged woman. "Marge is our camouflage expert," he said. "And Avery Whitlock." One of those guys who produces stuff they read in the university literature courses. Introduced as Whit. He smiled easily and nodded. He was pleased to meet Kellie and Digger. Firm grip, nice clothes, exquisite diction. Touch of New England somewhere.

"And, of course, Julie."

Julie was taller than he'd expected her to be. It was sometimes hard to tell when the only communication you had was electronic. She was redheaded and, he thought, very young. Barely out of her teens.

After the pleasantries had been completed Digger looked hopefully at Marge. "Can you really hide them?" he asked.

"I can put a cloud cover over them," she said. "After that, it's anybody's guess."

Knowing Whitlock was coming, Digger had taken time to read some of his work. He was a naturalist by trade, and he wrote essays with titles like "The Mastodon in the Basement" and "It's a Bug's Life." Digger had been put off by the titles. People who write about academic subjects should not try to appeal to the masses. But he'd enjoyed the work and was pleased to meet the author.

They were all saying it was hard to believe they were actually here. Whit kept looking out at the arc of the planet and shaking his head. "Where is the *Intigo*?" he asked.

"Can't see it from here," said Kellie, taking a peek to be sure. "It's on the other side of the planet."

"When can we go down?"

Until that moment, Digger had forgotten the long-ago message from Hutchins, informing them that Whit would want a tour, and that they were to accommodate him in every way possible, but were under no circumstances to lose him or let him get hurt.

"I guess we have some work to do before we can even think about that," said Collingdale, looking toward Julie.

"Not really," she said. "Everything's on automatic." She smiled, opened a channel to Bill, and told him to deliver the cargo.

One by one, the cylinders attached to the *Hawksbill* hull were released. A pair of thrusters was attached to each, and Digger watched as the units adjusted their positions, moving well away from each other and from the ships.

"What are they?" Digger asked Marge.

"Chimneys," she said. "Rainmakers."

If she said so.

A cargo door opened, and a helicopter floated out, its propellers folded. Then a pair of landers. "There are two more," Marge told him, "packed on the AV3."

The AV3 was a heavy-duty hauler, designed to move capital equipment in and out of orbit. It came next, a large, black vehicle, with massive wheels rather than the treads that the smaller landers used. Antigrav engines were located in twin pods outside the hull. Its vertical thrusters could be rotated out onto the wings so they could fire past large loads slung beneath the vehicle, as would be the case with the rainmaker packages.

"Aren't the Goompahs going to see all this stuff?" asked Digger. "I thought you'd make the clouds by using some sort of electronic thing you could just fire from orbit."

"Sorry," she said. "We're all out of those."

"And these are really rainmakers?" asked Kellie.

"Yes. They look a bit clumsy. But don't worry. They'll work fine."

Digger kept thinking how he and Kellie had been pussyfooting around on the ground to avoid being seen. "And all this is going down to the surface?"

"Only if you want cloudy weather."

"Marge, they'll *see* it."

"The Goompahs?"

"Of course the Goompahs. Who else are we worried about?"

"The landers are equipped with lightbenders."

"The hauler, too?"

"Too big. But we'll be doing everything at night. So I don't think you need to worry."

He sighed. "Okay. When did you want to start?"

"As soon as possible."

"Will you need help?"

"Nope. Just Julie here, to get me around." She smiled at him. "You can relax and watch, Dig."

AND THE BIG moment had arrived.

Kellie nodded at Digger, excused herself, and stepped out into the passageway. Julie followed a few moments later. When Julie came back she was wearing a formal white jacket, complete with epaulets and a pair of eagles, the symbol of her rank. Kellie showed up on one of the screens. "Dr. Conway," she said, "gentlemen, I'd like you to be aware that there has been a change in command, and that Captain Carson is now the commanding officer of the *William B. Jenkins*. Thank you very much for your attention."

Julie gazed around at them. "As my first official act," she said, "I am going to preside over the wedding of two of the company."

Collingdale made a face and looked at the time. "I don't want to be a spoilsport," he said, "but I assumed we were going to do this after we got back."

"From where?" asked Digger, making no effort to conceal his annoyance.

"From sidetracking the cloud. Digger, I understand how important this is to you, but the cloud is closing in. We have no time to spare."

"Actually," said Julie, "the most efficient orbital window is an hour away. Make yourself comfortable." She studied them for a few moments, as if decisions needed to be made. "Digger," she said, "over here, please. On my right. Marge, you'll be our matron of honor. And Whit, at the request of the groom, you'll serve as best man."

Whit came up and stood by Digger.

"David, we'd like you to act as witness to the proceedings."

Collingdale nodded and managed to look pleased.

Bill's image popped on-screen. He was in formal whites, seated at a keyboard. Julie pointed at him, and he began playing the "Wedding March *Lohengrin.*" The door to the passageway opened and Kellie appeared in full bridal regalia, flanked by Mark Stevens.

Digger's heartbeat went up a couple of notches.

Bill brought the march up full. Kellie and her escort strode into the room. Someone had given Marge a veil. She donned it and fell in behind the bride. Digger slipped the rings to Whit, experienced the momentary doubt that strikes anyone who's been a bachelor too many years, and wondered if Kellie was thinking the same thing.

But by the time Julie asked whether he wanted her for his wife, all hesitation had fled.

DIGGER TOOK A couple of minutes to kiss the bride, then was told that was enough and he should get to work. There were four hundred projectors to be set up in designated locations on the isthmus. Whit volunteered to assist.

That idea looked a bit shaky to Digger. He'd expected to do the distribution himself, without having someone else along that he'd have to look after. It wasn't that Whit wouldn't be good company, but he wasn't young, and he was just getting into an e-suit for the first time. He had no experience with lightbenders. He didn't really understand how things worked on the ground, and it was easy to imagine him bumping into one of the Goompahs and causing an incident. Digger knew the hazards quite well.

Still, he was a VIP, and they had a responsibility to keep him happy.

Meantime, David Collingdale was trying to get his show on the road. That meant good-bye to Kellie for a few days. "Enjoyed the honeymoon," he told her.

"You've had your honeymoon," she said. "Now it's time to earn your pay." She kissed him, hugged him, and looked up at him with shining eyes. "I love you, Digby," she said. "Keep your head up when you get down there."

"You, too, Kel. Take no chances. I don't really like this very much."

"I'll be careful."

Another smooch, and she was gone. E-suit, air tanks, go-pack, and she was swimming out the airlock with Collingdale, headed for the *Hawksbill.* He could have continued his conversation with her on the link, but it seemed easier not to. He watched them disappear through the cargo carrier's main hatch. Then she fired up, drifted away, and disappeared into the night. A few minutes later, Stevens told Digger he wished he could stay for the show, eased the *Cumberland* out of orbit, and started back to Broadside.

Digger sighed and wandered back up to A Deck. Time to sit down with Whit and show him what they'd be doing.

T'MINGLETEP WAS LOCATED on the western side of the lower continent, where a major river emptied into the sea. A narrow island hugged the shoreline, turning the strait into a marsh. A bridge connected the city and the island.

In terms of both geographical size and population, it was probably the largest of the eleven cities. The same mountain range that dominated the isthmus passed through the region a few kilometers to the east. That was where they wanted the Goompahs to be when the omega hit. The trek over there wouldn't be too bad. There was no road, but the ground was flat and easily passable. All that would be necessary was to persuade them to go.

A few ships were docked or anchored in the harbor, and one was just setting out, turning north. Julie engaged the lander's lightbender, and Whit looked out and watched the stubby wing of the spacecraft vanish. "Makes my head spin," he said.

Digger smiled. "You'll get used to it."

They settled onto a stretch of beach north of the city. Whit and Digger got out and activated their infrared lenses so they could see each other. "That's much better," said Whit.

They'd divided forty-eight micros between them, stuffing them into their vests. "I'll head for the mountains," Julie said. "If you need me, just call." When they were clear, she closed the lock, and Digger watched the spacecraft lift away.

Whit gazed around him, at the sea, the mountains, the sky. At a seashell, at a crablike creature digging busily in the sand. At the gulls. At a thorny green plant. "Why does it happen here," he said, "and so few other places?"

"Pardon?" asked Digger.

"We used to think that any world with the right chemicals, good temperatures, and some water, would produce elephants. And trees. And the whole Darwinian show." He shook his head. "In fact, it rarely happens."

"Don't know," said Digger.

"We're still missing a big piece of the puzzle. Some enabling mechanism that gets the whole process started."

They trudged up the beach toward a cluster of trees. The sand turned to hard earth, and they broke through onto a long avenue. A group of Goompahs, not quite fully grown, were gathered in a courtyard. They were bundled in heavy shirts and vests and pullover knitted caps. A couple wore animal-hide gloves.

"Can we go listen?" asked Whit. "For a minute."

"Do you understand the language?" asked Digger.

"Not really. I've tried, but I'm afraid my linguistic skills, whatever they might once have been, have deserted me. But it's okay. I'd just like to hear them speaking."

"All right," said Digger. "I guess we're not all that pressed for time."

It was routine stuff. They were all males, and it was strictly sex. Who was game for sack time and who should be avoided.

Whit was disappointed when Digger provided a carefully phrased translation. "Seems mundane," he said. "I expected more." But he adjusted his thinking quickly as they moved away. "Maybe it's what would happen with any intelligent species developing in a reasonably free society." But it was clear he'd have preferred to find them discussing philosophy or ethics.

"Do they talk much about the cloud?" he asked.

"Some." Digger thought about the fear he witnessed every day. "At night, especially, when they can see it. In the sunlight, I think it's kind of unreal."

"Has there been an increase in religious reaction?"

"That would be a better question for Collingdale. Other than the sacrificial ceremony we told you about, we haven't really seen anything. But they don't seem to be big on religious services. They don't go to the temple and participate in ceremonies or listen to sermons."

"But they do visit the temples?"

"Yes. Some do."

Whit was full of questions: "They sent off the round-the-world mission, but does the individual Goompah really care whether the world is round or not?"

The ones that showed up for the *sloshen* got pretty excited about it.

"They seem to have few or no prohibitions regarding sexual activity. What sort of contraceptives have they?"

Not something Digger had gotten into. Didn't know.

"They've been on the isthmus for millennia? Why haven't they expanded?"

Didn't know.

"Why haven't they been forced to expand by sheer population growth?"

Didn't know that either.

"What a marvelous place this is," he said at last, apparently giving up on Digger's intellectual curiosity. "A land in which the inhabitants are just coming awake."

They had arrived at their first destination. It was a wide thoroughfare, lined with merchants and eating places. The shutters were all closed against the cool air. Fires burned in the shops and the cafés. Digger did a quick survey. "There." He pointed at a spot a few meters off the ground, above some toddlers who were chasing each other in circles. "Ideal place for an apparition." He selected a cross-post that supported the roof of a bread shop, reached into his vest, produced a projector, recorded its number, angled the lens, and placed it as high up on the post as he could reach. It was inconspicuous, and there wouldn't be any Goompahs who could take it down without a ladder. He opened a channel to the lander. "Julie."

"Go ahead, Digger."

"Two-two-seven."

"Wait one."

Digger kept an eye on Whit. His fuzzy silhouette was back out of the way, between the side of a garment shop and an open culvert with running water. But he was bent forward, almost like a stalking cat, watching the crowds pass.

The *Intigo* was home to a seabird, a long-billed gray creature with large hang-down ears that almost looked like a second pair of wings. Called a *bogulok*, it was found in large numbers throughout the isthmus area. The name, freely translated, meant *floppy ears*.

Digger activated the unit and a *bogulok* blinked into existence above the crowd, at the point Digger had targeted. It was in midflight, and it got only a few meters before it vanished.

"Good," Digger told his commlink. "It's perfect." No one seemed to have noticed anything unusual.

"I'll lock it in," said Julie.

Digger collected Whit and went looking for a second site.

HE PLANTED FOUR projectors in the market area, three outside public buildings, six more inside theaters and meeting halls, and five at various locations along the main thoroughfares. Kellie had spotted what they thought was the equivalent of an executive office building, which was staffed day and night, and they installed two more there, one inside and one outside. On each occasion he checked back with the lander to make sure they had a good angle.

The bridge connecting the island to the mainland was about a half kilometer long. It consisted of wooden planks and supports. There was nothing else, no handrails, no braces. If you didn't pay attention to what you were doing, you could walk right off into the ocean.

It *was* wide. There were some draft animals on it, and they had no trouble finding room to pass everything without any undue bumping. "Not bad engineering," said Whit. Digger hadn't been impressed until Whit pointed out that the bridge's supports were embedded in ooze, and had to withstand tides generated by two moons. "Must require constant maintenance," he added. He got down on his knees and peeked underneath.

They got across and planted another projector in a tree at the end of the bridge, aiming it up so the apparition would appear in the branches, visible from all directions.

Whit had become a kid in a toy store, stopping to look at everything and everyone. "They're beautiful," he said, referring to the inhabitants. "So innocent." He laughed. "They all look like Boomer."

"You need to watch one of the orgies," Digger said.

"That's my point. If they weren't innocent, they wouldn't have orgies."

Digger didn't even ask him to explain that one.

THEY FINISHED UP shortly after sundown. Digger had expected Whit to be exhausted, but he seemed disappointed that the day was ending. "Marvelous," he said. "Experience of a lifetime."

The lander met them outside town, on the south side, where the isthmus road began. They stood at the edge of the Goompah world. Beyond lay impossibly rough country, a mountain range that looked impassable, dense forest, and, ultimately, the southern ice cap.

Julie was supposed to get back to the *Jenkins*, pick up Marge, and start installing the rainmakers. She was running late or maybe she just didn't feel she had time to spare. Digger was barely buckled into his seat before they were aloft, heading for orbit. "Are you really going to be able to do this?" Digger asked her.

"I'll manage," she said.

"You're going to work all night?"

"I expect so."

"And tomorrow you're going to be taking us to *Savakol*."

"Yes."

"All day."

"More or less."

"And then another round with Marge. When are you going to sleep?"

She had trouble restraining a smile. "I've already slept."

"When?"

They were rising through billowing cumulus. "Today. All day."

"Today? How'd that happen? I was on the circuit with you every fifteen minutes."

"No, you weren't," she said. "You were on with Bill."

"Bill?"

"I guess he used my voice." She smiled. "Don't worry about me, Dig. I have the easiest job in the operation."

Avery Whitlock's Notebooks

. . . What I find particularly striking, after this first day of walking the streets of a civilization erected by another species, is how few young there are. This is a society that seems to glory in parks, in throwing balls around and splashing through fountains. And yet there seemed as many mothers and fathers as children. Primitive societies at home always produce large families. It does not seem to be the case here. I saw only a few parents with two offspring. If there were any with three, I missed them.

I wonder why that is.

—December 4

"ARE WE READY to go?"

In fact, Marge had been ready for hours. She'd sat by the comm board listening to the conversations from below, going over her checklists, and trying unsuccessfully to sleep.

"Yes," she said. "Armed and ready."

And at last she and Julie strapped on e-suits and air tanks and went out the cargo airlock.

Marge didn't show it much, but she was delighted to be there. There'd been, God knew, a lot of time to think on the way out, especially after Collingdale came aboard. And she'd spent much of it reviewing her life. Loads of talent, her father had told her. You'll be whatever you want to be.

In fact she'd found everything too easy. She'd become an M.D., had gotten bored, and taken a second doctorate in climatology. She'd been more interested in power than research. She hadn't realized it before making this voyage, but it was the truth. Whenever there had been a choice between administration and pure science she'd gone for administration. Take over. Move up. Get the corner office. She had a natural talent for it. It had paid well, felt good, and yet it had left her eminently dissatisfied.

Probably as a direct result, she'd used a wrecking ball on each of her three marriages. Well, that was overstating it, but she'd attributed her disappointment with her various careers to each of her spouses in turn, and when the extension time came, the relationships had been discontinued. More or less by mutual agreement. Good luck. No hard feelings. Been good to know you.

Her dancing career, which had arced between the end of her college days and the beginning of her medical years, had been the same. Too easy, no patience with the routine work needed to rise to the top of the profession, find something else.

She'd even taken a fling at martial arts. She was good at it, and knew she could have picked up a black belt had she been willing to invest the time.

The problem with her life, she'd decided shortly after Collingdale had come aboard, was that there had never been a serious challenge. No use for a black belt in the great game of life because she could find nobody she wanted to clobber.

And now here came the cloud.

Collingdale thought of it as a kind of personal antagonist. It was his great white whale, the thing that had crushed the crystal cities of Moonlight. When this was over, when he got back, he was going to lead a crusade to find a way to destroy the things. He thought the experience at Lookout, which had generated worldwide sympathy for the Goompahs, would make this the right time.

It was an effort she would probably join. In any case, she was finally in a fight she wasn't sure she could win. And it was an exhilarating feeling.

The AV3 was waiting. Like the *Hawksbill*, it wasn't compatible with the *Moorhead*, so Julie had parked it a hundred meters away. The chimney packages floated in the night like so many barrels of beer. Marge had been in hostile environments before in the e-suit, but always on a planetary surface. Floating in the void, tethered to Julie, was a bit different, but not as disorienting as she'd been led to expect.

The hauler's airlock opened as they approached, and Julie took them in. Lights went on, more hatches opened and closed, and they were in the cabin.

Green lamps glowed as the hauler came out of sleep mode. Julie got coffee for them, and Marge settled into the right-hand seat and got out her notebook.

"Anybody ever try this before?" Julie asked.

"Cloud-making?"

"Yes."

"Oh, sure. The technique's been used to modify droughts."

"How come I never heard of it?"

"I don't know. How much time do you spend at home?"

THEY TOOK TWO landers on the first flight. And a Benson Brothers water pump. "Got a big, dry lawn? Depend on Benson." They could have saved time by having Bill simply take over the controls on all four landers and pilot them down, but AIs were notoriously deficient if it became necessary to respond to a surprise, like a sudden storm. Especially if they were trying to do too many things at once. It was the price paid for artificial intelligence. Like biological intelligence, its higher functions produced a single consciousness. Or at least, they seemed to. Multiple tasks requiring simultaneous judgment could lead to trouble. They were too far from home to risk losing a vehicle. If one went down, the operation would be over.

Marge had spent much of the voyage to Lookout reviewing weather and topographical maps she'd constructed from information forwarded by the *Jenkins* and deciding where to place the rainmakers. The target area for the first one was on the eastern side of the upper continent, midway between *Roka* and *Hopgop*. (How, she wondered, could you take anyone seriously who named a city *Hopgop*?)

It was dark, and the omega was just rising when they descended toward the edge of a heavy forest. Beyond, scattered trees and hills ran unbroken to the sea. A small stream, its source somewhere in the high country, wound through the area. There was no sign of nearby habitation.

"Enough water?" Julie asked.

"It'll do," said Marge. "Take her down."

Julie put them as close to the trees as she could, shearing off a few in the process. The forest was loud with insects. "Anything here that bites?" asked Marge.

"Not that we've been told about."

They switched on their night-vision lenses. The trees were of several types, but all were tall, spindly, not much to look at. Marge would have preferred something with a bit more trunk.

"What do you think?" asked Julie.

The wood seemed solid enough. "They'll have to do," she said. She headed directly for a section she'd spotted from the air, a cluster of trees forming an irregular circle, roughly forty meters in diameter. There were a few other growths within the perimeter, which they dropped with laser cutters.

"Got a question for you," said Julie.

"Go ahead."

"Why do we need the landers? If the hauler has enough lift to bring the rainmaker packages down, why isn't it enough to support one of them when it's extended? It won't weigh any more."

"When it's extended," she said, "the chimney will encounter resistance from air currents. It would take more than the hauler to keep it stable."

They got back inside the AV3, and Julie touched a presspad. The cargo door in the rear opened. "Bill," she said, "put the landers under cover of the trees."

"Yes, Julie. I'll take care of it."

The AI used a dolly to move the landers outside, then activated them and flew them into the shadow of the forest. Meantime, the dolly unloaded the pump.

Marge saw lightning in the west. "Maybe you won't need the chimneys," said Julie.

"Unlikely," she said.

                              *   *   *

THEY PICKED UP the second pair of landers and delivered them to the same site. They still needed a chimney package and the helicopter. They'd run simulations on what would happen if they tried moving both on the same flight. It was tempting to try it, and save time. But the simulations weren't encouraging. The chimney was heavy, and the load didn't balance right. Given almost any kind of aerial disturbance, they would go down in flames.

So they would make the additional flight. "To be honest," Julie told her, as they approached one of the cylinders floating off the *Jenkins's* port bow, "getting down with this thing slung on our belly will be enough of a battle."

The package *was* big. A large cylinder more than thirty meters wide, maybe forty-five meters long. Marge had been impressed with Julie's cool performance as she locked onto the rim, attaching it so that the narrow mouth of the cylinder faced down. Listening to the heavy *bang* as the clamps engaged, she decided the pilot's caution was justified.

The unit was equipped with guidance thrusters, which she now jettisoned. The *Jenkins* could retrieve them later.

They were on the night side, approaching the terminator, chasing the sun. "Not the best planning," Julie said. "We'll have to go around once before we start our descent."

At this point it didn't matter. Marge sat back to enjoy the ride. The skies were clear and bright. The omega was behind them somewhere, not visible unless they called it up on the scopes. The rising sun picked out a couple of islands and a few drifting clouds.

They were passing through daylight. Marge watched the oceans and landmasses rotating beneath, thinking how green it all was, how lovely, and she began to wonder whether it would draw settlers eventually, people who would argue that the Goompahs only used a small part of the world anyhow, so why not? It occurred to her for the first time that terrestrial governments might eventually find themselves unable to enforce their edicts about interfering with other civilizations. Might not even be able to stop groups of exploiters from seizing distant real estate.

Ah, well. That was a problem for another age.

Behind them, the sun sank below the horizon and they soared through the night. "Starting down in five minutes," said Julie.

It was okay by Marge.

MOMENTS BEFORE THEY entered the atmosphere, Julie switched on the spike, reducing the gravity drag. Marge noticed that they'd dropped out of orbit earlier than the point where they'd started the other three descents. "Losing weight isn't the same as losing mass," Julie explained. "We're still carrying a load, and we need more space to get down."

There were a few clouds over the area, and she didn't see the shoreline until they were directly over it. Then they raced inland, over rolling hills and, finally, the forest. The omega had set, and the eastern sky was beginning to brighten.

Julie eased the vehicle down among the cluster of trees where they'd landed earlier. When her cargo touched the ground she held steady, keeping the weight of the AV3 off it. "Okay, Bill," she said, "release the package."

Marge felt it come free.

They continued to hover immediately overhead. "Bill," Julie said, "peel the wrapper."

Marge watched the tarp protecting the rainmaker fall away. Grapplers took it up and stored it in the cargo bay.

When it was done, Julie banked off to one side so they could see. The chimney was made of ultralight, highly reflective cloth. It was a flexible mirror, and it was virtually invisible.

And that was it for the night. It was getting too close to sunrise to try to do any more. The next day, when they came back, they would bring the helicopter.

The mood has changed. You can't really miss it. Everywhere you go at night, Goompahs are looking up over their shoulders at the thing in the sky that won't go away and gets bigger every day. The sense of something deadly, of something supernatural, *coming this way has become a palpable part of everyday life here. The streets aren't as crowded at night as they used to be. And the Goompahs talk in hushed tones, as if they were afraid the monster overhead might hear them.*

It might be that the most disquieting aspect of the thing is that it looks like a squid. The Goompahs are familiar with squids, or with something very like a squid. They're a delicacy here, as they used to be in some cultures at home. But the Goompahs, like us, are struck by their grasping capabilities, and they, too, find the creatures unsettling. I overheard a group of them today describing an incident that is probably apocryphal, but which they were convinced was true: Someone in a fishing boat was seized by a squid and dragged overboard while his comrades watched, too frightened to assist. Did it really happen? I don't know. The interesting thing is that the story surfaces just as the time when a celestial squid seems to be coming after the entire Intigo.

Something else has changed: They don't call it T'Klot *anymore. The Hole. It's become instead* T'Elan. *The Thing. The Nameless.*

—*Digger Dunn, Journal*
Thursday, December 4

chapter 36

On board the *Hawksbill*.
Friday, December 5.

KELLIE COLLIER WASN'T comfortable with Dave Collingdale. He never laughed, never eased up. He sat beside her on the bridge, staring at the images of the cloud in stony silence.

"We never took the clouds seriously," she said finally, trying to start a conversation. "People who think we can just ignore them and they'll go away should come out here and take a look at one close up."

"I know." And he just sat there.

She asked him an innocuous question about the flight out, but that didn't go well either.

He turned aside every effort to lighten the atmosphere. Ask him how things were going, and he told you the position of the cloud. Ask how he was feeling, and he told you how he was going to enjoy doing it to the cloud.

Doing it to the cloud.

She got the sense that he would have used stronger terminology had she been a male.

But however he might have said it, it carried the clear implication that the cloud was alive.

"I am going to get it," he said.

Not decoy it.

Not turn it aside.

Get it.

THERE WAS AN industrial-sized projector mounted on the belly of the *Hawksbill* and a twin unit housed in the shuttle. Hutch, who had apparently thought up this whole idea, had warned her that the *Hawksbill* was the wrong shape for working around omegas, and she was sorry but they'd needed to pack so much stuff on board there'd been no help for that. Keep your distance, Hutch had said. Watch out.

She intended to.

The jets boiling off the cloud's surface raced thousands of kilometers ahead of it. The omega was coming in from slightly above the plane of the system, so most of its upper surface was in shadow. She'd arced around and come in from the rear. They were three hundred kilometers above the cloud. The mist stretched to the horizon in all directions. It was quiet, placid, attractive. And there was an illusion, quite compelling, that there was a solid surface just beneath. That one could have walked on it.

"How big is it, Bill?" she asked. "Upper surface area?"

"*Eighty-nine billion square kilometers, Kellie.*" Seventy-five hundred times the size of the NAU, which combined the old United States and Canada. "*This is a good time to launch the monitors.*"

"Do it."

There were six of them, packages of sensors and scopes that would run with the cloud and keep an eye on it.

Collingdale stood behind her, watching, grunting approvingly as the lamps came on, indicating first that the units were away, and then that they had become operational. "Dave," she said, "we'll be ready to go in about ten minutes."

"Okay," he said. He took his own chair and brought up an image of the shuttle, waiting in the launch bay with its LCYC projector. The LCYC was a duplicate of the one bolted to the ship's hull.

Dead ahead, slightly blurred by mist, she could see Lookout. There was just the hint of a disk. And the two moons. Permanently suspended in the omega sky, as though they were just rising.

"When this is over," he said, the tension suddenly gone from his voice, "I'm going to push to get this problem taken care of. If we organize the right people, make some noise in the media, we can get funding and get the research under way."

"To get rid of these things, you mean?"

"Of course. Nobody's serious. But that's going to change when I get home." He looked down at the cloudscape.

They were moving faster than the omega, and as she watched they swept out over the horizon, and it fell away. But it was still braking, and the vast jets thrown forward by the action rolled past her.

"Okay, David," she said. "Let's line up."

She took them down among the jets and set the *Hawksbill* directly in front of the cloud.

"*Electrical activity increasing,*" said Bill.

She saw some lightning. "That coming out of the main body?" she asked.

"*Yes,*" said Bill.

"Directed at us?"

"*I believe it is random.*"

Collingdale got up again and stood by the viewport. Man couldn't stay still. "It knows we're here," he said.

More illumination flickered through the cloud.

She felt chilled. Wished Digger were there.

"It's okay," he said soothingly, apparently sensing her disquiet, but not understanding the reason. "We're going to be fine." His eyes were hard, and a smile played at the corners of his lips. *He's enjoying this.*

"I need you to sit down and belt in, David," she said. "Maneuver coming up."

He tapped the viewport as if, yes, everything was indeed under control, and resumed his seat.

She didn't like being so close to the damned thing. She could very nearly have reached out the airlock and stuck an arm into one of the jets.

"*Range approaching 250,*" said Bill.

"Match velocity."

The retros fired. The same technology that provided artificial gravity served to damp the effects of maneuvering. But they still existed, and for about twenty seconds her body pushed against the forward restraints. Then the pressure eased.

"*Done,*" said Bill.

The problem for Kellie was to find adequate operating space away from the plumes. He waited with studied patience while she did so.

"Bill," she said, "begin relaying data to *Jenkins.*" Just in case. Bill confirmed, and she turned to Collingdale. "Dave, we are ready to launch the shuttle."

THE LCYC PROJECTORS were industrial units with a variety of uses, ranging from entertainment to environmental and architectural planning. They were configured, when used in tandem, to create a larger, more clearly defined image than either could have done alone.

The shuttle left the ship and moved out to a range of seven hundred kilometers, where it assumed a parallel course with the *Hawksbill.*

"*In position,*" said Bill.

"Bill," she said, "take direction from David."

"*Confirmed.*"

"Bill," said David, "start the program."

The AI, looking about twenty-two, dashing and handsome, appeared near the viewport. He looked out and smiled. "*Program is initiated,*" he said.

Midway between the *Hawksbill* and the shuttle, a giant hedgehog blinked into existence. It looked *real*. It looked like a piece of intricately carved rock. Gray hard spines rose out of it, and it turned slowly on its axis.

Beautiful.

"How big is it?" Kellie asked.

"Five hundred thirty kilometers diameter."

"A little bit bigger than the original."

"Oh, yes. We wanted to be sure the bastard didn't miss it."

It glittered in the sunlight, gray and cold. She'd never seen a hologram anywhere close to these dimensions before.

Collingdale smiled at the cloud. "Okay, you son of a bitch," he said. "Come get it."

More lightning off to port. They'd wandered too close to a jet. It was a flood, a gusher of mist and dust, streaming past. "At the rate the cloud's coming apart," she said, "maybe there won't be anything left by the time it gets to Lookout."

"Don't count on it," said Collingdale.

Another bolt rippled past. A big one. They both ducked. So did Bill. His image vanished.

Maybe they were drawing the dragon's attention. "I think we should get started," she said.

Collingdale nodded. "Yes. I was just savoring the moment."

Right. She was glad somebody was enjoying it.

"Bill," Collingdale said, "let's go left three degrees."

Bill complied. The *Hawksbill*, the shuttle, and the virtual hedgehog all turned to port. Images of the cloud played across four screens.

The bridge fell silent, save for the muffled chatter of electronics. Collingdale sat quietly, watching the monitors, calm, almost serene.

Off to starboard, the hedgehog sparkled in sunlight. From somewhere, lightning flickered, touched the image, passed through it.

"It'll probably take a while," said Collingdale, "for it to react. To start to turn away."

She'd become aware of her heartbeat. "Probably."

The shuttle was an RY2, lots of curves, no sharply drawn lines, nothing to attract the lightning. Only the oversize *Hawksbill* needed to worry about that. Target of the day. Maybe they should have ridden in the shuttle. Suddenly it struck her that they should have thought things out better. Of course they should be in the shuttle.

Collingdale's gray eyes drifted toward the overhead.

Digger would have thought of it in a minute. Never ride in the target vehicle, he'd have said.

"Bill?" said Collingdale.

"Nothing yet."

"Maybe we need to wiggle a little bit," he said. "Do something to get its attention."

"Maybe." Why don't you lean out the airlock and wave? "Bill," she said, "down angle three degrees."

"Complying," said Bill.

The face of the cloud was torn by fissures and ridges. One dark slice ran jagged like a gaping wound across the length of the thing. Gradually, the cloud was retreating from the center of the screens as the *Hawksbill* continued to pull away from it.

THEY WAITED SIX hours. The *Hawksbill* and its shuttle and the virtual hedgehog drew steadily away from the cloud, which continued on course for Lookout. Collingdale's mood had darkened. He sat smoldering in his seat. When he spoke at all, it was to the omega, calling its attention to the hedgehog. "Don't you see it, you dumb son of a bitch?"

"Hey, you're going the wrong way."

"We're *here*. Over here."

For the most part, though, he watched in stricken silence. Finally, he literally threw himself out of the chair, a dangerous move in the low gravity of a superluminal. "Hell with this," he said. He brought the AI up onscreen. "Bill, go to the next one."

The hedgehog vanished. A city appeared in its place. It was on the same order of magnitude.

This was a city unlike any she'd seen, an unearthly place of crystal towers and globes and chess piece symmetry.

"It's Moonlight," said Collingdale. "We know the thing'll go after this one." He gazed at the omega's image on the overhead.

But if the omega cared, or even noticed, there was no indication. Collingdale paced the bridge for hours, eyes blazing, his jaw clamped tight. He was talking to the cloud, cajoling it, challenging it, cursing it. And then apologizing to Kellie. "I'm sorry," he said. "It's goddam frustrating." Somewhere he'd picked up a wrench and he stalked about with it gripped in one fist, as if he'd use it on the omega.

Kellie watched.

"Nobody's afraid of you, you bastard."

THEY WERE GETTING too far away from the cloud, so she cut the image, took the shuttle back on board, swung around behind the omega, and repeated her earlier maneuver, easing the *Hawksbill* down directly in its path again.

She also suggested they board the shuttle, and run the operation from there.

"No," he said. "You go if you want. But the shuttle's too small. Too much lightning out there. It gets hit once, and it's over."

She thought about ordering him to comply. She was, after all, the vessel's captain. But they were running an operation, and that was his responsibility. His testosterone was involved, and she knew he'd resist, refuse, defy her. The last thing she needed at the moment was a confrontation. She relaunched and repositioned the vehicle, making a great show of it.

"I think it's a mistake," she said.

He shook his head. "Let's just get the job done."

"Have it your way. We're ready to go."

Collingdale stared hard at the navigation screen, on which an image of the shuttle floated. "Bill," he said, "let's have the cube."

A box appeared. It was silver, and someone had added the legend BITE ME on one side. Its dimensions were similar to those of the hedgehog and the city.

But it didn't matter.

Kellie put down a sandwich and some coffee while they waited. Collingdale wasn't hungry, thanks. He hadn't eaten all day.

He ran the cube in a fixed position, and he ran it tumbling. They were pulling away from the cloud again, and Kellie watched while Collingdale changed the colors on the visual, from orange, to blue, to pink.

"I guess," he said finally, "it knows we're just showing it pictures."

"I guess."

"Okay," he said, "let's recall the shuttle. We'll try the kite."

"Tomorrow," she said. "We don't do anything else until we've both had some sleep."

ARCHIVE

We'll try again in a few hours, Mary. We have to swing around and get back in position. And it's the middle of the night, so we're going to shut down for a while. Stupid damned thing. But we'll get it yet. If Hutchins is right and it really chases the hedgehogs, it'll chase the kite.

—David Collingdale to Mary Clank
Friday, December 5

BLACK CAT REPORT

Thanks, Ron. This is Rose Beetem, onboard the *Calvin Clyde*, now about one week from Lookout. Our latest information is that the omega is still on course to attack the Goompahs in nine days. When it does, the Black Cat will be there, and so will everybody in our audience. We're hoping the Academy team can do something to distract this monster, but we'll just have to wait to see.

Back to you, Ron—

chapter 37

JULIE SAT IN the lander, which was perched on a sea-bound rock too small to describe as an island, and watched the transmissions coming in from the *Hawksbill*. She followed the flight across the top of the omega, felt a thrill when the hedgehog came to life directly in front of it, held her breath when the ship and the shuttle began their turn to port. She kept Digger and Whit informed, talked with Marge on the *Jenkins*, and shared her disappointment when the omega failed to take the bait. She had expected the projections to work; had not in fact been able to see any chance they would fail. But there it was.

The next phase of the operation, deploying the kite, would not start for several hours, and Julie was going to be up all night helping Marge. So she kicked her seat back and closed her eyes. Once she woke to see sails passing in the distance, but she knew that if anyone got close, Bill would alert her.

Gulls wheeled overhead. In the background she could hear Bill talking, sometimes with Whit, sometimes with Digger. At Digger's insistence, he was using his own voice.

Savakol was one of the smaller cities, and there was consequently less walking around to be done. They expected to be finished by midafternoon.

This was Julie's first mission of consequence. She'd talked to some of the older Academy people before coming to Lookout, and most of them had never done *anything* that was close to being this significant. Her father had led the mission that first discovered the omegas; and she enjoyed being part of the first effort to rescue someone from them.

Ordinarily, the Lookout flight would have been offered to a senior captain first, but apparently either no one was available or, more likely, nobody was interested in a two-year operation. She'd applied and, to her surprise, gotten the assignment. She'd had mixed feelings when it came through, second thoughts about whether she really wanted to do it. But she was committed and saw no easy way out. Especially when her folks had called and tried to dissuade her. In the end they'd said okay, have your own way, but be careful, stay clear of the cloud.

That seemed a long time ago, and if her social life had fallen off a bit, she was nevertheless feeling good about what she was doing. She'd have preferred staying with the *Hawksbill* and going after the omega with Collingdale. It would have been nice to go home and tell her father she'd helped shoo the thing off. But this was okay. She was close to the action, and that was really sufficient.

Half asleep, she watched Whit record a boating regatta at a lakefront. He was putting everything he could find into his notebook, capturing ball games, debates in the park, haggling over prices at the merchants' stalls. The regatta featured half-dressed Goompah females paddling boats while a crowd cheered them on. They all wore green and white, which seemed to have some special significance because green and white banners were on display everywhere.

Digger explained that the seminudity was traditional with these events. He didn't know why, and no one seemed unduly excited by it. The females did wear wide-brimmed white hats, however, which—to the delight of the crowd—were forever flying off.

Julie drifted into sleep, and dreamed that she was back at the University of Tacoma, listening to somebody lecture about Beowulf, how Grendel represented natural forces, the dark side of life, the things people have no control over. Then she was awake again listening to the sea and the gulls and Digger.

"—*Having a problem,*" Digger was saying. "*Julie, do you hear me?*"

"What's wrong?" she asked, awake and surveying the screens. There were five of them, carrying an image of the omega, a satellite view of the three sailing vessels the Goompahs had sent east, a picture of the rainmaker they'd delivered the previous night, a revolving picture of the open sea around her, and, from an imager carried by Digger—

—A torchlight parade. Of Goompahs.

They were on a beach. Some were wearing robes. Others stood watching.

"*I think they're going to do another sacrifice,*" he said.

Julie knew about the Goompah who'd walked into the sea. He'd worn a white robe, and everyone else had worn black. There was a single white robe among the marchers. Worn by—it looked like—an elderly female.

"*I'm on my way,*" said Whit, breaking in.

"Aren't you guys together?"

"*No,*" said Digger. "*We split up to cover more ground.*"

Black-robed Goompahs were chanting. And a crowd spread across the beach, growing, and joining in. Julie couldn't understand a word of it.

Digger was frantic: *"I'm not going to stand by and watch it happen again."*

Whit had broken into a run. He wasn't in great shape, and pretty soon he was breathing hard.

Julie should have kept quiet. But she opened a channel. "Hey," she said, "keep in mind these aren't people."

The screen with the torchlight marchers went blank.

"Digger," said Whit, *"you okay?"*

"Fine. Don't have time for the imager."

"What's happening?" asked Julie.

"The head Goompah's making for the water."

Digger had begun to run across the beach. She could hear his shoes crunching the sand.

Whit gasped that he was close by, and Digger shouldn't do anything until he got there, and Digger replied that there wasn't time and he wasn't going to sit still again.

"Hey," she said. "This is not my business, but we're supposed to stay out of it."

"She's right." Whit again. *"Religious ceremony."* Blowing hard. *"The Protocol."*

"Forget the Protocol."

"Does she have a sword?" asked Julie.

"They have a javelin. And she's in the water. Up to her hips. Doesn't look as if she can swim a stroke."

"I see them," said Whit. *"Javelin's in the air."*

"Julie." Digger's voice. *"How soon can you get here?"*

Julie's harness was descending around her shoulders. She started punching buttons. "I'm just over the horizon."

"You got a tether handy?" asked Digger.

"Bill," she said, "let's go. What's the tether situation?"

"There's an ample supply of cable in the locker."

"Good. Activate the lightbender."

"Handing the javelin off," said Whit.

She could hear Digger charging into the water. *"Get here,"* he said, *"as quickly as you can."*

SHE LIFTED OFF the rock, staying only a few meters above the surface, and turned toward shore. It was early afternoon, a gray, depressing day, the sun hidden in a slate sky. The mountains that lay immediately west of *Savakol* dominated the horizon.

One of the satellites was over the scene, and she was able to get a picture of the beach. The white-robed Goompah was wallowing in the surf, but pushing doggedly forward. There was, of course, no sign of the invisible Digger.

"There are some," said Bill, *"who do not want her to do it."*

A few Goompahs were in the surf with her. One had reached her and was trying to restrain her, but one of the black robes pulled the would-be rescuer away.

"Her name is Tayma," said Bill.

"How do you know?"

"They're calling it out. Telling her to stop."

One of the Goompahs threw itself down on the beach and began to beat the sand.

Julie turned away from the screen. The ocean raced beneath the spacecraft.

"We are leaving a wake," said Bill.

"Doesn't matter. Nobody here to see it."

The chants ended. Silence fell across the beach, save for the protesters. The coastline was taking shape ahead. A pair of islands rippled past.

"Bill," she said, "you got the conn."

"I have it."

She slipped out of her seat, climbed into the rear of the cabin, opened the main storage locker, and began hauling out cable. She sorted through, found a five-meter length, and pulled it clear.

Tayma was off her feet now, alternately getting pushed in and dragged back by the surf. *"Not a very dignified way to go,"* said Bill.

"I'm close to her now," said Digger. He was breathing hard, too. She could hear a lot of splashing.

And suddenly there was a yowling coming over circuit.

"What's *that*?" she asked. "What's going on?"

"It's the crowd," said Whit. *"Dig's in the water, headed right for her. But they can see the splashes. You know what it looks like?"*

"No."

"To me it looks like something in the ocean stalking her."

The cries had become shrieks. Bloodcurdling screams.

Tayma hadn't seen it yet. A big wave came in, and she floated over the top, came down the far side, and went back to struggling against the drag. The crowd was making a lot of noise, and she must have heard it but probably thought they were expressing their sorrow for her. Or maybe she'd locked them out.

The lander arced in over the coastline. Julie saw the city and the long white beach.

"I've got her," said Digger. Then *he* screamed.

"Dig, are you okay?"

"*Let go!*" said Digger. There was a thunk and he gasped.

"Digger?" Whatever was happening, it sounded as if he was losing.

"*The crowd's getting scared,*" said Whit. "*They don't know what's going on.*"

"Neither do I. Where's Digger?"

The lander slowed and began circling over the scene.

Whit said something but it didn't matter anymore because she could see for herself now. The Goompah was well out in the water, and she was struggling fiercely with her invisible rescuer.

"*—Trying to save you,*" said Dig. "*You nit—*"

"*Doesn't want to be rescued,*" cried Whit. "*Let her go.*"

Julie turned the lander around so the hatch couldn't be seen from the beach. Then she opened up. Four thrusters along the hull rotated into vertical position and fired, providing additional lift.

"What are you going to do?" she asked Digger.

"*You find that tether?*"

"I've got a piece of cable."

"*Use it.*"

She was already at work. She'd secured one end of the line, and stepped into the open hatchway. "Good luck," she said, and dropped the other end into the water.

The struggle in the surf went on. The Goompahs, moaning and shrieking, crowded to the edge of the water. The cable twisted and turned. Julie saw more water kicking up near the beach and realized that Whit was about to join the fray. But before he got anywhere close, Digger announced that he'd secured the line around the female. "*Lift,*" he said.

Julie told Whit to go back, everything was under control. She stayed in the airlock and directed Bill to take the lander up. "But slowly," she said. "Gently." The line tightened, and the deck tilted under the weight.

The Goompah came out of the water, the line looped around her left arm. It was, despite everything, the most ridiculous sight Julie had ever seen.

"*Go,*" said Digger. "*Get her ashore.*"

"You okay?" There was a depression in the water where Digger was floating. The currents looked strong, and the beach kept getting farther away.

"*I'm fine.*"

"You're sure?"

"*Will you get moving?*" He sounded exasperated.

"*We're making a miracle,*" said Whit, who'd retreated back to the beach. The crowd had gone absolutely rock-still silent. The Goompah, Tayma, kept rising higher, secured by a line that, from their perspective, must have vanished in midair. Some had fallen to their knees.

"*Lift her gently,*" said Digger. "*Don't jerk her or anything.*"

"Right."

"*Do it the way the gods would.*"

"How the hell would the gods do it?"

"*Where do you want to put her?*" asked Bill.

"Empty section of beach at the east end. Take her there."

She could *see* Julie. God knew what she thought. The poor creature was already half out of her mind with fear, and there directly above her she was looking at a circle of light in midair with somebody hanging out of it.

"*Don't let her see you,*" said Digger. "*They're scared of people.*"

Too late. She'd heard that, forgotten, didn't really care at this point. The lander glided over the waves and east across the beach.

"*How do we know,*" Bill asked, "*she won't just walk back into the ocean?*"

"Next one's on her. Dig, how are you doing?"

"*Still afloat.*"

"I'll be right back."

"*Better make it quick.*"

She didn't like the sound of that and almost cut the Goompah loose.

"*Here?*" asked Bill.

"Good. Let her down."

She heard a sound that might have been a cheer.

"*I'm going after him,*" said Whit.

"No," she said. "Stay where you are. I won't have time to rescue two."

DIGGER HAD NEVER been the world's best swimmer. And he was out of shape. He had known when he splashed through the shallows and dived in after the unfortunate Tayma that he was making a mistake. But he had seen something in her face, and it told him she was terrified. In some absurd way, she was doing her duty, but she didn't want to do it.

The earlier suicide was with him still, the Goompah pushing out through the waves and struggling against the tide and finally sinking.

But Julie had been slower coming to the rescue than he'd expected. He'd exhausted himself reaching the *woman.* (Somehow, he was willing to extend the term to the Goompah.) The tide had been dragging them both out, and he'd made the typical inexperienced error of fighting it. And then fighting her. And finally had come the struggle to get the line around her shoulder.

His arms were desperately tired and heavy. He'd thought he could let himself slip under, that he was inside the e-suit and could rest in the depths for a few minutes until Julie got back. But he'd forgotten that he was wear-ing a converter and not air tanks. If he went under, he'd smother.

He had the satisfaction of seeing Tayma lifted from the ocean, of hearing cheers behind him, of watching her apparently glide through the air toward the beach.

But the currents were pulling him out to sea. And he was tired. God help him he was tired. Needed to get onto a physical regimen. Take better care of himself. Would do that when this was over.

He closed his eyes and tried to rest. Just for a few moments.

It occurred to him to turn off the lightbender so they could see him. He fumbled at the control on his wrist, but it was hard to find.

Hell with it. She had goggles. He closed his eyes and thought about Kellie as the water closed over him.

WHIT WATCHED TAYMA come gently down at the edge of the surf. The line fell after her, a longer cable than had been visible a moment before. Then he heard Julie trying to raise Digger on the circuit. Silence roared back. *"Where'd he go?"* Julie demanded.

It was all happening too fast.

THERE'D BE ENOUGH air left in the hard shell covering his face to keep him alive for a couple of minutes, to keep the water out of his lungs. As long as she could find him quickly.

Find him. "Digger," she said, terrified, "if you can hear me, shut off the lightbender."

No answer.

"Whit—?

"Look where you were before, Julie."

Where the hell was that?

"—Straight out. More to your right."

She was wearing goggles by then, hanging out the airlock again with a fresh piece of cable, searching frantically for a sign of the swimmer. While she looked, she secured one end of it and dropped the other into the water. But there was nothing.

"Do you see him?" asked Whit.

"Not yet." He'd gone under. "Bill, try the sensors."

The water looked quiet. She saw no indication of anything splashing around.

"Negative," said Bill.

The goggles weren't doing any good under these circumstances. "Do we have anything on the hull that will pick up sound?"

"Sure. Antenna's up forward, atop the hull." He showed her.

She recalled a story her father had told her. How Hutchins had been on foot one night looking for a lander that they'd parked and lost, and she'd found it by having someone call it and yell so she could listen for the sounds. "Okay, get as low as you can. Just over the waves."

"I'll put her down on the water."

"No." That could kill Dig. "Keep some space."

She grabbed a wrench and a strip of electrical cable out of the equipment bin and hustled through the airlock. "Bill," she said, "shut down the light-bender."

There was a brief change in the sound generated by the power grid. *"Done,"* said Bill. *"Lot of wind out here."*

Whit shouted a warning, thinking the vehicle had become visible by accident. "It's okay," she told him.

"You can't do that."

She had drawn the attention of every native in sight. "I don't have time at the moment, Whit." She climbed out onto the ladder and quickly hoisted herself onto the hull. The antenna was a few paces forward. "Bill, is this thing going to work if I rip it off and throw it in the water?"

"I'm optimistic it will. What are we going to do?"

She used the wrench to pry it loose, disconnected it, and connected the cable. Then she pitched it over the side into the ocean. "Is it working?"

"It is functioning. What good will it do?"

"I want you to listen up, Bill." She opened her channel to Digger. "Okay, Bill, if you can hear this through the receiver, give me an angle."

"I'm listening, Julie. But I do not hear anything."

She rapped the wrench on the link. "Can you hear it now?"

"Negative."

"All right. Got a better idea. Tie me in with the *Jenkins* library."

The Goompahs along the beach were pushing and shoving. Some were starting into the water, others were running off in all directions. Well, she was sure beating hell out of the Protocol.

"Done," said Bill.

"Okay. Let's have the *1812*. Lots of volume."

"Which movement did you want?"

"The part with the cannons. Fire off the cannons."

It exploded, drums, guns, bugles, and cavalry charges. It thundered across the water, and of course she was only listening to a rendition from her wrist unit. It would also be filling Digger's shell.

"You'll deafen him."

"Can you hear it, Bill?"

"*Yes.*" The lander moved forward, a bit farther out to sea. Slowed. Edged sideways. Retreated a bit. "*He should be right below you.*"

"*Have you found him?*" asked Whit. "*You're getting half the town out here.*" The lander was being buffeted by the wind, and hundreds of Goompahs poured onto the beach.

"Can't help that." She dropped into the water, kicked down, and heard the muffled chords of the overture. She swam toward the sound and saw his shimmering form ahead. A leg. She found his knee and juggled him while she decided which end was up. Hard to tell in the green depths. Then she got hold of his vest and headed for the surface. Meantime she switched off the lightbender. And she could see him. His eyes were closed, his skin was gray, and he looked not good.

"Bill," she said, "kill the *1812.*"

She got in front of him, caught the control on his left wrist, and the safety on his right shoulder, and shut off the e-suit.

He didn't look as if he was breathing.

"Bill, reactivate the lightbender. And set down in the water. Try not to sink."

The lander vanished again, save for the open hatch. She and Digger were visible from the beach. Another shock for the home folks.

"*Julie, I'm reluctant to put the lander in the water. I can't see where you are.*"

"It's okay. We're clear."

"*Julie,*" said Whit, "*do you have him?*"

"I've got him."

"*How is he?*"

She heard the lander touch down, saw the water *press* down. It looked as if a ditch had opened in the sea. "Can't tell yet."

"*Is he alive?*"

"I don't know." She looped the line around his waist, wrapped it around the hatch, and secured it so he wouldn't sink. Then she scrambled into the airlock, stayed on her knees, and dragged him in behind her.

He had a heartbeat, but it was faint. She started mouth-to-mouth.

IT WAS AN up and down day for the Goompahs. They'd been inspired— there was no other word for it—by the miraculous rescue of Tayma. But then the lander had appeared, a sleek gray *thing* floating in air, and then the humans had shown up, first Julie, and then Digger, both coming out of nowhere. Whit knew that the human physiognomy spooked the locals, but he'd hoped that, under the circumstances, they would adjust. They didn't. They howled and either ran or stumbled off the beach. A few stopped to help Tayma, who looked completely disoriented. In the end all had retreated to what could only be described as a respectful distance.

Whit stood watching the piece of airlock and lander's interior, rounded off by the open hatch hanging above the waves.

"*Got a pulse,*" said Julie.

"Is he okay?"

"*I think so. Is this the way you guys always behave?*"

"I don't know," he said. "I'm new in these parts. By the way, when you get a chance, you might want to close the hatch."

She looked out at him, and the spectacle narrowed and vanished.

That brought another series of grunts and pointing from the Goompahs. Tayma, meantime, supported by a half dozen friends, limped away.

HE WAS BREATHING again. It was shallow, and his pulse was weak, but he was *alive.* She called his name, propped him up and held her hands against his cheeks and rubbed them until his eyes opened. He looked confused.

"Hi, Digger," she said.

He tried to speak, but nothing came.

"Take your time," she said.

He mumbled something she couldn't make out. And then his eyes focused on her and looked past her at the bulkhead. "What happened?" he asked finally. "How—here?"

"I pulled you out of the water."

"Water?" His hands went to his clothes.

"What's your name?" she asked gently.

"Dunn. My name's Dunn." He tried to sit up, but, she pushed him back down. "She okay?"

"Tayma? She's fine. You saved her."

"Good. Thanks, Kellie."

"Kellie? Do you know who I am?"

"Kellie," he said.

"No. Kellie's with the *Hawksbill.* Try again."

ARCHIVE

(From the Goompah Recordings,
Savakol, Translated by Ginko Amagawa)

I'm no public speaker and I don't like being up here. If you want to know what happened today at *Barkat* Beach, I'll tell you what I saw, or what I thought I saw. And I'll leave you to draw your own conclusions about explanations.

I went because I'd heard the *keelots* were going to be there, and that they would perform the *kelma*. I went with Quet. We were standing near the front, close to the water.

They went through the ceremony without any problems, and Tayma started out into the ocean. She was praying as she went, and had gotten about ten or fifteen paces when something began to chase her. I don't know what it was. Something in the water but we couldn't see it.

She didn't notice it, but just kept going. We were yelling for her to look out, but she probably thought we were trying to persuade her to come back.

We could see it was going to catch her, and everybody screamed louder. A few cleared out. What happened next is hard to describe. But there was a big fight and then a window opened in the sky . . .

chapter 38

MARGE AND JULIE descended beside the rainmaker they'd brought down
the previous night, ready to go to work.

They'd rehearsed often on the way out, and they fell to with a minimum
of wasted effort. The rainmaker was already centered among the eight trees
that would serve as moorings. Marge did a quick measurement among tree
trunks to determine a flight path for the helicopter. When she was satisfied
she had it, she released the anchor cables. Julie meantime dropped a feed
line in the stream, attached it to a set of four sprinklers, and inserted the
sprinklers in the ground around the chimney. Then she connected the line
to the pump.

Next they attached the cables to the trees, arranging the slack so that,
when the time came, the chimney would be able to rise evenly to a height
of about ten meters. Then they disconnected the vertical lines that held the
package together. And that was it. It looked like a wide, sky-colored cylinder, made of plastic, open at top and bottom.

"Ready to go?" asked Julie.

Marge nodded. "Yes, indeed." She was proud of her rainmakers, but trying to look as though this were all in a day's work.

"Bill," said Julie, "Get the landers and the helicopter ready."

"They are primed and waiting."

Marge planted a pickup on a tree trunk so they could watch the action
on the ground. When she'd finished, they got back into the hauler and Julie
took them up, directly over the top of the chimney.

They did a quick inspection, and Marge pronounced everything in order.
"Let's go," she said.

Julie descended gently until they touched the top of the chimney. "That's
good," she told Bill. "Reconnect."

Marge felt the magnetic clamps take hold.

"Done," said Bill.

Marge started the pump. On the ground, a fine spray rose into the air and descended around the rainmaker. "That's not really going to make the clouds happen, is it?"

"It'll speed things along," said Marge.

Julie grinned. "The wonders of modern technology." She swung round in her seat. "Here we go."

She engaged the spike, the vertical thrusters fired, and they started up. The top of the rainmaker rose with them, extending like an accordion.

"You ever have a problem with these things?" asked Julie.

"Not so far. Of course, this is the first time we've tried to use them off-world."

"Should work better than at home," Julie said. "Less gravity." And then, to the AI: "Bill, let's get the first lander aloft."

The interior of the chimney was braced with microscopically thin light-weight ribs, and crosspieces supported the structure every eighty-six meters. A screen guarded the bottom of the chimney, to prevent small animals from getting sucked up inside. (Larger creatures, like Goompahs, would be inconvenienced if they got too close, would lose their hats, but not their lives.)

As they gained altitude, the omega rose with them. For the first time, Marge could see lightning bolts flickering within the cloud mass.

"*Four hundred meters,*" said Bill, giving them the altitude.

There was an external support ring two hundred meters below the top of the chimney. The first of the four landers, under Bill's control, rose alongside and linked to the ring.

"*Connection complete,*" said the AI. Both vehicles, working in concert, continued drawing the chimney up.

Marge could see lights in *Hopgop*, on the east along the sea. The big moon was up, and it was moving slowly across the face of the omega.

"*Seven hundred meters,*" said Bill.

The ship swayed. "Atmosphere's pushing at the chimney," said Marge. "Don't worry. It'll get smoother as we go higher."

"*The other landers are in the air.*"

It struck Marge that the cloud looked most ominous, most portentous, when it was rising. She didn't know why that was. Maybe it was connected with the disappointed hope, each evening, that it wouldn't be there in the morning. Maybe it was simply the sense of something evil climbing into the sky. She shook it off, thinking how the Goompahs must be affected if it bothered her.

"I have a question," said Julie.

"Go ahead."

"When it's all over, how do we get them down? The chimneys?"

"When the omega hits, we push a button, and the omega blows them into the sea."

Julie frowned. "They won't drag? Cause some damage on the ground?"

"I doubt it. In any case, it's a necessary risk." The construction materials were biodegradable, and within a few months there'd be no trace of the chimneys anywhere.

They were getting high. *Hopgop* looked far away. Overhead, the stars were bright.

"Twelve hundred meters."

Near ground level, a second lander moved in alongside the chimney and tied onto a support ring on the opposite side from the first. *"Second linkup complete,"* said Bill. *"All units ascending."*

At twenty-two hundred meters, the third lander joined the effort, connecting with a ring at right angles to the other two. Marge was sitting comfortably, reassuring Julie when the hauler occasionally rocked as the weather pushed at the chimney. Julie had never done anything like this, and when she put on goggles and saw the chimney trailing all the way to the ground, her instincts screamed that it was too much, that the weight had to drag the hauler out of the air. It came down to Marge's assurances against the evidence of her eyes.

"Keep in mind," Marge said, "it's the same thing you brought down out of orbit. It's no heavier now than it was then."

"Except now it's unrolled."

"Doesn't change the mass. Relax. Everything's going to be fine."

At thirty-seven hundred meters, they began to slow. By then the fourth lander had joined the support group, and they were approaching the chimney's extension limit. When the pickup they'd left behind showed them they had exactly the situation they wanted, the anchor lines pulled tight, and the base of the chimney off the ground, they halted the ascent.

"Bill," said Julie, "activate the helicopter and put it in position."

Bill acknowledged.

The helicopter was a gleaming antique unit, a Falcon, which had become legendary during the long struggle with international terrorists during the later years of the last century. CANADIAN FORCES was stenciled on its hull. It was equipped with lasers and particle beam weapons, but of course none was functional.

Bill started the engine and engaged its silent-running capability, which wasn't really all that silent. When it was ready, he lifted it a couple of meters into the air, navigated it between the two trees Marge had selected, and inserted it directly beneath the base of the chimney.

"Ready," said Bill.

"Okay." Julie was doing a decent job hiding her qualms. "We want the blades turning as fast as possible, but we don't want it off the ground."

"*Ground idle,*" said Bill.

"Yes. That sounds right."

The blades picked up speed. The helicopter strained upward and Bill cut back slightly. "Perfect," Marge said.

"What next?" asked Julie.

Marge smiled. "I think from here we can just relax and enjoy the show."

The helicopter pushed a column of warm moist air skyward. Up the chimney. More warm air rushed in to fill the vacuum, and gradually the flow took over on its own. Bill had to cut the blade rotation back again to keep the Falcon from lifting off.

"*Moving along nicely,*" he reported. And, finally: "*I believe it is self-sustaining now.*"

Marge gave it a few more minutes, then Julie directed Bill to move the helicopter away. "Be careful," she added.

Bill brought the Falcon out, squeezing past the same two trees. When it was clear, he gunned the engines, and it lifted off into the steady winds that were racing around the chimney. It fought its way into the sky and turned west toward Utopia.

Avery Whitlock's Notebooks

The ship is asleep.

Digger seems to be okay. We were worried for a while that there might be some brain damage. He still doesn't have his memory back completely, can't recall how he got into the ocean, or even being on the beach. But Bill says that's not an unusual result in cases like this. I guess we'll know for sure in the morning.

I haven't been able to sleep. It's not so much that I'm worried about Digger, because I think he'll be okay. But watching a creature that one thinks of as rational try to end its life for the most irrational of purposes . . . I cannot get it out of my mind. Knowing that it happens, has happened to us, and seeing it in action . . . It gives me a sense of how far we've come. Of what civilization truly means.

—*December 5*

chapter 39

"*LEVEL OF CONVECTION is sufficient,*" said Bill.

"All right." Marge rubbed her hands together. "Now we do the magic." She glanced out at the sky. The chimney, which they'd been supporting for several hours, was all but invisible to the naked eye. Julie had noticed that the drag on the AV3 had lessened, had in fact all but disappeared. "Cut them loose," she said. "Cut everything loose."

"The landers, too?"

"Everything. Send them to Utopia."

Julie knew how it was supposed to work. But this kind of operation flew in the face of common sense. And she had a bad feeling about what would happen when she released her grip on the chimney. Ah, well. "Bill," she said, "do it."

The AI acknowledged. She felt the clamps release the chimney, watched the status board light up with reports that the four landers had simultaneously turned loose, heard Bill say that the action was completed. And all her instincts told her that the elongated structure they'd so laboriously hauled up several thousand kilometers would now collapse, crash down on the countryside and, God help them, maybe on *Hopgop*.

Marge was smiling broadly. "Let's take a look," she said.

Julie took the hauler around in a large arc so they could see. The chimney was constructed of stealth materials. When she looked through the goggles, it was voilà all the way to the ground. It was standing on its own, a great round cylinder extending down through the clouds, supported by no visible means.

She knew the theory. Surface air is warmer, heavier, and more humid than air at altitude. It wants to rise but generally can't do so in any organized fashion, or in sufficient volume to create clouds unless there's substantial pressure or a temperature gradient. Nightfall and pressure fronts provide that in nature.

To do it artificially, a chimney was needed. Once it was in place, the warm air started up on its own. It kept moving up because there was no place else for it to go. They'd put the Falcon at the base to provide a fan, to help things along. Once the system got going, the chimney became an oversize siphon, perfectly capable of keeping itself inflated.

At the moment, warm moist air was spreading out from the top of the rainmaker. It would shortly begin to create clouds.

"We just have time," Marge said, "to get the next package and run it down to the *Sakmarung* site so we can be ready to go tomorrow night."

That would leave enough time for Julie to get back to the *Jenkins* and pick up her two caballeros, who'd be looking forward to another day of planting their projectors and getting ready for the big show. She wasn't entirely sure Digger would be able to go back down, and in fact she thought he should stay put. Since Whit was too inexperienced to go down alone, that meant both of them should take a day off.

But Digger had insisted the night before that he was okay, that he would be able to go back in the morning. Then he'd passed out, helped along by some medication. It occurred to Julie that she should let Kellie know what had happened.

"Better to wait," said Marge.

"Why?"

"Wait till you get back to the ship. Make sure he's really okay. She'll want to know, and you won't want to be telling her you *think* he's fine."

But Kellie called *her* and the issue became moot.

"Bill says he's fine," she told Kellie. "Not to worry."

Kellie thanked her and said she hoped Digger would take it easy for a bit.

Whit seemed to have been affected by events there. His rational, cautious, and thoughtful self had been replaced by someone more romantic, more willing to take a risk. He was in love with the idea of helping rescue the Goompahs. But she wondered how he'd react if things didn't go well.

THEY COLLECTED THE second chimney, and, as dawn was breaking over the *Intigo*, delivered it to an island thirty kilometers west of Sakmarung. Julie's first act was to look in on Digger, who was sleeping peacefully. Bill assured her he was fine, all signs normal.

WHIT HAD DEVELOPED a hobby. He loved being invisible, and he never missed an opportunity to record the Goompahs at work, at play, or during their frequent gambols. He watched them frolicking in the parks, families coming down to the pier to see ships coming and going, young ones playing ball games. It was all of a piece. Life in the *Intigo* seemed to be one long celebration.

And he watched it with a joy born of the sure and certain knowledge that this civilization was too vibrant, too alive, to be taken out by an artifact that had no purpose, no reason to be, and might be older than man. Collingdale would take it for a ride, if anyone could do it. And if not, they'd make Digger's avatars do the work. But one way or another, they and the Goompahs would come through it.

"How can you be so sure?" Julie asked him.

"You believe in destiny?"

"I don't think so," she said.

"I do." He looked at her, his dark face wreathed in thought. "Sometimes you can feel history moving a certain way. People are always saying that history turns on little things, Alexander dies too young to take out Rome, Churchill survives a plane crash and lives to save the Western world. But sometimes the wheels just go round, and you know, absolutely know, certain things have to happen. We had to have Rome. Hitler had to be stopped."

"And where is history taking us now?"

"You want to know what I really think?"

"Of course."

"Julie, the Goompahs are a remarkable race. I think they, and we, have a rendezvous up ahead somewhere. And I think we'll all be better for it."

Avery Whitlock's Notebooks

Dave told me today he thinks they can make the kite work. Maybe he can, maybe not. But I've had a lot of time on my flight out here to stay up with those who pretend to comment on the state of the human race. Most of them, people like Hazhure and MacAllister, think we are a despicable lot, interested only in power, sex, and money. They maintain, in addition, that we're cowardly and selfish. Today, I listened to Dave Collingdale, and I watched Julie and Marge come in after starting a rainstorm that might, just might, hide Hopgop from the omega. Anybody who's listening, be on notice: I'm a card-carrying human being. And I've never been prouder of that fact.

—December 6

LIBRARY ENTRY

Everybody else talks about the weather. We do something about it.

—Motto of the International Bureau of the Climate

chapter 40

ALL THEY HAD left was the kite. And Kellie's intuition warned her it would take more than that to sidetrack the omega.

Collingdale either didn't share her feeling or wouldn't admit to his doubts. He behaved as if there were no question that the kite would work fine. But it was sufficient for her to look out the viewport, and to recognize they were buzzing around that thing like a fly, to know just how uneven a contest they were in.

Collingdale had been plunged in a black mood since she'd found him that morning, pacing the bridge, drinking coffee by the gallon. He insisted he'd slept soundly, but he had rings under his eyes, and he literally looked in pain.

She checked in with Julie, who was in the process of activating the first rainmaker. Julie listened, looked sympathetic, raised her hand in a gesture that signaled affection, resignation, optimism. Here we go. *"We're rooting for you."* Then: *"Something you should know about."*

Her tone was scary.

"He's okay, but we had a close call with Digger yesterday." She described how he had plunged into the sea to rescue a Goompah, how the effort had succeeded, but that he had almost drowned. *"I should have told you yesterday, but to be honest I wanted to wait until we were sure he was all right. No point having you worry when you couldn't do anything."*

"You're sure he's okay?"

"Bill says he's fine. Not to worry. He's asleep at the moment, but I'll have him get on the circuit when he wakes up."

"Thanks, Julie."

THEY WERE IN front of the cloud again.

"With all flags flying," said Collingdale.

Ahead, Lookout and its big moon had grown brighter. And were right in the crosshairs. Nine days away.

The omega was continuing to decelerate.

"We're ready when you are," said Kellie.

Collingdale nodded. "Okay. Bill," he said, "start the launch process."

"*Opening the rear doors,*" Bill said.

The kite consisted of thousands of square meters of film folded carefully on a platform that was anchored to the cargo deck.

"*Launching the package.*"

Bill sprayed a lubricant across the deck, released the platform, and accelerated. The platform slid aft and started through the doors. At that precise moment, they cut the main engines so they would not incinerate the package. It drifted out of the ship and fell behind. A pair of tethers, five kilometers long, secured it to the ship. As the range between the ship and the package increased, they started to draw taut.

Retros cut in, and they braked before the lines had completely tightened, adjusting velocity so that both the *Hawksbill* and the package were moving at precisely the same rate.

Within the film, canisters of compressed air acted as thrusters, separating the folds. Other thruster packages carried the platform away, where it could do no damage. Support rods inside the kite telescoped open, connected with each other, and snapped into braces. Crosspieces swung out from brackets and stabilized the supports. The canisters became exhausted and were jettisoned. Gradually, over the next few hours, the world's foremost box kite took shape. When it was done, it trailed them, glistening in the sunlight, still connected to the twin tethers.

The box was forty-by-twenty-by-twenty kilometers. Rearrange Berlin a little bit, and it would almost fit inside. With plenty of air space. There was room for Everest, with substantial clearance.

The tethers looked fragile. But the manufacturer had assured them they would hold. Just be careful, Collingdale had told her. "Any sudden yanks, and we might lose it all."

At that moment, Digger came on the circuit. She was delighted to hear his voice, proud that he had tried to rescue the Goompah, angry that he had risked his life in so foolhardy a manner. "You're all right?" she asked.

"*I'm fine,*" he said.

"Okay. Don't do anything like that again."

"*I'll be careful.*"

"Promise."

"*I promise.*"

"Okay. We're busy. I have to sign off."

"*Go.*"

"I'm glad you're okay."

"Me too. Be careful yourself."

Collingdale had not seemed to pay any attention, but she'd seen his jaw muscles move. More important things to do now than personal conversations. But he smiled. "I'm glad he got through it okay."

"Thanks, Dave." Bill's image appeared on-screen. He was wearing *Hawksbill* coveralls and looked quite heroic. This was Bill at about thirty-five, with thick brown hair and piercing blue eyes and a dashing mien. She couldn't restrain a smile, but Bill didn't react. "How," she asked him, "is velocity vis-à-vis the cloud?"

"Identical. We're doing fine." His voice had gotten deeper.

Collingdale nodded. "Crunch time," he said. "Let's make our turn."

"Bill," she said, "let's do like last time. Three points to port. Ease into it."

Thrusters burped. And burped again.

The cables tightened.

And they settled back to wait.

KELLIE WAS BRIGHT and easygoing, but she talked a little too much. She'd encouraged him to tell her about his days as an Academy pilot and his life at the University of Chicago and how he had gotten involved in the omega hunt. He gave short, irritated answers, and she shrugged finally, said okay, as in okay if you want to sit in your room, that's fine with me. And she went into a sulk and stayed there.

It left him feeling guilty. That was a surprise. Where social blundering was concerned, he'd beaten his conscience into submission years earlier. He didn't much care whether people liked him, so long as they respected him. But it was clear that Kellie thought he was a jerk. And not very smart.

"I'm sorry," he said, while they waited for Bill to tell them the cloud was turning in their direction.

"For what?" Her eyes were dark and cold, and he saw no flexibility in them.

"You wanted to talk."

"Not really." She had a book on-screen and her gaze drifted back to it.

"What are you reading?"

"Lamb's essays."

"Really." That seemed odd. "Are you working on a degree?"

"No," she said.

"Then why—?"

"I like him." Slight emphasis on the *him*.

"I've never read him," he said. He never read anything that wasn't work-related.

She shrugged.

"I'll have to try him sometime."

She passed her hand over the screen, and the book vanished. "He's good company," she said.

He got the point. "Look, we've got another couple of days out here, Kellie. I'm sorry if I've created a problem. I didn't mean to. It's hard to think about anything right now other than *that* goddam thing." He gestured toward the after section of the ship. In the direction of the cloud.

"It's okay. I understand."

He asked how she had come to be there, at the most remote place humans had ever visited. And before they were finished, she'd told him why Digger was such an extraordinary person, and he'd told her about Mary, and about how sorry he was for Judy Sternberg and her team of Goompahs-in-training.

He learned that she loved Offenbach. "Barcarolle," from *The Tales of Hoffmann*, was playing in the background while they talked. They discovered a mutual interest in politics, although they disagreed on basic philosophy. But it was all right because they found common cause in the conviction that democratic government was, by its nature, corrupt, and had to be steam-cleaned every once in a while.

She liked live theater, and had thought she'd like to act on the stage, but she was too shy. "I get scared in front of an audience," she told him sheepishly. He found that hard to believe.

Collingdale had acted in a couple of shows during his undergraduate days. His biggest role had been playing Octavius in *Man and Superman*.

He wondered why she had chosen so solitary a profession. "You must run into a lot of people like me," he said. "Unsociable types."

"Not really," she said. "Not out here. Everybody loosens up. You can't be alone in a place like this unless you're literally, physically, alone." She flashed the first truly warm smile he'd seen. "I love what I do for a living," she added.

"*Kellie.*" Bill's voice crackled out of the speaker.

"Go ahead."

"*It's throwing off a big slug of cloud to starboard.*"

She looked at Collingdale.

"You sure?" he asked.

"*Here's the picture.*"

Bill put it on the navigation screen, the largest monitor on the bridge. A large plume was erupting off the right side. "It's turning," Collingdale said. He raised a triumphant fist. "The son of a bitch is *turning*!"

"You really think?" asked Kellie.

"No question. It turns left by throwing dust and gas off to the right." He was out of his seat, charging around the bridge, unable to contain himself. "It's taken the bait. It's trying to chase us. It has a hard time turning, but it's trying." His gaze fell on Kellie. "I believe I love you," he said. "Digger's got it exactly right. I wish you a long and happy marriage."

ARCHIVE

The beast is in pursuit.

—Ship's Log, NCY *Hawksbill*
December 6

chapter 41

THE NEWS THAT the omega was turning ignited a minor celebration, and induced Digger and Whit to take the day off. They were sitting in the common room, congratulating one another, when Bill broke in. *"Digger, your friend Macao is onstage again,"* he said. *"—In Kulnar."*

"Doing a *slosh*?" he asked.

"Yes. Would you like to watch?"

"Actually, Bill, I'm half-asleep. But Whit might enjoy seeing it."

Whit looked at him curiously. "Who's Macao? What's a *slosh*?"

"Whit, you'd be interested. A *slosh* is a kind of public debate. And Macao is the female I told you about."

"The one you talked to?"

"Yes."

"Okay. Yes, I'd like very much to see it."

Digger signaled Bill to start the feed.

Macao's image appeared on-screen. She was in blue and white and was waving her arms in a way that Digger immediately saw signaled frustration. *"—Not claiming that,"* she said. *"But what I am saying is that we should be ready. It's a storm, like any other storm. Except it's bigger."*

The biggest Goompah that Digger had seen was already on his feet. *"But how do you know, Macao?"* he demanded. *"How could you possibly know?"*

There was only one pickup, and it was positioned so that it caught her in profile. There were about two hundred Goompahs in view, but he guessed they were only half the audience.

"Forget what I know or don't know, Pagwah," she said. *"Ask yourself what you can lose by moving your family to high ground."*

Digger translated for Whit.

"What we can lose is that we sit on a mountain and get rained on for three or four days."

Another voice broke in, from someone off-screen: *"Maybe if you were to tell us how you know what you say you know, we could make more sense of it."*

The Goompahs pounded their chairs.

"*There have been signs,*" Macao said. "*Devils on the road, whispers in the night.*"

Whit chuckled. "Wait till she hears about what happened in *Savakol.*"

"*Devils on the road.*" A female about six rows back got to her feet. "*You're the one always tells us there are no such things.*"

"*I was wrong.*"

"*Come on, Macao, do we believe in spirits now? Or do we not?*"

Digger could see her hesitate. "*I believe they exist,*" she said.

"*I almost think you mean it.*" Again, Digger couldn't see who was speaking.

"*I do mean it.*"

"*That's quite a change of heart.*" This one was difficult to translate. Literally, the speaker said, "That's not the way you used to put on your pants."

"*Nevertheless it's true.*"

They laughed at her. There was a smattering of applause, possibly for her courage, or maybe because she'd provided a good evening's entertainment. But the mood was different from any of the *sloshen* Digger had seen previously. The others had been lighthearted, even the more serious events. But some of these creatures were *angry.*

"*It may be coming,*" she persisted.

"*But you're not sure.*"

"*There's no way to be sure.*"

"*When is it coming?*"

"*In a few more days.*"

"*Macao.*" Pagwah again. The big one. "*Macao, I'm embarrassed for you, that you would play on everyone's fears at a time like this. I wouldn't have expected it from you.*"

It ended in pushing and shoving and disgruntled patrons stalking out. One of the Goompahs fell down. Some stayed in their seats and pounded their chair arms. Macao thanked them over the general confusion and then she, too, was gone.

She reappeared moments later, at a side door, followed by a small group. They were engaged for a minute or two in animated conversation. Then they left, and the place was empty. An attendant entered, moved across to the far side, and the lamps began to go out.

"Magnificent," said Whit. "This is the kind of stuff I came to see." He produced a notebook and gazed at it. "I'd like to capture as much of this as I can. *Sloshen*. Uh, that's the correct term, right?"

"Yes."

"Wonderful," he said.

"What's wonderful? How do you mean?"

"Nothing seems to be sacred here. They can get up and talk about anything. The audience screams and yells, but the police do not come to get you." His eyes glowed. "You thought of this place as Athens when you first saw it."

"Well, not exactly, Whit. That was *Brackel*."

"I'm talking about the civilization, not merely this particular city." He fell silent for a few moments. Then: "They have more freedom than the Athenians did. More even than *we* do."

That annoyed Digger. He liked Whit, but he had no patience with crazy academics making charges no one could understand. "How could they have more freedom than we do?" he demanded. "We don't have thought police running around."

"Sure we do," he said.

"Whit." Digger raised his eyes to the overhead. "What kind of speech is prohibited? Other than yelling fire in a crowded place?"

Digger smiled. "Almost everything," he said.

He was baffled. "Whit, that's crazy. When's the last time anybody was jailed for speaking out on something?"

"You don't get jailed. But you have to be careful nonetheless not to offend people. We're programmed, all of us, to take offense. Who can go in front of a mixed audience and say what he truly believes without concern that he will offend someone's heritage, someone's religion, someone's politics. We are always on guard."

"Well," said Digger, "that's different."

"No it isn't," said Whit. "It's different only in degree. At my prep school, it was drilled into us that good manners required we avoid talking politics or religion. Since almost everything in the domain of human behavior falls within one or the other of those two categories, we would seem to be left with the weather." He looked momentarily bleak. "We have too much respect for unsubstantiated opinion. We enshrine it, we tiptoe cautiously around it, and we avoid challenging it. To our shame.

"Somewhere we taught ourselves that our opinions are more significant than the facts. And somehow we get our egos and our opinions and Truth all mixed up in a single package, so that when something does challenge one of the notions to which we subscribe, we react as if it challenges *us*.

"We've just watched Macao go in front of an audience and admit that a belief she's probably held all her life, that the world can be explained by reason, is wrong. How many humans do you know who would be capable of doing that?"

"But she was right the first time, Whit. Now she's got it backward."

"Irrelevant. She's flexible, Digger. It looks as if they all are. Show them the evidence, and they're willing to rethink their position." He shook his head. "I think there's much to recommend these creatures."

The actions of the gods are everywhere around us. We have but to look. What are the stars, if not divine fire? How does one explain the mechanism that carries the sun from the western ocean, where we see it sink each evening, to the eastern sky, where it reappears in all its glory each morning? How else can we account for the presence of plants and animals, which provide our subsistence? Or for the water that we drink? Or the eyes by which we see? The gods have been kind to us, and I sometimes wonder at their patience with those who cannot see their presence, and who deny their bounty.

—*Gesper of* Sakmarung
The Travels
(Translated by Ginko Amagawa)

chapter 42

THE CLOUD HAD been shedding velocity for months, possibly years. Because the *Hawksbill* was moving at a steady clip, the cloud was falling behind. Collingdale wished they could shed some velocity themselves.

But they couldn't. Not without bumping, and probably collapsing, the kite.

He wondered when they would reach a point from which the cloud would no longer be able to get an approach angle on Lookout. "*Insufficient data,*" said Bill, when he asked the AI. The truth was they simply knew too little about the cloud's capabilities.

Collingdale played with the numbers, but he wasn't much of a mathematician, and it was all guesswork anyhow. It was just past noon on the second day of the pursuit. He thought that if they could get through the rest of the day, and through the next, to about midnight, it would be over. The cloud would be so far off course that no recovery would be possible.

But the omega was becoming steadily smaller on the overhead. It was now eight-hundred kilometers back, almost three times as far as it had been when it turned to follow them.

He was exhausted. He needed some sleep. Needed to think about something else for a while. He'd done nothing since they'd left orbit over Lookout except sit and worry while his adrenaline ran.

Bill announced that Julie was on the circuit.

"*Good news,*" Julie said. She looked tired too. "*Ten-day forecast for* Hopgop, Mandigol, *and the entire northern end of the* Intigo: *Rain and more rain. With lots of low visibility.*"

"How about that?" said Collingdale. "I guess Marge knows her stuff."

"Apparently."

It was a memorable moment. Everything seemed to be working.

*　*　*

HE TRIED TO read, tried to work on his notes, tried to play chess with Bill. He talked with Kellie. The only release for his tension came when she admitted to similar feelings. Be glad when it's over. Dump the thing and wave good-bye.

He promised that when they went back to Lookout they'd do a proper celebration of her wedding. "I guess I pretty much put a cloud over everything."

"Not really," she said, but her tone said otherwise.

"Well, we sort of cleared out. Not much of a honeymoon."

"No. It wasn't."

"Probably the first time a woman got married and ran off for several days with another man."

THEY HAD AN early dinner and watched *The Mile-High Murders*. Kellie guessed after twenty minutes who did it. She was quite good at puzzles and mysteries. Collingdale wondered why she hadn't made more of herself. But she was young. Still plenty of time.

When it was over he excused himself and retired. An hour later he was back on the bridge clad in a robe. At about midnight Kellie joined him. "Wide awake," she said. "I keep asking Bill if the cloud's still behind us. If the kite's still in place."

It was eleven hundred klicks back now.

At about 3:00 A.M., when both were dozing, Bill broke in: *"The cloud has begun throwing jets out to the rear."*

Thank God. "Excellent," said Collingdale.

Kellie was still trying to get awake. "Why?" she asked.

"It's accelerating. It wants to catch us. Or, rather, catch the kite."

She looked at him, and smiled. "I guess it's over."

Collingdale shook his head. Don't get excited yet. "Another twenty hours or so," he said. "Then I think it will be time to declare victory."

Bill put the images from the monitors on-screen. A couple of plumes had indeed appeared at the rear of the cloud and were growing as they watched.

HE DOZED OFF again, and woke to find her gone. "Bill," he said.

"Yes, David?"

"Is it still there?"

"Yes, David."

"Range?"

"Twelve-fifty. It is still losing ground, but not quite as quickly."

"Excellent, Bill. Good show."

"*Thank you, sir.*"

"You're not really aware of any of this, are you? I mean, you don't know what we've actually accomplished, do you?"

"*In fact, I do, David.*"

"Are you as pleased as I?"

"*I have no way to gauge the level of your pleasure.*"

He thought about it a moment. "I wonder if you're really there."

"*Of course I am, sir.*"

"Well, I'm glad to hear it."

Kellie came back. "I heard voices," she said. "Everything okay?"

"So far."

AT MIDMORNING, THE *Jenkins* reported that Digger and Whit had decided to play it safe, and were back on the ground positioning projectors. This had happened, Julie said, not because anyone had any doubts that the *Hawksbill* had turned the cloud aside, but because Whit enjoyed wandering invisible among the theaters and cafés. And Digger wanted to keep him happy.

"She doth protest too much," said Kellie.

But it was a good idea. Collingdale felt that he was in control, but caution back at Lookout couldn't hurt.

They ate an early breakfast, took turns napping, and watched another sim, a musical, *The Baghdad Follies.* When it was over, Kellie suggested lunch, but neither of them was hungry. Their package of daily newscasts and specialty shows arrived during the early afternoon. The newscasts consisted of the usual array of political shenanigans, corporate scandal, and occasional murder. A pair of Holy Balu parents had run off with their desperately ill child rather than allow doctors to cure him, using a technique that required infusion of synthetic blood. Kosmik, Inc., the terraforming and transportation giant, had collapsed amid charges of theft, profiteering, and collusion at the top. A battle had broken out over implants that could increase one's intelligence, or maybe not, depending on how one defined the word.

By late afternoon they were beginning to feel safe.

"Bill," said Collingdale, "how about giving us another two degrees? To port?" Jerk the son of a bitch around a little bit more.

Kellie confirmed the order.

"*Executing,*" said Bill.

The thrusters realigned themselves and fired briefly. The ship angled a bit farther away from Lookout.

The viewports lit up. Lightning out there somewhere. But that was nothing new.

"I'll be right back," Kellie said.

She left him alone on the bridge. It was a good moment, filled with a sense of victory, of having beaten long odds. Of having taken a measure of vengeance for Moonlight.

Kellie came back carrying a bottle of chablis and two glasses. She filled both and held one out for him. "Sorry," she said. "The champagne supply is depleted."

He took his glass and looked at it. She raised hers. "To the Goompahs," she said.

It would have been hard to find a man less given to superstition than David Collingdale. And yet—he raised his own. "May their luck hold," he said, and drank.

As if the comment had stirred him, Bill's voice broke through the mood. *"The cloud is turning to starboard."*

"You mean to port," said Kellie.

"To starboard. It is turning back toward its original course."

Collingdale's blood froze. "Bill, are you sure?"

"Yes. It's throwing off more plumes. To port. And forward. I do believe it's trying to brake again."

Kellie looked at him. "Dave, can it still get to Lookout?"

"I don't know. How the hell can I tell what the damned thing can do?"

She centered the cloud's vector on the navigation screen, then added the kite's image. The kite, which had been centered, was off to the left. The omega *was* turning.

They informed Digger.

"What happened?" he demanded. His voice suggested it was Collingdale's fault.

"We think we got too far away from it."

"Can't you slow down? Get back in front of it again? Dangle the kite in its nose?"

"Negative," said Kellie. "We can't maneuver with the kite tied on our rear end. It's sitting right behind the tubes."

"Well, what the hell—"

"There is good news," said Bill. *"We have thrown it off its timetable. On its original trajectory, it would have arrived directly over the* Intigo. *Preliminary projection suggests that, if it can reach Lookout at all, it will get there a day and a half later."*

"Oh," said Digger. *"A day and a half. Well, that makes all the difference in the world."*

"No." Kellie pressed an index finger to her lips. "That means it hits the back side of Lookout."

"That's correct," said Collingdale.

They listened to Digger breathing. *"Okay,"* he said finally. *"You guys better just get out of there. We'll do what we can on this end."*

COLLINGDALE COULDN'T SEE any difference in the cloud, couldn't see that it had changed course, couldn't see that it had thrown on its brakes and was doing the equivalent of a sharp right turn. It would be a few hours before the change became noticeable.

"There might be something we could try," he said. "How about we cut the kite loose so we can move around a little."

"And then what?"

"Kellie, the *Hawksbill* is a big, oversize box of a ship. We could take it around and dangle ourselves in front of the thing, see if we can distract it."

"Dangle *ourselves*?"

Bad choice of phrase there. "The ship. Dangle the ship."

"I'm not sure I see the difference."

"Listen, if we get closer to it, and line ourselves up with the kite, which we can do if we move quickly, it'll be looking at *two* boxes. It might be enough to draw it away."

"It might get us killed."

He let her see that he understood what she was saying. "It might make all the difference. If we can push it a bit farther, just a little bit, maybe just a hesitation on its part, it might save everything—"

"—How close were you thinking of going?"

"Whatever it takes."

"Damn it, David. The *Hawksbill* is a target. We are exactly what that thing has for breakfast. What it might do is gobble us up and keep going."

"Okay." He allowed the contempt he felt to show in his voice. "Okay, let's go home."

She looked at him suspiciously.

"I mean it," he said. "You're the captain."

"Bill," she said, "release the kite and retract the cables. We're going back to Lookout."

"In a few days, though," he continued, "when that thing rolls in on the Goompahs, and kills them by the tens of thousands, you're going to remember you had a chance to stop it."

She froze at that, as he knew she would. "Collingdale," she said, "you are a son of a bitch."

"Kite released," said Bill.

"You know I'm right without my having to say it. If I weren't here, if you were alone, you'd do it."

He thought he saw fear in her eyes. But she pulled herself together. "Buckle in," she told him. They waited in a silence you could have hit with a sledgehammer until Bill announced that the cables were safely withdrawn.

"This way," he said, listening to his words echo around the bridge, "we won't have to fight a guilty conscience. Either of us."

She ignored him. "Bill," she said, "get us well away from the kite. When we can use the main engines, put us back in front of the cloud. I want to come in over the top again, from the rear, and I want to drop down in front of it, match course and speed, and line up between the face of the thing and the kite."

"How close do you wish to cut it, Kellie?"

"I'll let you know when we get there," she said.

SHE SETTLED IN front of the cloud at a range of three hundred klicks. Ahead, the box kite was a bright star. But the cloud was visibly leaning to starboard.

They sat in frozen silence. Vast plumes were boiling out of the omega's forward section, marking its efforts to slow down. One approached as she watched, fascinated. It exploded past the ship, and minutes later, raced past the kite.

Collingdale waited, trying to be patient, watching the screen. Watching the gap widen between the cloud and the kite. Hoping to see the omega notice they were there and begin another pursuit. "Bill," he said, "are we picking up any change?"

"Negative," said the AI. *"The cloud is still braking, still angling to starboard."*

"It might take a while," said Kellie.

"No." He found himself wishing she were off the ship. Somewhere else. He could have handled things himself, but the rules required a licensed captain. If he were alone with the AI, everything would be much simpler. He wouldn't be risking anybody else. "We're too far away," he said. "We have to get closer to have a chance."

Whatever she was about to say to him, she swallowed. Instead she turned back to the AI. "Bill, I'm going to manual."

Bill didn't say anything. Didn't have to, probably. Kellie's fingers danced across her control board. Views from forward and aft telescopes appeared on-screen. A second jet fountained past. Retros fired, and Collingdale was forced forward against his restraints.

"How close do you want to go?" she asked.

"I don't know," he said. "We have to do this by the seat of our pants." Damn, she was irritating.

Lightning flickered.

And again.

"Maybe we're getting its attention," she said.

"I hope so."

She shut the retros down. "It's at 240 klicks," she said. "And closing."

"Okay. That's good. Let it keep coming."

Something crackled against the hull. It was like being hit by a sandstorm. "Dust," she said. "Part of the cloud. We may be getting too close."

The viewport lit up again and stayed that way. Something hit the ship, rolled it. Collingdale lurched against his harness. One of the screens exploded; the others went blank. There was a second shock, stronger than the first, driving the wind out of him. Glass and plastic rained down. The bridge went dark. For a few moments he could hear only the crackle of blowing circuits and the sound of his own breathing. He could smell things burning. "Kellie—"

"Hang on. Everything'll be back in a minute."

He hoped so. "What—?"

It was as far as he got. His chair shoved him hard forward, and he could almost hear the thunderclap, hear the shielding sizzling. The lights on the bridge blinked on, went back out. He started to float against his restraints.

"Controls are down," she said. "Get us out of here, Bill. Head for open sky."

The only response was a distant murmur.

"Bill?"

Somewhere in the bulkhead he could hear a fan. A lamp came on at Kellie's position. She was doing things with the status board. "Engines are out," she said.

So were the screens.

"Can you get them running again?"

"Trying."

"Are we still dropping back into the cloud?"

"Yes. Nothing we can do about that at the moment." She shook her head. Not good. "Junction box problem, looks like."

"Can you fix it?"

"I can replace it." Another bolt hit. The ship shuddered. Red warning lamps came on and glowed scarlet. "But not in fifteen minutes." Which was a generous estimate of the time they had left.

She got one of the tracking screens back up. That allowed him to watch the misty forward wall closing on them. Another jet was erupting. "It's still trying for Lookout," she said. He couldn't decide whether her voice carried a ring of sarcasm. "We just happen to be in the way."

"How about the jump engines?"

"Not without prep. They'll explode."

He looked at her. "What else have we got?"

"Not much." She was scrabbling in one of the utility drawers and came out with a lantern. "Grab an e-suit and some air tanks. We're leaving."

"To go where?"

"The shuttle."

THE *HAWKSBILL* WASN'T designed for convenience. The shuttle bay was down in cargo, which could receive life support, but seldom did. It depended on what the ship was hauling. Collingdale slipped into an e-suit, activated it, and pulled on a pair of air tanks. Kellie led the way through the airlock and down into the bowels of the ship.

"Power's off here," she said.

"What about the shuttle?"

"No way to know until we get there."

He hadn't had to move in a zero-gee environment in a long time, but the technique came back quickly. They passed along wire mesh, down a dark corridor, through the cavernous space in which Marge's equipment had been stored, and crossed into the lower cargo section, which also served as the launch bay for the shuttle. The bulkheads were filled with equipment for working outside, laser cutters, wrenches, gauges, coils of cable, and with go-packs as well as more air tanks.

The shuttle rested atop its dock. She activated it with a remote. To his relief, lights came on, and the engine began to purr. She opened the hatch, but before they climbed in she aimed the remote at the airlock and pressed it.

Nothing happened.

"Door doesn't work," she said. "Hold on a second."

He followed her across the bay. "You'll have to open it manually," he said.

"My thought exactly." She sounded annoyed. Nevertheless, he found the wall panel before she did.

"Here," he said.

She opened it and extracted the handle. He stepped in beside her and pulled it down. The inner doors irised open. They repeated the process, and an outer door rolled into the overhead.

He looked out at a river of dust and gas. It was one of the jets, streaming past, close enough to touch. The omega itself filled the sky behind them.

"It's on top of us," he said.

"Come on." Kellie stayed cool. She moved through the weightless environment like a dancer, soared into the shuttle, and urged him to hurry.

Collingdale was no slouch either, and he climbed in quickly beside her and shut the hatch. And saw immediately the look on her face. "What's wrong?"

"No power in the dock." She rolled her eyes. "Should have realized." She opened up again and got out. Collingdale needed a moment to understand. The shuttle was secured to its launch platform.

He jumped out behind her. "Has to be a manual release here somewhere."

"I don't see it."

The airlock was filling with mist. "Time's up," she said. She broke away from the shuttle, grabbed two pairs of air tanks from the bulkhead, and floated one his way.

"What's this for?" he asked. They were already wearing tanks.

"Extras," she said. "We're going to be out there for a while." She pulled a go-pack on over her shoulders.

"Kellie, what are you doing?"

"We're leaving."

"What? No! You can't possibly get clear in that."

"It's all we have. We can't stay here."

"They don't even know we're in trouble."

"They'll know our signal's been cut off."

He took a last desperate look for the manual release, did not see it, concluded it was in the bulkhead somewhere, thought how they should have taken more time to familiarize themselves with the ship, and turned back to her. The cloud was literally coming in the open airlock. Coming after him.

"It's not fast enough," he said. The go-pack. "You can't outrun it in that."

She apparently had lost all interest in arguing. She grabbed his shoulder and pushed him toward the exit, simultaneously shoving the go-pack into his midsection. But it was hopeless.

In that terrible moment, he realized suddenly, as if everything that had gone before had been simply a problem to be solved, that there was no solution. That he was going to die.

All that remained was to choose the method.

"Get out, Kellie," he said, and pulled away from her. He went back through the doorway and into the lower cargo section.

"*What are you doing, Dave?*" she demanded.

He found her lamp floating near the shuttle, turned it on, and began to search through the equipment.

"What are you looking for?"

"A laser cutter." And there they were, three of them, neatly stored side by side above a utility shelf at the dock. "Get as far away as you can," he said. He held the cutter up where she could see it and started for the engine room.

Her eyes widened. She understood perfectly what he had decided. She pleaded with him over the circuit, threatened him, told him he was a damned idiot. He wished her luck, told her he was sorry, and shut down all channels.

That would end it. She'd give up and do what she could to save herself. Through the airlock with an extra set of air tanks but a go-pack that wouldn't be able to take her far enough fast enough to outrun the cloud. Or to outrun what he was about to do.

He regretted that. In those last minutes he regretted a lot of things.

CARRYING THE LAMP and the laser, he hurried through the lower decks and the airlock they'd left open and emerged at last on the bridge. Here and there lights still worked, and the electronic systems were trying to come back. Once, the artificial gravity took hold, throwing him to the deck. Then it was gone again. Moments later, he thought he heard Bill's voice, deep in the ship.

Somewhere, a Klaxon began to sound.

He needed the remote, but he'd left it below in cargo. Or maybe Kellie still had it. There was usually a spare, and he searched through the storage cabinets for it. But he didn't see one. Well, he'd have to do without. Find another way. He ducked out of the bridge and headed aft.

He'd lived on the *Hawksbill* for two months, but the ship had changed in some subtle way. These dark corridors, with their shadows and their silence, were unfamiliar, places he'd never been before.

He caught another burst of gravity, stumbled, rolled, and came up running. Not bad for an old guy. Then it died again.

He could hear the sound of hatches closing. Sealing off compartments.

He had to open one, and then a second, to get into the engine room. They both closed automatically behind him.

The good news was that the lights were on and the jump engines had power. The fusion unit was down, dark, silent, useless. But that didn't matter. He had what he needed.

He felt oddly calm. Almost happy. He might not succeed in damaging the cloud, but he'd strike a blow. Make it recognize he was there.

And he wondered if, somewhere deeper than his conscious mind had been able to go, he had foreseen this eventuality, had almost planned it. It accounted for his intense interest in the *Hawksbill*, his drive to have Julie explain everything.

The possibility strengthened his resolve, suggested that he would be successful after all, that there was something at work here greater than he knew. A destiny, of sorts. He didn't believe in such nonsense, and yet now, in these final moments, it was a possibility to which he could cling.

He found the manual controls and flicked them on. Watched lights come up. He told it to activate the engines. Go to jump.

A voice, not Bill's, responded. *"Unable to comply. The unit is not charged."*

"Override all injunctions."

"Unable to comply."

"This is Juliet Carson. Override."

"Please enter code."

Well, he'd expected it. But the system was designed to prevent tinkering, and not outright sabotage.

There was an explosion up front somewhere. Near the bridge.

He aimed the laser cutter, ignited it, and took a long look at the engine. The design of these things hadn't changed much since his day.

He applied the torch to the metal and prayed for time. Cut through the outer housing. Cut through the protective shell. Get to the junction box, the same device that had failed in the fusion engines.

It was hard work because he needed the lamp to see into the housing. So he had to use a hand to hold the lamp, and a hand to hold the cutter, and a hand to keep from floating away.

But finally he was in.

And it was simply a matter of removing the flow control, and power would pass into the system and start the jump process. Or in this case, because the protective bubble wasn't adequately charged, it would release some antimatter fuel and blow the ship into oblivion. Maybe, if he was extraordinarily lucky, it would find a vulnerable spot in whatever system controlled the cloud. And put it out of action, too.

It wasn't much of a chance, but it could happen.

He thought of calling Kellie, of telling her how sorry he was, of letting her know it was moments away. But it would be better not to. More compassionate. Let it come as a surprise.

He would have preferred to wait until he got deeper into the cloud. But he had no way of knowing when the power would fail altogether. And then he'd have nothing.

Another Klaxon started, and shut down.

He sliced the flow control.

LIBRARY ENTRY

Sometime within the next few days, the civilization which refers to itself as *Korbikkan*, which we call Goompah, will be wiped out. The omega will collide with their world and devastate its handful of cities while we sit watching placidly.

So far, there is no word of any serious action being taken on their behalf, no indication we have planned anything except to try a decoy, and if that doesn't work, which it clearly won't, we'll make it rain, and then claim we tried to help. The problem is that the effort, such as it is, is being run by the usual bureaucrats.

It's too late for the Goompahs, I am sorry to say. And the day is coming when another crowd of bureaucrats of the same stripe will be charged with rescuing *us* from the same unhappy result. It gives one pause.

—Carolyn Magruder Reports
UNN broadcast
Monday, December 8, 2234

DIGGER HAD JUST finished inserting a projector under the roof overhang of a shop that sold fish when the news came.

"They're off the circuit." Julie's voice. *"All channels."*

It was probably just a transmitter glitch. But a terrible fear clawed at him. He should have refused to let her go. He'd known from the beginning that he should have kept her away from that thing. He could have simply raised so much hell that they'd have backed off. If Collingdale wanted to go, let him go. But let Bill take him. Why did he have to have Kellie along?

"Digger? Do you hear me?"

"Yes."

"It doesn't mean there's a major problem."

"I know." He was standing on top of a storage box, and he didn't want to come down. Didn't want to move. "Pick us up," he said. "I'll get Whit."

Whit tried to be reassuring, thing like this you always think the worst, she's a good pilot. They decided where they'd meet, and Digger passed the word to Julie. An hour later they were back on the *Jenkins*, leaving orbit.

THE RUN OUT to the cloud took four hours. It was a frantic four hours for Digger, who tried tirelessly to raise the *Hawksbill*, and for the others, who didn't know what to say to him.

When they arrived in its vicinity, they found the box kite, cruising quietly ahead of the omega, gradually pulling away from the giant. Bill reported that he was in contact with the surveillance packages the *Hawksbill* had been using to monitor the omega.

"But I do not see the Hawksbill *itself,"* he added.

There was no wreckage, no indication what could have happened.

They must have gotten too close.

Each of them, in turn, said much the same thing. Even Digger admitted the ship was lost, had to be lost, no other explanation for it. Yet he could not believe Kellie was gone. She was too smart. Too alive.

"They'd have let us know if they were in trouble, wouldn't they?" he demanded of Julie.

"Maybe they didn't have time. Maybe it happened too quickly."

For a while, they lived with the hope that the cloud was between them and the *Hawksbill*, that it had somehow blocked off the ship's transmissions as it was now preventing a visual sighting. But Digger knew the truth of it, although he would not accept it, as if refusing to do so kept her chances alive. He walked through the ship in a state of shock.

Julie invited him onto the bridge, tried to find things for him to do. In his heart he damned Collingdale, and damned Hutchins for sending him.

He could not have told anyone what time of day it was, or whether they were actively searching or just going through the motions, or whether there was anyplace left to look. He listened to Bill's reports, *negative, negative,* to Marge and Whit talking in whispers, to Julie talking with Bill and maybe sending off the news to Broadside.

And he became aware that they were waiting for him to say the word, to recognize that there was no way the *Hawksbill* could be intact without their knowing, that it was hopeless, but that they would not stop looking until he told them to do so.

There was always a chance they were in the shuttle, he told himself. The shuttle could easily be hidden among all the jets and dust and shreds and chunks of cloud, its relatively weak radio signal blown away by the electrical activity in the area.

It was possible.

THE FIRST INDICATION there might be something out there came in the form not of a radio signal, but, incredibly, of a sensor reading of a small metal object, glimpsed briefly and then lost.

"Metal," said Julie. "It was small."

"The shuttle?"

"Smaller than that."

The return of hope was somehow painful. He could lose her again.

"Where?" demanded Digger.

"Hold on." The area around the cloud was a vast debris field.

Bill drew a vector. "*Somewhere along that line.*"

They picked it up again. "*I believe,*" said the AI, "*it's a set of air tanks.*"

Air tanks? Then somebody was attached to them, right?

"*Negative,*" said Bill. "*Tanks only.*"

They tracked them and took them on board. Saw the *Hawksbill* label on the shoulder strap. Noted that they were exhausted.

"They're out there," said Digger. Julie nodded. Empty tanks meant some-one had used them for six hours, then discarded them. You only did that if you had a spare set of tanks.

At least one of them was still afloat.

They checked the time: ten and a half hours since the signal had been lost. Six hours to a set of tanks.

How many spares could you carry?

Then Bill announced he'd picked up a radio signal.

KELLIE BURST INTO tears when they hauled her inside. Tough, stoic, always in control, she let them remove her tanks and go-pack and shut off the suit, and she made no effort to restrain her emotions. Her right arm was broken, and she had a few torn ligaments and a bunch of bruises, but she was alive and that was all that mattered.

She smiled weakly at Digger and told Bill she wished he were human so she could kiss him.

Bill promptly appeared, his younger, lean, devil-may-care version, with dark hair and dark skin and dark eyes that literally flashed.

"He's gone," she said of Collingdale. "He stayed with the *Hawksbill.*" She explained how it had lost power, how Collingdale had refused to abandon it, had decided they couldn't survive, that he would ride it inside the cloud and detonate the Hazeltines.

"It doesn't look as if he did any lasting damage," said Whit.

"*No,*" agreed Bill. "*The cloud will make its rendezvous with Lookout.*"

Julie looked puzzled. "How'd you get clear? Of the blast and the cloud? You couldn't have done it with that." She was looking at the go-pack.

Whit handed her a painkiller, and they were taking her back to the med station.

"There was a plume," she said. "A jet stream. It only took a few minutes to get to it, and it blew me out of the neighborhood pretty quick." She looked at her arm. "That's where I took the damage."

ARCHIVE

The gulfs between the stars overwhelm us, as the eons overwhelm our paltry few years of sunlight. We are cast adrift on an endless sea, to no purpose, with no destination, bound where no one knows.

—Dmitri Restov
Last Rites

L I B R A R Y   E N T R Y

Mary,

I'm sorry to tell you that we lost David this morning. We all admired him, and everyone here shares your grief. I'm sure you'll be receiving official notification from the Academy in a few days.

It might console you to know that he died heroically, in the best of causes. His action here appears to have thrown the omega off schedule and thereby bought some time. It's likely that many who would have been lost at the *Intigo* will survive as a result of your fiancé's efforts.

—Julie Carson
December 8

PART FIVE

lykonda

chapter 44

THE SKY WAS blanketed by Marge's rain clouds. Three of her chimneys were up and running. The fourth would be erected that night on an island forty klicks off the west coast, midway between *Mandigol* and *Sakmarung*. Over the last two days, no one in *Hopgop* or *Roka*, or in the four cities located in the center of the isthmus, had seen the sun, the stars, or the apparition.

It was still visible from *T'Mingletep* and *Savakol* in the south, and from *Saniusar* in the far north. There, the Goompahs watched the omega grow visibly larger each night. It filled their sky, a terrifying vision, grim and churning and lit within by demon-fire.

Digger sat, concealed within his lightbender, in a pavilion in the middle of a rainswept park. The park was deserted, as were the surrounding streets. Whit was out positioning projectors. He'd gotten good at it, and obviously enjoyed the work.

They'd done the calculations again, and the cloud was not compensating for its new position, was probably unable to compensate, and would consequently reach Lookout when it was early afternoon on the *Intigo*. Since it was coming out of the night, that meant it should expend most of its energy on the far side of the world.

Halleluia! Add that to the cloud cover Marge was putting up, and the Goompahs had a decent chance.

"Don't get too confident," Whit had warned him. "Conditions here will still be extreme."

Digger had seen only the shimmering haze of Whit's lightbender, and considered how difficult it was to communicate when you couldn't see people's expressions. Was he becoming seriously pessimistic? Or cautious? Or was it just a reflex that you never claim victory lest you tempt the fates?

"And don't forget the round-the-world mission," he'd added, apparently determined to dampen the mood. He'd been like this since they'd lost Collingdale. The others had expressed their regrets, had been sorry; but Collingdale reportedly hadn't been easy to get to know. Digger, in fact, had barely had time to say hello as he passed through the wedding and took Kellie and the *Hawksbill* out to chase the omega. Kellie had spoken little about him since her return. He hoped she was too smart to assign any guilt to herself for the loss, but she had made it clear she didn't want to talk about the experience.

Whit, however, must have been closer to Collingdale than anyone had realized. He'd been visibly shaken by his death.

The round-the-world mission had been gone ten weeks. Bill was keeping an eye on them and reporting periodically. They'd lost a couple of sailors. One had fallen overboard; another had contracted a disease of some sort and been buried at sea. Otherwise, not much was happening. The wind stops, they stop. The wind picks up, and they're off again. *"They're steering crooked,"* Bill had been saying the last three days. *"They're off course. Had almost a week of bad weather, so I guess they can't see the stars to navigate."*

The ships were approaching the eastern continent and would soon, Digger thought, have to turn back.

The rain around the pavilion was almost torrential. It had been falling steadily for a night and a day. Marge, it seemed, was very good at what she did for a living.

A couple of signs were posted announcing an afternoon *slosh* at *Broka* Hall, giving the time by sundial. In the event of rain, bells would be rung at intervals. A *moraka* was also scheduled that evening at the edge of the park, weather permitting. Music and snacks. Compliments of the *Korkoran* Philosophical Society.

Whit had known what a *slosh* was. But he had not seen the term *moraka* previously.

"It's hard to explain," Digger had told him.

"Try."

"It's an orgy."

"Really?"

"Yes."

"The orgy starts at nine?"

"Something like that."

"Sponsored by the Philosophical Society?"

"Apparently so." Digger grinned.

"This place has some unique aspects."

There was no one about. He could see a Goompah adjusting shutters in one of the buildings lining the park, and another hurrying across a street. And that was it.

Bill broke into his musings. *"Weather update,"* he said in a voice copied from weather reports back home. He enjoyed doing that. *"Expect continued rain in the central sections of the isthmus at least until tomorrow."*

"Bill," he said, "we only have three chimneys up. Are they more effective than we thought?"

"I do not think so, Digger. I believe what we are seeing is partially due to natural meteorological conditions. The arrival of a low-pressure area from the west coincided—"

"—It's okay, I don't need the details. Is there any chance the rain will remain with us over the next few days?"

"Until the cloud arrives? No. The weather system will pass over the isthmus by midday tomorrow. After that, it will be up to Marge's chimneys."

The streets and cafés in the cities were virtually deserted. The Goompahs were staying home in substantial numbers.

Signs had been posted announcing *sloshen* to discuss "recent unsettling events." Digger and Whit had posted projectors at a couple of them so they could watch from the ship. Ironically, the unseasonable weather had added to native disquiet, as had reports of voices and disembodied eyes, mystical flashes in the sky (which might have been the chimneys or the AV3, or both). There'd been *zhoka* sightings on the highways and, most terrifying of all, the levitation of Tayma, the priestess at *Savakol*, followed by a window opening in midair. Witnessed by hundreds.

Digger, Whit, and Kellie had watched fully a dozen Goompahs rise and swear they were there, or knew someone who was there, when it happened. "She literally rose out of the sea," one bull-sized male had said, "and floated through thin air across the water, over the water, until she was set down by an unseen hand on the beach."

The consensus seemed to be that the confluence of supernatural events portended approaching catastrophe. But they wondered, if such a thing were actually about to happen, why the gods were permitting it. Where were they, anyhow? There was a palpable sense of irritation that the local deities were not on the job.

Earlier that day, Digger had stood outside a schoolroom and listened to the teacher and students discuss the approaching cloud. The students were probably a young-adolescent equivalent. It was hard to tell. But some of them wanted to know whether the teacher still believed that supernatural events did not happen.

"It is simply," the teacher had argued, "that there are parts of the natural world we do not yet understand."

The youth in *Avapol* may have been too polite to laugh, and too smart to argue: but even Digger, who had not yet begun to learn the nuances of nonverbal communication among this alien race, could see what they thought of that opinion.

As Whit put a projector in a tree, he caught a glimpse of Digger. When he'd finished, he turned, looked toward the pavilion, and waved. Digger waved back.

"That's the last one," Kellie told him. She was in the lander. This was her first day back at work, giving Julie a well-earned chance to sleep in a bed again.

The last one in *Avapol*. They still had two cities to visit.

It was getting tight. The Goompahs would have three more days of relative calm. During the midafternoon of the third day, the omega would hit the far side of the planet, and conditions would deteriorate. The cloud that had struck Moonlight had delivered most of its energy during the first seven hours. It had systematically picked out every city around the globe still standing and demolished it. Then it had abated.

On Lookout, the actions of the *Hawksbill* had thrown the omega off schedule. Furthermore, Marge's weather would hide the targets. The cloud, not knowing better, would raise hell on the other side of the planet, and the Goompahs, during the first few hours, would get their feet wet. During the course of the evening the *Intigo* would rotate beneath the main body of the storm, but by the time it arrived in the lethal zone, the thing would be starting to dissipate. And it would, they hoped, not even see the cities.

"You guys ready to come home?"

Digger watched Whit moving steadily through the rain. "Give us thirty minutes to get there."

She would pick them up on a hilltop on the northern edge of town. *"I'll be there,"* she said.

Digger got up from his bench.

"By the way," she said, *"the media have arrived."*

"Really?"

"The Black Cat Network, of all people." The Black Cat Network tended toward sensationalist journalism. *"They're asking permission to send in a ground team."*

"Tell them no. We have no authority."

"I already told them."

He sighed. He couldn't really blame them. This was a pretty big story. And they'd come a long way for it. He was tempted to tell them to go ahead, but if he did, Hutch would fry his rear end. "They can do whatever they need to with telescopes."

"Okay."

"And tell them they can have access to the pickups." He thought about that. Maybe it wasn't a good idea. For one thing, they'd undoubtedly find out about the *morakas.* "Do we have guidance from the Academy on any of this?"

"Hutch says cooperate, but they are not to set foot on the surface. If they do, they will be prosecuted. She says they've been warned."

"Okay. Tell them we'll help where we can. Don't mention the pickups."

"Good," she said. *"I think that's prudent."*

BLACK CAT REPORT

Thanks, Ron. This is Rose Beetem in the skies over Lookout. At the moment, we can't show you the cities of the Goompahs. They're under a heavy cover of rainstorms. I have to report to you that we have been asked not to land on the planetary surface, because of the Noninterference Protocol, and we are adhering to that request.

But we expect to be able to follow the action on the ground as the situation develops. Meantime, it is late evening over the Goompah cities, which are concentrated on a relatively small landmass in the southern hemisphere. What you are looking at now is the rim of the omega. It is just rising, and, as you can see, it is an incredible spectacle . . .

Avery Whitlock's Notebooks

It is hard not to conclude that my entire life has been a prelude to and a preparation for this moment. If we do not succeed here, nothing else I've done will have mattered very much.

—December 12

chapter 45

"WE'LL BE LEAVING *orbit in thirty minutes.*" Kellie's voice came over the speaker from the bridge. She'd resumed command of the *Jenkins*.

They were running through the night beneath the cloud. The *Intigo* was on the daylight side of the globe, approaching evening. In a couple of hours, when it rotated beneath the omega, and the ship had withdrawn to a safe distance from Lookout, they would put Digger's plan into effect and see whether the Goompahs could be persuaded to head for the high country. They'd have the night and much of the following day to get out of town. Then, at about midafternoon the omega would impact the far side, weather conditions would worsen, and the event would begin.

The projectors were in place, and the chimneys were up. Clouds were spreading out from *T'Mingletep* on the south to *Saniusar* in the north.

The situation was promising. The omega would, as predicted, hit the wrong side and spend the bulk of its fury before the cities of the *Intigo* rotated into its path.

Moody and dark and silent, lit by only an occasional flicker, it had almost completely blotted out the stars. The Goompahs could no longer see it, but the crew of the *Jenkins* knew. Digger hated looking at the thing. There was a tendency on the ship to walk softly, to hold one's breath, and to speak in low tones, as if a little noise might draw its attention.

The plumes reached well past Lookout and lost themselves in the dazzle of the sun. On the surface of the threatened world, seas had grown rough, in anticipation of the onslaught. Around the *Intigo*, the weather had grown cold and wet.

On the *Jenkins*, as they counted down the last few minutes, they talked about the ongoing debates over enhanced intelligence, about a report from Hutch that clouds did not survive their encounters with their hedgehogs, about an assassination attempt in the NAU Senate, about a new teaching system designed to bolster lagging literacy scores. The approaching omega was the elephant in the room, the thing no one mentioned.

The promised celebration of the marriage between Kellie and Digger never really happened. They'd had a few drinks and exchanged embraces all around, but that was about it. Maybe it seemed inappropriate after Collingdale's death, or maybe nobody really wanted to celebrate anything until they had the results on Lookout.

"*Daylight coming,*" said Kellie.

The sun rose over the rim of the world, and the omega dropped down the sky behind them and receded below the horizon until only the plumes remained visible, great dark towers soaring into the heavens.

"Good riddance," said Marge.

"Next time they want somebody to wrestle one of these things," Digger said, "they're going to have to find somebody else."

"Twelve minutes to departure," said Kellie. "Lockdown in eight. Anybody needs to do anything, this would be a good time."

Digger felt an enormous sense of relief to be putting some distance between himself and the omega.

Julie commented that she was having the time of her life, and they all looked at her as if she'd lost her mind. "Well," she said. "I haven't been around as long as some of you guys have, but if things go well, or even if they don't, I expect this will be the high point of my career. How often do you get involved in something that really matters?"

Mouths of babes, thought Digger. He was jiggling a puzzle on his monitor. Find your way out of the maze.

They were over ocean. Daylight sparkled off a few clouds, and he saw land in the north. In a little more than an hour it would be getting dark along the *Intigo*. Their last peaceful night.

Digger gave up on the maze—he'd never been good at puzzles anyhow—and headed for one of the acceleration couches. It felt good to lie down, punch the button, and feel the harness settle over him. The others laughed at him. "Anxious?" asked Whit.

"You bet."

"I guess we all are." Julie took one of the chairs; Marge, the other couch. Whit settled in beside Julie. "Congratulations," he said.

She smiled. There was a touch of innocence in it, and Digger couldn't help thinking again how young she looked. When they wrote the history of these proceedings, he suspected she'd get left out, pretty much. Collingdale would be seen as a hero who'd sacrificed himself to turn the cloud aside. He still didn't have the story from Kellie, but he suspected something else had been at work. Otherwise, she wouldn't have been so quiet. But it was okay. You always need heroes.

Marge would rank up there, too. And Jack, the first victim. That brought a rush of guilt. Killed by the stupidity of a colleague. If the historians ever got the truth, old Digger wouldn't look very good.

Bill's voice broke in. *"Marge, Kellie asked me to pass the current weather report along."*

He wondered why it mattered at that point.

"What've you got, Bill?" she asked.

"There's a storm system building to the west of the Intigo.*"*

"That's just what we want, isn't it?" said Digger. He glanced over at Marge and gave her a thumbs-up. "An assist for the little lady," he said.

She frowned. "Maybe not. Bill, what kind of storm?"

"Electrical. I'd say the isthmus is going to get heavy rains tonight."

Digger didn't like the way she looked. "What's wrong?" he asked. "Why is that not good news?"

"Think about it. How are you going to send signals to the projectors you've been planting all over the isthmus? During an electrical storm?"

Uh-oh.

"Isn't it a bit late in the season for thunderstorms?"

Marge shrugged. "Don't know. We've haven't really had a chance to look at climatic conditions here. In any case, they could be starting to feel the effects of the omega." The plumes had been burrowing into the atmosphere for a couple of days.

It didn't bother Julie. "I don't see that it makes that much difference," she said. "The thing isn't going to hit the cities anyhow. So even if they don't get out, they'll probably be okay."

"That's not so," persisted Marge. "The omega is going to kick up a very large storm. Think maybe tornado-force winds around the planet." She looked at Digger with frustration. "I don't know. We just don't have enough experience with these things."

She released her harness and went back to one of the stations and brought up an image of the *Intigo*. "The cities are all at or close to sea level. They're going to get high water. Maybe even tsunamis. If the population doesn't get to high ground, the losses are going to be substantial."

"Well," said Julie, "what about this? We can use the landers. They're still down there. Load the broadcast program into the landers now while conditions are good. Pick out four locations covering the eleven cities and have Bill move the landers. Right? One in each spot. Then when the time comes, just broadcast from the four sites. We can watch the storm and try to pick the best time for each."

"Sounds okay to me," said Digger. "I don't see any reason it wouldn't work."

Marge's expression never changed. "I don't think so," she said.

"Why not?" asked Digger.

"The landers are on Mt. Alpha at the moment."

"Where?" asked Whit.

"It's a mountain near *Hopgop*. Nice safe place. Nobody could get near it on foot."

"—And?"

"They're lashed down. To protect them from the winds. They aren't going anywhere."

"Well," said Julie, "I guess we didn't think this one through the way we should have."

"We can't release them from here?" asked Digger.

"They're just ordinary cables tied to trees." Marge looked uncomfortable. "Sorry. It didn't occur to me we'd need them again before this was over."

Julie took a deep breath. "It's out of our hands then. Whatever happens, happens. We've done everything we can."

Whit looked squarely at Digger. *No, we haven't.* But he didn't say it.

"*Two minutes,*" said Kellie. "*Marge, you need to belt down.*"

Digger had no idea where the isthmus was. There were too many clouds. The planet looked so *big*. Surely that little stretch of land with its cluster of cities would get by okay.

Whit was watching him, waiting for him to say something.

Digger sighed. "I'll go down," he said. "I can use the landers and run the signal from the ground. As opportunity permits."

Julie stared at him. "Have you lost your mind?"

"Kellie," he said, "hold off on departure."

"*Why? We'll lose our window.*"

"You're going to need another one."

"I'll go with you," Whit said.

"No." Digger had released his harness and was sitting up. "We'll only need one person on the ground."

"*What's going on back there?*" asked Kellie.

"The weather report created a problem," Julie told her. She looked at Digger. "You'll need a pilot."

Kids always think they're immortal. "Bill can take us down."

"That's not a good idea."

Whit was still watching him. "I'd take it amiss if you don't let me go along."

Digger saw no point in it, but he also saw that Whit was serious. "If you insist," he said. He was trying to think it out. The four landers were tied down on a mountaintop north of *Hopgop*. He'd need the AV3. And the helicopter. "Plus a pilot," he said reluctantly. "I guess you're in, Julie."

"Why do you need the hauler?" demanded Kellie, who had appeared in the doorway.

"It's got a better chance of surviving heavy weather."

"I can pilot the damned thing. There's no need to drag Julie along."

"You're not qualified."

"Digger—"

"We need all the edge we can get. And don't look at me like that. We don't have time to argue about it."

THEY HAD TO make another pass around the night side before they could get set up. Kellie told him it was a fool's errand, and he could see she was struggling to hold back tears. But she finally admitted it was the only thing they could do.

God knew Digger didn't want to go back down with the omega coming on. But he had too much invested in the Goompah cities to walk away from them now. "Listen," he told Kellie, "we've been reasonably confident they can get through it. If they can, we can."

He checked the prepared broadcast to be sure he hadn't overlooked anything, downloaded it onto disk, made an extra copy just in case, and put both in a pocket. The sun dropped behind them, and they plunged into the night. The cloud rose and filled the sky. Everyone was quiet. They'd all seen too many sims, where you go one extra time into danger and pay for it. But they came back out into the sunlight without incident.

When the ship was clear, and they were getting ready to leave, Kellie joined him, and for a long minute, put her hands on his arm, held on, but said nothing.

"It'll be okay," he told her.

Her eyes were damp. "I have to take the *Jenkins* out of orbit."

"I know."

"That means—"

"—I know what it means."

There was another long silence. "I won't ask you not to go, Dig. Just, please, come back." She looked around at the others, making her request binding on all.

"We will. We'll be okay."

"Don't do anything dumb."

"Nothing dumb. Check."

"And make for the high ground."

"Love," he said, taking her into his arms, "I'm already on the high ground."

"I'm serious."

"I know, Kel. Don't worry. I'll be careful. I've too much to come back to."

WHEN THE MOMENT arrived, she gave the word, and they slipped through the airlock, the three of them. They were tethered together, and Julie wore a go-pack. The AV3 was only a short burst away.

It was a big vehicle, but it was all storage space. Digger took a quick look in back to make sure the Falcon was there. The blades had been shortened somehow to save space. Otherwise, the oversize cargo hold was empty.

The cabin was no bigger than the one in the *Jenkins*'s lander. He climbed into the right-hand seat, Whit sat down in back, and the harnesses slid down over their shoulders. Julie settled in, turned on one of the monitors, and began powering up. Lamps blinked on, and Julie was talking to both Bill and Kellie.

Kellie gave her clearance to go, and she throttled up. "How are we going to do this?" she asked, as they slipped away and began their descent.

Digger explained what he wanted. They dropped through the cloud cover and emerged over the ocean. They were down among electrical storms, west of the isthmus, when Bill's elderly sea captain image appeared on the overhead. "*The* Jenkins *has left orbit*," he said.

Moments later Kellie was on the circuit. "*We're pulling out to a range of 3 million klicks. I don't want the ship anywhere near this place when the omega hits.*"

"That should be safe enough," said Julie. Her smooth features were expressionless in the glow of the instrument panel.

Digger twisted around but still couldn't really see Whit. "May I ask you a question?" he said.

"Sure."

"Why did you come? You don't have a dog in this race."

Whit looked momentarily offended. "I'm as involved as anyone else, Dig. I don't think I'd want to be on hand for this and have to tell my grandkids all I did was stand in the third row and watch."

It occurred to Digger that none of them would have been out of the third row had it not been for Whit's prompting. Digger didn't think he would have gone back to the *Intigo* on his own. But it was hard to stay aloof after Whit had made it clear that they were preparing to abandon the Goompahs.

"Hang tight," said Julie. "Rough weather ahead."

*   *   *

MOUNTAINS JUTTED OUT out of the clouds. "Mt. Alpha is that way"—Julie jabbed a finger—"and *Hopgop* over there." Off to the right. It was late afternoon in Goompah country.

"Do you want to wait until it's dark?" Julie asked.

"No. Too much to do, and we're too short on time."

Mt. Alpha was craggy, snow-covered, probably the tallest peak on the isthmus. It was sheer on the west side, as if something had taken a hot knife to it. The remainder was broken into notches, ridges, slopes, gullies, and buttresses.

Julie brought the hauler down cautiously atop the snow cover at the summit and quickly lifted off again when the ground gave way. "Not too steady up here," she commented. They made it on the second try.

The mountaintop was flat. A few trees were scattered about, and some bushes. It was about the size of a soccer field, maybe a little larger. A rock chimney rose out of the center, and a massive fissure had been gouged into the northern angle. Everything beyond it looked ready to plunge into the clouds below.

Two landers were parked on either side of the chimney, anchored to it, to a couple of trees, and to a spread of boulders.

"I think," said Digger, "they're safe from rising water up here."

"We thought so," she said, without a trace of a smile.

They released the cables and tossed them into the vehicles. Digger climbed inside each and uploaded the disk.

The third lander was in the shelter of a buttress, well down the side of the mountain. They were in the weather by then, lightning walking about, rain hammering down. It was secured to five trees. The fourth was in a clutch of forest in a saddle.

They piled out of the AV3 at the saddle and climbed into the lander. Julie activated the vehicle's lightbender, while Digger inserted the final disk.

They were ready to go looking for broadcast locations.

SANIUSAR **WAS EFFECTIVELY** isolated in the northwest, and needed a site of its own. They picked out a ridge in a remote area, and Bill started one of the landers forward. It turned out to be an unnerving experience because the storm kept loosening Bill's grip on the unmanned vehicle, and they almost lost it altogether while he was setting it down.

They settled on a second site midway across the *Intigo*, from which they could reach *Mandigol* and *Sakmarung* on the west coast, and *Hopgop* and *Roka* to the east. It had grown dark when they established a similar location farther south, which provided access to *Kulnar*, *Brackel*, *Avapol*, and *Kagly*.

Finally, in the late evening, they took the AV3 to a mountaintop, where the broadcast range covered *Savakol* and *T'Mingletep*.

LONG BEFORE THE landers were in place near *Brackel* and *T'Mingletep*, Digger had activated the programs in the north. Unlike *Saniusar*, which was a sprawling collection of towers and ornate houses and bridges and public buildings spread across several urban areas, *Hopgop* was a modest town with about a tenth the population and an inclination toward the austere. Where the western city was flamboyant and almost baroque, the New York of its world, *Hopgop* liked to think of itself as casual, informal, no-nonsense. Another Moscow. Its architecture was purely utilitarian; its literature (as the translators were already learning) was lucid, uncontrived, vigorous. Sometimes lurid. And often powerful. *Hopgop* was the intellectual center of the *Intigo*.

When Digger started the transmission, which occurred shortly after the torches were lit in both cities, anyone passing before the cutlery shop on *Hopgop*'s main avenue, or in any of the major parks of *Saniusar*, would have been startled to see a luminous apparition appear apparently from nowhere.

Macao had been in *Hopgop* for three days. She'd been performing, visiting relatives, attending shows. The real reason she was there was that she had not forgotten Digger's prediction. The timing was incorrect. The previous day had been the ninety-third day, the day it was all supposed to happen. She'd even talked her cousins and her brother into clearing out, into sitting on a nearby ridge under animal skins, while the rain came down and the sky remained in its accustomed place.

Still, she wondered if she might have misunderstood something. Whatever the truth might be, they had clearly fallen on ominous days, and, if Digger turned out to be belatedly right, she wanted to be with her family.

It was impossible to know what to make of events. Suddenly it seemed she lived in a world of *zhokas* and levitation and lights in the sky. A *zhoka* had been seen just a few days ago in *Avapol*. Of course, they had always been observed with some regularity, but that could usually be ascribed to an overabundance of piety or wine or imagination. Take your pick.

She wondered about the three ships, out in the night somewhere, on the wide ocean while terrible things were happening. She tried to console herself with the possibility that they were beyond the sunrise, and beyond the reach of the thing that seemed to be coming at them out of the night.

She was in her brother's villa on the southern edge of town, near *Klaktik* Square. They had been at dinner when the next-door neighbor came pounding on the door. "Something's in the sky," he roared. And then ran off, leaving them gaping.

They opened the shutters and looked out at the storm, which had consisted only of gray rain all day. But now there was a downpour, and the evening was full of lightning. "I don't see anything," said her brother.

But Macao had a feeling, and she remembered Digger Dunn, would never forget Digger Dunn. She went outside and looked up. And she saw it in the flickering light: a giant bird, but not a bird, a thing that moved somehow independent of the wind, that did not seem to use its wings. She watched it vanish into a cloud.

Then she went back into the house and told her brother what she'd seen. "It's hard to see in the storm," he said. "Maybe it was something else."

But it had been something not of this world. She knew that as surely as she knew the children were in bed.

AFTER ABOUT AN hour, the rain let up, and the thunder subsided. Macao was still wondering whether she should suggest they get the children and go out into the storm. Repeat the fiasco of the previous night.

Was it even possible the ocean could overflow the shoreline? Could such a thing happen?

She was thinking about it when a fresh commotion started in the street. Voices. Shouts. Running.

They hurried out, into the courtyard.

People were moving past. Toward *Klaktik* Square. "Miracle!" someone said. And another: "Have mercy on us."

Klaktik was a large park, with shops and a children's lake and a meeting house.

The street was full of shouts: "I don't know, but it's *her*."

"What's happening?"

"The goddess."

"Lykonda."

"Worst weather I've ever seen."

The commotion quieted as they approached the square. There were a hundred people standing in the rain. More than a hundred. And they were coming in from all directions.

Macao stood on her tiptoes, trying to make out what was happening. There was a glow in the trees. People were crowding toward the children's pool. Toward the light.

She couldn't make out what it was. The night grew quieter, and everything seemed to be slowing down, the people around her, the rain, the wind. Even the children.

A woman stood within the light. Incredibly, her feet rested on the air, unsupported.

It was hard to breathe.

The woman surveyed the crowd. She seemed utterly serene, sometimes solid, sometimes as insubstantial as the clouds.

She was dressed for the forest, in green leggings and a loose yellow blouse. And she carried a blazing torch.

People in front of Macao were removing their hats, whimpering, falling to their knees.

She was the most beautiful woman Macao had ever seen. And there was something eerily familiar about her.

The power that ran through the night, that brightened the skies, ran into Macao's mind. And she knew who the woman was.

Lykonda.

Goddess of the hunt. Patroness of the arts. Protector of *Brackel.*

Another being who should not exist.

But in that moment of darkness and confusion and fear, Macao welcomed her into her heart.

THE GODDESS SEEMED detached from the physical world. The wind pulled at the trees, but her garments remained unruffled. The rain sparkled when it touched her aura, but never seemed to touch *her.*

In all that assemblage, no one spoke.

Macao heard the boom of the distant surf and somewhere behind her the brief cackle of an *oona.* And she realized this was the supreme moment of her life. For the first time, she embraced the faith of the *Intigo,* and knew the joy that came with it.

She was vaguely aware that people were still coming into the park, but how big the crowd might have become, she could not have said. Nor did she care.

And then, shattering the mood, a voice: "O Goddess, why have you come among your servants?" The voice was male, with a strange accent. She was annoyed that anybody would presume to speak. And she thought it a voice she had heard before.

The light changed subtly, and Macao saw that the goddess's blouse was ripped, her leggings torn. And there was a smear on her right cheek that looked suspiciously like blood.

Lykonda switched the torch to her left hand and beckoned with the right. *"Hear my words,"* she said. *"A great storm is coming. You have seen it now for many months. We have been engaged with it, trying to subdue it, and we have reduced its power. But know that even we cannot vanquish it altogether, and you must now look to your safety."*

The crowd stirred. Some began to sob. Cries and moans went up.

"The waters will rise and flow across the land."

More lamentations.

"Take your family and your friends and hurry to high ground. Do not panic. There is time, but you must leave the city quickly. This is your last night before the storm breaks over you. Stay away from the city until the danger is past. Take supplies for six days."

"Goddess." It was the oddly accented voice again. "Many of us are old and weak and cannot make the trek you describe." Macao could not see who was speaking. But she knew the voice.

"Be of good courage. You will not see me, but I will be with you."

The whimpers turned to cries of thanks.

And then, abruptly, the light faded and went out, and Lykonda was gone.

IN *BRACKEL*, PARSY the librarian helped his *kirma*, his brother-husbands, get their twenty-two spouses to safety. He had witnessed, had been stunned by, the appearance of the goddess. Who would have thought such things actually happened? But he was, if anything, a prudent man. Having heard her words, he needed no additional encouragement.

Until this night, although he assumed the gods existed somewhere, that they kept the stars moving and brought the seasons and the harvest, he'd never thought much about them. To him, they tended to be occasional characters in the dramas, showing up to give advice, to move the plot along, to teach a much-needed lesson. He would be more cautious in the future. Whatever years were given him, he would reverence the gods and their ways, and he would walk in righteousness.

He stood on the crest of a hill within sight of *Brackel*. The roads between the city and the surrounding hills were narrow, and they were choked with the fleeing population. The dawn was near, although he didn't expect to be able to see the sun. The rain had finally stopped, but it had gotten cool. The children were wrapped in skins, and the new day would be long and trying. But they would get through it. How could they not, if Lykonda walked with them?

The signs of the coming hazard were everywhere: The wind was rising, the tide was unnaturally high, and the rivers were beginning to flood. Parsy had long since discovered that prudence always suggested he assume the worst, and that if he did so, he would seldom be either surprised or disappointed. So he had ordered his family to bring everything they could carry. Prepare for a siege on the hilltops. And get high. No matter that the climb was tiring.

Now it was done, and they were as safe as he could make them. So it was time to consider his second duty. "Who will come with me?" he asked.

"Let them go," said Kasha, his special mate, the woman with whom he shared his innermost thoughts. "In the end, they are only scrolls. They are not worth your life."

"You won't be able to get through *that*," said Chubolat, signifying the refugees pouring out of the city. Chubolat occasionally worked at the library.

"I have no choice," he said. "It is my responsibility."

Tupelo came forward and stood by his side. Reluctantly, but he came. And then Kasha. "Where you go, I will go," he said.

"No. I cannot allow it."

"You cannot stop me."

"And I," said Yakkim, with whom he spent so many of his evenings in conversation about the ancients.

And brown-eyed Chola. And Kamah, who was the most timid of all. And Lokar, who had never read anything in his life.

"I only need two," he said.

BLACK CAT REPORT

Ron, it's becoming hard to see any separation between the cloud and the planet. The bulk of it is over ocean at the moment. Our sensors indicate that rock and dust are being hurled into the atmosphere, that conditions in the atmosphere are becoming, to say the least, turbulent.

The good news is that the Goompah cities are moving away from it, out onto the other side of the world. For the moment, at least, they're shielded. They're beginning to get some flooding, but other than that they're still in pretty good shape. Tonight will be critical, Ron, when the Goompahs rotate into the heart of the storm.

This is Rose Beetem reporting from Lookout.

Avery Whitlock's Notebooks

It has been the fashion since Darwin to attack religious belief on grounds that it is oppressive, that it closes the mind, that it leads to intolerance and often to violence. And not least of all, that most of the faiths are necessarily wrong, as they contend against each other.

Yet there is much that is ennobling in the belief that there is, after all, a higher power. That there is a purpose to existence. That we owe loyalty to something greater than ourselves. And it strikes me that, even when we get the details wrong, that belief can produce a happy result.

chapter 46

"HOW COULD YOU tell them that?" demanded Julie.

"How could I tell them *what*?"

"That the goddess would be with them. They're on their own, and they'll find that out quickly enough."

Digger shook his head. "She'll be with them," he said. "They'll discover they're stronger and more capable than they ever thought. Anyhow, what would you have done? Tell them to go ahead and leave Grandma?"

Pictures were coming in. Throughout *Savakol* and the cities of the Triad in the south, in *Saniusar* and *Mandigol* and *Hopgop* in the north, across the midbelt of the *Intigo*, the Goompahs were on the move. Lykonda was appearing outside cafés and metalworking shops, theaters and public buildings, on bridges and docks. In *Roka*, she stood above the incoming tide; in *Kagly*, she showed up in the private home of the *squant*, a member of the town council. At *T'Mingetep* she took over the yardarm of a long-beached schooner. In *Mandigol* she stood on a river. Everywhere the word went through the streets. They got some interference from the storms, and occasionally the goddess broke up into an eruption of color. But it was working. They chose their times carefully, initiating the programs when the rains slackened and the lightning died down. To the Goompahs it must have seemed that the elements were bowing to her will.

"*Get to high ground.*"

It was Kellie's contralto. With, he thought, some majesty mixed in.

"*I will be with you.*"

THE WIND ROSE during the night.

They flew over *Kagly*, north up the coast. The shoreline curved almost due west between *Kagly* and *Avapol*, which was about forty kilometers away. There were a number of islands. Lykonda had appeared on one, and they noted with satisfaction that the sea was full of lights. A small flotilla was moving back and forth between the islands and the mainland. The word was getting around.

Near dawn they hovered over *Kulnar* and watched cold, tired masses of Goompahs plodding out of the city and climbing into the hills. The storm abated and the sky became quiet, but it was still heavy with Marge's clouds, cloaking the horror that hung over their heads.

The isthmus road was full of moving lights. The countryside, the crests of hills, trails leading into the uplands, were all alive with traffic. In the harbors, ships were pulling out, making for deep water.

Bill relayed pictures of the omega. It was coming alive, enormous lightning bolts rippling through it, crashing down into Lookout's upper atmosphere. The sun rose, and the bolts brightened the western sky. But they were falling behind as the isthmus rode into the dawn.

"Last day," said Julie, shivering.

Rain continued to fall in varying degrees of intensity across the peninsula. "This is the sort of thing," Whit said, "that constitutes the stuff of legends."

"You mean they'll tell this story to their grandkids," said Julie.

Digger smiled. "And nobody who wasn't here will believe it."

"Don't be too sure," said Whit. "One day this might all become part of a sacred scripture."

"Not on this world," insisted Digger. "I keep remembering a sign we saw at one of the schools. 'Think for yourself.' If they can really push that, I doubt any of their grandkids will believe Lykonda actually showed up."

"Pity," said Julie. "It's a lovely story."

Bill's features showed up on-screen. "*One of the chimneys is down,*" he said. "*In the south. Near* T'Mingletep."

Much of the western coastline was beginning to flood. Marge got on the circuit. "*The cloud is hitting the far side pretty hard,*" she said. "*The isthmus is already seeing the effects. Look for high winds, maybe tornadoes. God knows. It'll get worse during the day, and they'll get hammered tonight. Best for you is to skedaddle. Stay on the day side of the planet. Keep it between you and the omega.*"

In fact, the omega was enormously bigger than Lookout, and Digger knew that it would fold completely over the world. And then, finally exhausted, it would pass.

One night. The *Intigo* only had to get through one night.

THEY DRIFTED OVER *Mandigol*, which was lovely in the gray dawn. There was a waterfall to the northeast, fed by a lake roughly a hundred meters above sea level. A bank of white mist crept down from the lake, drifting over houses and parks, closing in on the center of the city. Some of it had already drifted out onto the docks, where a few torches and oil lamps burned. A half dozen boats floated at anchor, and a single large ship was headed out to sea.

Mandigol was a city of architects. The inhabitants obviously liked cupolas and rotundas. Most of the public buildings were domed, the westside indoor market area was domed, scores of homes were domed, even the park shelters were domed. Many of these were supported by fluted columns. Cornices and transverse arches were everywhere. Several structures boasted upper and lower galleries, and four steeples marked the corners of the city.

There was a host of trees and gardens. The inhabitants of *Mandigol* loved their gardens. Vegetation was an art form, and when the mist moved in to shroud walls and buildings, when everyone had fled so there was no distraction, it took on the appearance of a celestial dwelling place. When the gods retire, one Goompah sage had observed, they will come to *Mandigol*.

THE REMAINING RAINMAKERS all let go within a few minutes of each other and drifted away.

The exodus was painful to watch. Everywhere, exhausted Goompahs had collapsed on the trails. Younger ones, dragged from sleep, screamed. Some took charge and tried to direct traffic. They were drenched by intermittent rain, and they shivered in the autumn air. They carried clothing and food wrapped in skins and bags, drove *berbas* and other domestic animals before them, sat on wagons, and generally looked miserable.

"Some aren't going," said Whit.

Digger had seen that there were Goompahs in the windows of many of the houses. "Probably rather die at home," he said.

"Or maybe," said Julie grimly, "they're rationalists."

"Storm's going to get worse," said Dig.

Whit looked depressed. "I wish we could do something for them."

"There are limits to what you can do," said Julie. "Maybe even if you're a god. At some point they have to take responsibility for themselves."

"We could try running it again," said Digger. He wanted to go down into the town, bang on the doors, tell them for God's sake to get out.

"I think Julie's right," said Whit. "Deities don't make curtain calls."

THE ROADS LEADING out of *Mandigol* were strained to the limit. There were overturned carts, dead pack animals, abandoned supplies. But the Goompahs kept moving.

The city was fortunate. High ground lay on three sides, and it was neither far nor positioned in difficult terrain. It wouldn't be an easy night for refugees, and it was, of course, all uphill. But most should be able to get clear. A few looked up as they passed overhead, and Digger wondered if the lightbender had been inadvertently turned off. But the hull was invisible, and he suspected it was his imagination, or perhaps they'd heard the drive, which was quiet but not silent.

"Look down there," said Whit, pointing.

There was a commotion on a forest trail.

Julie took the lander down to treetop level.

Hundreds of refugees had gathered on the southern bank of the river the Goompahs called the *Orko*, which flowed down from the mountains north of *Saniusar* and emptied into the western ocean. To get to high ground, the population of *Mandigol* proper had to cross the river. The river was wide and deep, a Mississippi, and it was swollen. There was no bridge, and no place where it could be forded. Crossing was done by ferry.

To meet the emergency, the Goompahs had collected a small fleet of shallow-draft vessels, flatboats, sailboats, canoes, and rafts. It looked as if everything that could float and could be gotten upriver had been thrown into the effort. But one flatboat had been overloaded. It had foundered in the middle of the river and was sinking.

As they drew close, Digger saw a couple of Goompahs fall overboard. Ropes were thrown to them from the boat, but hauling them back would do no good: The vessel was minutes from going down. There were close to forty refugees packed onto it, maybe three times its capacity. The deck was half-submerged.

A small boat, not unlike an outrigger canoe, was hurrying to the rescue, but it was far too small to be able to help.

Digger activated his e-suit and strapped on the lightbender.

"What are you going to do?" asked Julie.

"Rescue drowning Goompahs," he said. "It's my specialty."

"Where are you going to put them? Anyhow, you damned near drowned yourself last time." She looked at Whit. "We're going to open up," she said.

Whit understood and activated his own suit. "Anything I can do to help?"

"Just stand by."

"You sure you can do this, Digger?" she asked.

"Are you serious?" In fact it looked a little scary, but he couldn't sit there and watch a boatload of Goompahs go down.

When the cabin pressure had equalized, she opened the airlock. Digger switched on his lightbender, activated his goggles so he'd be able to see the outside the spacecraft, and grabbed two coils of cable from the storage locker. He stuck his head through the outer hatch and looked down.

The vessel's anchor was a rock. It was tied to a line, located forward at the prow. The line was secured through a hole in the planking. Aft, the tiller had a housing that looked pretty solid. "Lower, Julie," he said.

She took him down onto the water and he opened the hatch wide. It may have been that the occupants of the boat were too preoccupied to notice the sudden appearance of a disembodied airlock. Whatever, they paid no attention.

He slipped out onto the treads and secured each of his two lines to the undercarriage, one toward the front, one in the rear.

"They told me you were a kind of bookish guy," Julie said.

"Books? Yep. That's me."

"I hope," she continued, *"you don't tear the bottom out of this thing."*

"Get us in front of the boat," he said.

She complied. *"I wish we could get a picture of this."*

Digger was in fact impressed with his own display of audacity. It was out of character. He'd always been willing to help when people needed it, but his enthusiasm usually ran in inverse proportion to any degree of personal risk. He wondered what was happening to him.

It would have been easier if he could have gotten onto the deck. But there was no room. Working off the tread, he leaned down, pushed one of the Goompahs aside, got hold of the anchor line, and tied the cable to it.

"Hurry," said Whit.

The prow was going under. Goompahs grunted and screamed. More fell into the river.

Julie took him to the after section on the flatboat, and he jumped into the water, hauled himself up near the tiller housing, and decided it wouldn't do. Up close it looked spindly.

He took the line and dived beneath the boat with it, came up on the other side, tried to measure it so he had as much slack as the front line had. Then he looped it around the tread.

"Okay, Julie," he said. "Lift."

The after section rose first and a couple more went into the river. He didn't have it quite right. But it was close enough. Most of the passengers hung on, although they were whimpering and sobbing.

Julie didn't actually lift the flatboat out of the water. In fact, she couldn't have even had she wished. The boat was far too heavy. But she was able to keep it afloat. Some of those in the water were picked up by the outrigger. But a few were swept downriver.

Gradually, with Digger hanging on to one side, the flatboat got across to the northern shore. Several of the survivors declared it a miracle.

DIGGER'S SURPRISE AT his own heroism was dampened by the knowledge that some of the refugees had been lost. But when he got back inside the lander, Julie insisted on delivering a passionate smooch, commenting that she knew Kellie wouldn't mind, and Whit shook his hand with obvious respect. It might have been the first time in his life that Digger had earned that kind of reaction from someone of Whitlock's stature. He began to feel he could do anything.

The winds were getting stronger. "Time to recall the landers," said Julie. Put everything back on Mt. Alpha and tie it down. And get back into the AV3. Put some heavy metal between themselves and the coming storm. They should, she said, take off and head west. Safety for the next twenty hours or so lay in daylight.

They returned the landers to Mt. Alpha and spent the rest of the morning securing them as best they could. Another thunderstorm rolled past at lower altitudes, and by noon they had boarded the AV3 and were ready to clear out.

Digger wondered about Macao, where she was, what she was thinking, and hoped she was okay. He would go back eventually, at least to assure himself that she'd survived. And maybe, if things had worked out reasonably well, he'd say hello.

Challa, Macao.

"We're forgetting something," Whit said, as they strapped in and prepared for flight.

"What's that?" asked Digger.

Whit heaved a long sigh. Bad news coming. "The round-the-world mission."

Digger hadn't really forgotten. He'd been aware of it, in some remote corner of his mind, but he'd been telling himself the three ships were already as safe as anything he could arrange. They were in deep water, and all they'd have to do was trim their sails, or take them down, or whatever it was you did in one of those things when the wind started to blow. And ride it out.

Julie brought the AI up. "Bill," she said, "what do we have on the round-the-world mission? Where are they?"

"Last sighting is twenty hours old," he said. *"At that time they were doing well. They have reached the coast of the eastern continent and are now sailing north, looking for a passage."*

Should be as safe as anybody could reasonably expect, thought Digger. *At least they're not standing on an island.*

THE GOOMPAHS, WHIT predicted, would later tell their children that Lykonda was everywhere on this night. She directed traffic in each of the eleven cities, assisted those who had fallen, used a torch to show the way around a flooded valley outside *Kulnar,* held a bridge in place until several hundred had crossed safely, lifted several who'd been stranded on a rapidly disappearing island, taking them into her hands and transporting them to safe ground. She will have found a lost child in the rising waters outside *Avapol*; provided light to those struggling along a narrow mountain ledge; returned to *Sakmarung* to help those who had refused to leave until the floodwaters came.

"The legend will grow," he said.

"It's the way religion is," said Digger.

"I suppose. But I prefer to think of it as the way human nature is. It's a great story. On the night when they most needed her, Lykonda came. It tells me that they are a lot more like us than would make some folks comfortable."

"I suppose," said Digger. "All in all, we've gotten a lot of use from her tonight."

"Maybe," he said.

"How do you mean?"

He shrugged. "Sometimes it's hard to be sure who's using whom."

BILL WAS PICKING up bits and pieces of transmissions from the omega monitors, and also from satellites placed in orbit by the *Jenkins*.

The cloud was such an amorphous object that it was impossible to say precisely when it made contact with Lookout. But what was clear was that, by midday on the *Intigo*, the planet was in its embrace. Rain and high winds swept across the Goompah cities.

The *Jenkins* stayed in contact. Giant storms, they said. Some loose rock that had been traveling with the cloud was coming down. The ocean surged from the west and, as they'd expected, submerged wide parcels of land. The river that flowed out of *T'Mingletep* overwhelmed its banks and spread out in all directions. The city on the island went underwater.

They were getting ready to depart Mt. Alpha when Bill reported an earthquake on the floor of the eastern ocean. *"Tsunamis coming."*

"How bad?"

"They look relatively small. I can't be certain at the moment because they're in deep water. But they're approaching an island chain, and I can let you know then. Just a few minutes."

"When are they going to get here?"

"Hour and a half."

He relayed satellite pictures of the islands. The weather seemed quiet. In fact, the sun was out and the beaches were gleaming. Long-legged birds strutted on the sand, which was bordered by forest. "This where the tsunami's headed?" Digger asked.

"Yes, Digger."

The picture broke up, came back, broke up again.

"There's a lot of interference," said Bill. *"The wave should be imminent,"* he added.

They saw the sea beginning to rise. A large wave became a wall of water and kept getting bigger. It raced across the surf. The birds scattered, and the ocean spilled onto the beach, submerged the trees, and crashed against a series of ridges.

"About twelve meters," Bill said.

Marge's voice broke in: *"It'll be about the same when it gets to the* Intigo."

Digger breathed a sigh of relief. It was high, and it would raise hell with the cities, but most of the refugees should be out of reach.

"There are at least three follow-on waves," Marge continued. *"All appear to be less of a threat."*

"What about the other direction?" asked Whit.

"How do you mean?" asked Julie.

"The round-the-world mission. Are they still cruising the coastline?"

"Skies are heavy in the region." said Bill. *"And we don't have a satellite in the area."*

"They'd have to be," said Digger. "Is that a problem?"

"Pretty much," said Marge. *"They need to be in deep water."*

Avery Whitlock's Notebooks

I cannot help wondering what has been, for the Goompahs, the more terrifying aspect of this business: The threat posed by the omega, or the appearance of the goddess?

—December 15

chapter 47

On board the *Regunto* on the eastern
ocean. Ninety-fifth day of the
voyage.

TELIO HAD BEEN hardly a week at sea when he was ready to turn and go back home. That reaction had surprised him, because he'd spent much of his adult life as a sailor and fisherman, moving up and down the coast of the *Intigo*. He'd even been on an exploratory mission ten years earlier, when they'd pushed into the regions where the sun was in the middle of the sky and the air became hot beyond what one could bear. It was the longest foray in modern history, made under Hagli Kopp, as fine a captain as ever sailed. He wished the current captain, who commanded all three vessels, were of his quality.

Not that he wasn't competent. But Mogul Krolley lacked the fire and presence of Kopp, whose sailors would have followed him anywhere. In the stifling heat, Kopp had called them together. Scholars maintained that the boiling air did not go on forever, he said, that if one could break through the barrier, the seas would become cool again. The captain did not know for certain what conditions were like farther on. He suspected the scholars were correct, but he told the crew candidly they had reached a point from which going ahead would, in his view, be foolhardy. He did not wish to risk their lives. Or, he admitted with a chuckle, his own.

And so they had turned around and, as the first mate put it, lived to go home.

There were no natural barriers to an east–west voyage, no heat in one direction or ice in the other. But there was the haunting possibility that they were sailing on an endless sea. Or that there was an abrupt edge of things, as some warned. The notion that they could proceed east and eventually would come upon their own west coast had seemed plausible, and even likely, back in the cafés and *sloshen*. But out here, on the broad sea, it approached absurdity.

They had indeed found a continent, and they'd spent sixteen days examining its harbors and rivers, looking for *Saniusar* or *Mandigol* or *T'Mingletep*. But this was *Korbi* Incognita. Unknown country.

Should the occasion arise, Telio did not think Krolley would have the self-assurance to admit failure, to recognize reality and accept defeat. It was more likely that he would press on, that if this wasn't the *Intigo*, he'd look for a way to pass through it, a river, a series of lakes, whatever was needed. He was rumored to have considered the possibility of abandoning the ships, if necessary, to travel overland, and build new vessels when they found the sea again on the far side. If indeed there was a far side.

That had led to talk that the world might not be constructed in the form of an infinite sea with scattered landmasses, that Korbs only thought that because they lived near ocean. But it could well be that it was *land* that went on forever, with occasional stretches of water. Who knew? Telio was certain only that he was ready to concede failure and go home. He thought of himself as being as courageous as the next person, but he also knew that, when the evidence was in, it was prudent to draw the proper conclusions and react accordingly. There was no point in being an idiot. The way was blocked.

Which brought him back to Captain Krolley.

The thought of a mutiny never crossed his mind. It would never have occurred on any Korb ship. It wasn't that authority was held inviolate, but that a contract entered into voluntarily was sacred, regardless of circumstance.

They had adequate water and stores on board, having just filled up a few days earlier. And the only immediate problem they faced was that many of the sailors, like Telio, had had enough of the open sea and simply yearned to go home.

Telio missed Moorka, missed all the females in his *genus*, missed the evenings on the Boulevard with his brothers, missed his son, now about to have a child of his own.

He hadn't realized it would be this way. He'd expected to be gone for a couple of years, but he'd thought the time would be spent pushing forward across an open sea, and not poking into endless bays and rivers along a vast landmass. Moorka had asked him not to go, but he'd explained how he'd always wanted to sail past the sunrise, to be part of the great mission that people always talked about but never seemed to get around to launching. He had joined a group years earlier for such an effort, but funding had never appeared. And he'd spent his life since regretting the lost opportunity.

Well, he'd gotten past that piece of stupidity, at least. When he got home, he'd stay there and enjoy his family, and never again sail out of sight of the *Intigo*. And he'd leave the adventuring to those young enough, and dumb enough, to want it.

He wondered what Moorka was doing. That was most difficult of all, lost ut here on the sea and no one near with whom he could slake his passions. No luminous eyes watching him in the night, no soft cheek on the pillow eside him. It was an unnatural way to live, and it reminded him of the old rgument that the gods had given the *Intigo* to the Korbs with the understanding that everything else was a divine realm, that the Korbs were to tay in their assigned lands. And to remind them of that truth, the gods had ealed it off, heat to the north and ice to the south, and the boundless ocean n either side.

He looked up at the sky. The sun was bright, but a storm was coming. Ie could smell it in the wind. And he was almost grateful. The heavy clouds vould conceal them from the thing in the night sky. Almost everyone beeved that the apparition was intended to warn them to go back. To remind nem of the Covenant.

It was impossible to know what Krolley thought. Few of the men would ave dared mention their doubts to him. Although Telio had made up his nind that *he* would do it, next time he had the opportunity. He'd asked the fficer of the rigging whether *he* thought they'd come too far, that they'd ffended the gods, and the officer had smiled and shrugged it off. Ridiculous, e'd said. Don't worry about it, Telio. If a divine ordinance prohibited what ney were doing, did he think they'd still be afloat?

But afterward he'd seen him talking seriously to the executive officer.

The ships had been moving south along the new continent. And, as at ome, it was getting colder with each passing day.

Telio watched the wild coastline drift by on his left. The *Hasker* was runing behind them, closer to shore and out of their wake. The *Benventa* stood rther out to sea.

The plan was to proceed south until they could round the continent, or, ; the crewmen said, until they froze. Whichever came first.

If any candidate for a passage through the continent presented itself, they ould try that, but there'd been nothing even remotely promising for sev-al days. Many of Telio's compatriots back home would be surprised to arn there was another major landmass. Most thought there was only the ne on which the Korbs lived. It had, at one time, been an article of faith.

They'd sent landing parties in twice since arriving on these shores. The ater was good, and there was plenty of game. But the animals were unlike ny they had seen before. The trees were different; as were many of the ushes and shrubs. And one of the crewmen had been attacked and killed y a terrible creature of enormous size. His companions had riddled it with rows, and they'd dragged the thing down to the beach for everyone to wk at. It had fangs and claws and fur the color of the woods in which it aveled. Witnesses to the attack said it had reared up on its hind legs.

It reminded Telio of the *keeba*, which could be found in the lands north of *Saniusar*. But this thing was bigger, even in death. Well, it wasn't as if the captain hadn't warned them to be careful. There'll be wild beasts, he'd told them before the first group went ashore. *And there might even be tribes of savage Korbs.*

Now there was a chilling thought.

TELIO WAS SUPPOSED to be mending sails, but one of the crew had fallen from a spar and sprained his wrist. Telio had some experience as an apothecary, and he doubled sometimes as ship's surgeon. There was a fully qualified surgeon on the voyage, but he was on the *Hasker*, and would only be called in the event of serious injury.

Telio put soothing gel on the damaged limb, wrapped it, and warned the crewman not to try to use it until Telio had looked at it again. He was just putting away his ointments and wraps when a sudden burst of wind struck the ship. It came without warning and was of such violence that it almost capsized them.

The captain ordered the fleet to haul down some sail. The sky began to darken. The blow was out of the east, a change in direction for they'd been riding with the westerlies throughout the voyage. The sea had been rough all day, but it had gotten abruptly worse while Telio was below mending the crewman. The ship rode up one side of a wave and crashed down the other. As he watched, all three ships turned to starboard, to put distance between themselves and the shoreline.

Rain began to fall and quickly became torrential. The crew secured the hatches and tied everything down. Lightning ran through the sky.

There was no longer anyone on the *Regunto* who did not fear the sunset. Night would bring *T'Klot*, rising black and terrible over the new continent. It was impossible to set aside the notion it was coming after them.

After a time the rain blew off, and they were running again before a gentle northwesterly wind. The sea turned to glass, and the world grew quiet.

The *Regunto* adjusted its sails and glided beside silver cliffs.

The captain came out on deck, wandering among his deckhands, reassuring them, finding things to laugh about. Telio watched for an opportunity to take him aside.

When it came, he asked if he might have a moment of his time. "If you'll excuse my brashness, sir."

"Of course," he said, glancing at the deck lieutenant, who framed Telio's name with his lips. "That was a quick storm, wasn't it?" And, without waiting for an answer: "What can I do for you, Telio?"

Telio looked up at the *Korbs* working in the masts, adjusting the sails. "Indeed it was, sir," he said.

Krolley was tall, lean, with mottled skin and a serene disposition. There was much of the scholar about him: deliberate speech, careful diction, intelligent eyes with a golden cast. He was always impeccably dressed. His posture was perfect, his expression composed. Even now, after a heavy storm during which he certainly had not had time to change, he looked well turned out. It was almost as if he was always ready for someone to carve his image.

"Captain, some of us are worried about *T'Klot*."

Krolley bobbed his head up and down. "Ah. Yes." He smiled at the deck lieutenant, a smile that indicated this is the sort of triviality about which the seamen concern themselves. The lower classes. Not to be taken too seriously. "It's all right, Telio. It's simply a weather phenomenon. It will be passing us by in a few more days."

"Captain—"

He patted Telio on the shoulder. "It's nothing to fret over. Just pay it no attention, and I think you'll find it will pay none to you."

He started to walk away, but Telio stayed with him. "Captain, the thing is not natural. It isn't just a storm we can run from. There is some suspicion among the crew that it is after *us*."

The deck lieutenant tried to interpose himself, and gave Telio a strong look. He'd be scraping down the decks for the next few days. "Telio." Krolley was being careful because a number of the crewmen had gathered around and were listening. "You're a scholar. An apothecary. You know, as I do, that the world is not governed by supernatural forces."

"I'm not so sure anymore, sir," he said.

"Pity." The captain studied him closely. "Keep your nerve, Telio. And your good sense."

BLACK CAT REPORT

Ron, it's early afternoon on the *Intigo*. The pictures you see are courtesy of surveillance equipment inserted by the Academy of Science and Technology. This is a view of the harbor area at *Roka*. There's a map available on our alternate channel.

Anyhow, it's quiet there now. The rain has stopped—it's been raining across the isthmus on and off all day. We don't see anyone out on foot. There are still some Goompahs who've stayed behind. Probably older ones. And it looks as if some who might otherwise have gotten out have stayed with them.

This is the way it looks all across the *Intigo*. I'm tempted to say there's a sense of waiting for something to happen. But that's subjective. I know tidal waves are coming. The inhabitants have no idea. Although they are certainly aware that they are facing a severe hazard tonight.

This is Rose Beetem, near Lookout.

ARCHIVE

We are adrift in a divine tide. Those whom the gods love will find themselves carried to a friendly and amicable shore. Others, not so fortunate, will be dragged into the depths. The terrible reality is that those of us embarked on life's journey cannot readily separate one from the other, nor have we any idea which will claim us.

—Gesper of *Sakmarung*
The Travels
(Translated by Nick Harcourt)

chapter 48

Lookout. En route across the
eastern ocean.
Monday, December 15.

THEY WERE THREE hours out from the *Intigo* and threading their way
through storms, crosswinds, and downdrafts, when Bill informed them they
were passing over the eastbound tsunamis. The sky had cleared off, save for
occasional clouds and lightning. The ocean was churning, but there was no
sign of giant waves. "*Don't expect to see much,*" said Bill. "*We're over deep water.*"

Tsunamis only manifest themselves in shallows. Digger had been researching Bill's library, and there were stories of people in small boats going
over them without ever knowing it. That happened because the bulk of the
wave was submerged. When the ocean became shallow, the water had no
place to go, and, consequently, it pushed high into the air, forming the
wave.

"*Traveling at 630 kps,*" said Bill. "*I still make out three of them. Big one's in
front. They'll hit about fifteen minutes apart.*"

"One for each ship," said Julie. "Tell me again how we're going to do
this."

Digger had seen her disapproval the first time he'd explained the plan.
Same way we did things on the isthmus. We'll use the Lykonda projection."

"Okay. What is she going to tell them?"

"Bill," he said, "run the program for Julie."

Lykonda appeared on the overhead. The implication that she'd been
through a struggle was gone. Her garments were white and soft, and an
aura blazed around her. She said that it was essential for the ships to turn
west and to continue straight out to sea until she told them to do otherwise.

When he'd translated for Julie, she frowned again. "What happens," she
asked, "if the wind is blowing in the wrong direction?"

He hadn't thought of that. "I'm not sure," he said. "Can't they tack against
the wind or something?"

"I don't think so," said Whit.

She smiled patiently. "If a goddess gave me that kind of command, I'd expect she would supply the wind."

Digger didn't know which way the wind would be blowing when they reached the eastern continent. He did know that where they were it seemed to be blowing out of all directions at once.

He'd been considering another idea: They had a sim library on board, which would unquestionably include the previous year's big horror hit, *Fang*. The show had featured batwinged horrors that would have scared the pants off the Goompahs. If those things came out of the forests and seemed to be attacking the ships, there was no question which way the ships would turn. It would save a lot of talk. But it still wouldn't work if the winds weren't right.

"We need Marge," said Whit. But they'd lost all contact with the *Jenkins*.

"Something else to think about," said Julie. "The waves are going to get there less than an hour after we do. These are only sailing ships. Even with a good wind behind them, they aren't going to get far in an hour." She sighed and shook her head. "Small wooden boats. I wouldn't give them much of a chance."

"You have a better suggestion?"

"I'd tell them to land and climb trees."

Digger was tired and unnerved. He knew Goompahs were going to die in substantial numbers before this was over, and he was in no mood for Julie's acerbic humor. "Just let it go, will you?" he said.

Whit caught his eye and sent him a silent message. Cool down. She's telling you stuff you don't want to hear, but you'd better listen.

As they proceeded east they were headed into the late afternoon. Digger wanted to bring off the warning, do whatever they could, and get clear before night came.

He saw lightning ahead and thick dark clouds.

"Hang on," Julie said. "It's going to get a bit rough."

"Can we go around it?" asked Whit.

"If we had time to spare, sure."

They got hit before they even got into the storm. Digger heard things sizzle, lights went out, an alarm sounded, and it was free fall, grab the arms of your chair, and hang on. Julie fought the yoke and stabbed at her panels, and the lamps blinked on and off. He smelled something burning. The sea spun around them, and Julie damned the spacecraft to hell. Then he was settling back into his seat. They continued dropping toward the sea, but she finally gained control, more or less. Digger started breathing again and looked out the window, and the ocean looked very close.

She leveled off just over the waves. "Room to spare," she said. "Every-body okay?"

We're fine. Whit laughed and commented he'd never been so scared in his life. Thought it was over.

Digger'd had a few bad moments himself, but he wasn't admitting it. Didn't want Julie to think he didn't have confidence in her. The cabin seemed extraordinarily quiet. He couldn't hear anything except heartbeats.

"It hit the tail," she said.

"Are we okay?" asked Digger.

Her fingers moved across the status screen. "Yes. We're okay. We can stay in the air. Some of our sensors are out. Long-range communications are down."

"That's not good," said Whit.

"Doesn't matter. We haven't been able to talk to anybody anyway. I can jury-rig something later."

"Okay."

A frown creased her forehead. "But I think we've lost Bill."

A large sea animal surfaced near them, a thing that seemed mostly ten-acles. Then it slipped back beneath the surface.

"Bill? Do you hear me?"

More lamps blinked.

Digger realized what a good thing it was to have a human pilot along. "Can you fix him?"

More fingers across the screen. "No. He's gone."

Digger felt a wave of remorse.

"It's only a software program," she reminded him.

"I know."

"When we get to one of the other landers, he'll be there."

"Can we still find the mission?" asked Whit.

"That shouldn't be a problem." She went back to her status screen, changed the display, and made a face. "There is one thing, though—"

The moment stretched out. She continued poking at the screen while Digger waited, holding his breath.

"We've lost Bill's memory banks. I should have realized."

"Why's that a problem?" asked Digger.

"That's where Lykonda was stored."

"Are you saying we can't use her?"

Julie nodded. "She's *kaput*."

Whit looked over at him, having assumed his most reassuring face. "We'll have to talk to them directly."

"Won't work," said Digger. "We've had experience with that."

"What else do you suggest?" Whit was wearing a bright green shirt, as close as he could get to the styles favored by the Goompahs, and a coffee-colored vest.

"What do you think would happen if they saw the lander?" Julie asked.

"Don't know," said Digger. "They'd probably panic. Jump overboard."

Another bolt hit nearby. They were passing over an island chain. "Pity," said Whit. "A whole world to explore. The ultimate odyssey, and they run into one of these clouds." He gazed at the islands. There were eight or nine of them, big, covered with forests. Rivers cut through them. As they passed overhead, hordes of birds rose from treetops.

Digger was more concerned that they'd take a second bolt up the rear end and wind up fried or in the drink.

"*Odyssey*," said Whit.

Digger looked at him. "Pardon?"

He was opening his notebook. "I have a thought."

THE THREE SHIPS were moving steadily, if slowly, south. Trees and shrub-bery pushed down to the water's edge and spilled into the ocean. The sun was approaching the horizon.

The *Regunto* was immersed in a sense of foreboding, a conviction that the thing in the sky was on top of them, that it would come for them that night. Krolley was on deck constantly, strolling about as casually as if there were nothing to worry about. Telio had to concede he feared nothing. But under the circumstances, courage and defiance were not virtues.

A few of Telio's shipmates were gathered aft, talking idly. A couple were in the rigging, getting ready to come down. No one was supposed to be up there after dark, unless specifically ordered.

The night before, when they'd passed beneath the cloud, the sky had been black and threatening and streaked with lightning in a way he had never seen before. He would not be on duty again until morning, and he thought it would be a good night to spend in his bunk, belowdecks, away from the spectacle.

The *Hasker* was still running behind them, shoreward; and the *Benvent* was off to starboard. But the three ships had uncustomarily pulled close together as night approached.

There was a sudden commotion near the rail. Several crewmen were jabbering and pointing inshore. Toward the *Hasker*. He joined them and was surprised to see that the other ship had put up a signal and was engaged in turning toward shore.

The signal consisted of three pennants, two red, one white, the white on the left, signaling a turn to port and requesting the other vessels to follow.

As Telio watched, they dropped anchor, and began preparations to put a boat over the side.

That was extraordinary behavior since the fleet commander was on the *Regunto*.

One of the officers went after the captain, who'd just gone below.

There was a harbor coming up just ahead, and the *Hasker* seemed to be heading for it.

Then Telio saw what appeared to be a canoe, a couple of canoes, running alongside the *Hasker*.

"What's going on?" demanded Krolley, who appeared on deck like a summer thunderstorm. He was not happy.

Everyone pointed.

Three young females sat in each of the two canoes. They were half-naked, despite the coolness of the evening. But incredibly, they wore the green-and-white colors of *Savakol*!

He stared.

"We're home," said one of the crew. And a cheer went up. They'd done it. Completed the mission.

But it wasn't true. Telio wasn't the only one there who knew the home coast too well to mistake it for this wilderness. But how then did one account for the Korb females and their *Savakol* colors?

He scanned the shore and saw nothing but forest and hills. The canoes were turning into the harbor and apparently making for shore. Beyond it, atop one of the ridges, he saw flames begin to flicker. Someone was building a campfire.

"Hard to port," said the captain. "Bekka, signal the *Benventa*. We'll lay up alongside the *Hasker*."

The sailors cheered again.

A second fire started near the first, and Telio heard distant voices singing. Young females again. Doing one of the mating chants from back home.

"We're obviously not the first to reach here," said the captain, sounding disappointed. If he was, he was alone.

"I think it's from up there," said one of the officers, indicating the fires. A drum began to beat. And then several more joined in.

Barbar Markane, who found trouble with everything, shook his head and said they would be prudent to stay away. Stay on the ship, he advised. It's *Shol's* work. "Don't go there."

THE CREW OF the *Benventa* had to run for their lives. They had just reached shore when someone spotted the blue line on the horizon, just visible in the encroaching twilight. At the top of the ridge, the crews of the *Hasker* and the *Regunto* were trying to figure out why someone had made a pair of large fires, then abandoned them and, stranger still, where the females had gone, and how they had managed to hide their canoes. The drums and the voices had fallen silent, and except for the fires, it was as if none of this had happened.

It was hard to say how the seamen and their officers might have reacted to so unsettling an event, had their thoughts not been instantly diverted: The *Benventa* crew was scrambling desperately up the side of the ridge, yelling at the tops of their lungs about the ocean.

The ocean. Telio turned and looked in its direction and watched in horror as the sea rose up, swallowed their three ships, roared inshore, crashed into the harbor, and surged up the ridge. Some of the crewmen tumbled down the other side in a desperate effort to get away from it.

The top of the wave boiled over the crest. It knocked Telio down, put out both fires, and then, exhausted, began to recede.

The chief mate, who'd thrown himself behind a small boulder, got unsteadily to his feet and looked around. Some of his mates were on the ground; others clung to trees. "A miracle," he said.

"But the ships are gone," cried the sailors.

Everyone watched the water go down. The captains stared aghast at the magnitude of the disaster and, responding quickly, assigned their officers to find out who was missing. A quick count indicated they'd lost about twenty, including Markane. It was sad, heartbreaking, but had it not been for the intervention of the *Savakol* females, they would all have been lost.

How did one explain such a thing?

While Krolley considered the implications, a voice, a *male* voice, spoke out of the wind. "Stay as high as you can," it said, in an odd accent. "There are more coming."

BLACK CAT REPORT

Ron, we're watching a tidal wave approach *Brackel*. I'm sorry to report there are still a lot of Goompahs who elected to stay inside the city. This view is from a surveillance package that we've been told was inserted along the waterfront. You can see the wave in the distance. Our information is that it'll be about three stories high when it arrives. The real problem, though, is that it's traveling hundreds of kilometers per hour, so the chances of the folks inside the city aren't good.

The picture keeps breaking up because there are numerous electrical storms in the area. But we're going to try to stay with it. If you look closely, you can see that there are a few residents who are over in the shelter of that large building at the end of the pier. They seem to be watching the wave.

Ron, I wish there were something we could do—

chapter 49

BLACK CINDERS WERE falling out of the sky, trailing fire. Something ripped into the sea out near the horizon and sent yet another wave—though much less ferocious than the others—against the shore. The wind howled, sometimes from the east, sometimes cold and icy out of the south. The ocean maintained a steady roar.

The sun disappeared into a thunderstorm, and the world got dark.

The AV3 was on the eastern side of a ridge, shielded from the waves, across the harbor from the Goompah sailors. Julie had recommended they not try to fly the damaged craft through the storm-laden skies, so they'd lashed it down, and she'd gone outside and replaced the long-range antenna. Not that it mattered. The evening was so full of interference that they couldn't hear anything anyhow. When she was finished, as though it were a signal, the weather got abruptly worse. They huddled in the cabin, lights out, waiting for the night to pass, hoping not to attract the attention of the omega. "I know that sounds paranoid," said Julie, "but the one at Delta tried to destroy the lander my father was in."

Nobody was going to sleep well. Rain hammered on the hull and the winds howled around them.

"In the morning," said Julie, "when you talk to the Goompahs again, what are you going to tell them?"

"If there are any left," said Digger.

"There'll be some left. You need to figure out what you're going to say."

"Why say anything?"

"Because," said Whit, "they're going through a terrifying experience. When it's over, a little reassurance wouldn't be out of place."

"Hell, I don't know." Digger looked around the cabin. "How about, 'My children, all is well. Come down off the hill.' How's that?"

"Okay," she said. "I was talking about their ships. About going home. Are you going to tell them the planet's round, but it's too big for sails? That they wouldn't have made a successful voyage anyhow?"

Whit's features softened. He canted his head and waited for Digger's answer.

"No," Dig said. "If the situation has calmed down, I'll just tell them it's over, and let them decide what they want to do."

She let him see she didn't approve.

"It's not up to us to tell them what they're capable of, Julie," he continued. "How do we know they can't make it around the globe?"

"Well, it's not going to happen now, anyway," she said. "Whatever you tell them."

That was true. If they were able to construct a fresh set of ships, they'd go home. At least, they would if they had any sense.

Outside, something broke and fell heavily to the ground. A tree.

Whit took a long sip from his coffee cup. "Are we going to be able to fly this thing when the storm's over?" he asked.

"I'll let you know," she said.

DIGGER SAT IN the dark, trying to sleep, trying to think about something else. Well after midnight, he heard a distant explosion. It blended with the continuous thunder, and the lander shook. Lightning filled the sky.

They talked for hours while the storm raged. About how none of them had ever been through anything like this, about the Goompahs on the other side of the harbor and the Goompahs on the *Intigo*, about books they'd read and places they'd been, about how it couldn't last much longer, about how glad they were to have the AV3. Whit said it reminded him a little of a rainy evening he'd spent in a cabin when he was a Boy Scout.

Eventually it dissipated. The night grew quiet, the winds subsided, and there was only the steady beat of the rain.

Julie came to attention. "Listen," she said.

He heard a burst of radio interference and then Kellie's voice: *"—breaking up—when you can—clouds—"*

It was her standard professional tone. Level, unemotional. *"—storm—"*

Dawn was about two hours away. That meant it was a bit after midnight on the *Intigo*. The cloud was directly over the cities.

"—total—"

"We were lucky," Digger said.

"How do you mean?" asked Whit.

"The lightning strike. If we'd used Lykonda to warn the ships to go to deeper water, they might have survived the waves, but they wouldn't have gotten through the storm."

Whit passed his cup forward for a refill. "No luck involved. You and Julie made the right decision."

*   *   *

THERE WAS NO dawn. The sky stayed dark. Sometimes the wind and rain slacked off completely, and the night became still, but both inevitably came back with a rush.

He sat with his eyes closed, dozing, but still aware of his surroundings. Julie had put her seat into its recline position and had finally drifted off. Whit was busily tapping on his notebook. Eventually, he too slept.

Digger listened to the weather and the sea. If the storm was bad here, in this out-of-the-way place, he wondered what it would be like to be in the crosshairs. Not a stone upon a stone, he suspected.

THE INTENSITY OF the storm decreased after sunrise, but weather conditions remained too severe to attempt a flight. So they sat it out through the daylight hours and into another night.

At dawn on the second day, the winds finally abated, the rain slowed and stopped, and the sun came up.

"I think we're over the hump," Julie said.

They were too washed out to congratulate one another. Julie went outside to inspect and repair the lander, while Digger and Whit slogged over to see how the Goompahs had managed. They were scattered across the ridge, squatting exhausted and frightened in the mud. Some were injured. A few had descended to the lower levels and were fishing. Others were scavenging for fruit or small animals.

He would have liked to tell them it was all right to abandon their refuge, but the ground was so muddy he couldn't approach without making large footprints. In the end he cornered his old friend Telio and stood behind a fallen tree. "Telio," he said, "it is over." He'd planned to say no more, but decided on the spot that Julie was right. "Rebuild your ships and return home."

The Goompah looked for the source of the voice. "Who are you?" he asked, frightened.

Might as well play it through. "I am sent by Lykonda," he said.

Telio fell to his knees and Digger was stuck, unable to move without giving himself away. He waited, and finally Telio asked in a low voice whether he was still there and, getting no answer, muttered his thanks and returned to his comrades.

"And God bless," Digger added, uncharacteristically.

The three ships lay shattered and covered with mud. Two were on their sides in shallow water; one had been jammed into the trees. They were so badly wrecked that he wondered whether the Goompahs could tell them apart.

Trees were down everywhere, some from the waves, some blackened by lightning.

Later, when he told Whit what he'd done, the older man frowned. "They'll go back with the idea their gods don't want them to leave the isthmus."

"Maybe," said Digger. "But they'll have a much better chance to *go* back. Right now, it's all I care about."

At the lander, Julie told them she'd been in touch with the *Jenkins*. "The channel's down again," she said, "but it should only be temporary. *Roka* and *Kulnar* are pretty well destroyed. *T'Mingletep* took a major hit. But Kellie says the rest of the *Intigo* looks pretty good.

"Marge said there was a substantial storm surge, as well. Seven, eight meters of water across much of the isthmus."

"How about the Goompahs?"

"They can't tell for sure. It looks as if a lot of them should be okay. The ones who were smart enough to do what the goddess told them." She smiled, nodded at Digger, and broke out a bottle. Drinks all around. "Gentlemen." She raised her glass. "To the defenders of the weak." It was a French cordial. Where had she been hiding it?

THE BEACH WAS covered with dead fish and shells and debris. The smell was terrible, but Telio was grateful that he was still alive. And ecstatic that the celestial powers knew him by name. And cared about him.

The captains had formed a small party, and they were inspecting the three hulks. There'd already been talk that they would be taken apart and the wood used to make new vessels. Some of the crew had brought in fresh water. They had plenty of fish, and they'd discovered a fruit very like the *kulpas*. And some of the local game had proven to be quite savory.

He was going to be busy taking care of the injured over the next few days. That was a task that would be difficult because his medicines had been lost with the ship. There were a few strains and some broken bones to tend, and one case of a sweating illness that would probably respond to cold compresses and rest.

But it was over, whatever it had been, and most of them were still alive. *T'Klot* was still visible in the sky, both night and day, but not as a thunderhead. Rather it was now simply shreds of cloud.

Under ordinary circumstances, with their ships wrecked and the mission in ruins, he suspected they'd all have given in to despair. But he had heard the voice in the wind, and his comrades wanted to believe him. They knew now what they had not known before, that the gods were with them. The road home would not be easy, but Telio had no doubt he would see it again.

Avery Whitlock's Notebooks

Tonight, perhaps for the first time, I can see the true value of faith. It strikes me as a priceless gift. Those of us who have traded it for a mechanical universe may have gotten closer to the actual state of things, but we have paid a substantial price. It makes me wonder about the value of truth.

—*December 17*

chapter 50

THE RETURN TO the *Intigo* was painful. The cities were filled with mud and debris. Buildings were smashed, towers knocked over, fields flooded. The eastern cities, where the waves had hit, had been virtually swept away.

And there were corpses.

"No way you can get through something like this without losing people," said Whit. "The consolation is that there are survivors."

Yes. But somehow Digger had thought they would do better. He could see the Korbs beginning to file back down from the ridges and mountain slopes.

THEY GOT COMMUNICATIONS back with the *Jenkins*. Kellie and Marge had also been sobered by the carnage, but they were nevertheless putting the best face on things. "*We saved the bulk of them,*" Marge told them. "*I think we did pretty well.*"

In the midafternoon sky, the last pieces of the omega were drifting sunward. Whit gazed after it. "When can they expect another one?" he asked.

"If the pattern holds," said Digger, "about eight thousand years."

"Long enough," he said. "Good-bye, farewell, amen."

He wrote something in his notebook, frowned at it, shook his head, rewrote it, and entered it with a flourish. Then he sat back and looked outside at the flooded land below.

Digger found himself thinking about Jack. He'd have been pleased they'd done as well as they had. In fact, he suspected Jack would have been surprised that Digger had come up with a workable plan.

"Problem?" asked Julie, glancing over at him.

"No," he said. "Just thinking about the ride home."

THE *JENKINS* WAS on its way back to Lookout. Kellie reported that a fleet of ships, loaded with supplies, would begin arriving in a few days.

Julie took them to Mt. Alpha, where they traded in the AV3 for one of the smaller landers.

They switched on the lightbender and, at Whit's request, made for the temple at *Brackel*.

The city itself wasn't as severely damaged as they'd expected. A lot of buildings were down and areas flooded, but a substantial number of structures, occupying the wide arc of hills that circled the inner city, had escaped the worst of the water damage.

The temple had also come through reasonably well. A few Korbs were there, wandering through the grounds, looking dazed and battered. The walkways were covered with fallen trees and limbs and an ocean of sludge. A section of roof had been blown off, the interior was flooded, and several statues had been broken. But Lykonda still stood proud, her torch raised. A circle of Korbs stood respectfully around her, and someone had planted a small tree at her base.

ON HER HILLTOP outside *Hopgop*, Macao pulled an animal skin around her shoulders and tried to smile bravely for the children. Pasak, her cousin, had returned with an armload of *cabaros*. Ordinarily, *cabaros* weren't considered very tasty. But there wasn't enough fish to go around, and everything else was pretty much depleted. It looked as if it was going to get pretty hungry in the neighborhood over the next few days.

Nevertheless, she would have been ungrateful to complain. She was *alive*. As was most of her family. A few names were missing, including one of her cousins, but when she thought about the nature of the disaster that had overtaken them, she realized how fortunate they had been. Had they been in their homes when the storm surge came, few of them would have survived.

Everyone was giving thanks to the gods. As if they weren't equally responsible for the storm that had drowned the land. Yet Lykonda had come to their aid. She'd seen the goddess herself.

It had been a Lykonda who somehow resembled Macao.

Well, that had been a trick of the light. But how did one explain the rest of it?

Behind her, someone threw a few more branches on the fire.

She looked out at the ocean, cold and gray. She had never before thought of it as a monster that could hurl giant waves at them. Who would have believed such things could happen? None among them, not even the oldest, knew of any similar occurrence. Nor was there anything in the Archives.

Yet it was precisely what the *zhoka* had predicted. Except that he'd had the wrong night.

How was that possible? Why would a demonic creature try to help them? She'd told her story over and over during the last couple of days, while the rains were pouring down, how the *zhoka* had warned her they needed to get to high ground, that *T'Klot* was a terrible storm. So many had seen the goddess in the streets that they were now prepared to believe anything. Unlike the audiences that had debated her over her tall tales, people now accepted her story, and assigned everything, good and ill, to celestial powers.

For Macao, the problem went deeper. Her view of reality had been shattered. The world was no longer a mechanical place, a place controlled by physical laws that were accessible by reason. There were gods and demon-storms and a creature called *Digger Dunn* and who knew what else?

She shuddered, pulled the animal skin close round her shoulders, and leaned closer to the fire.

Avery Whitlock's Notebooks

Eventually, we will discover that honest communication with the Korbs will be to the benefit of both species. But that day is far off, because it will require more wisdom than we now possess. And more experience than they now have. Meantime, we can take pride in the fact that we have done what we could, and that the Korbs will, one assumes, still be here when that far-off day arrives.

—December 19

chapter 51

THE REPORT FROM Lookout arrived, as it always seemed to, at 2:00 A.M. It was the best possible news: as much success on the ground as they could reasonably have hoped for. There'd been substantial casualties among the Korbs, but an estimated 80 percent of them, thanks to Digger's inventiveness, had taken to the hills. Of those the vast majority had survived. And her own people had come away with no additional casualties. Hutch never got back to sleep.

The staff came to work knowing that the Academy had a new set of heroes, and emotions ran high through the morning. The commissioner called a press conference, the politicians were delighted, and, because it was Christmas Eve, everyone went home early.

Hutch, of course, was ecstatic. The Korbs would live, and it was possible to assign meaning to the deaths of Jack Markover and Dave Collingdale.

She spent the afternoon toting Maureen through the malls for some last-minute shopping. Then, reluctantly, she went home, knowing the media would be there.

Did it seem like coincidence that the good news had come on Christmas Eve?

Was it true that the Academy teams had violated the Protocol?

No, she replied to both questions. And added *not exactly* to the latter.

They crowded up onto her front porch. A few neighbors wandered over to see what was happening. Drinks appeared from somewhere. Bells jingled.

What could she tell them about this Digger Dunn? Had he really masqueraded as a god? Wasn't that—?

Digger was a good man. Pretty creative, wouldn't you say? Saved tens of thousands of lives.

The porch was big and enclosed, and it turned into a party. Season's best. Happy Hannukah. Merry Christmas. To us and to the Goompahs. To the Korbs.

"By the way," asked the UNN representative, "have we figured out yet what those clouds are? Any idea at all?"

"We're working on it," she said. They shook their heads and rolled their eyes.

Later, when everyone had gone home, she relaxed with a drink and watched Tor and Maureen trying to get a kite into the air. They weren't having much luck. Tor, who seemed to have no idea how it was done, charged about the lawn while the kite whipped in circles behind him. Maureen trailed along with all due seriousness, only to break out giggling every time the thing crashed.

In his way, Tor possessed the same innocence as the child. It was part of his charm, his sense that the world was essentially a good place, that if you worked hard and paid attention to business, everything would work out. He'd explained to her that he'd grown up with two ambitions: to become a professional golfer, and to create art for a living. He liked golf because it was leisurely, and you always went to summery places to participate. But the truth was that she had a better swing than he did.

Art, though, was a different matter altogether. Give him a brush, and put him near a passing comet, and he was a genius. When you aim high, she decided, one out of two wasn't bad.

Actually, he was luckier than most people, and not because he had talent. What he really possessed was an ability to enjoy life on its most basic levels. He loved having Maureen chase him around the lawn, enjoyed slapstick comedy, talked endlessly about his camping experiences with the local Boy Scout troop (where he was an assistant scoutmaster), and he could never get enough ice cream. He was a big kid.

He pretended to be modest about his work, to look surprised when he was nominated for the Delmar Award, or the Fitzgibbon. And when one of the media did a piece on him, he was thrilled.

She watched the kite arc high. It had gotten dark, and the Christmas lights were coming on. A virtual stable blinked into existence on the lawn at the Harbisons'. Complete with kneeling shepherds, camels, and a blazing star a few meters overhead.

Projectors came on all over the neighborhood. Santa and his sleigh were just landing on Jerry Adams's roof. A river of soft blue-and-white stars floated past the Proctors' place. No red or orange or green for Hal Proctor, who claimed to believe in the power of understatement. At the far end of the lane, three camels were approaching with wise men in the saddle.

It was all a bit much, but Hutch never said anything, knowing she'd be perceived as having no spirit. Still, she wondered what invisible aliens, had they been there somewhere, would have made of it all.

"By the way, have we figured out yet what those clouds are? Any idea at all?"

A group of carolers were wandering from door to door.

Tor gave the kite more string and a quick pull, probably a mistake. It turned over in midflight and crashed. Maureen exploded with giggles.

She pleaded for a chance to try, and Tor let her have the string. She raced off, still screaming with laughter, dragging the kite behind her.

Tor joined Hutch on the porch. "You're woolgathering again," he said.

She laughed. "You really look good out there."

"One of my many talents." Maureen charged by, squealing with delight. "You okay?"

"Oh, yes. I'm fine. Couldn't be better." An elf turned methodical somersaults on her lawn. And a blue lantern glowed in a window. They were her sole concessions to the lighting frenzy.

"It's over," he said gently.

"We still have a supply problem. I'll feel safer after Judy gets there. When we've begun to get some help to the Goompahs."

"You think?"

"What else?"

"I don't know. You seem restless."

"I wish Harold were here."

Tor rocked back and forth a few times. "He may not have known anything."

"It's not that. I'd just like to see him again."

What had he known?

They talked about inconsequentials. Then Tor asked whether Charlie Wilson had gotten any closer to a solution.

Charlie was a good guy, but he wasn't the right person to figure it out. Charlie was an analysis guy. Here's the data. Here's what it tells us. But he was not equipped to make the kind of imaginative leap that Harold might have done. "No. I think Charlie feels we don't have enough information yet. He's like you. Doesn't believe Harold really had anything." She shook her head. "Maybe that's right. Maybe Harold was going to say that the omegas are a gigantic research project of some sort, probably gone wrong but maybe not, and that would have been it. No big secret. That's, by the way, pretty much what Charlie thinks. But as to what sort of research, he says there's no way to know."

The reindeer atop the Adams house appeared to be gamboling, enjoying themselves, anxious to get to their next stop.

"Everything's showbiz," she said.

Tor's eyes darkened momentarily. "Sometimes you're a bit hard on people. Showbiz is what life is about."

Lights appeared in George Brauschwitz's array of hedges, green and white and gold, and began to ripple in waves through the gathering twilight. Green and white and gold.

A myriad of color, hypnotic in its effect. It was hard to draw her eyes away. "I wonder," she said. "Maybe there's a connection with the George-own Gallery after all." A possibility had occurred to her. But it was so outrageous that it seemed impossible. Yet right from the beginning they'd noted that the tewks showed up in clusters.

Tor watched her while she surveyed the stable, the camels, the hedge, Santa.

"We've assumed all along," she said, "that, in some way, the clouds were connected with research. Or that they were a weapons system run amok, or a slum clearance project run amok. These were things we could understand."

"Okay."

"Were they performing light experiments? Testing weapons?" She pushed back in her chair. Maureen tumbled over, scrambled back to her feet, looked puzzled, and began to cry. Hutch hurried to her side. "Skinned your knee," she told the child. "Does it hurt?"

Maureen couldn't get an answer past the sobs.

Hutch took her into the house, repaired the damage, got her some ice cream, and took a little for herself. She read to the child for a while. Lobo Louie. As she did, she considered the possibility that had occurred to her, and began to wonder if she might have the answer.

Tor came in and built a fire. "So what are they?" he asked.

She smiled at him. The house smelled of pine.

"Showbiz," she said.

He laughed.

"I'm serious. The arts are all about perspective, right? Angle of light. Point of view. What the artist chooses to put in the foreground. Or in shadow."

"I'm sorry, Hutch," he said. "I don't think I see where this is leading."

"Do you remember how Maureen reacted to the tewks?"

"She liked them. Thought they were attractive."

" 'They're pretty,' she said."

"So—?" Maureen was arranging her dolls, seating them on the floor, their backs against a chair, positioning them so they could see the tree.

"We've been watching them from God's point of view."

"How do you mean?"

"By eliminating distance, we've looked at them as they actually exploded—if that's the right term—to try to get a perspective on what was really happening. We ruled out the possibility that time and distance might be part of the equation."

Tor tilted his head. "Plain English, please."

"Think about the art gallery."

"What about it?"

"I missed the point. It didn't affect Harold because of something he saw inside it—"

Tor's brow creased. "—But because it was *there*."

"Yes."

"So what does that tell us?"

SHE SLIPPED THE disk into the reader, and a cross section of the Orion Arm blinked on.

"I've always believed," said Tor, "that the whole thing was a project by some sort of cosmic megalomaniac who just wanted to blow things up." He had mixed two white tigers for them. "But you don't think that?"

"No. I don't."

"Why not?"

"The method's too inefficient. There are a lot of omegas out there. Thousands, maybe. And only a handful that will actually destroy anything." She tried the drink. It was warm and sweet and made with a bit more lemon than the recipe called for. Just the way she liked it. "Tor, it doesn't *feel* malicious."

"It feels dumb."

"Yes." She gathered up Maureen, and they threaded their way through the constellations to the sofa. "Exactly what I've thought from the very beginning."

"Like Santa's sleigh over at the Adams house."

"Well, okay. It feels showy. Pretentious." She drew her legs up, tucked them under, and turned off the tree lights. A log crashed into the fire. Sparks flew and mixed with the stars. Maureen wanted to know what was happening.

"We're going to watch the sim for a few minutes, Love." And to the AI: "George, run the patterns. Fast forward."

Among the stars, tewks blinked on and off. A few here, a couple there, a few more over by the window. A half dozen or so by the tree. A cluster near the bookcase, a group by the curtains. Some on this side, some on the far side. Altogether, there were now 117 recorded tewk events.

"What are we looking for?"

"Bear with me a bit. George, change the viewing angle. Pick a site at the galactic core. More or less where the clouds would be originating."

The stars shifted. The familiar constellations vanished.

"Run them again, George."

They sat and watched. Lights blinked on and off. Some here, some there, a few over near the clock.

"There's a pattern," she said.

"I don't see it." Tor's hand touched hers. "What sort of pattern?"

"I don't know. You get a little bit in one place, but then it breaks down everywhere else. George, take us out to the rim. Let's have a look from, uh, Capella."

The starfield shifted again. *"Run it?"* asked George.

"Yes. Please."

Again the lights winked on and off around the room. She had to swing around to see everything. Tor gave up and edged off the sofa onto one knee, from which it was easier to follow the images.

"What's the time span here?" he asked.

"From start to finish," she said, "about twenty thousand years."

"How long do you think it's been going on?"

"No idea," she said. "Could be millions, I suppose." And to George: "Try it again, George. From the Pleiades."

And: "From Antares."

And: "From Arcturus."

Maureen got down off the sofa and headed into the kitchen.

Tor resumed his seat, but made no further effort to see into the far corners of the room. "You give up?" she asked.

"I'm tired twisting around to see everything. We'd do better to go sit by the door."

"George," she said, "can you make out a pattern here anywhere?"

"Please specify parameters."

"Never mind." She heard the refrigerator open.

Tor started to get up, but she pulled him back down. "It's okay," she said. "I've got it."

SHE GOT SNACKS for all of them, chocolate cake for Maureen and herself, ice cream for Tor and when the child had finished, she put Maureen to bed. Later they had visitors, Tor's brother and his wife, who lived in Alexandria, and MacAllister, who brought an armload of presents. More reporters showed up, and Michael Asquith called to tell her that she was invited to the White House for dinner Friday.

"You're on top of the world," Tor told her. "Enjoy it."

She was doing that. It was a nice feeling to be the toast of the town. She understood she was getting credit for what other people had done, but that was okay. She'd be careful to spread it around when the opportunity of-fered.

Finally, at about 2:00 A.M., things quieted down, and they found them-selves alone. They brought Maureen's presents out of the closet, put them under the tree, and went to bed. On her way up the stairs, Hutch was still thinking about the tewks. Somewhere, she'd missed something.

Tor headed for the shower. Hutch brushed her teeth and decided to let her own ablutions go until morning. She changed into a sheer nightgown, thinking it would be nice to celebrate properly. But as soon as she slipped into bed, her eyes closed, and her head sank back into the pillows.

The tewks went off in various series. A pattern of sorts. A few here, a few there. Why?

She got up, went back out, and stared down into the living room, its outlines just visible in the soft glow of the night-light.

"What's wrong?" asked Tor, appearing suddenly at her side.

"What did you say?" she asked.

"I asked what was wrong." He was pulling his robe around his shoulders.

"No. Before that."

He shrugged. "I have no idea."

"You said, when you're on top of the world, make it count. Or something like that. And earlier you said we'd do better to go sit by the door. That's what I'm going to do."

His hand touched her shoulder tentatively. "Priscilla, my love, what are we talking about now?"

"Point of view," she said. "We've been looking for a pattern while we're sitting *inside* it. George?"

"*Yes, Hutch?*"

"George, I want to run the program again."

"From what perspective?"

"Try from *above* the Orion Arm. Maybe twenty thousand light-years or so."

THE TEWK EVENTS exploded in glorious rhythm, one-two-three, magnifi-cent eruptions, a few seconds apart, and then six blue lights flaring in se-quence near the picture of Maureen, and a series of green flashes, erupting in perfect sync, up and down in a zigzag pattern just over the armchair. And four more, blood red, a vampire's eyes, near the windows.

It went on and on. There were parts missing, of course. The great bulk of it was missing, if she was correct in assuming that all the clouds in time would become part of the same incredible light show. The ultimate work

ɔf art. What they were looking at was no more than a few fragments, a
:hord here and there. But magnificent nonetheless.

"My God," he said.

"It's the way it would look if you were sitting sixteen thousand light-
years above the Milky Way, and you had a different sort of time sense. And
ʼou liked fireworks."

"But who—?"

"Don't know. Maybe long dead. Maybe not. But I suspect, whoever they
are, they aren't very bright."

"They *have* to be," he said. "Look at the engineering involved."

She looked down on the grandeur of the Milky Way, watched the tewks-
ury objects blaze in a kind of luminous choreography, and thought it was
ɔne of the loveliest and most majestic things she'd ever seen.

"Well," she said. "Not very bright. Or don't give a damn. Take your pick."

LIBRARY ENTRY

. . . We continue to pour resources into star travel.

The question no one ever asks is why we should do this. What
possible benefit has the human race received from the fact that it can
visit Alpha Serengetti or some such place. We are told that knowledge is its own reward. And that there have been practical benefits
as well. That household AIs work better because we can travel faster
than light, that we know more about nutrition, that we would not have
developed artificial gravity, that our shoes are more comfortable, and
that we have a better grasp of our own psychology, all because some
of us have gone to these impossibly distant places.

But which of the above advantages could not have been secured
by direct research? And who would even need artificial gravity if we
had the good sense to stay home?

We have yet to find a new Earth. And one might argue sensibly
that we have no need of one.

Maybe it's time to call a halt, and to rethink the entire effort. Before
the assorted crazies who want to go to Epsilon Eridani, at taxpayer
expense, ruin us all.

—*Paris Review*
December 27

chapter 52

Brackel. Twenty-fourth day after
T'Klot.

THE LIBRARY WAS finally ready to receive the scrolls that Parsy had rescue
the night of the storm.

The walls had been refurbished; the floor had been replaced. New chair
and tables had been brought in; the librarians' counter rebuilt. New shutter
installed, compliments of one of the library's several support groups. Peopl
had contributed lamps and pens and parchment. Several of those who ha
died on that terrible night had left bequests of which the library had bee
the beneficiary. He'd ordered a statue of Lykonda to be placed at the en
trance.

Tupelo and Yakkim came in with the scrolls, which had been carefull
stored at the villa. There would be a reopening ceremony the next day, an
Parsy was determined that the library would look good. Two new map
were up, to replace the ones that had been ruined. The scrolls would b
back in the inner room, where they would be available once more, and tw
fresh sets, a history of intellectual thought during the current century b
Pelimon, and a collection of essays by Rikat Domo, would be contribute
by the Society of Transcribers. To further mark the event—

—What was that?

Yakkim had seen it, too. A tube lay atop the table at the head librarian
station. "Where did that come from?" Yakkim asked. "It wasn't there ye
terday."

Tupelo frowned. Parsy signaled him to open it.

There was a scroll inside.

"Must be another donation," Yakkim said.

Tupelo removed the roll of parchment. Parsy, who knew the work of a
the master transcribers, did not recognize the hand. "Maybe one of th
workmen left it," Tupelo said. He handed it to Parsy.

"That's very odd," Parsy said.

"It's a play," said Yakkim. "But I do not know the author."

Nor did Parsy. Here was the cast of characters, and there the setting. I the palace at Thebes. He studied the page a long time, reading down the lines. The form of the play was unfamiliar. "Where is Thebes?" he asked.

Tupelo had no idea.

"It must be fictitious," said Yakkim. "There is no such place." He looked over Parsy's shoulder. "What do we do with it? Shall we add it to the holdings?"

"I'll ask around. See if anyone is familiar with it." He laid it down. Strange title, too. *Antigone.*

"*Antigone?* That's a curious word."

"It's the name of one of the characters."

"It sounds made-up."

"Indeed." He looked around. "Well, we have a lot to do. We can look at his later."

MACAO, MY NAME is Tasker. I'm a visitor to *Kulnar.* Never heard you speak before, but the regulars tell me you're prone to exaggerate."

"Not this time."

"Of course. But you really want us to believe you saw a *zhoka?*"

"Believe as you wish, Tasker. And no, I am not sure that it was a *zhoka.* t looked like one."

"What form did it take? Was it flesh and blood? Was it a spiritual entity? A ghost of some sort?"

"It was solid enough." She signaled to someone in back. "Pakka? Did you ave a question?"

"Yes. I've been here many times. As you know."

"I know."

"Heard you often."

"As we all know." That brought a laugh from the audience. Over the ears, Pakka had developed into a good-natured antagonist, instantly recgnizable to anyone who attended Macao's events.

"Yes. Well, however that may be, can we assume you are now willing to dmit that the world operates under divine governance."

"I never denied it."

"You've always said all things are open to reason."

"Yes." She hesitated. "I have, haven't I?"

"Do you wish to change your position?"

There was nothing for it, in the light of recent events. "I suppose I shall ave to reconsider."

"It is good of you to say so."

She smiled. "An open mind is of the essence, Pakka." It was in fact the eginning of wisdom. Accept nothing on faith. Verify the facts, and draw the logical conclusions. She found herself fingering the necklace given her by the *zhoka*. "It appears the world is more complicated than we thought."

The audience, most of it, nodded their agreement.

Tasker was on his feet again. "Tell us," he said, "why you think this *Digger Dunn*—that was his name, right?—"

"Yes."

"An odd name, don't you think?"

"Who am I to criticize the names of such beings?"

"Yes. Of course. But you say that, despite his appearance, you doubt that he was a *zhoka*. Would you tell us why?"

She looked out over the hall. It was on relatively high ground, fortunately, and had survived almost intact the floods that had ruined so much of *Kulnar*. "Yes," she said. "I will tell you why. Because *Digger Dunn* warned me about the cloud. Wanted me to warn everyone. To get the word out, to get the city evacuated."

"But you said he lied about the date."

"I prefer to think he was simply wrong about the date. It hardly matters. What does matter is that he tried to help. And I—" She trembled. Her voice shook, and tears came to her eyes. "I refused to believe."

The hall became very quiet.

"Unlike him, I failed to help."

WHEN IT WAS over, when her listeners had drifted away, she lingered, until only the service personnel were in the room with her, putting out the lamps, checking the fire screens, picking up whatever trash had been left behind. And then they, too, were gone.

The entire business was so fantastic that she would have ascribed it all to too much wine if she could. But the destruction had been real. And thousands had seen Lykonda.

She slipped her necklace over her head and gazed at it.

Incredible workmanship. A tiny silver chain unlike any she had seen before. And a strange circular jewel that glittered in the firelight. She could not escape the sense that it was somehow *alive*, that it watched her.

Even had she gone to the authorities, they would never have believed her story. Wouldn't have acted on it if they had. You don't accede to the wishes of a *zhoka*. Unless you are very foolish.

Or perhaps unless the *zhoka*'s name is *Digger Dunn*.

She sighed and wandered out of the auditorium into the corridor and out through the main entrance. The stars were very bright, and a cold chop blew off the sea. Winter was beginning in earnest.

Pakka and Tasker and several others were waiting for her a few steps away. It was traditional to take the guest speaker out for drinks and a good time after the *slosh*. But she hesitated in the doorway. Something, a breath of wind, an air current, brushed her arm.

"*Challa*, Macao."

The greeting had come from nearby, a pace or two. But she saw no one.

"I'm glad you came through it okay."

She knew the voice, and tried to speak, but her tongue caught to the roof of her mouth.

"I enjoyed the show," he said.

"*Digger Dunn*, where are you?"

"I'm right here."

She reached out and touched an *arm*. It was a curious sensation, solid yet not solid, rather like putting her hand against running water. But her hand remained dry. "Why have you come?"

"To say good-bye," he said. "And to thank you."

"To thank me? Why would you wish to thank me? I am sorry to say so, but I did not believe you when you told me about *T'Klot*."

"You tried. That was as much as I could ask. It's hard to fight lifelong reflexes." He seemed to be looking for the right word. "—Lifelong habits of thought." And here he used a word she did not understand. It sounded like *programming*.

"*Digger Dunn*, can I persuade you to do a *slosh* with me?"

He laughed, and the sound was loud enough to draw the attention of those who waited for her.

"I'm serious," she said. "We would be wonderful."

"I think we would cause a panic."

He was right, of course.

"I'd better go," he said.

"Wait." She removed the necklace and held it out for him. It was difficult because she wasn't sure precisely where he was standing. "This is yours."

"Actually," he said, "it belongs to someone very much like you. And I think she'd like you to keep it." A pair of lips pressed against her cheek. "Good-bye, Mac," he said.

She reached out, but he was gone. "Thank you, *Digger Dunn*," she said. "Do not forget me."

epilogue

ONE OF THE aspects of *Korbikkan* life that particularly fascinated and baffled xenologists was the apparent lack of warfare in a history now known to be ten thousand years long. Even stranger to human eyes was the fact that the Korbs showed no inclination to expand away from their tiny isthmus. It was true that the land to the north was sealed off by jungle and desert, and to the south by an unforgiving mountain range. But this was an intelligent species that never got above the equator, that showed no interest in spreading out through the island groups east and west of their homeland.

It's a curiosity of history that they launched a major exploration mission at the very moment that humans arrived. But it was only a coincidence. They have attempted similar voyages on other occasions. Several have returned from the direction in which they set out. To our knowledge, none has ever circled the globe. And none was ever followed up by a serious attempt at colonization.

Also puzzling was the Korbs' freewheeling treatment of sex. This was a society whose standards shocked most human observers, themselves from a society that thought sex a private matter and, at least officially, subscribed to monogamy.

Also difficult to explain was the lack of technology. The Korbs thought of chariots as bending the landscape. Yet they predated the Sumerians by millennia.

It now appears that all of these anomalies, the lack of organized warfare, the failure to expand, the open sex, the lack of technology, derive from a single factor: Korb women are capable of closing off their fallopian tubes. They have no unwanted children and no surprises.

Because living conditions on the isthmus are reasonably comfortable—fruit, vegetables, game, and fish can be had quite easily—there has never been pressure to produce large families. The population on the isthmus appears to have remained relatively stable for millennia. This fact has rendered intertribal competition pointless. It has also prevented technological development. Civilizations do not advance without population pressures.

BEST ESTIMATES ARE that fewer than 20 percent of the total population of the *Intigo* were lost during the encounter with the omega. When the far side of *Korbikkan* was examined, where the omega had vented its fury, analysts concluded that, had it struck the *Intigo* directly, the destruction of property and the loss of life would have been nearly total.

Food, blankets, and other supplies sent forward by the Academy arrived at the critical moment. They were landed by night in remote sites, and distributed by Judy Sternberg and her linguists. The recipients were told that the supplies were donated by the *Korbikkan* Relief Association, which was true enough, and it seemed to satisfy the natives' curiosity.

In recognition of their efforts, Sternberg's likeness has been enshrined in the Museum Humana in Berlin, and a *Shironi Kulp* plaza will be opened next year in Pentagon Park.

The real coordinator behind the bulk of the contributions was, of course, Dr. Alva Emerson, who tried unsuccessfully to deflect the credit by awarding a medal to Priscilla Hutchins. Hutchins accepted, but it may have meant more to her when Dr. Alva took her aside and confessed that, whatever impression she might have had originally, she had concluded Hutchins to be "rather a decent human being after all."

Tor drew up a formal certificate, citing the phrase. Although the certificate is confined to her bedroom, she owns no document of which she is more proud.

The round-the-world mission, stranded on the eastern continent, needed almost a year to build new ships. But they completed the task and, as of this writing, are on their way back to the *Intigo*.

Marge, Digger, Kellie, and Julie Carson received formal recognition for their accomplishments not only from the Academy, but from the media at large. Jack Markover was posthumously awarded the Legion of Honor from the French government, and David Collingdale received the President's Medal.

On the anniversary of the omega strike, a memorial ceremony was held on the Academy grounds at Arlington to honor the memory of Collingdale and Markover. Markover's brother James and Collingdale's fiancée, Mary Clank, were brought in for the event, and they helped dedicate the new Korbikkan wing to their memory.

AFTER THE MARKOVER-COLLINGDALE ceremony, Digger asked Hutch whether the Academy was now ready to put some serious effort into doing research on the omegas, so that, as he put it, "what we went through at Lookout won't happen again."

"I think we've learned, Digger," she said. "I surely hope so."

HUTCH'S NOTION THAT the tewk events were actually an effort to create a kind of cosmic symphony has not been generally accepted, although it's difficult to explain in any other way the visual results if one happens to be seated at the proper place above the Orion Arm.

Whatever the official view, however, a synthetic hedgehog is on its way to the local cloud, and by the time this is published, will have, one hopes, already ignited it and disposed of the thing. Hutchins is pushing for mass production of hedgehogs, which she would like to see used wherever possible to explode the omegas. To get rid of them. And, she added recently in an interview with UNN: "To ruin the show for the idiots who sent them. To point out that there are women and children here."

There are even some who are arguing that, since we know where the omega engineers live, we should send them more pointed sentiments.

Avery Whitlock's Notebooks

But I wonder what we would have done had they been barbarians. Or looked like insects.

is all about—not fancy footwork or clever phrase-making, but things leading to other things. Whose cooperation did the acquiring bank need in order to do business in Colorado? That of state officials. And what influences state officials? Public opinion. And what moves public opinion? Media attention. And what focuses media attention? Properly applied spin.

> **Damage control is only a last resort; see if the damage itself can somehow be undone.**

We had done much the same thing a few years earlier on behalf of a successful high-tech outfit that unexpectedly became the object of a hostile takeover attempt. Our clients in this case were literally rocket scientists, but they couldn't figure out how to keep this other firm from gaining control of their company.

They had called in Sitrick and Company to fashion some sort of publicity campaign on their behalf. But publicity wasn't really what they wanted or needed. What they really wanted was for their unwanted suitors to go away and leave them alone.

Recognizing this, I sat down with the company's harried CEO and asked him a series of questions. Basically, I was trying to find out what might cause the takeover attempt to fall apart.

After a bit of back and forth, the CEO came up with something specific. "If they were to lose their financing," he said, referring to the other company, "they wouldn't be able to do the deal."

"Okay," I replied. "And what might cause them to lose their financing?"

"Well," he said, "if we lost some of our government contracts, that would make us look a lot less attractive to the banks."

"And what might cause you to lose your government contracts?" I asked.

He thought about it for a long moment. "I suppose if some of our key people were to leave, it would make the Defense Department very unhappy."

I nodded. "So tell me—what do you think would happen if some of your key scientists put out a press release in which they said they had serious concerns about this takeover and weren't really sure they'd want to continue working for the company if the deal were to go through?"

The CEO brightened. "Obviously, that would make the banks very nervous," he said. "At the very least, they'd wonder if we'd still be able to get government work."

As it turned out, we didn't issue any such release. While most of the company's key people were indeed very unhappy at the prospect of being taken over, not all of them were willing to go on the record with their misgivings. So instead we leaked a story to a major local newspaper saying merely that a number of the company's most important researchers and designers were thinking of leaving if the takeover went through. A few of them were willing to talk, though not for attribution. That was all it took. As predicted, the banks got nervous, canceled their financing, and the takeover attempt collapsed.

As with Purgatory, thinking strategically got us to the heart of the matter, where a solution to the client's fundamental problem was waiting to be uncovered. What did our client really want? To get rid of the hostile bid. How do you get rid of a hostile bid? By making the item in question (in this case, our client's company) look less attractive to the potential buyer. And so on and so forth. What was tricky in this case was coming up with a way of making the company look less alluring without (1) violating securities laws, and (2) actually doing it any real damage. Once the CEO gave me the information I needed to figure that out, the rest was nothing more than setting up a row of dominoes and then knocking them down—or as we put it before, a simple matter of letting one thing lead to another.

■ ■ ■

If thinking strategically means anything, it means refusing to accept situations at face value. Whether it's something as specific as a client's initial description of what he thinks he needs, or something as general as the conventional wisdom about some ongoing controversy, the smart spin doctor makes a point of trying to look beneath the surface of events.

One of my favorite examples of this sort of thing is what became known as the frog taco story. The episode was actually a pretty funny one, though I don't think any of the participants found it particularly amusing at the time.

Early in November 1995, I got a call from a longtime client. Among other things, his company owned a major interest in the El Torito restaurant chain. He wanted to know if I'd read that morning's *Orange County Register*.

"Not yet," I said.

"Well, there's a story in there about a guy who claims that he bit into a beef taco in one of our restaurants and wound up chewing on a frog."

"You're kidding," I said.

"Nope. The guy says there was a frog in his taco."

However comical it may have sounded (and I *did* have to stifle a smile), there is nothing more devastating to a restaurant than the suggestion that its kitchen might be contaminated. If word gets around that strange things have been turning up in your bouillabaisse, forget it—you're out of business.

I quickly got a copy of the *Register*. There it was, on the front page of the Metro section: "Diner Finds Frog in His Beef Taco." The story was about as bad as it could be. The previous Saturday, it reported, a local man had taken his family to dinner at an El Torito in Orange, California. At first, everything was fine. But then, the newspaper noted, "it hit him—in one sobering flash—that the taco in his No. 7 combo was chewier than it ought to be."

"So I spit it out," the *Register* quoted the man as saying, "and there was a frog. I couldn't believe it. I bit the damn head off."

There's an old journalism cliché that says if a dog bites a man, it's not news, but if a man bites a dog, it is. Apparently, it's even bigger news if a man bites a frog. Whatever the reason, the frog-in-the-taco story spread through the media like wildfire. It was retold on literally hundreds of radio and television stations throughout the country, on the national news, and in newspapers from Maine to Hawaii. Both Jay Leno and David Letterman did bits on it in the opening monologues on their late-night talk shows—not just the first night, but the second night as well. (Among other things, Leno claimed to have visited El Torito to try the chain's new Kermit Taco Supreme, while Letterman said the frog was the slimiest thing served in the restaurant since O.J. Simpson's defense team had lunch there.)

I had only two questions for the El Torito people. The first was, what did we know about the man making the claim? The second was, did we have the frog?

The answer to my first query was "not much, at least not yet," but the chain's security people were checking out his background. The answer to the second was, happily, yes. The restaurant manager had fought the man for the suspect amphibian and placed it in a freezer for safekeeping. Interestingly enough, contrary to the man's statement, the frog's head was still very much attached to its body. Nor, it seemed, had the frog been cooked. If it really had been in the taco, as the man claimed, it had to have been placed there deliberately, after the taco had come off the grill.

Obviously, something fishy was going on here. Either a cook with an extremely warped sense of humor had played a practical joke—which was possible but not likely—or there was something wrong with the man's story.

My first recommendation, while we waited to find out about the man's background, was that we send the frog out for testing—not to a commercial laboratory, as the El Torito people had originally been prepared to do, but to a university lab, whose objectivity and integrity would be beyond reproach. While we waited for the results—of both the lab tests and the background check—we put out a statement reiterating El Torito's commitment to quality control and pledging to get to the bottom of this "very serious matter."

It didn't take long for the background check to raise serious questions about the man's motives. By the middle of the week, the media had somehow gotten this information and were reporting that he had filed for bankruptcy and was wanted by police in Utah for credit-card fraud and other crimes. What's more, reporters were tipped to a former woman friend of his who was quoted as saying that he had spoken to her repeatedly "about how finding a roach or piece of glass in his food would be a great way to make money."

At the same time, the results of the lab tests on the frog came back, adding to our suspicions about his veracity. Among other things, they confirmed that contrary to the man's story, the frog had not been chewed, there was no evidence of teeth marks on it, its head was still attached to its body, and it had not been cooked.

Given the huge play the man's charges had received and their impact on the public's mind, I felt it was important to stretch out the rebuttal cycle of the story over at least two days. So we held the lab results for twenty-four hours, letting the news of the man's bankruptcy and criminal background dominate the midweek head-lines. We finally released the lab report on Thursday along with a short but strongly worded statement about its implications— specifically that the frog "was not chewed," that it bore "no evi-dence of teeth marks," that the frog's head was "still attached to the body," and that the frog had "not been cooked." "Something appears very, very wrong here," our statement noted. "The more we look into this thing, the more [the man's] story—as reported— just doesn't ring true. An investigation into the operations of the restaurant in question has led us to the conclusion that it is highly unlikely that El Torito or any of its employees had anything to do with the frog getting on [the man's] plate. At this point, that's really all we can say."

At the same time, I sent a letter to Leno and Letterman, point-ing out that El Torito's reputation had been unjustly maligned. I specifically avoided making any kind of legal threats, appealing instead solely to the two comedians' sense of fair play. "I know you are having fun with this frog-in-the-taco thing," I told each of them, "but I thought you should have the facts."

Sure enough, on Friday night, both late-night hosts included bits in their opening monologues pointing out that the frog charges had turned out to be fraudulent. ("Finally," Leno exclaimed, "a case Gil Garcetti can win!" Added Letterman, in a joking correc-tion that one of El Torito's competitors no doubt could have done without: "Don't worry, though—if you want a frog in your taco, you can still go to Taco Bell.")

By then, the press was flogging the fraud aspect of the story with nearly the same fervor it had devoted to the original supposed scandal. By the weekend, the tables had been turned completely. What on Monday had looked like an unmitigated disaster for El Torito had by Friday evaporated into a hearty if somewhat rueful laugh, and the chain was back to business as usual.

As in the Purgatory case, the key here to successful spin was thinking strategically—that is, looking beyond the superficial distractions to the big picture, and focusing our efforts on solving the fundamental problem. A traditional PR person would probably have approached the El Torito situation by asking, "How can I save the restaurant's reputation?" A strategically-minded spin doctor, by contrast, poses a more basic question: "Has the client really done anything wrong?" The answer in this case was no, so instead of having to undertake an awkward and embarrassing campaign of damage control, all we needed to do was set the record straight.

CHAPTER 10

▌ Find a Lead Steer...

... and the media herd will follow.

THE MOVIE STAR WAS PERCHED on a sofa in her lawyer's office, literally shaking with nerves. Her husband sat beside her, his dark eyes glittering with barely suppressed rage and frustration. She was recounting her version of the appalling events that over the past year had turned her life upside down—threatening to torpedo a promising career and ruin her financially, in addition to provoking an avalanche of abusive tabloid headlines.

If the press was to be believed, this sultry but surprisingly fragile-looking actress was a spoiled, self-indulgent brat who only got what was coming to her when six months earlier she lost a highly publicized law suit. To hear the media tell it, the jury's order that the actress pay the plaintiff millions of dollars in damages represented nothing less than the triumph of a hard-working little guy over an irresponsible and imperious Hollywood princess. As for the actress's horrified protests that she was being punished for something she hadn't done—and that there was no way she could afford to pay such a huge judgment—according to news accounts, these were merely the disingenuous bleatings of "a poor little rich girl" (as a Reuters dispatch described her) trying to weasel her way out of her obligations.

Not surprisingly, the story the actress herself had to relate was somewhat different. Indeed, it was so different from what the media had been almost unanimously saying for the past few months that countering it would require a very particular and unusual strategy.

■ ■ ■

The actress's account of her troubles left me feeling both sympathy and amazement—sympathy that she had been put through such an appalling ordeal, amazement that the media situation had gotten so out of control. The actress told me that the lawyers handling her appeal were confident that the judgment against her would eventually be overturned. But the appeals process grinds painfully slowly; it might be a year or more before her name was finally cleared. By then, her career might be irrevocably damaged. Obviously, she couldn't wait that long for relief.

Our only real hope of restoring her reputation lay with the press. The press, however, wasn't exactly an ally. As is so often the case, it was stampeding en masse in one direction—from our point of view, the wrong direction. We had to change that before the actress became a forgotten footnote. But how?

The answer lay in that metaphor I just used to describe the situation: *The press was stampeding*. It's a description we've all heard (and perhaps even employed) more times than we can remember. The phrase tends to irritate newspeople, but after a drink or two the best of them will concede that the unpleasant image is not entirely inapt.

For all their competitive-ness and iconoclasm, news-people, in fact, tend to seek safety in numbers. They prefer to hunt in packs, and when

> **One well-timed, well-placed story can—with a little finesse—reverse a media stampede.**

they are off on their own, they feel distinctly uncomfortable. Indeed, perhaps the single greatest accomplishment of the *Washington Post* in the early days of its Watergate coverage was summoning the courage to stay the course when not one other news organization believed in the story.

Journalists, in short, are herd animals, and so it doesn't take a lot to whip them up into a full-tilt stampede.

Understanding this aspect of the journalistic character is the key to figuring out what to do when the prevailing tone or direction in the coverage of a given story is going against you. As insulting or simplistic as it may seem, the image of the press as a stampeding herd is not only often accurate, it can also be a useful guide to action. After all, if you think of reporters as a single-minded pack of steers engaged in headlong flight, it's bound to occur to you that jumping out in front of them and yelling and waving your arms is not likely to accomplish anything so much as get you gored and trampled.

So how *can* you stop a stampede? The short answer is that you can't—but you can change its direction. The trick is finding a lead steer.

The curious thing about herd animals—say, cattle—is that even as they gallop with the group, they sometimes find themselves wondering uneasily if perhaps they're being taken for a ride. Not so much, mind you, that they'll actually break away from the crowd, but enough to keep them watching to see if anyone else feels the same way. All it takes, in this situation, is for one steer to change direction on his own, and the entire herd may wind up executing a complete about-face without missing a stride.

It's not all that different with journalists. All you have to do is find one reporter willing to push the story in a different direction, and the entire media pack may change its perspective in the blink of a news cycle.

This contrarian reporter is the "lead steer." To be sure, not just anyone in the press corps can play the role. It's got to be a journalist who enjoys the respect of his or her peers—or at least works for a news organization that does. That's because the lead steer's real audience is not so much the folks at home as it is his or her colleagues in the press room. The idea is not to change public attitudes in one fell swoop (that not really being possible) but to influence future coverage.

■ ■ ■

By the time the actress finished telling me her tale of woe, there was no doubt in my mind that if the public knew her side of things, the general hostility she'd been encountering would melt away virtually overnight. The problem, I explained, was twofold. First, hers was a complicated story that couldn't be related in short news bursts, but rather had to be told in depth. Second, as we'd seen, the media were arrayed against her pretty solidly.

That didn't mean we were stuck. With an appropriate lead steer, we could solve both problems at once. "What we're going to do," I told her, "is find the right reporter to do a major 'factual' story about you, someone you can sit down with and really open yourself up to, so they can see who you really are." In part, I explained, the point of the story would be to restore her reputation generally, but at bottom it would be aimed at influencing the rest of the

> **The lead-steer technique can also be used to *start* media stampedes.**

media. Thus, the key would be to find a journalist whom the rest of the press corps held in high regard—someone they felt confident couldn't be snowed, about whom they could say, "Wow, if this person believes it, it must be true." We also needed a venue that made sense—a publication that had credibility both within the media community and among the sort of people whose opinion mattered professionally to a movie actress.

"So tell me," I asked her, "what's the most important publication to you? The *Wall Street Journal*? *Variety*? The *New York Times*?"

She and her husband exchanged a glance. "Well," she said, "if I had to pick one, it would probably be the Calendar section of the *Los Angeles Times*."

It was a good call. In addition to being one of the nation's most important news organizations, the *Los Angeles Times* also happens to be the movie industry's hometown newspaper. As such, its Calendar section, which contains its arts and entertainment coverage, is read by everyone who is anyone in Hollywood. What's more, major Calendar stories not only reach industry movers and shakers, but because of the *Times*'s stature they also help set (and sometimes re-set) the journalistic agenda of the entire Hollywood press corps.

The question then became who could we get to write what we hoped would be a sympathetic yet credible profile of the actress.

My associate Mike Kolbenschlag came up with the answer. One of the Calendar section's best-regarded contributors happened to be a longtime acquaintance of his, and as Mike saw it, she had just the qualities we were looking for. A Pulitzer Prize–winner, she was respected by her peers. Though a bit cynical ("Definitely not the kind of reporter who can be spun," Mike said), she was also something of an iconoclast, not averse to questioning the conventional wisdom. Equally important, she was willing to give a beleaguered subject the benefit of the doubt. And that's really all we wanted—an even break. As Mike told the reporter, "Look, all we're asking is that you come at this with an open mind and see what you find."

I prepared the actress with a warning I often give people in her position. "The danger in sitting down with someone like this reporter," I told her, "is that she's not one of these sycophants you're probably used to being interviewed by. People in the business know who those reporters are, and their stories don't have any impact. So this is not going to be one of those situations where your publicist can browbeat the writer or the newspaper into submission. You have to understand that parts of the story might make you cringe."

The actress said she understood.

"Good," I replied, "because if you're not prepared for that, you should bail out now."

It wasn't easy, but she hung in there. She and her husband spent hours with the reporter over the following weeks, telling their story, answering her questions, and generally demonstrating that they weren't the monsters the media had been having so much fun portraying them as being.

Like any good journalist, the Calendar reporter also spent a fair amount of time talking to the other side, interviewing the man who had sued our client, as well as numerous other people our client knew and for whom she had worked over the years. In the end, she wound up writing what became a 5,200-word cover story for the Calendar section's prestigious Sunday edition. The cover image of our client, looking vulnerable but determined under an extremely sympathetic headline, said it all. The piece transformed her from villain to victim (though it quoted her as insisting that she didn't see herself "as some victim or martyr—I hate those words, they're so pathetic"). What's more, it totally changed the media's attitude toward her. No longer the spoiled princess, she now began to be consistently portrayed as a hard-working professional who had been wronged.

When, a year and a half later, the appeals court finally got around to throwing out the civil judgment against her, virtually no one in the press or the public was surprised by the news.

■   ■   ■

Using one well-timed, well-placed story to reverse a media stampede takes a certain amount of finesse and a fair bit of experience, but when done properly, it can be enormously effective.

The lead-steer technique can also be used to *start* stampedes. For example, there was the time, a few years ago, when Sitrick and Company worked with the giant Hollywood talent agency International Creative Management (ICM) to help it make a point against its cross-town rival, Creative Artists Agency (CAA).

It was the early spring of 1993. ICM had been talking to us on and off for several months about whether we might be interested in advising it on how to raise its public profile.

Though it was by far the larger and more diversified agency, ICM was not nearly as well known to the general public as CAA, then at the height of its power and mystique under the almost cult-like leadership of superagent Michael Ovitz.

Finally, one Friday evening at the beginning of April, I got a phone call from ICM chairman Jeff Berg. A lanky, intense, and extremely intelligent twenty-five-year veteran of the agency business, Berg said he and ICM president Jim Wiatt had decided to retain us formally—"and by the way," he added, "I think you should know that I've just given a series of interviews to the *Wall Street Journal* and *Variety* and the *Los Angeles Times* in which I called Mike Ovitz's representation of Credit Lyonnais a conflict of interest."

> **We used the lead-steer technique to help the abused ex-wife of a major star.**

Berg was referring to news that had Hollywood abuzz. The previous week Credit Lyonnais—the big Paris-based bank that for more than a decade had been the number one lender to independent Hollywood film companies—had announced that it had hired CAA as a consultant on what it described as "matters regarding the bank's worldwide entertainment industry activities." In addition, it said, CAA "would provide advice to the bank regarding its future entertainment portfolio."

Now Ovitz had been actively promoting and expanding the corporate consulting aspects of CAA's business for some time. Indeed, in 1989 the agency had advised Sony Corporation in its $3.5 billion purchase of Columbia Pictures. A few years later, it was hired by Matsushita to help the huge Japanese conglomerate with its acquisition of MCA/Universal. So it wasn't merely that a big foreign bank was willing to pay for CAA's expertise that had raised some industry eyebrows.

What had people talking—and what Berg was loudly complaining about—was that CAA's newest client happened to own a 98.5 percent interest in Metro-Goldwyn-Mayer, Incorporated. In the view of some (most prominently, Berg), that put Ovitz on both sides of the table, advising the owners of a movie studio, which was in the business of buying talent, while running an agency, which was in the business of selling talent.

As far as Berg was concerned, the conflict of interest was obvious. CAA and its ambitious leader, he felt, should decide whether they wanted to be talent agents or corporate insiders. They couldn't be both, he felt—at least not without violating federal antitrust regulations, not to mention Screen Actors Guild rules that bar talent agencies from being involved with production companies.

Berg's arguments certainly made sense to me. But there was something about the line-up of newspapers to whom he had spoken that I found troubling. "You talked to the *Los Angeles Times*, the *Journal*, and *Variety*," I said. "What about the *Hollywood Reporter*? Did you talk to them?"

"Well, no," he replied.

That was a mistake. The entertainment industry has two major trade papers, the *Hollywood Reporter* and *Variety*. Not surprisingly, they are deadly rivals. To talk to one of them, as Berg had done, without talking to the other is like talking to *Time* without talking to *Newsweek*.

"Jeff," I said, "the *Reporter* is going to kill you. It's one thing to give a paper an exclusive, but it's another thing to talk to three of them and exclude the *Reporter*."

Though Berg protested that he hadn't left the *Reporter* out intentionally, he'd been in the business long enough to know that in situations like these, intentions didn't really count. "So what do we do now?" he asked me.

Fortunately, neither *Variety* nor the *Wall Street Journal* publishes on Saturday or Sunday, so we still had two days before the *Reporter* would discover it was out in the cold. Quickly, I phoned some people I knew at the *Reporter* and arranged to bring Berg down to their offices on Sunday morning so he could explain in person his position on CAA's relationship with Credit Lyonnais.

As it turned out, Berg's session at the *Reporter* proved to be the most in-depth interview he did with anyone. It also turned out to be something of a lifesaver. While *Variety* and the *Journal* and the *Los Angeles Times* all ran stories about Berg's attack on CAA, none of them made much of it. The *Reporter*, by contrast, took Berg's charges seriously, putting them on page one under the banner headline "ICM Blasts CAA's Bank Ties."

The length and depth of the *Reporter* story—not to mention its dramatic play—totally shifted the press corps's take on the subject. Where before there had been almost no media interest in Berg's views, now he was a hot topic. Indeed, the *Los Angeles Times* felt moved to give the controversy a second, more serious look a few days later, while newspapers from Sacramento to Cleveland suddenly decided the story was worth finding space for. The *Reporter* turned out in the end to be our lead steer, and the result of our hasty cultivation was a small but extremely gratifying media stampede.

■   ■   ■

It would, of course, be disingenuous to pretend there isn't a certain satisfaction to be gleaned from watching virtually the entire press corps change direction midflight. Nonetheless, what makes such stampedes so welcome is not simply that they can be generated, but that they can be used to accomplish something worthwhile—to force an action, say, that somehow rights a wrong. Public embarrassment, particularly the sort that comes with massive media coverage, is a powerful lever; when wielded properly, it can move even the toughest adversary to cry uncle. Indeed, I've noticed over the years that even confirmed hard-noses who are left cold and unmoved by the most appalling charges made against them in court pleadings will cut and run when the very same statements are repeated in the public press.

Such was certainly the case when we used the lead-steer technique to help the abused ex-wife of a major star achieve a modicum of justice.

She had come to Sitrick and Company on the eve of filing charges in what her attorney described as the worst case of spousal brutality he'd ever seen. The lawyer wasn't exaggerating. According to the depositions he showed me, the woman's ex-husband, a star of major proportions, beat her regularly and savagely throughout their five-year relationship—once so badly, she said, that she "flopped on the floor like a fish." On several occasions, he nearly killed her; one time, after being battered into unconsciousness, her suit alleged, she "awoke in a hospital to learn she had been injected with heroin and cocaine and had gone into cardiac arrest."

The first thing we did was ensure that the woman's lawsuit got media attention. Frankly, given the defendant's prominence and the lurid nature of the charges against him, it didn't take a great deal of effort on our part to attract extensive press coverage. Still, it didn't have much impact; like the fabled River Platte, it may have been a mile wide, but it was only one inch deep. There were literally hundreds of one- and two-paragraph first-day news stories, and no second-day attention at all. By the third day, the lawsuit was ancient history, at least as far as the press was concerned.

That was hardly unexpected, for our client, who was in an extremely fragile emotional state, didn't want to give any interviews—or, indeed, even provide the press with new pictures of herself. (She was terrified that her ex-husband or one of his fans might try to do her harm.) As a result, once they had covered the initial filing, there was really nothing more for the media to report—nor was there likely to be until the suit eventually came before a judge and jury. And that was probably months, if not years, off. In the meantime, without any new developments to hold its attention, the media spotlight was bound to drift elsewhere.

This fact of media life suited our client's ex-husband and his lawyers just fine. Their strategy was simple and brutal. They intended to stiff-arm the woman—basically, to ignore her, refusing even to discuss a settlement, in the hope that her limited resources would force her to drop the suit long before it ever got to trial.

The strategy was hardly fair—indeed, given the nature of her charges, it was scandalous—but it was perfectly legal, and there seemed little if anything she could do about it.

Now it's true that unhappy ex-spouses tend to make all sorts of wild charges about each other, and as a rule, I make a point of taking everything I am told in such situations with a grain of salt. Unless I can corroborate a client's charges independently, I am careful never to represent them as anything more than allegations. "This is what we've been told," is the way I put it to reporters when I haven't been able to confirm for myself the truth of a particular accusation. In this case, however, her attorney, an extremely well-respected lawyer whom I happened to know quite well, was able to obtain independent confirmation of the woman's charges, which left me more convinced than ever that hers was a story that deserved more than one-day coverage—and because it would also bring pressure on her ex-husband to take her seriously, if not settle.

So once again we found ourselves wanting to get the media moving on a story conventional wisdom said was moribund. The obvious solution was to find a lead steer. Normally, a behind-the-scenes account of a star's lurid misbehavior might seem to be of interest only to the tabloid press. But there was another element in play here, an issue of genuine social concern—namely, domestic violence. Given the growing public interest in the subject, if I could persuade our client to cooperate (which meant agreeing to be interviewed and sitting for a photo session), I was confident I could persuade a major mainstream magazine to run with our story.

The publication I had in mind was the nation's number one journal of celebrity news and human-interest features: *People* magazine. A story in *People*—ideally, a cover story—would not only have enormous impact on the public consciousness, it would also galvanize the rest of the press, serving notice that there was more at issue here than just some celebrity backbiting.

To my mind, the story—with its mixture of insider gossip and serious subtext—was perfect for *People*. So as soon as my client said she felt strong enough to do what would be required, I was on the phone to an editor I knew there. As it happened, my instincts turned out to be right on target. The editors at *People* loved the idea and quickly assigned a team of writers and correspondents to pull it together.

We spent several weeks working with the reporters from *People*—laying out the court filings, lining up acquaintances and eyewitnesses who could confirm our client's account of her abusive relationship with the star. The story that resulted was so powerful that the magazine's editors wound up deciding to make it a cover, in addition to splashing it across six full pages inside.

The impact was predictably huge. Immediately after the story appeared, the rest of the press seemed collectively to rediscover its interest in my client's woes. Shortly after that, as the media stampede gathered momentum, her ex-husband's lawyers decided it was time to sit down again and talk. They eventually settled. Our lead steer had brought us very real results.

CHAPTER 11

▌ Fight Back

When and where it's called for, don't be afraid to put your adversaries under the wheel of pain.

THERE ARE MANY WAYS TO describe life in and around the public arena—exciting, rewarding, unpredictable, challenging—but one adjective you rarely hear is genteel. That's hardly surprising, for as anyone who has spent any time in the media spotlight can attest, the rough-and-tumble of public life is intense, continuous, and often nothing short of vicious. Dog eat dog may be putting it mildly. As Lyndon Johnson once observed, "If you're not doing it to them, then they're doing it to you."

To survive in such a world—much less, to prevail—it's not enough simply to have the ability to roll with the punches. When the situation demands it, you've got to be able to throw a few yourself. This capacity is particularly important when you're facing an adversary who seems intent on using the press as a club to beat you into submission, someone who has no scruples about crossing the line that separates vigorous contention from unabashed mudslinging.

Now it goes without saying (or at least it should) that mudslinging is not something a sensible person ever wants to get involved in. The former U.S. Army chief of staff General Creighton Abrams used to cite a doctrine he called the Pig Rule: "Never wrestle with pigs—you get dirty and they enjoy it."

> **It's not always enough to roll with the punches; sometimes, you've got to throw a few yourself.**

Nonetheless, there are occasions when it may be advisable to come down from the high ground and try to level the playing field—when you have no choice but to fight fire with fire.

We had a client once who was involved in a horrendous lawsuit with a woman he had lived with for many years. She also worked for his company, and the intermingling of their personal and professional affairs—always an explosive mixture—provided her with a hook to feed the media a series of unfair and inaccurate stories that were destroying his reputation. In short, she was trying the case in the press, and she was winning.

As it happened, the woman's own professional behavior had been somewhat less than impeccable. Indeed, our client had more than enough evidence at least to pique the interest of law-enforcement authorities. But at first, he resisted my suggestion that we turn the evidence over to the government and file charges against her.

"Look," he said, "you know and I know what sort of a woman she is. But even if she's convicted, she'll never go to jail."

"That doesn't matter," I replied. "The point is that the press will report the charges, and before long everyone she knows will be aware that she's been accused of some pretty awful things. At the very least, it will shut her up." I went on to explain that what I was proposing to do was something we refer to as putting your enemy under the wheel of pain. It's a particularly unpleasant tactic that should be employed only when absolutely necessary—and even then only when you are absolutely certain of your facts. But when those conditions are satisfied, it can bring almost instantaneous results.

Though the wheel of pain resembles nothing so much as a personal assault, it is every bit as much a technique of spin as any of the other rules enumerated in this book. Like all the others, this tactic is designed to change someone's mind (and sometimes his life). The only difference is that in this case the "someone" happens not to be the public or the press but your adversary himself, and what you're trying to convince him of is that in taking you on, he's gotten in way over his head—that he hasn't got a chance of winning and should throw in the towel.

Specifically, what you want to do is make your adversary understand that you're going to defend yourself—and that he is going to feel some real pain if he persists in provoking you. It's not simply a matter of making your accusations sufficiently horrific (the nature of the charges, after all, depends entirely on the facts of the case); rather, it's what you do with those accusations that gives this tactic its power. In the most extreme case, you're going to make sure that not only the target's business associates become aware of your charges, but also his spouse, his children, and his minister. Every time his wife goes to the grocery store, the cashier is going to say, "Oh, Mrs. Smith, we're all so sorry about this terrible business that your husband is involved in. I hope you know that none of us here believes all those terrible things they're saying about him."

Before long, of course, Mr. Smith will be worrying about his kids reading the worst about Daddy—not to mention what his friends at the country club are saying about him behind his back. And not long after that he will begin wondering whether it's really worth it to continue that suit or doing whatever else it is that you happen to want him to think twice about.

I laid out this scenario to my client and asked him how he thought his former girlfriend would react to that sort of pressure.

"My God," he said, "she'll be devastated. She'll be a basket case."

I nodded. "It will make her think twice the next time she's tempted to try this case in the media, won't it?"

My client was still dubious, so I bet him my fee—double or nothing—that the tactic would work.

He didn't take the bet, which was just as well for him, for if he had, I'd have won.

■ ■ ■

Using the wheel of pain is a delicate business. If you're not careful, it can wind up hurting you as much as anyone else. To wield this weapon effectively, you need to understand your adversary's threshold of pain. If your opponent's tolerance for pain is high—or if you employ too much force—he might successfully counterspin himself as a martyr.

Above all, you must be absolutely certain of your facts. There's nothing worse—legally, tactically, or morally—than going after someone tooth and nail, only to discover (or, more likely, have someone else discover) that what you're saying about him simply isn't true. That's a calamity from which there is no recovering. Spin is about persuasion, and persuasion depends on credibility. Once you've shown yourself to be someone whose word can't always be trusted (whether because you're an out-and-out liar or simply have a tendency to go off half-cocked), you'll find it extremely difficult, if not impossible, to persuade anyone of anything.

For these and other reasons, the wheel-of-pain technique tends to be used only by the hardest of the hard-nosed in the most extreme of situations, when the stakes are at their highest. That pretty well describes the circumstances in which the tactic was successfully employed by a client of mine, the founder of a major public company. Just as

> **The wheel of pain is employed sparingly, and only when you are absolutely certain of your facts.**

this fellow was emerging from a horrific business battle that had torn his family apart, he was viciously attacked by one of his sons, an erstwhile ally, who pummeled him mercilessly in the press as he mounted a boardroom coup against the old man. Brought in to help defend the embattled patriarch, we became convinced that the attacker's strategy was simply to harass our client to the point at which he would no longer feel the struggle was worth the effort. The only possible response, we concluded, was for my client to show his son how it felt—to demonstrate that two could play the same game, and to attack his attacker with every bit as much abandon as his attacker had attacked him.

It was an ugly and unfortunate situation. Our client had, at great sacrifice to himself, built an enormously successful business, giving his son everything he could want—only to have his boy turn on him. In a series of questionable corporate maneuvers, he had his father removed as chairman of the company and stripped of his control. The aim was to install himself as head of the company, and for a time it seemed there wasn't anything he wouldn't do to have his way. Going after his father in a particularly vengeful *ad hominem* fashion—using words like dishonest, irrational, and criminal—the son seemed determined to embarrass his father into submission.

It was at this point that Sitrick and Company was brought into the picture. Our assignment was to help the father level the playing field. Once we'd assessed the lay of the land, our recommendation was obvious: It was time to shut this media circus down. As it happened, our client said he had evidence that his son had improperly diverted several million dollars of the company's funds. So after making sure there was a real basis for the accusation, we immediately issued a press release announcing that our client was thinking about asking the appropriate government authorities to consider bringing criminal charges. He followed up by filing a civil suit accusing his son of "misappropriation of funds, securities violations, and self-dealing"—as well as trying to steal control of the company to cover up what he'd done.

The immediate result was an avalanche of news stories in the local as well as national media, both broadcast and print. And we made sure the uproar didn't die down too quickly. For the next few weeks, we worked to keep the press focused on our side of the story—the lawsuit and other charges. Among other things, we got our client on a national TV interview show, where he came out swinging with both fists, startling the host—and, presumably, thousands of viewers as well—by charging that his son had engaged in "extortion, blackmail, bribery, fraud, misappropriation, hiding funds, false statements, and taking assets without authorization." The son's response, after months of attacking his father in the press, was to attempt to get a court order prohibiting both him and his father from speaking to the media. The judge, however, turned him down. Faced with the prospect of a continuing barrage of unfavorable coverage, the son decided to start behaving himself—at least in public and with the press. Our client was delighted.

At that point, we could have buried the son. But that wasn't the point. For all the bad blood between them, he was still our client's flesh and blood, and our client wasn't interested in destroying him. He simply wanted to get his side of the story out and send the boy a message—to wit, "Enough is enough."

As it turned out, our client's suit proved to be more than just a tactical feint. Eventually, a jury concluded that the son had overstepped himself in seizing control of the family company the way he had and awarded our client many millions of dollars in damages. Three months after that, a judge confirmed the verdict. Ruling that the son had acted with "willful, wanton, and reckless disregard" of his father's rights, he ordered control of the company returned to our client. The son and his colleagues "simply had no right to do what they did," the judge said, "and, therefore, what they did cannot stand."

The son appealed the verdict, but a few months later he and his father reached an out-of-court settlement that seemed to end the dispute once and for all. Instead of rolling over as his son had hoped he would, our client had fought back hard—proving in the process the truth of the old cliché that the best defense is a good offense.

In general, this approach reflects my old southside Chicago mentality. If you come at me with a fist, I'm going to hit you back with a brick. It may not be pretty, but it works.

∎ ∎ ∎

Though it should be employed sparingly, the wheel-of-pain technique is not reserved exclusively for situations in which you're trying

to stop someone from slinging mud at you. Its use can also be justified when you find yourself confronted with an adversary who is
much bigger than you and, as a result, thinks he can ignore your complaints with impunity. In the face of this kind of disdain, the PR
equivalent of a sharp stick in the eye can be a speedy and effective
means of cutting even the most high-handed antagonist down to size.

For example, there was the time Sitrick and Company was

The wheel of pain can handle even the largest and most arrogant of adversaries.

asked to help a Beverly Hills real-
estate developer who became the
subject of egregious discrimination by a major California bank.
The client, an American citizen
of Mexican descent, was in the
midst of a major building project in Las Vegas when, without warning, the bank abruptly refused to renew his line of credit. The reason, a loan officer told him, was that the bank did not like lending
money to Mexicans. "For all we know," the executive sneered, "you
could be in Mexico tomorrow."

Outraged by this treatment, the developer had filed a lawsuit
in state court, charging the bank with discriminatory loan practices. As usual, however, the wheels of justice were grinding slowly,
and while they did, his Las Vegas project was falling apart. If he was
to survive, he needed to do something immediately to show the
bank's senior management that he was not to be trifled with. As far
as we were concerned, there was only one way to get the bankers'
attention quickly enough: We had to strap them to the wheel of
pain. But how?

As it happened, the bank's annual meeting was coming up in a
few weeks, and that gave us an idea. Annual meetings are generally
regarded with dread by the senior executives of publicly held firms,

because they provide stockholders—no matter how small—with an opportunity to put questions about the operations of "their" company directly to top management. What makes executives particularly sensitive about these ordeals is that they occur in the open, often with reporters in attendance. An awkward question—or, worse, an ill-considered answer—can thus have serious consequences.

For the most part, corporate officers try to avoid embarrassment by rushing through the question-and-answer part of their annual meetings as quickly as possible, making an effort to charm (or, failing that, to intimidate) stockholders out of asking anything too painful. Nonetheless, a properly prepared stockholder who is determined to stand his ground can raise a considerable ruckus. Our client, we decided, would be just such a stockholder.

The first thing we did was have him purchase one hundred shares of the bank's common stock, so he would be eligible to speak at its annual meeting. Then we prepared a list of questions for him to ask. There were three in all: What is the policy of the bank with regard to loans to minorities? How did management explain the comments of the loan officer who said the bank did not like lending money to Mexicans? And would management allow the bank's board of directors to conduct a high-level investigation of the bank's lending practices?

The day before the meeting, we put out a press release announcing that our client had filed complaints with the Federal Deposit Insurance Corporation, the Justice Department's civil-rights division, and the California state banking department, asking the three agencies to look into his discrimination charges. We also alerted the media that the bank's annual meeting—normally an uneventful affair—might be worth covering this time.

Our *pièce de résistance* was an advertisement we had our

client place in the *Los Angeles Times* on the morning of the meeting. In big bold letters, it charged the bank with refusing to loan him money because of his Hispanic heritage and asked those who felt the bank had discriminated against them to contact him regarding a possible class-action suit.

In the end, the meeting and the resulting coverage played out just as we had planned. Our client got the floor and asked his three questions. The bank's general counsel, sweating nervously as he cited the exigencies of pending litigation, refused to answer them. The media took it all in and wound up having a field day. The Associated Press headline was typical: "Real Estate Investor Accuses Bank of Racial Bias."

Stung by the unflattering publicity, the bank quickly reversed itself and decided to reach an accommodation with our client. Within a few weeks, he was back in business. Once again, the wheel of pain had proved its ability to make even the largest and most arrogant of adversaries think twice about its behavior.

CHAPTER 12

▌ Face Forward

Don't defend past mistakes or get bogged down in apologies; instead, explain how you'll make the future better.

UP TO THIS POINT, WE'VE focused mainly on how the techniques of spin can help turn the tables when you've been misunderstood, unfairly maligned, or dishonestly attacked in the public arena—situations, in short, in which through no fault of your own, you find your good name dragged through the mud by what may seem to be an ill-informed or undiscriminating press. Occasionally, however, there are times when you are attacked or criticized for good reason—times, if truth be told, when you're not an innocent victim but have actually done something wrong, times when bad press is no more or less than what you deserve. Can spin help you then?

The answer is yes... and no. No, spin cannot undo a blunder or a misdeed, nor can it turn bad news into good or permanently distract the public from a genuine problem. Nonetheless, it can be hugely helpful in extricating you from a hole you've stumbled into—even if it's one you happen to have dug yourself. Indeed, the techniques of spin can both give you a leg up out of the hole and also help you figure out what direction you should head once you've found your feet again.

▮ **Spin cannot undo a blunder, but it can help extricate you from a hole you've stumbled into.**

Imagine you're the CEO of a national retail chain who has just been informed that, according to government investigators, the subcontractor who manufactures your house brand of leisure wear has been producing the stuff in illegal sweatshops with child labor. The news will almost certainly be featured that evening on each of the nightly network news shows, and again the next morning on the front pages of most of the nation's newspapers. Your company's reputation, in other words, is about to be shredded. The subtleties of spin may seem to offer precious little comfort at such a time, but the fact is, if properly applied, spin can help salvage your good name. Indeed, as horrified as both the public and press will no doubt be, there is no question that an appropriately crafted response on your part can put the embarrassing incident behind you quickly and cleanly.

What kind of response could possibly be appropriate in the aftermath of such a potentially disastrous revelation? In a nutshell, one that anticipates the needs of both the public and the press in these sorts of situations. Pundits often stress how important it is for companies to take responsibility and apologize to the public when they've done wrong. But while such responses may be necessary if public trust is to be maintained, confessions of guilt and expressions of sorrow alone are hardly sufficient.

That's because, as a rule, people don't care nearly as much

about what happened in the past as they do about what's going to happen in the future. It's the same with the media. Some elements of the press may love to spend time finger-pointing and assessing blame in the aftermath of a disaster (PR or otherwise), but most newspeople grow tired of rehashing the same old information. What excites them far more than stirring the ashes of a dying fire is the prospect of being offered some new development they can use to freshen a story that may be growing stale.

For anyone who finds himself called to account by the media for some mishap or misbehavior, the implications of these realities ought to be clear. Going on about how sorry you are for whatever it was that you did wrong is nice, but it will only get you so far. Without a doubt, the most important thing you can do to recover from your misstep is to emphasize to the public exactly what actions you intend to take to ensure nothing like it ever happens again.

In the case of our embarrassed retail chain, that would mean undertaking an aggressive and very public series of actions. First, the company would announce it was immediately suspending the contractor who had been caught using child labor. At the same time, it would publicize the launch of an intensive investigation of labor practices at its other subcontractors. The results of both these inquiries would be released to the media, and based on what was found the company would then devise, implement, and announce an array of reforms.

Assuming the company was sincere in its efforts—and its new safeguards made sense to the public—this kind of open, forward-looking response would have enormous impact. At the very least, the sight of the company dealing with its problems, rather than denying their existence, would mollify concerned customers. And the new procedures would give the press something else to write about besides the heart-breaking plight of underage workers. The public outrage generated by the initial headlines would quickly evaporate, and the crisis would be defused.

I have used this technique often, spinning a story forward in order to put it behind us—helping both individuals and institutions rebound from what might otherwise be fatal transgressions. One of my favorite examples of this approach involves a health-care company that had been accused of lapses that bordered on the macabre. What was accomplished (by everyone involved) in this case might well be characterized as *the* corporate turnaround of the 1990s.

The company was National Medical Enterprises (NME). Founded by an erstwhile tax attorney with just six hospitals and a $25 million public stock offering in 1969, NME had ridden the revolution in employee and taxpayer health-care programs in the 1970s and 1980s to become one of the fastest-growing and most profitable hospital chains in the nation. By 1991, with well over one hundred acute-care and psychiatric facilities on four continents, it was earning close to $600 million a year on annual revenues of nearly $4 billion. But storm clouds were gathering. For one thing, the double-digit growth rates that had propelled the company through the previous two decades were proving impossible to sustain. For another, the billing and patient-admissions practices that had produced those growth rates were becoming the subject of both government and insurance-company investigations—as well as fodder for lawyers representing countless former patients, scores of whom were suing the company on a wide range of charges, including that patients had been held against their will in NME psychiatric facilities until their hospitalization coverage had been exhausted.

Things really started to unravel at the beginning of 1993,

when the *Wall Street Journal* published a devastating front-page report on the company's woes. At the time, NME was facing more than one hundred lawsuits brought by former patients. In addition, some nineteen insurance companies were accusing it of over-billing them by as much as $1 billion, and no fewer than fourteen separate federal and state investigations were under

> **Correcting a problem is necessary but, alas, rarely sufficient; that is where spin comes in.**

way against it. The rap on the company was straightforward—and ugly. As the *Journal* described it, NME was a classic example of the tendency of commercial hospital operators "to place profits above the needs of patients." A few months later, *Business Week* suggested that the company's "top management instructed hospital administrators to adopt 'intake' goals designed to lure patients into NME hospitals for lengthy and unnecessary treatments."

The crisis seemed to come to a head at the end of April 1993, when the company's founder, Richard K. Eamer, resigned as chief executive. Two months later, he gave up his post as chairman as well. He was replaced in both jobs by a forty-nine-year-old invest-ment banker, Jeffrey C. Barbakow. Barbakow had been a member of NME's board of directors but otherwise had no health-care expe-rience. Still, he was extremely smart and unflappable—and he was determined to get the company back on track. In the weeks follow-ing his appointment as CEO, he shook up the top management, announced a restructuring of the company, and settled some of the suits brought by former patients.

But NME was not out of the woods. On a Thursday morning late in August 1993, hundreds of federal agents descended on NME offices and hospitals in more than twenty cities from Washington to

San Diego. At the company's Santa Monica, California, headquarters, some forty agents swarmed through the corridors, brandishing search warrants and seizing files. In all, investigators carted off hundreds of boxes of documents, further bolstering the media's belief that NME had been guilty of criminal acts ranging from widespread overbilling to concocting fraudulent diagnoses in order to keep healthy patients from checking out of its lucrative psychiatric facilities. Coming as they did immediately after a White House announcement that the Clinton administration was going to make the fight against fraud a significant part of its embattled health-care reform package, the dramatic raids not only made headlines in virtually every major newspaper in the nation, they also generated extensive coverage on radio and television, including each of the nightly network news shows. In one fell swoop, the complicated charges against NME had been elevated beyond mere business-section boiler plate; now the company's woes were front-page news, and its continued existence was suddenly in doubt.

It was against this backdrop that Jeff Barbakow called me. "I don't know if you've been following what's been happening with our company," Jeff said to me, "but we had a visit from the FBI yesterday."

"I'd have to have been on Mars to have missed it," I replied.

Jeff continued without missing a beat. "I *asked* my people several times to phone you—to get your firm involved," he continued. "Well, now I have *told* them. You'll be getting a call shortly from one of my executive vice presidents. If you're free, I'd be grateful if you could come over to our offices and speak with a group of our management people."

To tell the truth, I wasn't completely surprised by the request, for Jeff and I weren't exactly strangers. I had met him earlier that year, before he took over NME, just after I'd signed on to help Kirk

Kerkorian in his battle with Credit Lyonnais. Jeff, who was one of the defendants in the Credit Lyonnais suit, had also worked for Kerkorian. In 1988 the financier had hired him away from Merrill Lynch, to become CEO of what was then known as MGM/UA Communications Corporation. It was Jeff who negotiated the 1990 sale of the studio to Giancarlo Parretti. He had then gone back to investment banking, joining Donaldson, Lufkin & Jenrette as a managing director—which was what he was doing when we first met. I thought he was a thoroughgoing professional, and he was extremely complimentary of our work on the Credit Lyonnais matter.

In any event, as Jeff had promised, I soon received a formal phone invitation to advise NME. Thirty minutes later, my associate Mike Kolbenschlag and I were sitting in the NME boardroom with top company executives and a bevy of attorneys.

After we had been briefed, it was clear what needed to be done. "Look," I said, "from the media reports I've seen, there's no question your company must act immediately to assure your various constituents that, guilty or not, there will be no improprieties in the future. We need to work through the weekend to come up with a plan. As things stand now, your constituents have no confidence in you. The insurance companies are suing you. Hundreds of your patients are suing you. The government—well, let's just say they don't send six hundred FBI agents to make a social call. As for your employees, they've been reading about the company's problems for months, and at the very least, they've got to be terribly demoralized."

No one at the table disputed my assessment. But it left at least one person unmoved. Certainly, he didn't seem particularly seized with any sense of urgency. "The thing is," this executive said, "we're really bushed. I think we should take a break and reconvene on Monday. After all, the media have already done their stories."

Another executive echoed agreement. "We've had an exhausting twenty-four hours here," he said. "The press has written all they're going to write about this. I mean, what else are they going to say?"

"Look," I replied, "this is not a one-day story. It is a major news event that will be generating headlines for days, if not weeks, to come.

> **To get the press to stop focusing on what you did wrong yesterday, you've got to do something right today.**

My God, the media reported that you had six hundred government agents swarming all over your facilities yesterday. I promise you, come Monday morning there will be a whole slew of follow-up stories—and most of them are being written right now. If you don't give those reporters something new to talk about, they are simply going to wind up rehashing all the old allegations, making guesses about what else might go wrong, and speculating about whether the company can survive."

"Oh come on," the same person said. "There's no way that's going to happen."

"I disagree," I responded. "What we need to do is reconvene not on Monday but at 7:30 tomorrow morning to figure out what sort of actions we can announce to the press that will convince all of NME's different constituencies that whether or not the company is guilty of anything, what you've been accused of cannot and will not happen in the future."

This prompted another round of side discussions—followed by a polite request that Mike Kolbenschlag and I leave the room for a few minutes. "Well," I said to Mike as the doors closed behind us, "that might have been the shortest assignment we've ever had."

Of course, it wasn't. We did, however, have to agree to one

compromise: our proposed Saturday morning meeting was pushed back to 8 AM.

Even so, it wound up yielding excellent results. Working through the weekend, the crisis-management team came up with a five-point plan that Jeff Barbakow was able to unveil on Sunday during interviews we scheduled with the *Wall Street Journal*, the *New York Times*, and the *Los Angeles Times*. Among other things, the plan included the appointment of an independent task force to monitor patient admissions and referrals, the establishment of local governing boards in all NME hospitals, tighter billing and documentation procedures, and the installation of a toll-free "patient satisfaction line" over which patients and their relatives could report any problems or improprieties.

The plan was specific, well reasoned, and credible, and the media responded to it just as we had hoped they would. Instead of focusing on the FBI raids and speculation that NME was doomed, the second-day coverage had the company acting decisively to restore confidence. The *Los Angeles Times* headline said it all: "NME Promises to Beef Up Oversight of Its Hospitals." After nearly a year of almost completely negative coverage, this headline marked a radical departure in the press's view of the company. A similar sea change was reflected in a follow-up profile in the *Wall Street Journal* a few days later. The headline proclaimed: "Barbakow's Mission at National Medical: Resolve Litigation, Strengthen Business." The story noted approvingly Jeff Barbakow's "ability to appear calm and reassuring in a crisis" and his efforts to "restore confidence and send a message that any past illegal or unethical practices won't be tolerated."

Interestingly enough, as the media tide turned, so did the government's attitude (helped along by a lot of hard and brilliant work by NME's lawyers). The Justice Department was evidently impressed that NME was taking measures to correct what it openly conceded had been areas of abuse.

We spent the next few months getting the word out to patients, doctors, and staff—not to mention Wall Street and government regulators—about what the company was doing. We talked about how Barbakow had set up two separate management groups within NME: one to concentrate on cleaning up all the old messes, the other to make sure the company's ongoing businesses didn't suffer in the process. We also began to promote the positive things going on at NME, including various profit-improvement, debt-reduction, and repositioning programs.

At the same time, the company undertook an aggressive effort to put its myriad legal problems behind it. And indeed, by the following summer, it had resolved virtually all of the cases that had been brought against it—including, most significantly, the huge government fraud investigation that had prompted the embarrassing FBI raid. In June 1994, NME reached a landmark $380 million settlement with the federal government and twenty-eight states, under which the two-year-old probe was dropped, allowing the company to face the future unencumbered by the consequences of its long-ago misdeeds.

Its troubles finally behind it, NME—which eventually moved its headquarters to Santa Barbara and changed its name to Tenet Healthcare—went from strength to strength. By 1997 its stock had quintupled in value from its 1993 low, and the company had come to be widely regarded as the very model of a modern major health-care company. Indeed, the best indication of the firm's total rehabilitation was the fact that when the nation's largest hospital chain, Columbia/HCA, became the target of federal investigators in the summer of 1997, Tenet was held up as an example of how the for-profit hospital business should be practiced—and was widely touted as a potential rescuer of its embattled rival. As the *New York Times* noted, "That Tenet even has a good name to bestow on a huge combined entity is evidence of its recovery from its own scandals...."

At bottom, what made the recovery effort at NME so successful wasn't spin, of course, but that its management was extremely competent and completely sincere. Barbakow and his people really were genuinely determined to reform the company. That was crucial, for as I warned everyone at the beginning of the process, while cleverly phrased announcements of thirty-, sixty-, and ninety-day improvement timetables can buy you a little breathing room, the media have an annoying habit of remembering self-imposed deadlines. So while you may get a bit of a break at the beginning, if you don't actually get your corrective programs up and running in earnest, you're going to be in big trouble thirty or sixty or ninety days hence when the press comes back to check up on how it's all going.

Without substantive action, in other words, forward-facing spin is bound to fall flat. But as we've seen elsewhere, while doing the right thing is essential, it is, alas, almost never sufficient. Word of your rehabilitative efforts has got to get out—and, equally important, be portrayed in a way that both engages the public's interest and strikes people as believable. In order to make sure that happens, you've got to understand media dynamics well enough to be able to predict how a particular story is bound to develop—that is, what direction reporters are going to want to take it, and where the press as a whole is likely to wind up.

Making those sorts of predictions is much more of an art than a science. The first question I always ask when I find myself in a situation like the one we faced at NME is, What's relevant? What's the real news today, and what is it likely to be tomorrow? In order to answer such questions correctly, you must consider the media's mixed mindset, the fact that the press sees itself not merely as a conduit—the straightforward reporter of the facts—but also as a watchdog or guardian of the public interest. Hence, the burden of proof is always going to be on you, the alleged wrongdoer, and silence on your part will invariably be taken as a tacit admission of everyone's worst suspicions. At bottom, however, the fundamental principle at work in these sorts of situations is quite simple—namely, that new is what makes news. When all is said and done, in order to get the press to stop focusing on what you did wrong yesterday, you've got to do something right today.

CHAPTER 13

The Most Important Rule

Credibility is the spin doctor's ultimate resource.

THE EIGHT RULES OF SPIN we've laid out in the preceding chapters are not meant to comprise an exhaustive list. There are literally hundreds of techniques, strategies, and prescriptions that you could quite reasonably label as rules of spin—everything from practical advice like "don't wear a striped shirt and polka-dot tie on television" to such time-honored maxims as "quit while you're ahead." Nor are our rules meant to be taken literally—at least not in the sense that any of them should be regarded as a complete recipe for handling a given situation. The reality of media relations is far too complicated for cookbook chemistry; effective responses to real situations (including most of the examples we've used in this book) invariably involve a mixture of several techniques, as well as the ability, experience, and expertise to know what to do when and how—and more important, to know what not to do.

No, what our rules really amount to is a kind of map—a running description, if you will—of the manners and methods of the modern news media. At their heart, they reflect the nature of the information culture in which we live—in particular, the idea that the press is neither an inscrutable force of nature nor a craven pack of hyenas, but rather a very human institution driven by an entirely comprehensible set of motivations and aversions. From this key concept flows the realization that what the inexperienced participant may regard as a chaotic media frenzy is actually a predictable (and hence manageable) process—and that if you understand this process and act accordingly, you can transform the media from a hostile adversary into a powerful ally.

The rules also reflect a particular understanding of the nature of spin itself. Popular impressions to the contrary, our notion of spin has nothing to do with obfuscation and misdirection. (Or as Harry Truman once put it, "If you can't convince 'em, confuse 'em.") Rather, it's built on the recognition that, while you're not likely to win in the long run if the facts are against you, simply having the facts on your side is not enough. In order to carry the day, you must also know how to present them effectively. That, in a nutshell, is all spin is—effective presentation.

That may sound simple, and on some levels it is. Indeed, provided the stakes aren't too high and the pressure isn't too intense, virtually any alert, imaginative individual can be his own spin doctor. Spinning is not so much a matter of arcane knowledge or esoteric techniques as it is one of common sense and sound judgment. From a tactical point of view, it requires little more than a solid grasp of cause and effect. How is a particular story likely to play?

What is the likely action if I do this? What is the likely reaction? What is the likely action if I do that? What is the likely reaction?

Nonprofessionals who want to try spinning on their own should nonetheless keep in mind a few basic caveats before they step in front of the microphones. Probably the most important is to think before you speak. This is good advice in general, but particularly so when your audience is the press and public. Work out in advance what you want to say and how you want to say it, and then stick to your script. Remember, what differentiates spin from mere press-agentry is that spin always has a point, an objective beyond simply getting your name in the paper. Keep yours in mind. Remember, too, that when it comes to ill-considered remarks, the media can be astonishingly unforgiving. Once you've said something, it's out there—and if it turns out to be a major gaffe, all the "clarifications" and "explanations" in the world will not expunge it from public consciousness. Nor can you get off the hook by complaining later, as do so many victims of foot-in-mouth disease, that you were "quoted out of context." All that accomplishes is to underscore your ineptitude.

> ▌ **Spin, in a nutshell, is effective presentation.**

Another key rule of thumb is to treat every media inquiry as if it were critical. That means answering every inquiry as quickly as possible. Think before you act—but in the end, always act. If you can't respond personally, have a secretary, assistant, or colleague return the call, and promise that you'll follow up yourself as soon as you have the time. If you simply can't return the call at all, delegate a surrogate to offer a response to the inquiry. But don't hide behind others for too long; after two or three deferrals, even the most understanding reporter will begin to wonder if you've got something to hide.

It's also important to educate yourself about the media. Make a point of noticing reporters' bylines, and learn who covers the beats that matter to you (for example, your company and your company's industry or product line). Most major cities have publicity clubs that publish local media directories. Buy the one that lists the news organizations in your area, and drop an introductory note to the relevant reporters and editors, offering yourself as a source for information and commentary on appropriate topics. In addition, whenever you are at an event where key journalists are present, make a point of introducing yourself.

And don't dismiss what you might regard as minor-league media. A positive story in even the smallest of local papers or trade publications can have enormous value. Almost everything published these days becomes part of computerized media databases like Lexis-Nexis, which national reporters use to develop their own stories. Your appearance in a local story can lead directly to a mention—or even a major story—in the national press. In addition, reporters from small publications often move on to larger ones.

■ ■ ■

All this notwithstanding, at its highest levels, spinning probably should be left to the professionals. For the most part, complicated problems require sophisticated solutions, and it takes a fair amount of experience and expertise to be able to predict accurately the probable attitudes and responses of media professionals. Just as you hire legal specialists to handle complicated legal problems, you should turn to media specialists to handle complicated media or communications problems. As noted earlier, once you've spoken publicly, you can't take it back. What's more, the ground rules and unspoken protocols that govern much of the press's behavior are rarely obvious or even logical. Amateurs venture into these rarefied precincts at their peril.

Of course, whether it's practiced by a professional or by an amateur, the ultimate aim of spin is always the same. The spinner wants some audience—his friends, his customers, the community at large—to come to believe something: that his company's stock would make an excellent investment, that his plan for cleaning up Lake Michigan is better than anyone else's, that

> **No matter what, don't lie—lying is the one sin the media will neither tolerate nor forgive.**

he's not the terrible guy his enemies claim he is. In essence, then, the spinner is a persuader; his task is to persuade a particular public to accept his version of reality.

This simple (and probably obvious) fact leads us to perhaps the most important of all the so-called rules of spin. As we have seen, there are countless techniques a spin doctor can employ to achieve his goals. Which one (or ones) he chooses depends on the nature of the situation. But regardless of the circumstances, there is one tool that no spin doctor can do without—credibility. Eloquence, technical expertise, a sense of drama—all these qualities help. But without credibility, they're nothing.

Credibility, of course, is not a technique. It is an empirical characteristic, a quality that comes from consistently demonstrated truthfulness—which is to say that it is as fragile as it is powerful. Once it has been called into question, it can take years to restore. The implications of this fact of public life are obvious (or should be). The smart spin doctor never does anything that could damage his credibility. Above all, he never lies to the press, no matter how expedient it may seem at the time.

There are, of course, much larger reasons for being truthful than merely its practical value in the court of public opinion. To put it plainly, lying is wrong. It is immoral, unethical, and contrary to the core values on which our civilization is based. (When the Bible commands, "Thou shalt not bear false witness," it is not referring to testifying in court.)

For our purposes, however, it should suffice to note that lying simply doesn't work. From a PR point of view, it's a miserable strategy and a highly questionable tactic. Indeed, more than being merely ineffective, lying can be actively counterproductive. To be sure, a lie can have short-term utility, getting you out of a potentially awkward situation, allowing you to dance around an inconvenient fact. But as noted earlier, PR is about relationships, not one-night stands, and in public as well as private life, good relationships are impossible without trust and credibility. Given the relentless pressure of media scrutiny, a lie will sooner or later be exposed for what it is. When that happens, a reputation that took a lifetime to build can crumble in an instant, with consequences that are bound to extend far beyond the issue at hand. What's more, the press, which does not take at all kindly to being misled, generally responds with a ferocity that can lead to a situation far worse than anything the lie was designed to prevent. Among other things, this was one of the chief lessons of the Watergate scandal, and the logic behind the now commonplace political observation that the cover-up is invariably more damaging than the original crime.

■   ■   ■

This then is the ultimate rule of spin: No matter how dire the circumstances, don't lie—for lying is the one sin the media will neither tolerate nor forgive. Yes, being truthful can sometimes be painful. But unlike the alternative, it has the practical virtue of not coming back to blow up in your face. Moreover, spin that's based on the facts is spin that's hard to refute. For all the bells and whistles and sophisticated techniques of modern media relations, if there is a single principle on which the art of spin can be said to be based, it is surely that.

The classical Greek tragedian Sophocles had it right some five centuries before Christ. "The truth," he noted, "is always the strongest argument." Nearly 2,500 years later, would-be spin doctors ignore his advice at their peril.

∎ Acknowledgments

THE CASE HISTORIES IN THIS book are not the work of any one individual, but of a team: my coworkers and colleagues at Sitrick and Company, a group I consider to be without peer in this business. If I do say so myself, one of my greatest skills as a manager has been my ability to identify what makes a good public-relations executive, and I am fortunate to have surrounded myself with the best. Managing directors Mike Kolbenschlag, Sandi Sternberg, Jeff Lloyd, and Rivian Bell were involved in many of the cases discussed here, as well as a myriad of other cases handled by our firm, as were Anne DeWolfe, Donna Walters, Ann Julsen, David McAdam (now a vice president of communications for a client company), Steve Hawkins, David Lawton, John Grimaldi, Anne Djordjevic, Brenda Adrian, Anita Marie Hill, Jim Bourne, Julie

Fahn, and more than a dozen other people. In all, we have some thirty professionals in our offices in Los Angeles and New York, and each one of them has contributed to the firm and its success.

I would be remiss if I didn't also acknowledge and thank our back-office staff. In particular, I would like to thank my administrative assistant Stephanie Pion for helping to keep me organized and on track during this ordeal; her back-up, Audra Bonacki; and Joan Woods, our controller, for making sure everyone got both billed and paid.

People often ask me what sort of professional backgrounds seem to lead to success in our business. All I can do by way of answering is to point to the backgrounds of the people who comprise Sitrick and Company. Some come from the business world, others from the print and broadcast media.

The corporate veterans include former senior executives from a variety of Fortune 500 companies—including Wickes Companies, National Can, Tenneco, Great Western Financial, and Kaufman & Broad—as well as brokerage firms and mutual funds such as Merrill Lynch and the Pilgrim Group.

In the print world, Sitrick staffers have held such positions as senior editor of *Newsweek*; associate editor of *Forbes*; Chicago and Paris bureau chief for *Business Week*; page-one editor of the *Asian Wall Street Journal*; West Coast bureau chief of *U.S. News & World Report*; business and metro editor of the *Orange County Register*; U.S. correspondent of the *Economist*; assistant business editor and news editor of the *Oakland Tribune*; business editor of the *Contra Costa Times*; copy editor of the *San Francisco Examiner*; New York news and features editor of United Press International; and foreign correspondent for the *Washington Post*. Additionally, the firm has people who have served as reporters for a number of major-market daily newspapers and trade publications. Two of the firm's professionals have won Pulitzer Prizes for their reporting; another's work won the National Magazine Award.

On the broadcast side, our people have served as producer for *The MacNeil/Lehrer News Hour*, KCBS-TV News (Los Angeles), and KNBC-TV News (Los Angeles); executive producer for KCBS-TV's investigative unit and KNBC-TV News; city editor for KCBS-TV; West Coast newsmanager for NBC-TV News and director of news for KNBC-TV; European producer, news editor, and writer for *The Huntley-Brinkley Report*; and news writer and producer for WNBC-TV News (New York).

Of course, Sitrick and Company is not a typical public-relations firm. We concentrate our practice in only four areas: corporate, financial, transactional, and crisis communications. Although we are probably best known for our work in mergers and acquisitions and other sensitive situations, we have an extensive and successful practice in each of our specialty areas. Indeed, our experience runs the spectrum of what's come to be known as strategic PR, including litigation support, emergency executive transitions, sexual harassment and sex discrimination cases, labor issues, personal and business litigation, criminal indictments, insurance fraud, Medicare and Medicaid fraud, U.S. Justice Department inquiries and indictments, Securities and Exchange Commission inquiries and indictments, Federal Trade Commission problems, Environmental Protection Agency allegations, product recalls, warranty and product-liability claims, fraudulent conveyance cases, trade disputes, environmental problems, and a variety of sensitive financial issues, including bankruptcies and out-of-court restructurings.

■ ■ ■

Finding a collaborator to work with when you undertake a project like this is both a difficult and, if it works out, a rewarding proposition. It is especially difficult if you have a work schedule like mine. I was thus very fortunate to find someone as smart, talented, hardworking, and easy to work with as Allan Mayer, without whose efforts this book would not have been possible. Allan is not only a talented reporter, writer, and editor, but when it came to the subject of spin, he "got it" right away. Having been an award-winning journalist (a reporter at the *Wall Street Journal*; a writer, foreign correspondent, and senior editor for *Newsweek*; and the founding editor-in-chief of *Buzz* magazine) certainly helped. So did his willingness to meet with me every Sunday morning at the crack of dawn. Given all that, I am particularly pleased to be able to report that at the conclusion of this project, I was able to persuade him to join our firm.

There are also some other very important people in my life who deserve thanks: my parents, who in my early years made it possible for me to learn, strive, and achieve, and who encouraged me every step of the way. It is to my mother—who used to tell me, "Sick, schmick, go to work, go to school"—that I guess I owe my work ethic. And it is to my father—who very early in my career told me, "Your job is not to go to your bosses with a problem, your job is to go to them with a solution"—that I owe much of what I know about business. He is and has always been my mentor.

Finally, this book would be no more complete than my life without thanks to my partner and best friend—my wife, Nancy, who has put up with me and my absolutely crazy work schedule for nearly thirty years now. Knowing that Nancy would be at our children's parent–teacher meetings, school plays, and the like while I was away fighting the good fight made it possible for me to do what I do. Not that I haven't felt a bit guilty, but as I told her many years ago, quoting Popeye, "I yam what I yam." Still, nothing I have accomplished would have been possible without her unfaltering love and support, and for this I will always be grateful. (I also have to thank my three daughters, Julie, Sheri, and Alison, for being so understanding about the fact that I couldn't be there for them as much as I would have liked.) It is impossible to overestimate the importance of having a stable and supportive family in allowing you to concentrate all your energies on getting the job done.

One more thing—this page will self-destruct thirty seconds after it is read so as not to ruin my reputation and give people the impression that I am a nice guy. To quote both my secretary and my wife on two separate occasions when I complained that they had hurt my feelings, "That's impossible. You have no feelings!"

How I am viewed is like everything else—it all depends on spin.

Index

A

Abrams, Creighton, 176
Accessibility, 123–145
Accountability, 6
Adversarial relationships with media, 6–7, 16–18, 36–37, 38, 41
Akin, Gump, Strauss, Hauer & Feld, 113
All the President's Men, 46
Archival material, 101, 107, 126, 129, 130, 200
AT&T, 9, 10–11
Audience, importance of knowing, 23, 29

B

Bankruptcy, 141;
    Barneys New York case, 62–77;
    Orange County case, 139–145

Barbakow, Jeffrey C., 189, 190–191, 193, 195
Barneys New York, 62–77
Barnum, P.T., 149
Basinger, Kim, 38
Beatrice Foods, 26
Bennett, Bruce, 143
Berg, Jeff, 168–170
Bernays, Edward, 10, 15–16
Bernstein, Carl, 47
Big top syndrome, 48
Bogdanoff, Lou, 143
Builders Emporium, 33
Bush, George, 55

C

CAA. *See* Creative Artists Agency
Chicago Department of Human Resources, 24–25
Christensen, Miller, Fink, Jacobs,

Glaser, Weil & Shapiro, 137
Christensen, Terry, 137
Cibber, Colley, 106
Citron, Robert L., 140, 144
Clinton, Bill, 53, 55, 56, 57
Columbia Pictures, 168
Columbia/HCA, 194–195
Committee on Public Information, 11–12, 14
Communication process, 3–8
Competition, 44–45
Confidentiality, x
Considine, Frank, 30–31
Cooke, Janet, 51
Corporate public relations, 10–11
CPI. *See* Committee on Public Information
Creative Artists Agency, 167–170
Credibility, 178–179, 197–203
Credit Lyonnais, 131, 136–139, 168–170, 191
Crisis management, 5–8, 16–18; *See also* Rules of spin

D
Daley, Richard J., 24
Damage control, 152, 159
Davis, John, 91–93
Davis, Marvin, 38, 91
Deadlines, 22
Deaver, Michael, 13–14, 53
Defining spin, 53–58
DFS, 76
Dickson Concepts, 76
Dionne, E.J., Jr., 56–57
Disney, Roy, 35
Djordjevic, Ann, 115
Dole, Bob, 56
Donaldson, Lufkin & Jenrette, 191
Donaldson, Sam, 116
Dooley, Martin, 39–40
Dowd, Maureen, 71

Drexel Burnham Lambert, 35, 132
Dunne, Finley Peter, 39–40, 42, 49

E
E.& J. Gallo, 77–80
Eamer, Richard K., 189
Educating the press, 123–145
El Torito restaurant chain, 155–159
Exclusivity, 44–45, 72–73

F
Financial filings, 119–122
Finke, Nikki, 17, 48
Floros, Leo, 26
Food Lion, 111–116
Ford Motor Co., 11
The Front Page, 46

G
General Electric, 9, 11, 13
Glaser, Patty, 137
Gold, Stanley, 35–36, 37
Grammer, Kelsey, 38

H
Halberstam, David, 47
Healey, Denis, 76
Heaven's Gate mass suicide, 43
Helmsley, Leona, 108
Hennigan Mercer Bennett, 143
Hine, Lewis, 15
Hoffman, Dustin, 47
Hollywood: abused ex-wife case, 171–174;
   actress case, 161–167;
   ICM case, 167–170;
   public relations and, 12–13;
   tabloid case, 91–93

I
ICM. *See* International Creative Management

Information Age, 5
Intel, 5
International Creative Management,
    167–170
Internet and public information, 130
Isetan, 62–76

J
Jackson, Jess, 77–80
Johnson, Lyndon, 175
Jones, Stephen, 97
Journalists: adversarial relationships
        with, 6–7, 16–18, 36–37, 38, 41;
    competition and, 44–45;
    cultivating, 200;
    drinking and, 42;
    egos of, 45–47, 91, 93–94;
    exclusivity and, 44–45, 72–73;
    getting along with, 39–51;
    idealism of, 49–51;
    liberalism of, 41;
    public's opinion of, 112;
    story concept, 42–44

K
Kalb, Marvin, 115–116
Kendall-Jackson Winery, 77–80
Kerkorian, Kirk, 38, 131, 136–139,
    190–191
King, Don, 38
Kipling, Rudyard, 18
Kolbenschlag, Mike, 78, 166, 191,
    192
Kosuge, Kuniyasu, 64–65, 66

L
Lee, Ivy, 9–10, 14
Leno, Jay, 156, 158
Letterman, David, 156, 158–159
Lexis-Nexis, 126, 129, 130, 143, 200
Lincoln, Abraham, 62
Lippmann, Walter, 15, 46

Locked in the Cabinet, 70
Ludlow Massacre, 9–10, 14

M
Matsushita, 168
McAdam, David, 149
MCA/Universal, 168
McVeigh, Timothy, 97
Merrill Lynch, 191
Metro-Goldwyn-Mayer, 136–139, 169
MGM. *See* Metro-Goldwyn-Mayer
MGM/UA Communications
    Corporation, 191
Miracle White, 26–29
Morris, Dick, 53
Murdoch, Rupert, 139

N
National Association of
    Manufacturers, 13
National Can Corporation, 29–31
National Medical Enterprises,
    188–196
New Deal, 12, 15
Nixon, Richard, 47, 49
NME. *See* National Medical
    Enterprises

O
Orange County, California, 139–145
Orwell, George, 53
Ovitz, Michael, 168–170

P
Parretti, Giancarlo, 136–139, 191
Perot, Ross, 56
Pig Rule, 176
Placement skills, 24–25
Poincaré, Henri, 123–124
Polaroid, 35–38
PolyGram, 139
Pope, Alexander, 106

Press agents, 10, 93
Pressman, Barney, 64
Pressman, Fred, 64
Pressman, Gene and Robert, 62–77
PrimeTime Live, 111–116
Procter & Gamble, 26
Product publicity, 26–29
Public relations: history of, 8–16;
    practicing, ix–x, 197–203; *See also*
    Rules of spin
Public relations, history of, 8–16
Public sector public relations, 11–12
Publicists, 10, 93
Purgatory Ski Resort, 147–152

R
Reagan, Ronald, 13–14, 55
Redford, Robert, 47
Reich, Robert B., 70
Roosevelt, Franklin D., 11, 12, 15
Rosen, Ira, 113
Rothenberg, Randall, 54, 56–57
Rules of spin: always respond, 81–101;
    explain the facts, 123–145;
    face forward, 185–196;
    feed the media, 61–80;
    fight back, 175–184;
    find a lead steer, 161–174;
    maintain credibility, 197–203;
    preempt the situation, 103–122;
    think strategically, 147–159

S
Sansweet, Steve, 16, 17, 44, 45
Sawyer, Diane, 116
Seabolt, Lee, 25–26
Selz, Seabolt & Associates, 25–29
Shamrock Holdings, 35–38
Sigoloff, Sanford, 32–34
Silbert, Steve, 137

Singer, Leo, 27–29, 29
Sitrick, David, 19
Sitrick, Michael S.: education of,
    19–22;
    job history, 22–38
Sitrick, Nancy, 20
Sitrick, Ronald, 19
Sitrick and Company: establishment
    of, 38;
    naming of, 35;
    profile and philosophy, 38
Sloan, Allan, 18, 45
Sony Corporation, 168
Sophocles, 203
Sternberg, Sandi, 75, 140
Story concept, 42–44
Strategic thinking, 147–159
Stutman, Treister & Glatt, 139, 143
Sun Tzu, 110
Sweetbaum, Henry, 34–35

T
Tabloid newspapers, 91–93
Tenet Healthcare, 194–195
Truman, Harry, 198
Truth: spin and, 53–58; *See also*
    Credibility
Turner, Lana, 12
Turner, Rich, 73–76
TWA, 6
Tylenol, 5

U
Unruh, Jesse, 44
USS *Coral Sea,* 3–4

V
Vail, Theodore Newton, 11, 14
ValuJet, 6
Vietnam, 46–47

W

Walters, Donna, 115
Watergate, 46–47, 49–50, 202
Wayne, John, 12
West, Rebecca, 61
Western Electric, 24
Wheel-of-pain technique, 177–184
Wiatt, Jim, 168
Wickes Companies, 31–34
Wilson, Woodrow, 11–12, 14
Womble, Carlyle, Sandridge & Rice,
    113
Woodward, Bob, 47
Wyatt, Richard, 113

Y

Yemenidjian, Alex, 137–138